MICHAEL ALLRED'S

¡IT GIRL!

ROUND ONE: "DARK STREETS, SNAP CITY"

WRITTEN BY
JAMIE S. RICH

ILLUSTRATED BY
MIKE NORTON

COLORED BY
ALLEN PASSALAQUA

LETTERS AND DESIGN BY
CRANK!

CHYNNA CLUGSTON FLORES
ARTIST, "HIS SPACE HOLIDAY"

MICHAEL & LAURA ALLRED
CHAPTER ART

AARON CONLEY, MICHAEL ALLRED, & LAURA ALLRED
FRONT COVER

EDITED BY
JAMIE S. RICH AND ERIC STEPHENSON

PIN-UPS BY
DARWYN COOKE, TERRY BLAS, MARC ELLERBY,
NICOLAS HITORI DE, NATALIE NOURIGAT,
AND ADAM CADWELL

ISBN: 978-1-60706-725-2

IMAGE COMICS, INC.
Robert Kirkman - chief operating officer
Erik Larsen - chief financial officer
Todd McFarlane - president
Marc Silvestri - chief executive officer
Jim Valentino - vice-president

Eric Stephenson - publisher
Ron Richards - director of business development
Jennifer de Guzman - pr & marketing director
Branwyn Bigglestone - accounts manager
Emily Miller - accounting assistant
Jamie Parreno - marketing assistant
Jenna Savage - administrative assistant
Kevin Yuen - digital rights coordinator
Jonathan Chan - production manager
Drew Gill - art director
Tyler Shainline - print manager
Monica Garcia - production artist
Vincent Kukua - production artist
Jana Cook - production artist
www.imagecomics.com

"CARRYING THE SUPERHERO TORCH"

An IT GIRL! introduction by Dean Haspiel

The ancient Greeks had their angry gods of wit, strength, speed, lightning bolts and betrayal, and the Norse had their bastion of immortals wielding swords, shields, hammers, lightning and lies, too. Moralistic mythologies that were, arguably, superhero stories for all ages. It wasn't until 1938 that America gave birth to its first sustainable superhero when DC Comics published Superman, arguably a god (albeit an alien immigrant), who "could leap tall buildings in a single bound." In 1941, a super soldier named Captain America punched Adolph Hitler in the chin and the success of comics with the Human Torch, Sub-Mariner, Wonder Woman, Batman, Captain Marvel, and so many more opened the floodgates to new superhero lore and comic books held sway. That is, until recently.

Before movies got good enough to pick up the gauntlet that 4-color print threw down on the racks of newspaper stands and suspended disbelief that a man could fly or that a team of empowered humans and mutants could assemble to save the world, the comic book industry had to build the library that our current tech-savvy storytelling mediums could poach from. Producing decades of monthly comics during a time when the unlimited budget of a blank page pushed the boundaries of what the mysteries of science and circumstance could do to our families and friends, and the moral questions those experiments asked, achieved a creative Babylon that, to this day, is unmatched in any other medium.

There is a narrative and budgeting concern in filmmaking called "killing your darlings," which means eliminating the dialogue and/or scenes that don't necessarily support the thesis of a story. In other words, some of the experimental stuff that comes out of left field and gobsmacks you upside your head. In comic books, we tend to indulge our darlings and explore them beyond their original intent. Sometimes a story escapes our grasp, unlocks our subconscious, and takes us to places we didn't see coming. For me, that's one of the few remaining things that still highly recommends comic books.

My favorite decade of superhero creation came from the masterminds that launched Marvel Comics in 1961 when the "House of Ideas" gave birth to a legacy of characters that made a cosmic impression upon our cultural zeitgeist. The 1960s was a defining era in our nation where equal rights and the rumblings of creators rights were debated and fought for while music and literature shed psychedelic light on our minds and in our fashion and some of our comics went underground and got personal and adult. And then mainstream comics got serious and, eventually, dark. Very dark. Alas, independent cartoonists responded to our industry struggles and our American mythology with their creator-owned inventions. In 1990, Michael Allred hopscotched the angst and kept the spirit of 1960s comics alive when he created Madman and Snap City, where, eventually, a team of spore-infected street beatniks called the Atomics would lead to It Girl!

Within the pages of Michael Allred's *It Girl and the Atomics*, Jamie Rich, Mike Norton, Chynna Clugston Flores, Allen Passalaqua, and Crank! pick up where Allred left off by carrying the superhero torch that was lit in 1938 but with a 2012 twist. "Dark Streets, Snap City" deals with multi-player video gaming, social networking, identity theft, cyberspace, alternate realities and, of course, good old fashioned sibling rivalry, resurrection, revenge, and redemption. The story stuff that superheroes have respectfully borrowed from science fiction, crime, mystery, romance, and horror, while challenging the tropes of misunderstood monsters and sexy freaks. *It Girl and the Atomics* keeps comics easy and fun but lets the reader take a neo-retro break from our current digital diatribes where thoughts and conversation are reduced to ticker-tape headlines and, instead, allows us to reflect on our world, express our imagination, and bend our minds with the power of comic books.

--Dean Haspiel, November 2012

Emmy Award-winner and Eisner Award-nominee Dean Haspiel created *Billy Dogma*, illustrated for HBO's "Bored To Death," received a residency at Yaddo, and was a Master Artist at the Atlantic Center for the Arts. Dino has written and drawn many superhero and semi-autobiographical comix, including *Spider-Man, Batman, X-Men, The Fantastic Four, Godzilla, Mars Attacks, American Splendor, Street Code,* and collaborations with Harvey Pekar, Jonathan Ames, Inverna Lockpez, Stan Lee, and Jonathan Lethem. Dino also curates and creates for TripCity.net.

Visit Dean at http://www.deanhaspiel.com/.

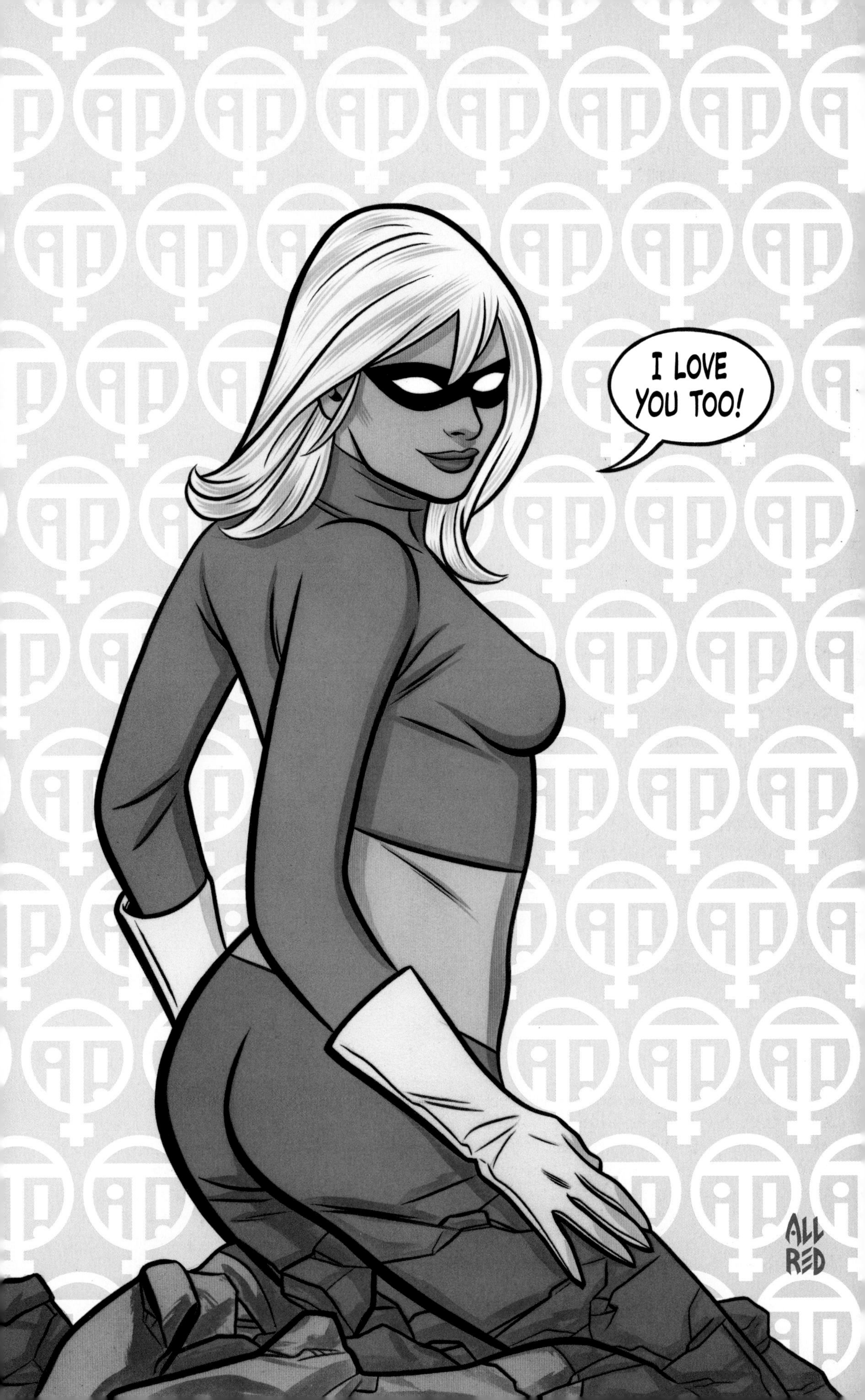
I LOVE YOU TOO!
ALLRED

MICHAEL ALLRED'S

iT GiRL!

AND THE ATOMICS

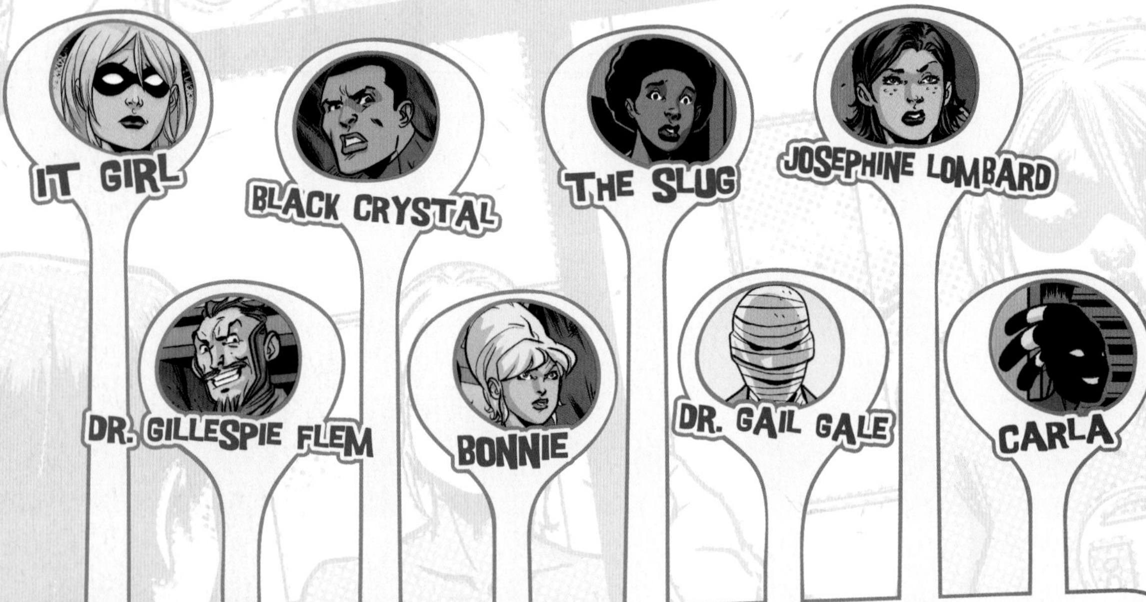
IT GIRL
BLACK CRYSTAL
THE SLUG
JOSEPHINE LOMBARD
DR. GILLESPIE FLEM
BONNIE
DR. GAIL GALE
CARLA

BACKGROUND · STORY SO FAR...

IN SNAP CITY, AN ALIEN SPORE TRANSFORMED A GROUP OF STREET BEATNIKS INTO THE SUPER-POWERED BAND OF HEROES KNOWN AS THE ATOMICS. THESE COSTUMED ADVENTURERS ALIGNED THEMSELVES WITH FRANK EINSTEIN, A.K.A. MADMAN. CURRENTLY, MADMAN AND TWO OTHER ATOMICS ARE ON AN INTERGALACTIC MUSIC TOUR WITH RED ROCKET 7, LEAVING THE REMAINING ATOMICS ON THEIR OWN ON EARTH. WHICH IS WHERE OUR STORY BEGINS...

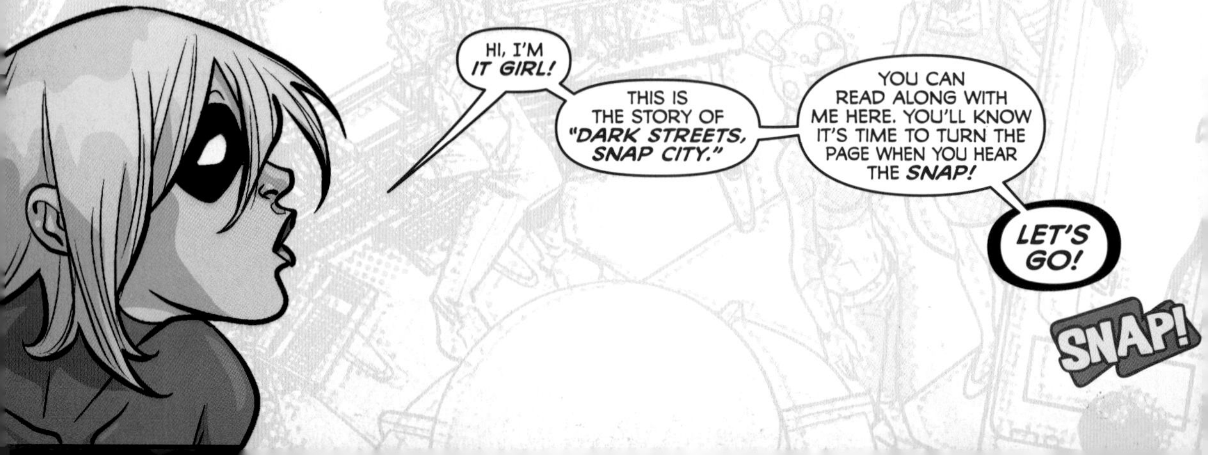
HI, I'M *IT GIRL!*
THIS IS THE STORY OF *"DARK STREETS, SNAP CITY."*
YOU CAN READ ALONG WITH ME HERE. YOU'LL KNOW IT'S TIME TO TURN THE PAGE WHEN YOU HEAR THE *SNAP!*
LET'S GO!
SNAP!

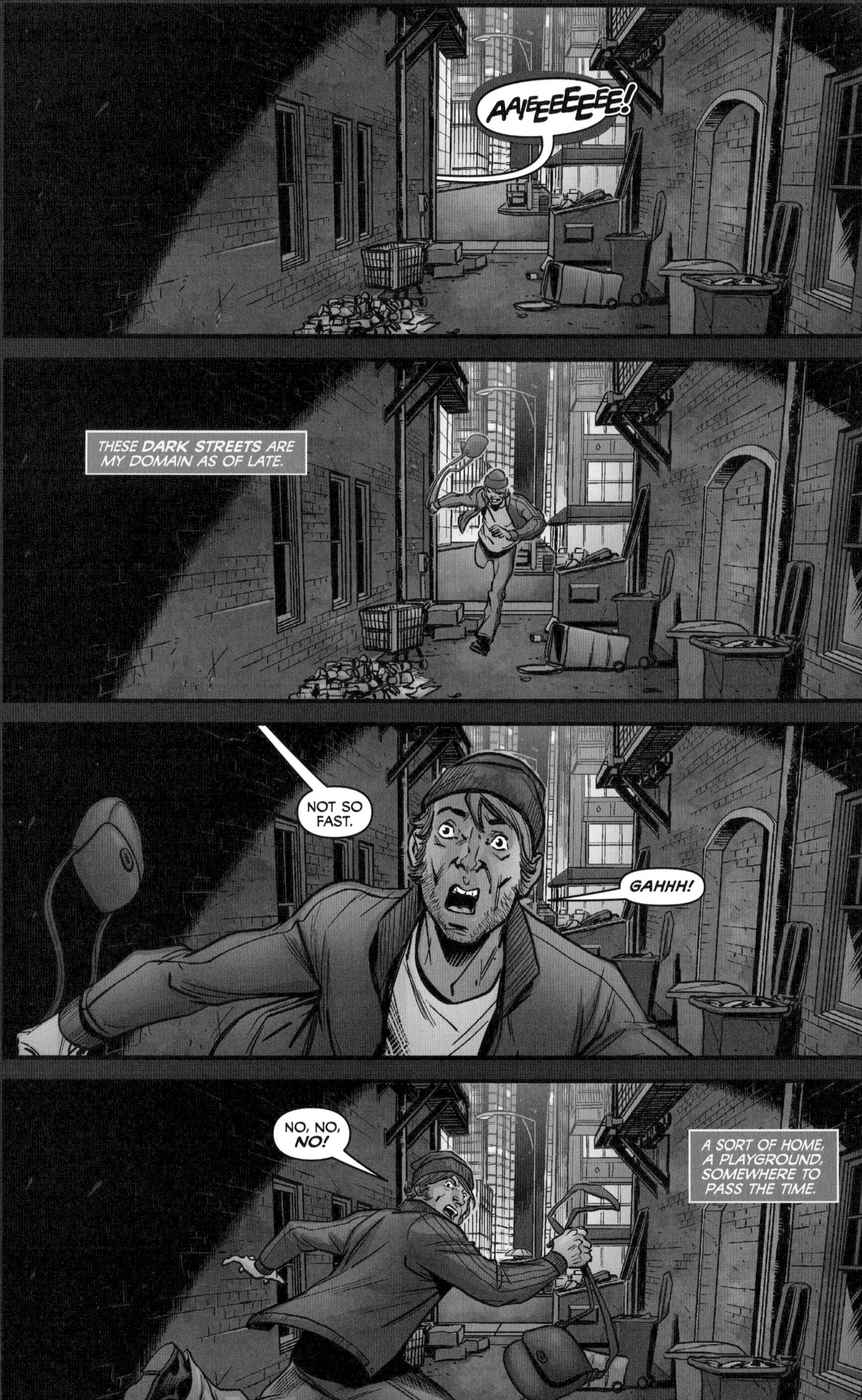
AAIEEEEEEE!
THESE DARK STREETS ARE MY DOMAIN AS OF LATE.
NOT SO FAST.
GAHHH!
NO, NO, NO!
A SORT OF HOME, A PLAYGROUND, SOMEWHERE TO PASS THE TIME.

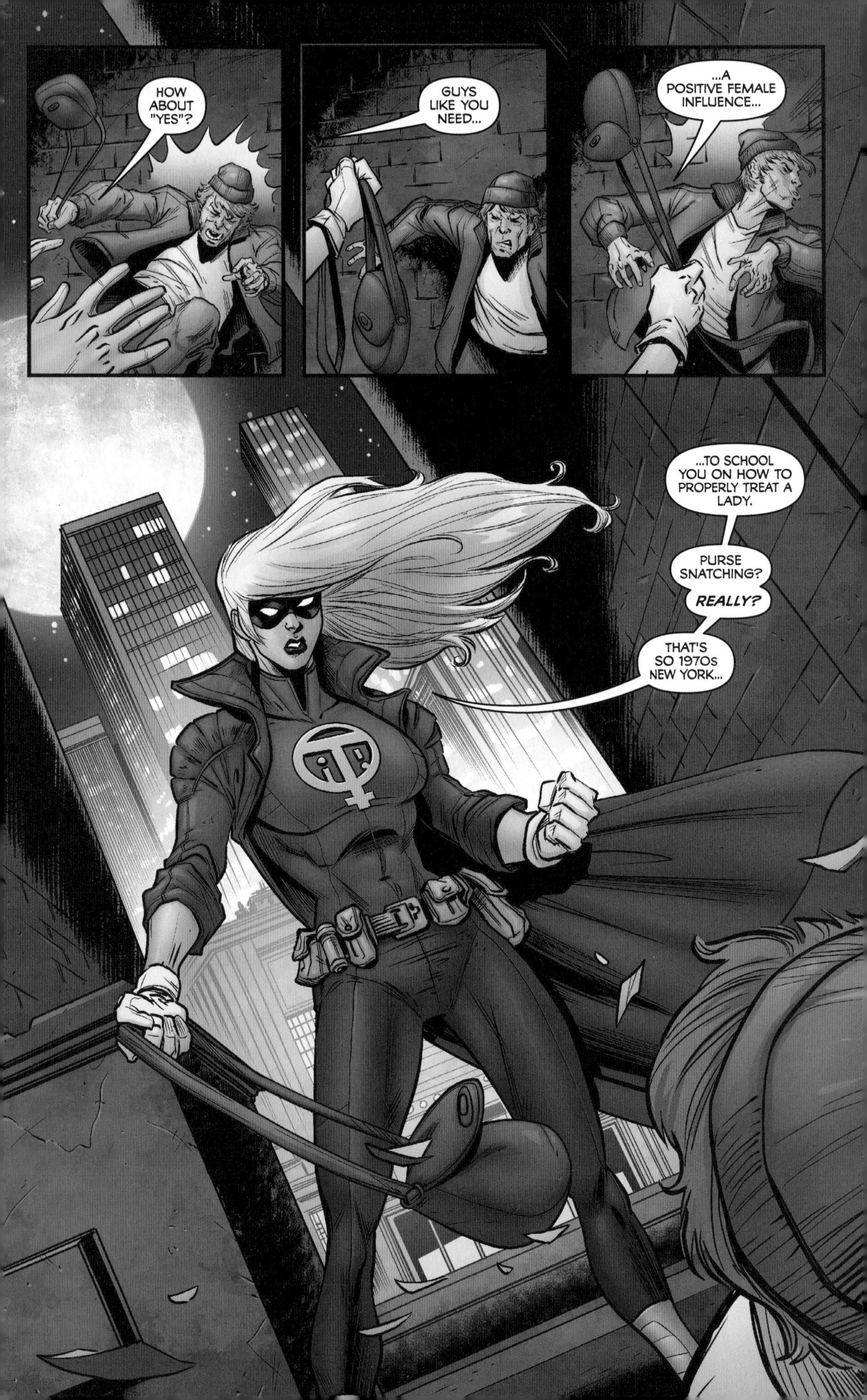
HOW ABOUT "YES"?
GUYS LIKE YOU NEED...
...A POSITIVE FEMALE INFLUENCE...
...TO SCHOOL YOU ON HOW TO PROPERLY TREAT A LADY.
PURSE SNATCHING?
REALLY?
THAT'S SO 1970s NEW YORK...

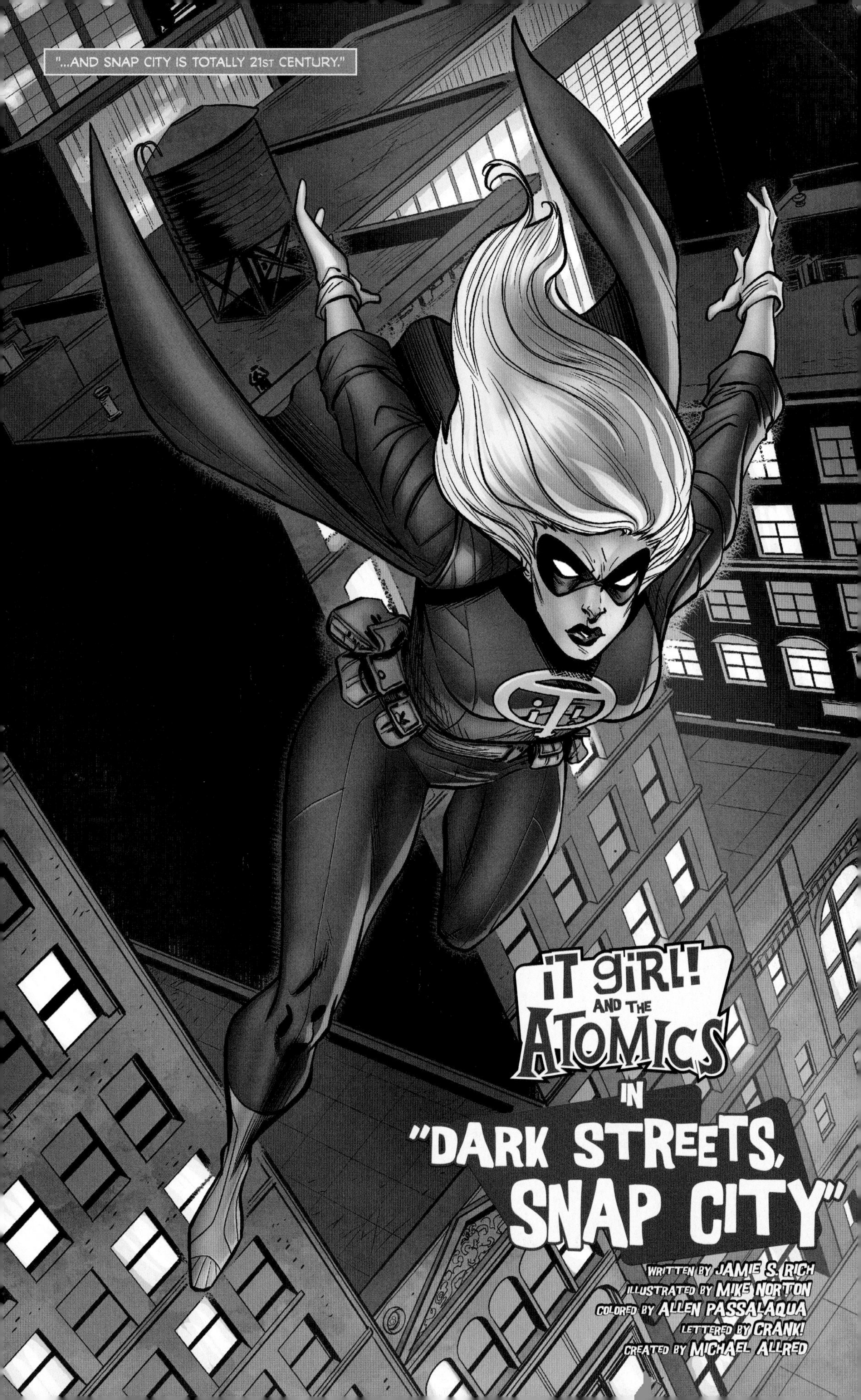
"...AND SNAP CITY IS TOTALLY 21ST CENTURY."
IT GIRL! AND THE ATOMICS
IN
"DARK STREETS, SNAP CITY"
WRITTEN BY JAMIE S. RICH
ILLUSTRATED BY MIKE NORTON
COLORED BY ALLEN PASSALAQUA
LETTERED BY CRANK!
CREATED BY MICHAEL ALLRED

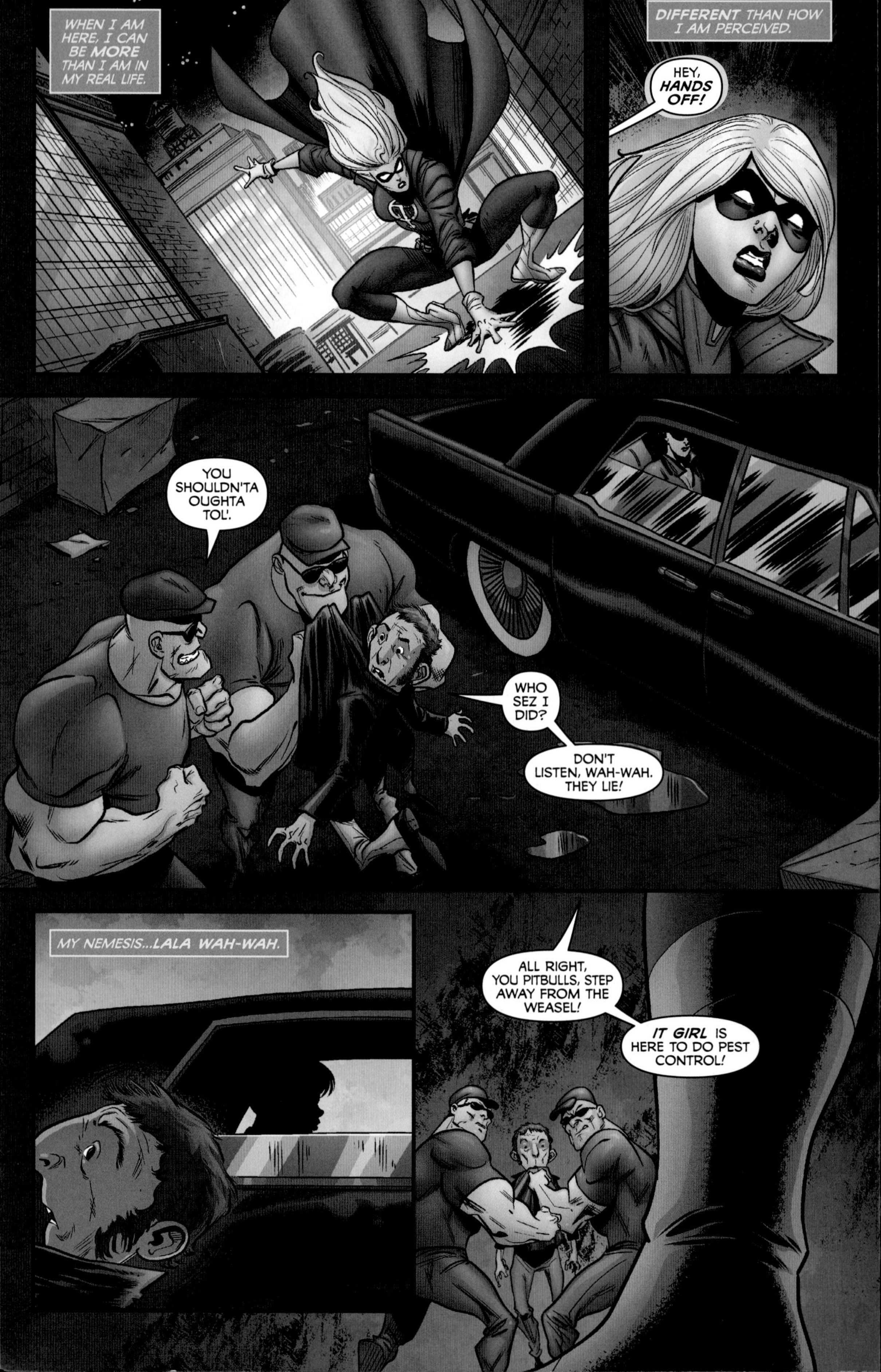
WHEN I AM HERE, I CAN BE MORE THAN I AM IN MY REAL LIFE.
DIFFERENT THAN HOW I AM PERCEIVED.
HEY, HANDS OFF!
YOU SHOULDN'TA OUGHTA TOL'.
WHO SEZ I DID?
DON'T LISTEN, WAH-WAH. THEY LIE!
MY NEMESIS...LALA WAH-WAH.
ALL RIGHT, YOU PITBULLS, STEP AWAY FROM THE WEASEL!
IT GIRL IS HERE TO DO PEST CONTROL!

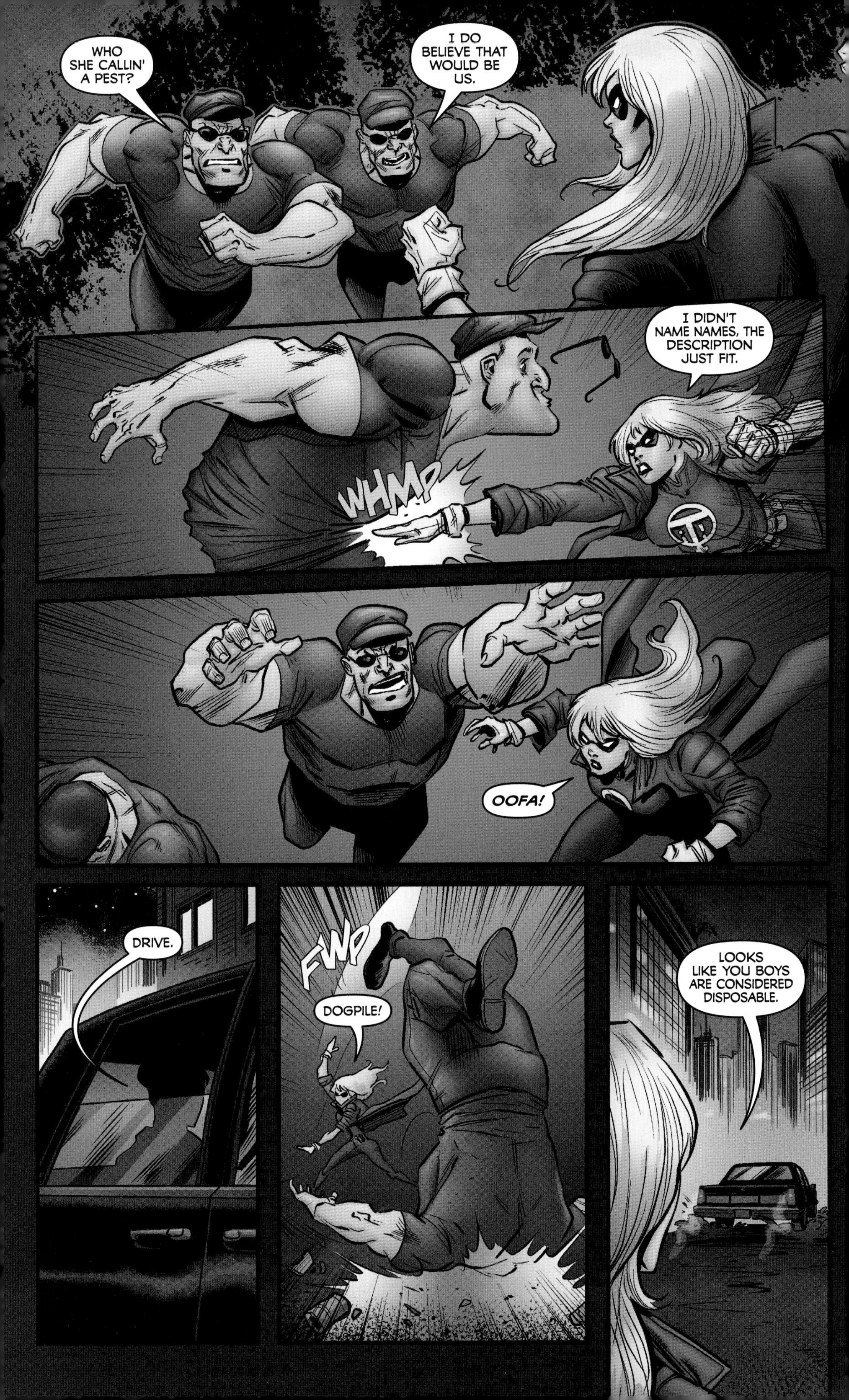
WHO SHE CALLIN' A PEST?
I DO BELIEVE THAT WOULD BE US.
I DIDN'T NAME NAMES, THE DESCRIPTION JUST FIT.
WHMP
OOFA!
DRIVE.
FWP
DOGPILE!
LOOKS LIKE YOU BOYS ARE CONSIDERED DISPOSABLE.

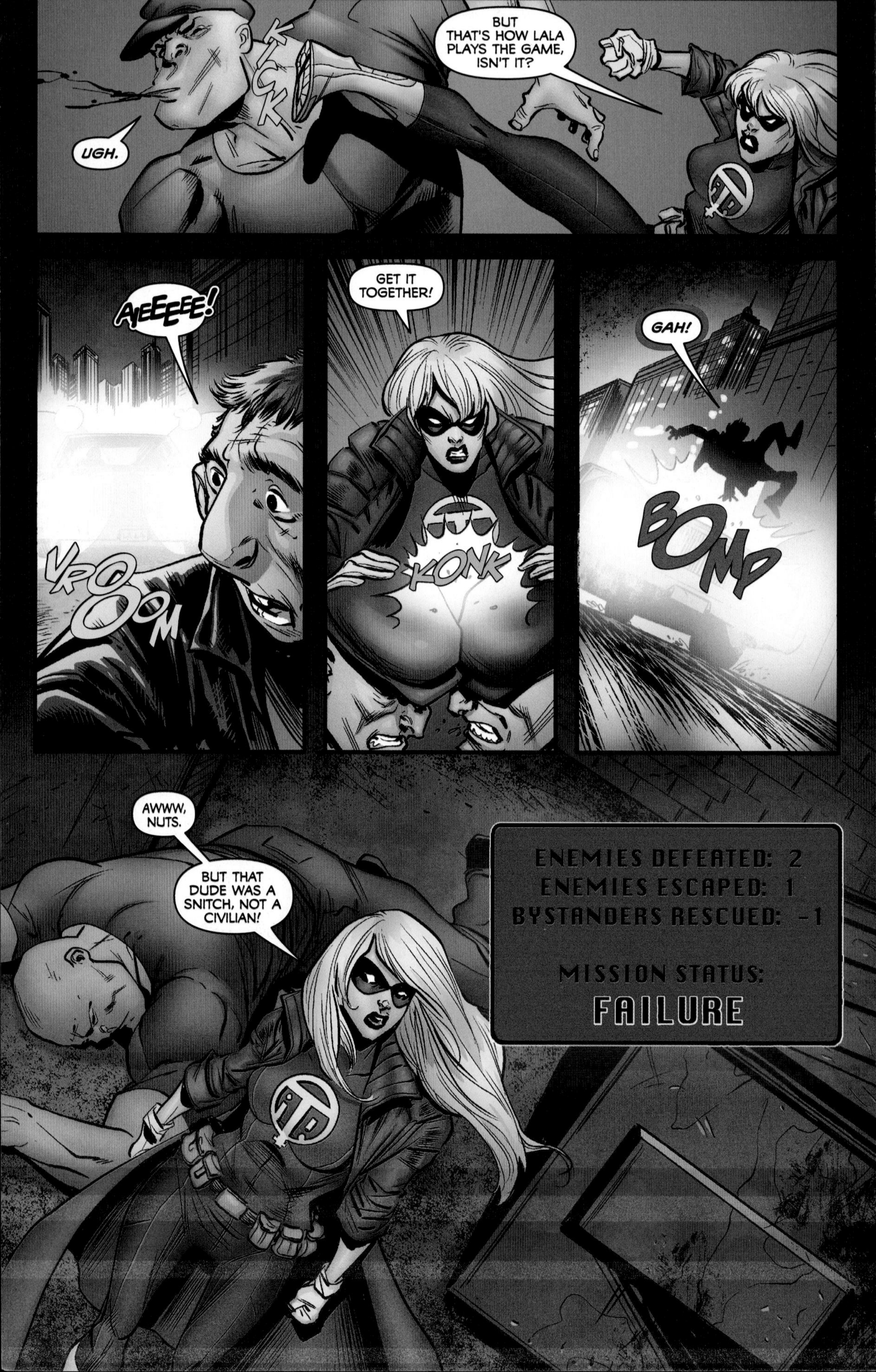
BUT THAT'S HOW LALA PLAYS THE GAME, ISN'T IT?
KICK
UGH.
AIEEEEE!
VROOOOM
GET IT TOGETHER!
KONK
GAH!
BOMD
AWWW, NUTS.
BUT THAT DUDE WAS A SNITCH, NOT A CIVILIAN!
ENEMIES DEFEATED: 2
ENEMIES ESCAPED: 1
BYSTANDERS RESCUED: -1
MISSION STATUS:
FAILURE

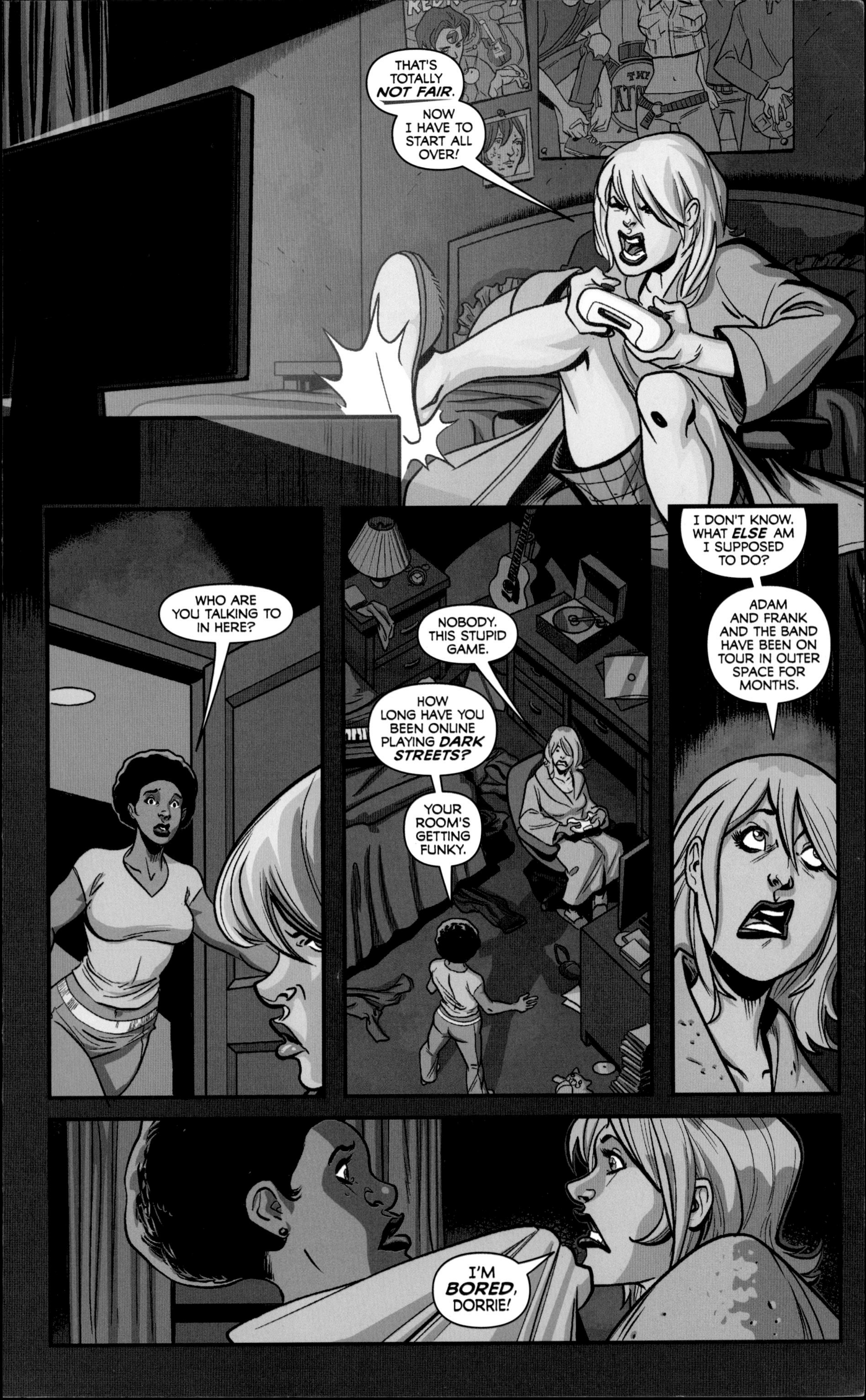

THAT'S TOTALLY NOT FAIR.
NOW I HAVE TO START ALL OVER!
WHO ARE YOU TALKING TO IN HERE?
NOBODY. THIS STUPID GAME.
HOW LONG HAVE YOU BEEN ONLINE PLAYING DARK STREETS?
YOUR ROOM'S GETTING FUNKY.
I DON'T KNOW. WHAT ELSE AM I SUPPOSED TO DO?
ADAM AND FRANK AND THE BAND HAVE BEEN ON TOUR IN OUTER SPACE FOR MONTHS.
I'M BORED, DORRIE!

WHEN WAS THE LAST TIME WE HAD AN ADVENTURE?

NOT SINCE BEFORE THEY LEFT.

RIGHT. BUT MORE IMPORTANTLY, NOT SINCE *MADMAN* LEFT.

I'M STARTING TO THINK FRANK IS SOME KIND OF *TROUBLE MAGNET.*

OOOH-*WEE!*

THAT'S BLINDING!

WELL, IF YOU'RE ITCHING FOR EXCITEMENT, QUIT LOOKING FOR IT IN A VIDEO GAME.

GET YOURSELF CLEANED UP AND GO BE A SUPERHERO FOR REAL.

OKAY, BUT LET ME SAVE MY SETTINGS FIRST.

NO! IT'S COLD-TURKEY TIME, YOU ADDICT!

BUT I JUST EARNED "ELECTRO BOOTS." WHAT IF ANOTHER PLAYER STEALS THEM?

ES DEFEAT
ES ESCAPE
ERS RESCUED

ION STATUS:
AILURE

TOUGH. IF YOU WON THEM ONCE, YOU CAN WIN THEM AGAIN.

BUT THEN I'D BE PLAYING MORE AND THAT WOULD DEFEAT THE PURPOSE!

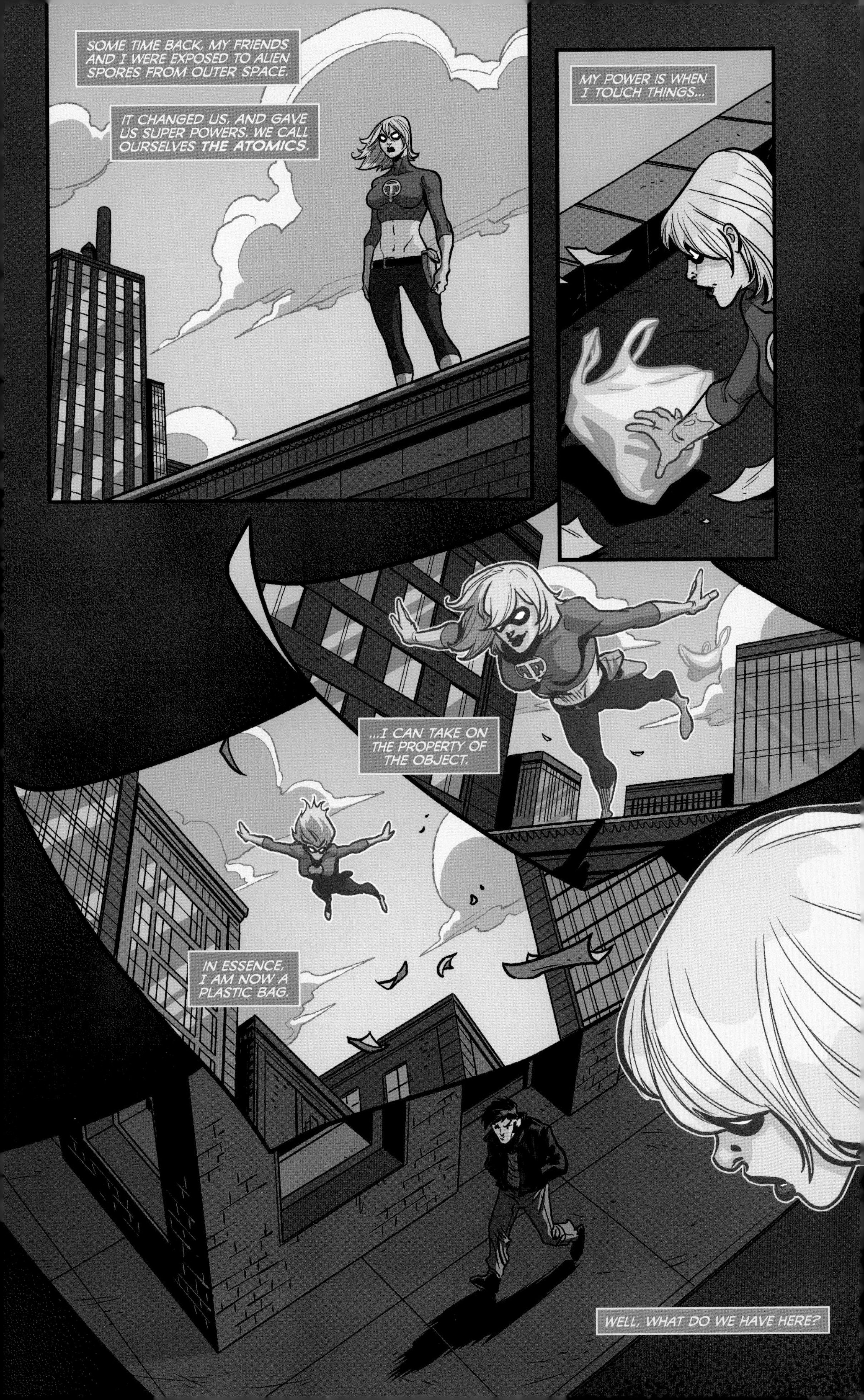
SOME TIME BACK, MY FRIENDS AND I WERE EXPOSED TO ALIEN SPORES FROM OUTER SPACE.
IT CHANGED US, AND GAVE US SUPER POWERS. WE CALL OURSELVES THE ATOMICS.
MY POWER IS WHEN I TOUCH THINGS...
...I CAN TAKE ON THE PROPERTY OF THE OBJECT.
IN ESSENCE, I AM NOW A PLASTIC BAG.
WELL, WHAT DO WE HAVE HERE?

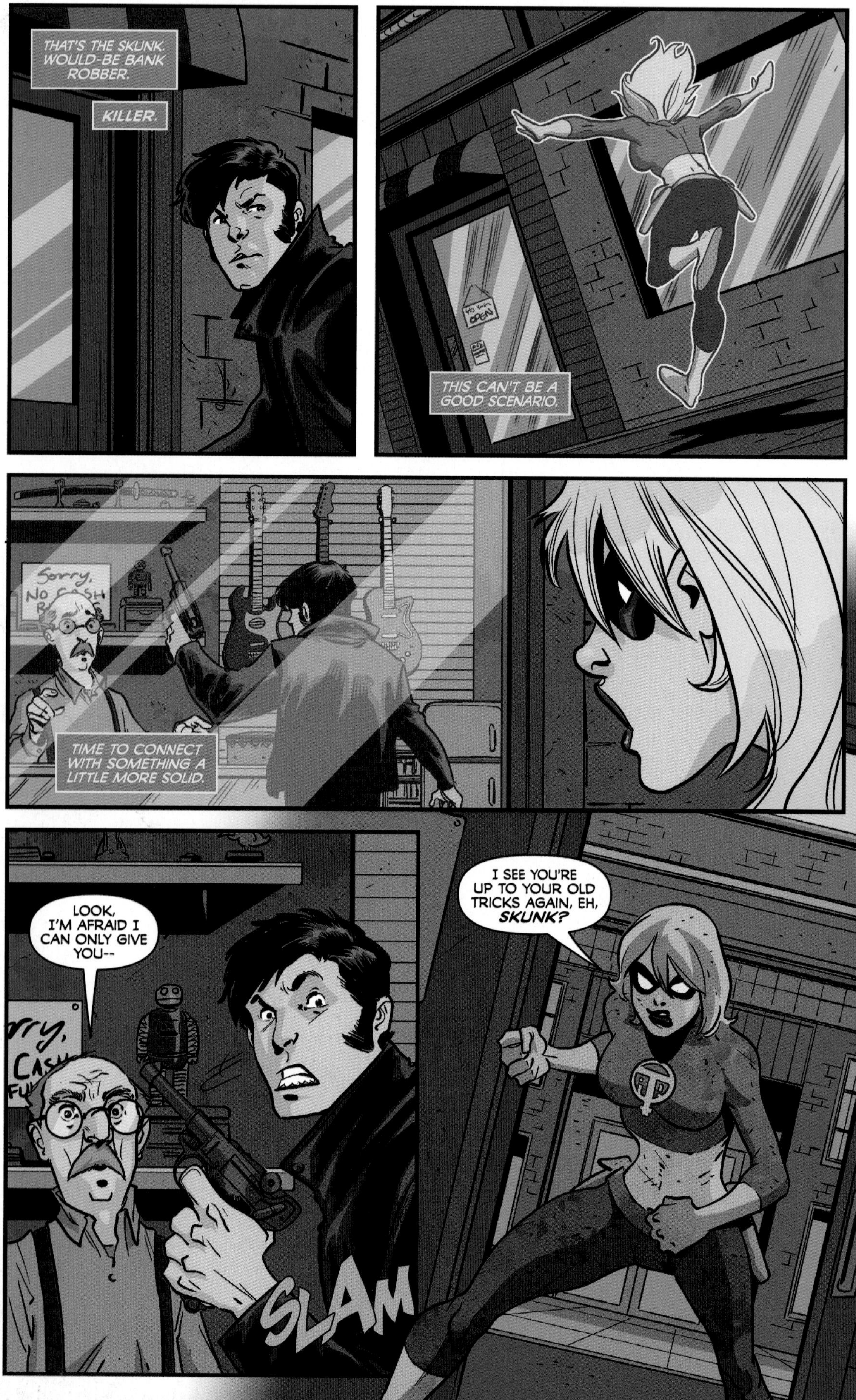
THAT'S THE SKUNK. WOULD-BE BANK ROBBER.
KILLER.
THIS CAN'T BE A GOOD SCENARIO.
Sorry,
TIME TO CONNECT WITH SOMETHING A LITTLE MORE SOLID.
LOOK, I'M AFRAID I CAN ONLY GIVE YOU--
I SEE YOU'RE UP TO YOUR OLD TRICKS AGAIN, EH, SKUNK?
SLAM

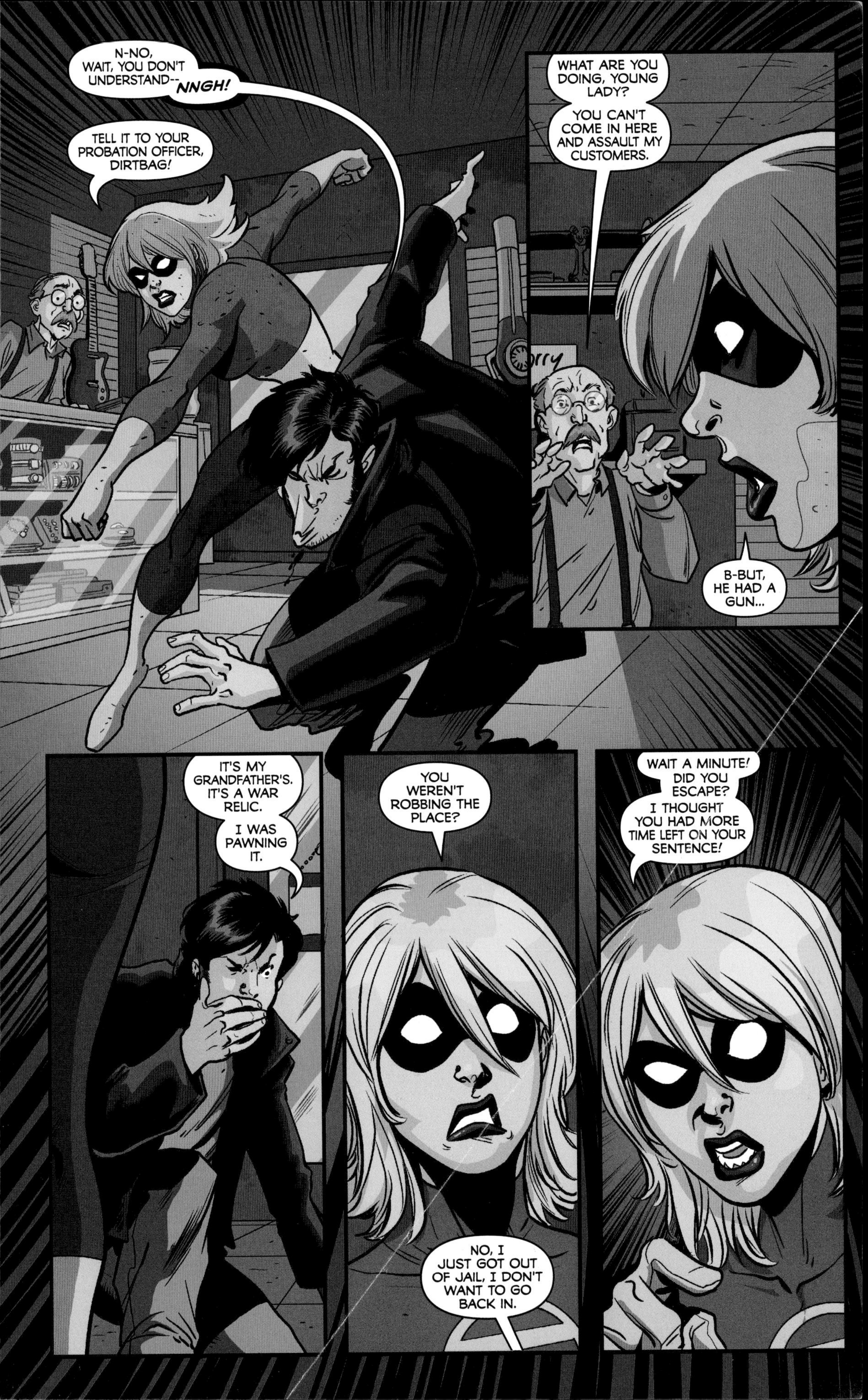
N-NO, WAIT, YOU DON'T UNDERSTAND--NNGH!
TELL IT TO YOUR PROBATION OFFICER, DIRTBAG!
WHAT ARE YOU DOING, YOUNG LADY?
YOU CAN'T COME IN HERE AND ASSAULT MY CUSTOMERS.
B-BUT, HE HAD A GUN...
IT'S MY GRANDFATHER'S. IT'S A WAR RELIC.
I WAS PAWNING IT.
YOU WEREN'T ROBBING THE PLACE?
NO, I JUST GOT OUT OF JAIL, I DON'T WANT TO GO BACK IN.
WAIT A MINUTE! DID YOU ESCAPE?
I THOUGHT YOU HAD MORE TIME LEFT ON YOUR SENTENCE!

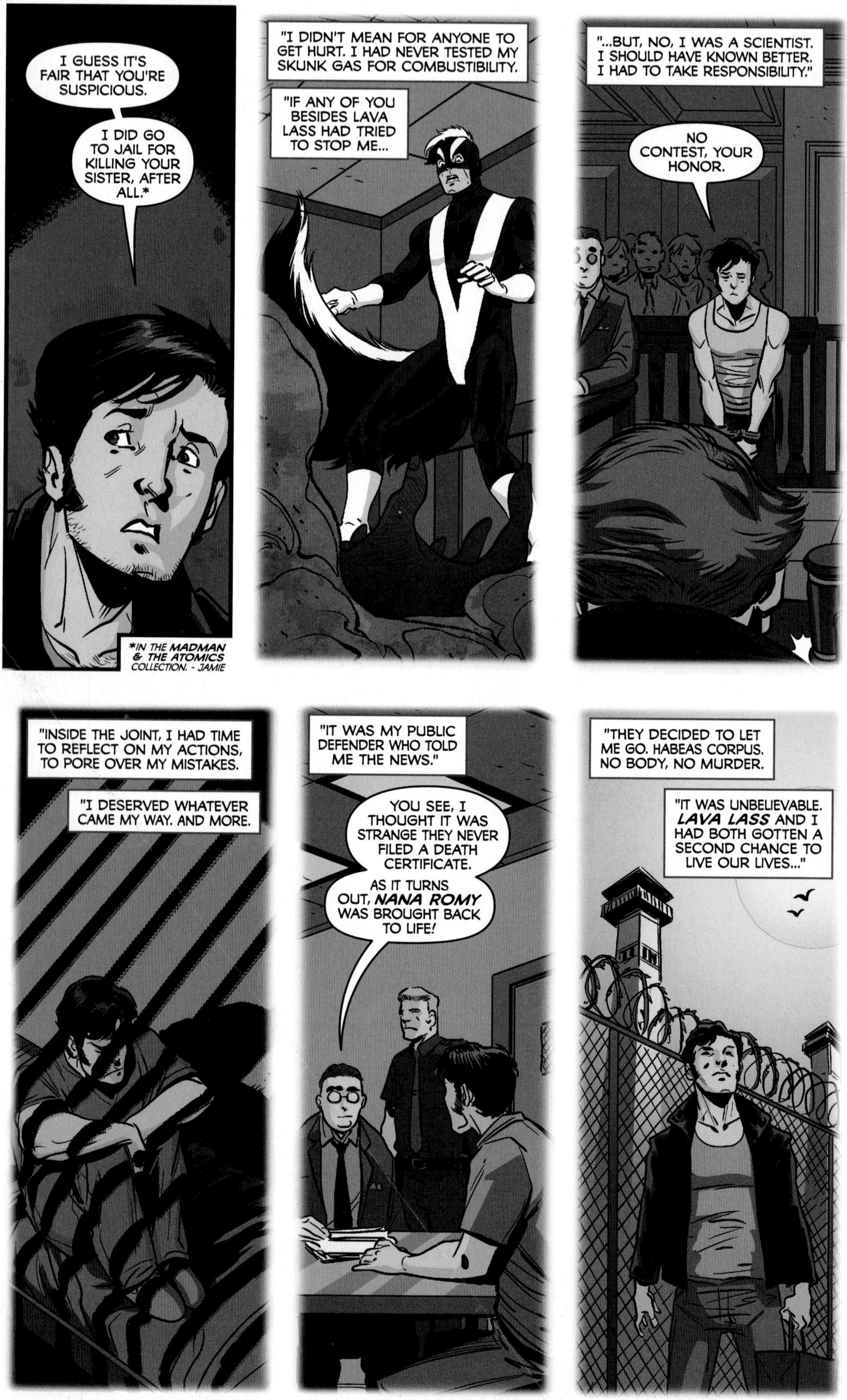
I GUESS IT'S FAIR THAT YOU'RE SUSPICIOUS.
I DID GO TO JAIL FOR KILLING YOUR SISTER, AFTER ALL.*
*IN THE MADMAN & THE ATOMICS COLLECTION. - JAMIE
"I DIDN'T MEAN FOR ANYONE TO GET HURT. I HAD NEVER TESTED MY SKUNK GAS FOR COMBUSTIBILITY.
"IF ANY OF YOU BESIDES LAVA LASS HAD TRIED TO STOP ME...
"...BUT, NO, I WAS A SCIENTIST. I SHOULD HAVE KNOWN BETTER. I HAD TO TAKE RESPONSIBILITY."
NO CONTEST, YOUR HONOR.
"INSIDE THE JOINT, I HAD TIME TO REFLECT ON MY ACTIONS, TO PORE OVER MY MISTAKES.
"I DESERVED WHATEVER CAME MY WAY. AND MORE.
"IT WAS MY PUBLIC DEFENDER WHO TOLD ME THE NEWS."
YOU SEE, I THOUGHT IT WAS STRANGE THEY NEVER FILED A DEATH CERTIFICATE.
AS IT TURNS OUT, NANA ROMY WAS BROUGHT BACK TO LIFE!
"THEY DECIDED TO LET ME GO. HABEAS CORPUS. NO BODY, NO MURDER.
"IT WAS UNBELIEVABLE. LAVA LASS AND I HAD BOTH GOTTEN A SECOND CHANCE TO LIVE OUR LIVES..."

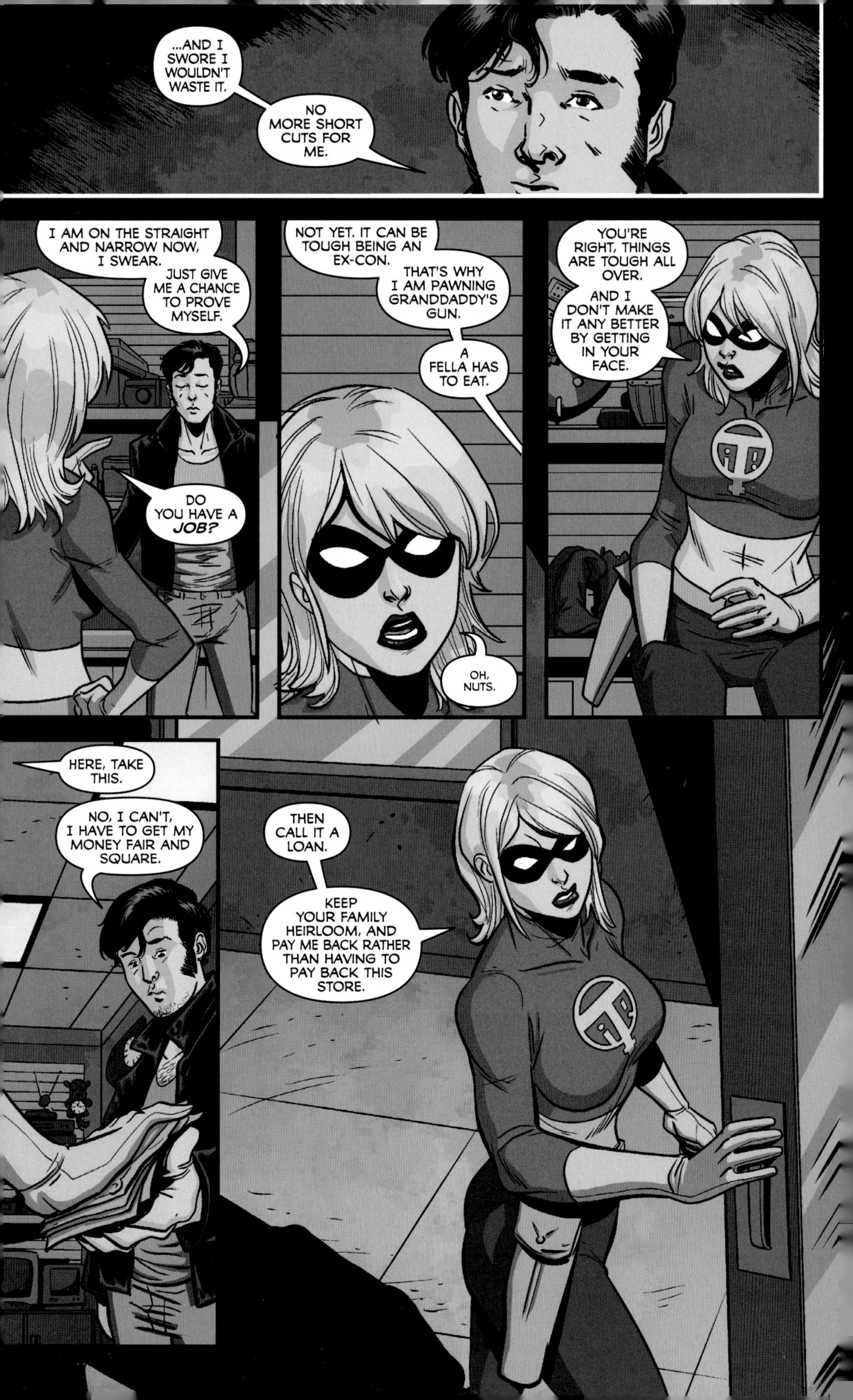
...AND I SWORE I WOULDN'T WASTE IT.
NO MORE SHORT CUTS FOR ME.
I AM ON THE STRAIGHT AND NARROW NOW, I SWEAR.
JUST GIVE ME A CHANCE TO PROVE MYSELF.
DO YOU HAVE A *JOB?*
NOT YET. IT CAN BE TOUGH BEING AN EX-CON.
THAT'S WHY I AM PAWNING GRANDDADDY'S GUN.
A FELLA HAS TO EAT.
OH, NUTS.
YOU'RE RIGHT, THINGS ARE TOUGH ALL OVER.
AND I DON'T MAKE IT ANY BETTER BY GETTING IN YOUR FACE.
HERE, TAKE THIS.
NO, I CAN'T, I HAVE TO GET MY MONEY FAIR AND SQUARE.
THEN CALL IT A LOAN.
KEEP YOUR FAMILY HEIRLOOM, AND PAY ME BACK RATHER THAN HAVING TO PAY BACK THIS STORE.

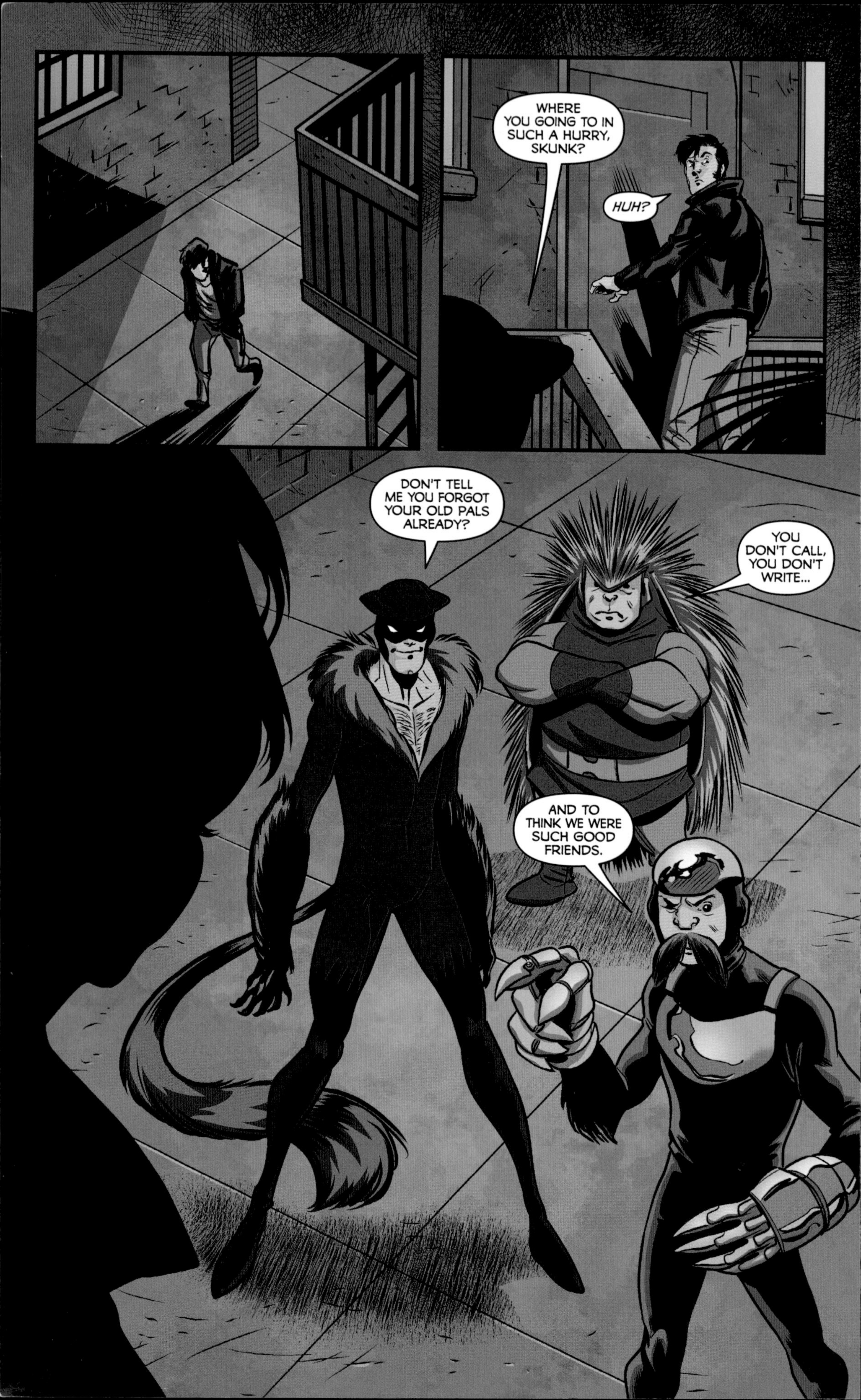
WHERE YOU GOING TO IN SUCH A HURRY, SKUNK?
HUH?
DON'T TELL ME YOU FORGOT YOUR OLD PALS ALREADY?
YOU DON'T CALL, YOU DON'T WRITE...
AND TO THINK WE WERE SUCH GOOD FRIENDS.

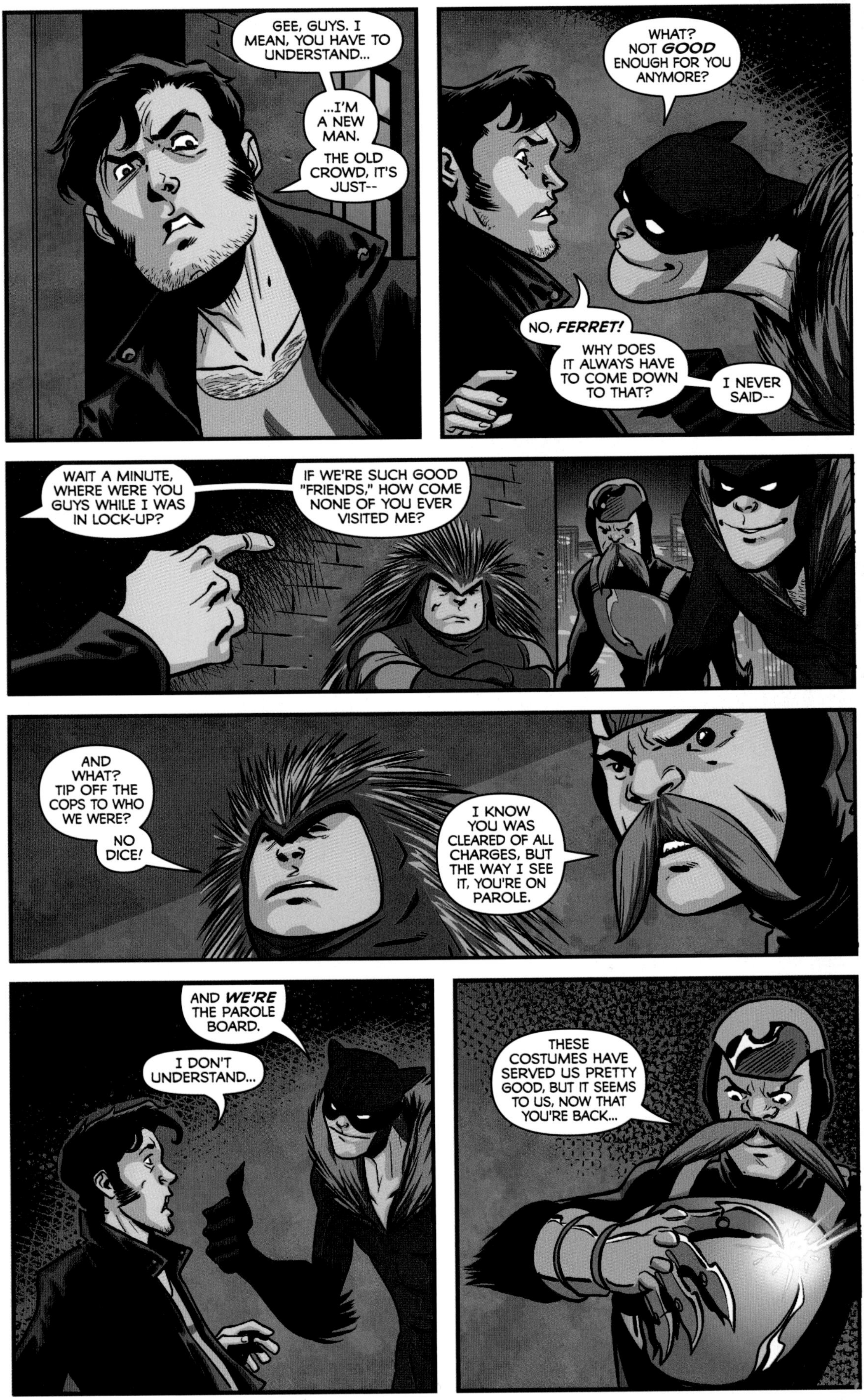
GEE, GUYS. I MEAN, YOU HAVE TO UNDERSTAND...
...I'M A NEW MAN.
THE OLD CROWD, IT'S JUST--
WHAT? NOT GOOD ENOUGH FOR YOU ANYMORE?
NO, FERRET!
WHY DOES IT ALWAYS HAVE TO COME DOWN TO THAT?
I NEVER SAID--
WAIT A MINUTE, WHERE WERE YOU GUYS WHILE I WAS IN LOCK-UP?
IF WE'RE SUCH GOOD "FRIENDS," HOW COME NONE OF YOU EVER VISITED ME?
AND WHAT? TIP OFF THE COPS TO WHO WE WERE?
NO DICE!
I KNOW YOU WAS CLEARED OF ALL CHARGES, BUT THE WAY I SEE IT, YOU'RE ON PAROLE.
AND WE'RE THE PAROLE BOARD.
I DON'T UNDERSTAND...
THESE COSTUMES HAVE SERVED US PRETTY GOOD, BUT IT SEEMS TO US, NOW THAT YOU'RE BACK...

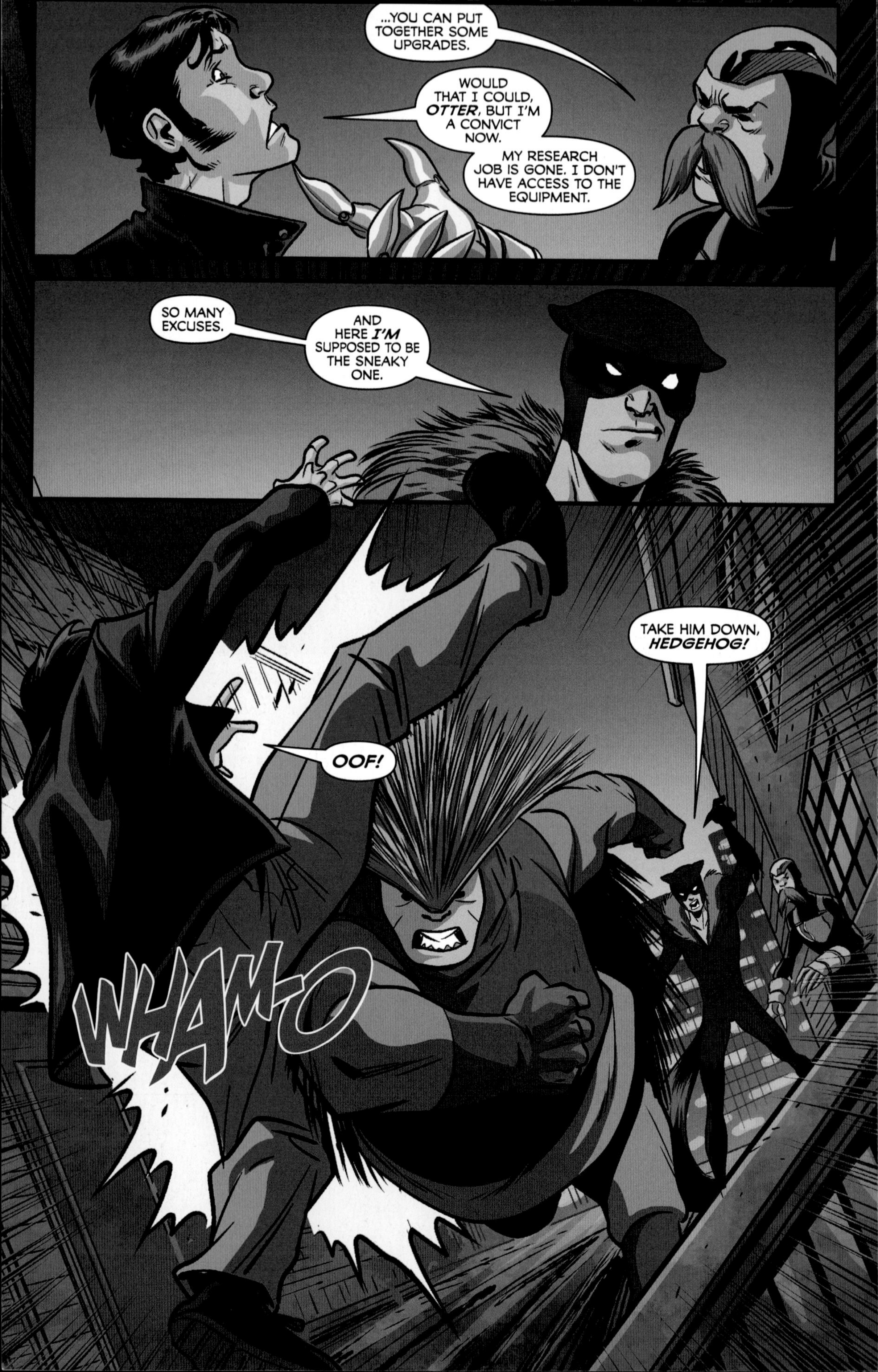
...YOU CAN PUT TOGETHER SOME UPGRADES.
WOULD THAT I COULD, OTTER, BUT I'M A CONVICT NOW.
MY RESEARCH JOB IS GONE. I DON'T HAVE ACCESS TO THE EQUIPMENT.
SO MANY EXCUSES.
AND HERE I'M SUPPOSED TO BE THE SNEAKY ONE.
TAKE HIM DOWN, HEDGEHOG!
OOF!
WHAM-O

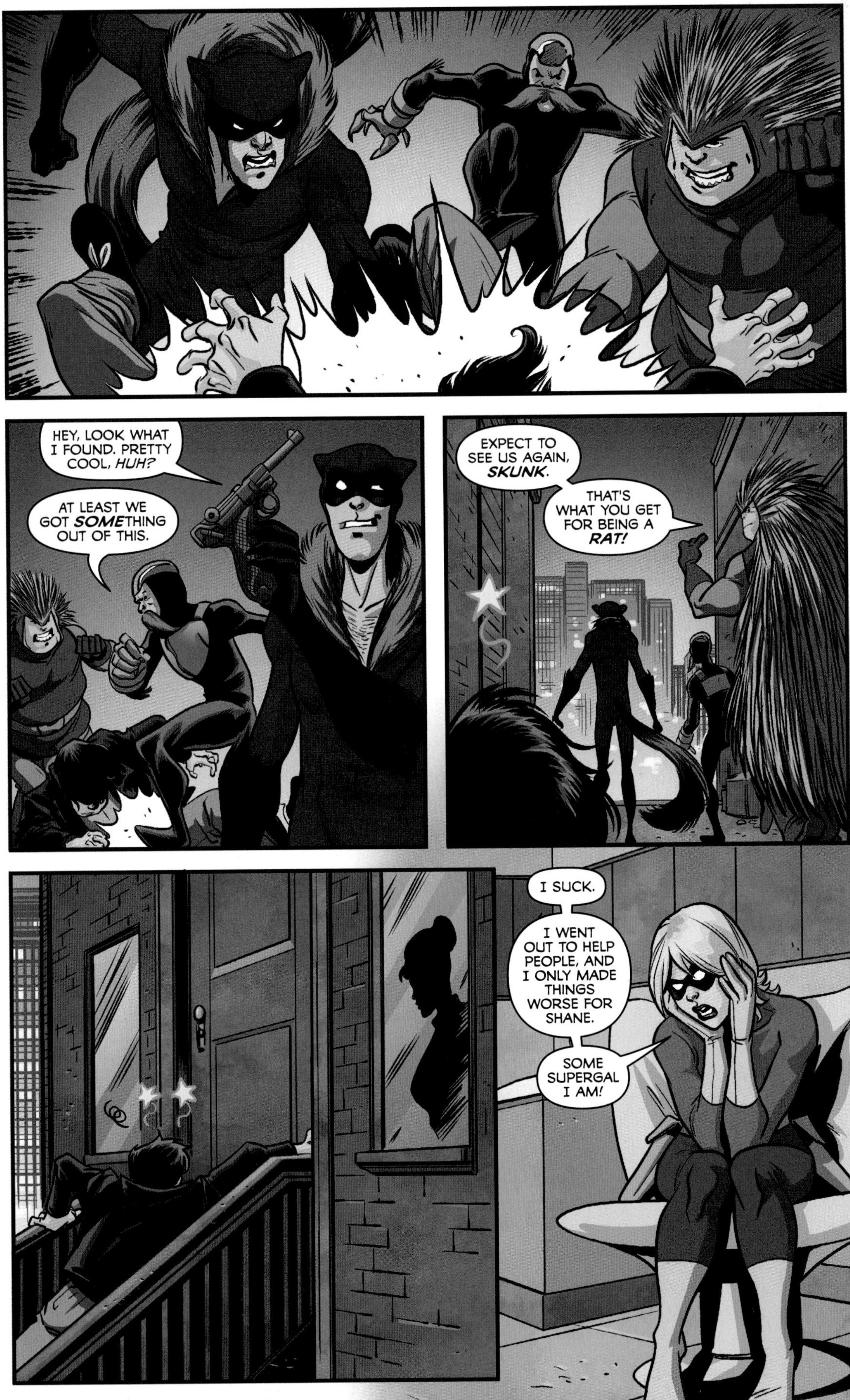
HEY, LOOK WHAT I FOUND. PRETTY COOL, *HUH?*
AT LEAST WE GOT ***SOME***THING OUT OF THIS.
EXPECT TO SEE US AGAIN, ***SKUNK***.
THAT'S WHAT YOU GET FOR BEING A ***RAT!***
I SUCK.
I WENT OUT TO HELP PEOPLE, AND I ONLY MADE THINGS WORSE FOR SHANE.
SOME SUPERGAL I AM!

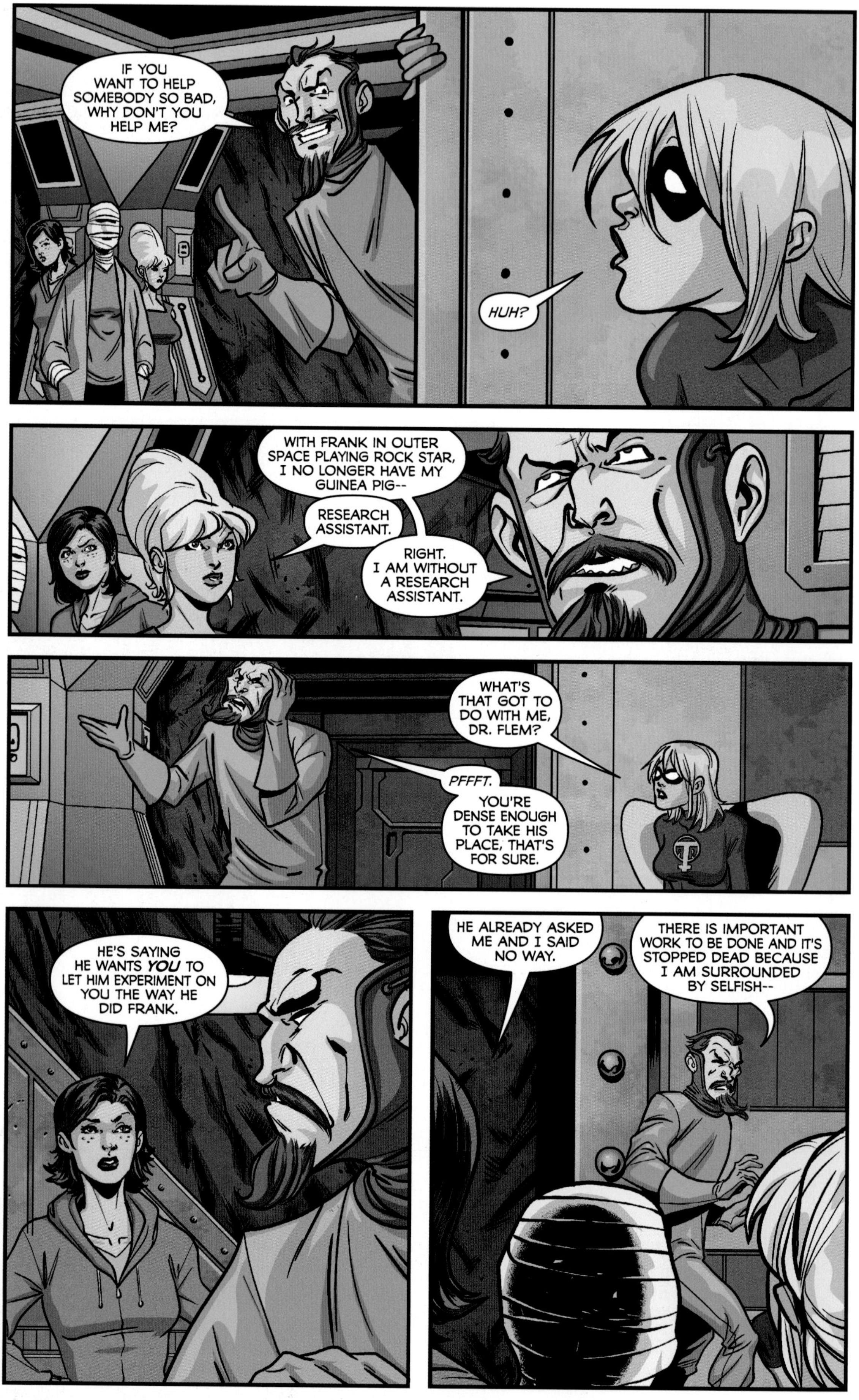
IF YOU WANT TO HELP SOMEBODY SO BAD, WHY DON'T YOU HELP ME?
HUH?
WITH FRANK IN OUTER SPACE PLAYING ROCK STAR, I NO LONGER HAVE MY GUINEA PIG--
RESEARCH ASSISTANT.
RIGHT. I AM WITHOUT A RESEARCH ASSISTANT.
WHAT'S THAT GOT TO DO WITH ME, DR. FLEM?
PFFFT.
YOU'RE DENSE ENOUGH TO TAKE HIS PLACE, THAT'S FOR SURE.
HE'S SAYING HE WANTS YOU TO LET HIM EXPERIMENT ON YOU THE WAY HE DID FRANK.
HE ALREADY ASKED ME AND I SAID NO WAY.
THERE IS IMPORTANT WORK TO BE DONE AND IT'S STOPPED DEAD BECAUSE I AM SURROUNDED BY SELFISH--

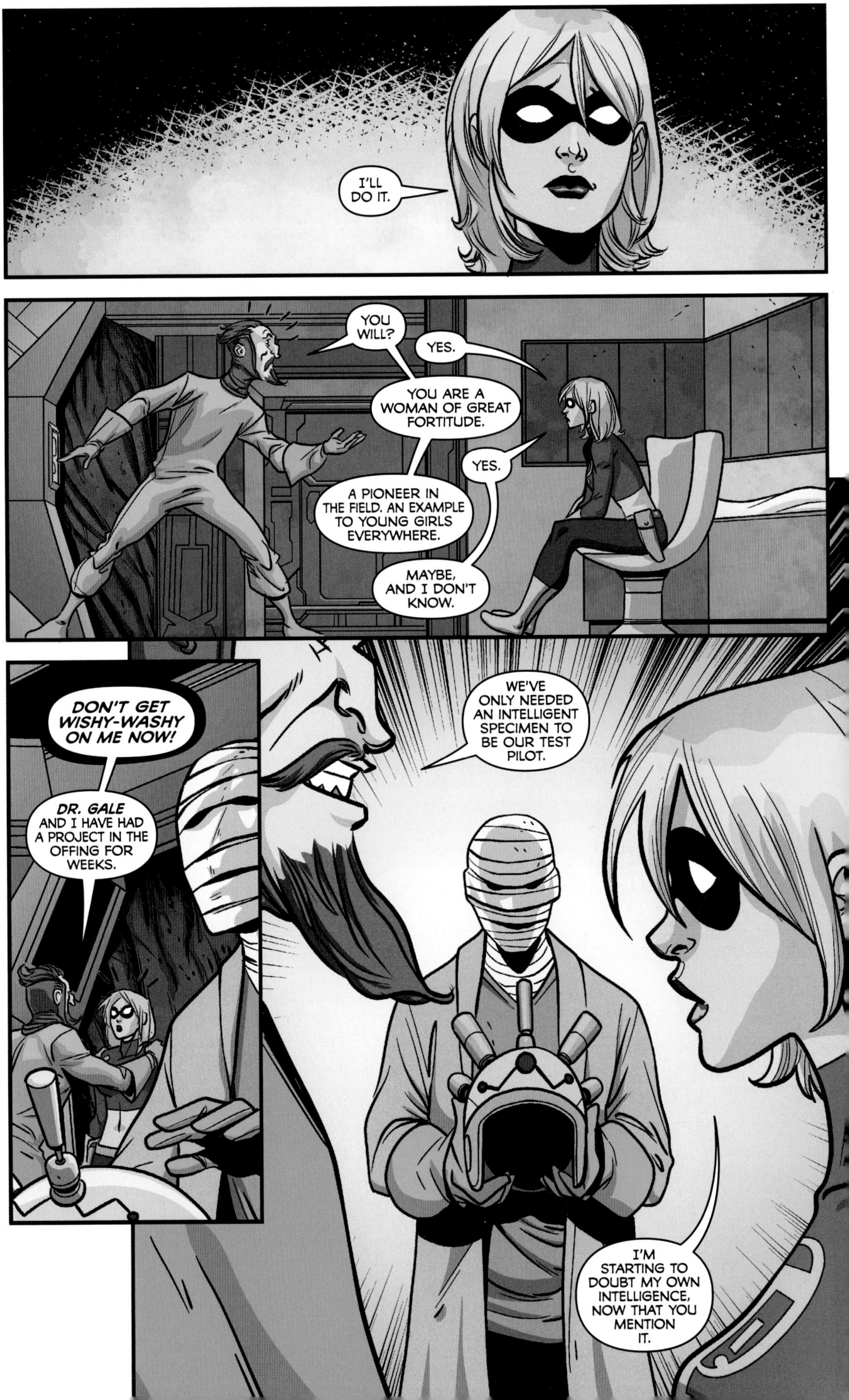
I'LL DO IT.
YOU WILL?
YES.
YOU ARE A WOMAN OF GREAT FORTITUDE.
YES.
A PIONEER IN THE FIELD. AN EXAMPLE TO YOUNG GIRLS EVERYWHERE.
MAYBE, AND I DON'T KNOW.
DON'T GET WISHY-WASHY ON ME NOW!
DR. GALE AND I HAVE HAD A PROJECT IN THE OFFING FOR WEEKS.
WE'VE ONLY NEEDED AN INTELLIGENT SPECIMEN TO BE OUR TEST PILOT.
I'M STARTING TO DOUBT MY OWN INTELLIGENCE, NOW THAT YOU MENTION IT.

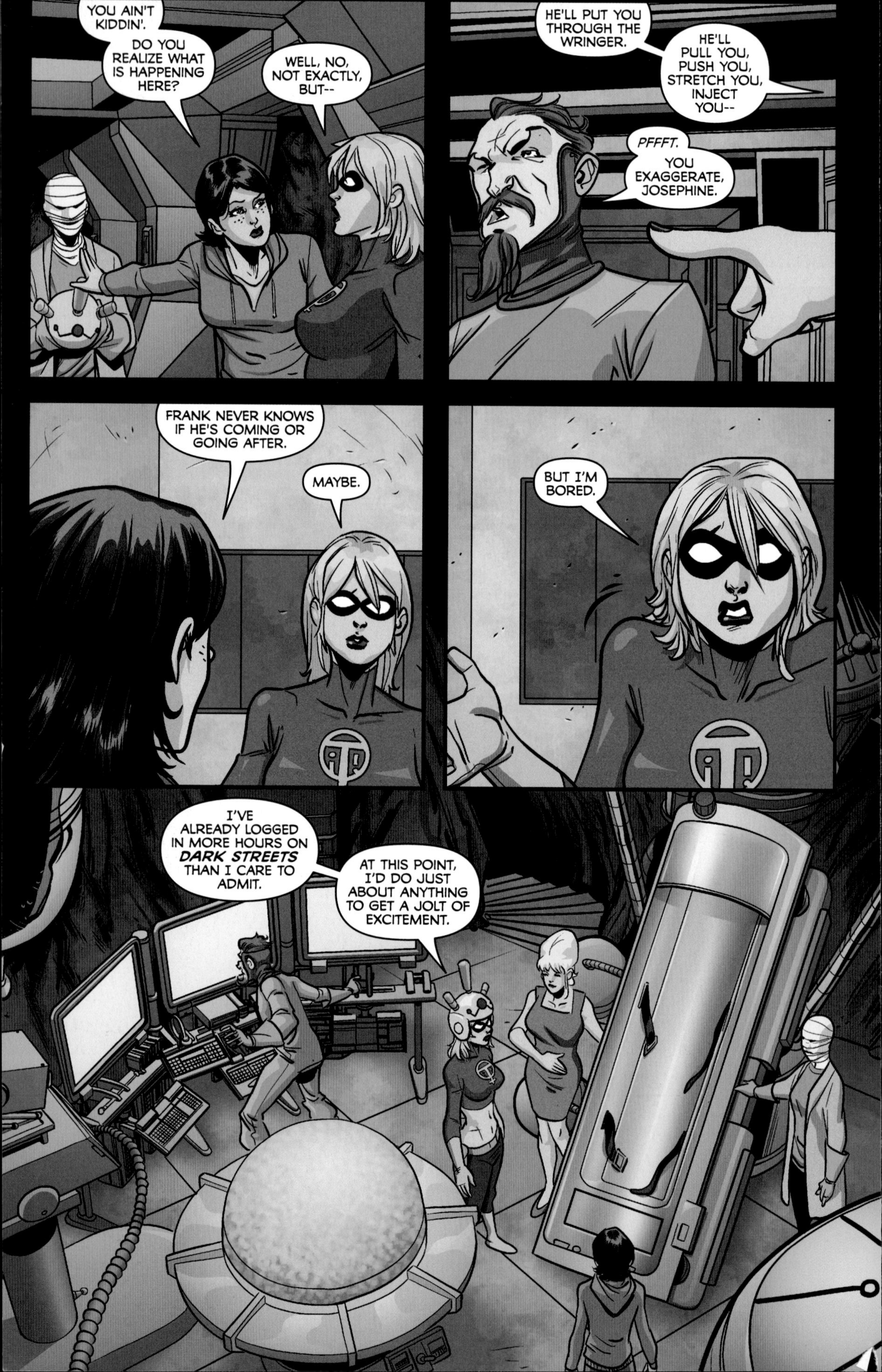
YOU AIN'T KIDDIN'.
DO YOU REALIZE WHAT IS HAPPENING HERE?
WELL, NO, NOT EXACTLY, BUT--
HE'LL PUT YOU THROUGH THE WRINGER.
HE'LL PULL YOU, PUSH YOU, STRETCH YOU, INJECT YOU--
PFFFT.
YOU EXAGGERATE, JOSEPHINE.
FRANK NEVER KNOWS IF HE'S COMING OR GOING AFTER.
MAYBE.
BUT I'M BORED.
I'VE ALREADY LOGGED IN MORE HOURS ON DARK STREETS THAN I CARE TO ADMIT.
AT THIS POINT, I'D DO JUST ABOUT ANYTHING TO GET A JOLT OF EXCITEMENT.

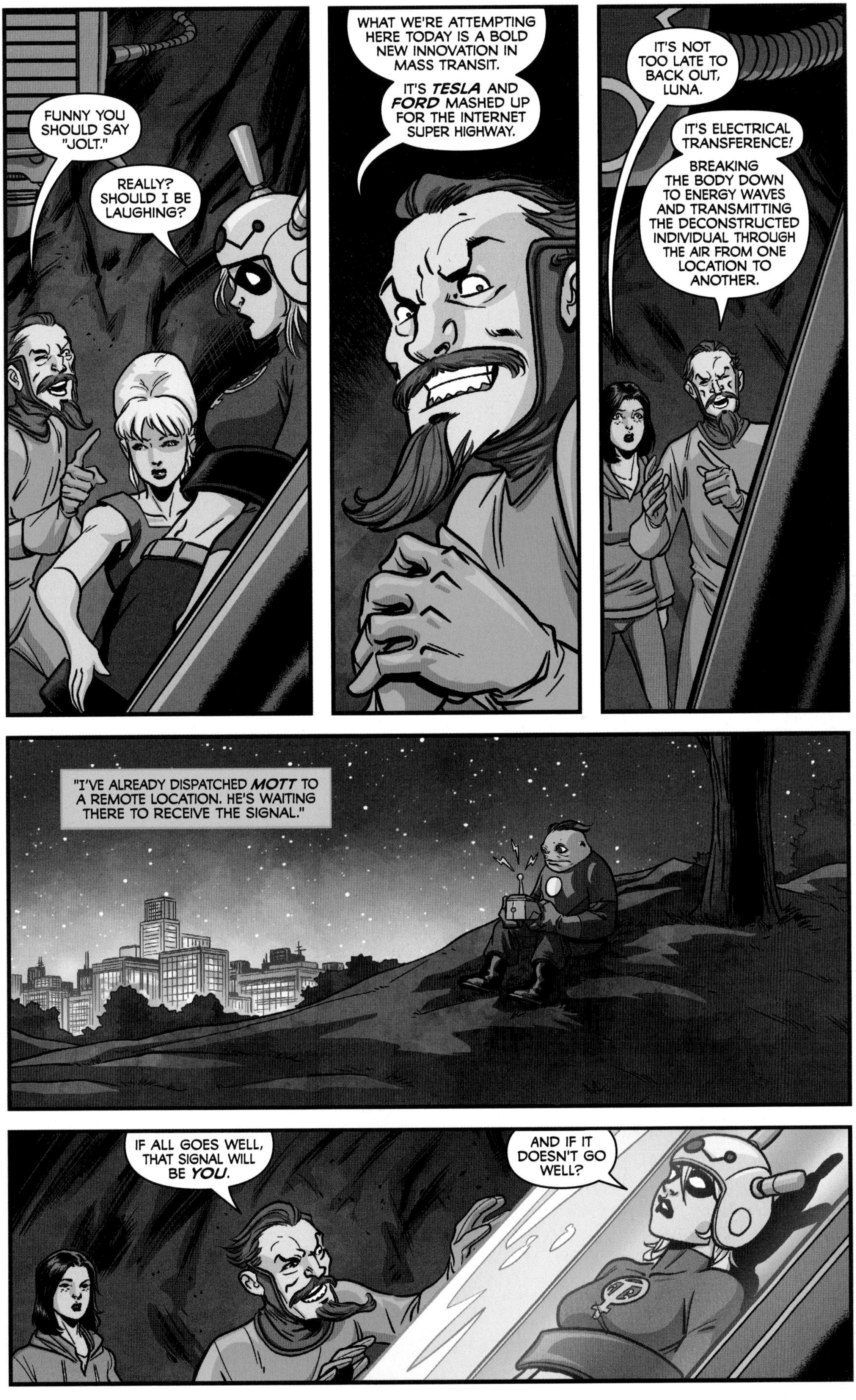
FUNNY YOU SHOULD SAY "JOLT."
REALLY? SHOULD I BE LAUGHING?
WHAT WE'RE ATTEMPTING HERE TODAY IS A BOLD NEW INNOVATION IN MASS TRANSIT.
IT'S *TESLA* AND *FORD* MASHED UP FOR THE INTERNET SUPER HIGHWAY.
IT'S NOT TOO LATE TO BACK OUT, LUNA.
IT'S ELECTRICAL TRANSFERENCE!
BREAKING THE BODY DOWN TO ENERGY WAVES AND TRANSMITTING THE DECONSTRUCTED INDIVIDUAL THROUGH THE AIR FROM ONE LOCATION TO ANOTHER.
"I'VE ALREADY DISPATCHED *MOTT* TO A REMOTE LOCATION. HE'S WAITING THERE TO RECEIVE THE SIGNAL."
IF ALL GOES WELL, THAT SIGNAL WILL BE *YOU*.
AND IF IT DOESN'T GO WELL?

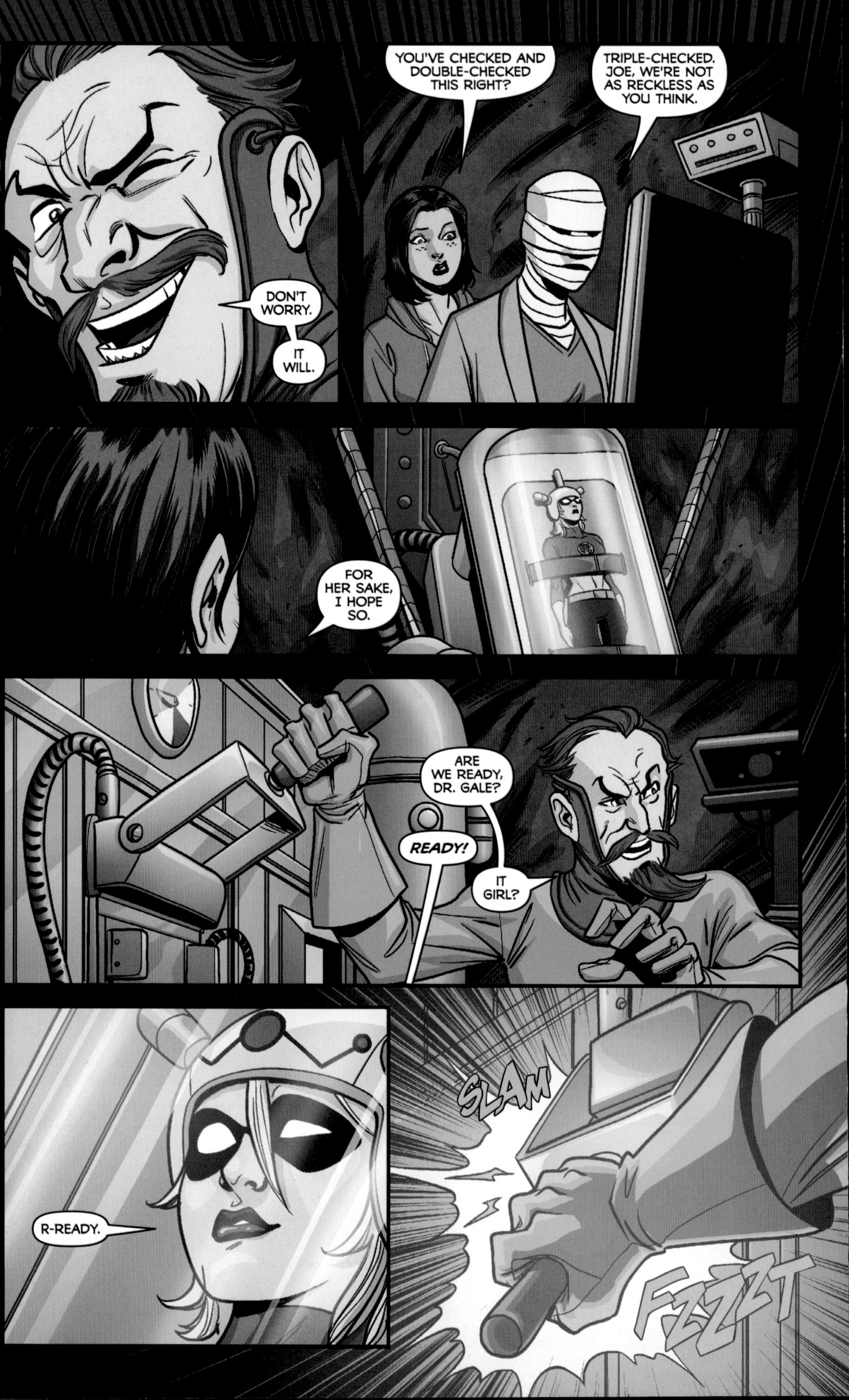
YOU'VE CHECKED AND DOUBLE-CHECKED THIS RIGHT?
TRIPLE-CHECKED. JOE, WE'RE NOT AS RECKLESS AS YOU THINK.
DON'T WORRY.
IT WILL.
FOR HER SAKE, I HOPE SO.
ARE WE READY, DR. GALE?
READY!
IT GIRL?
R-READY.
SLAM
FZZZT

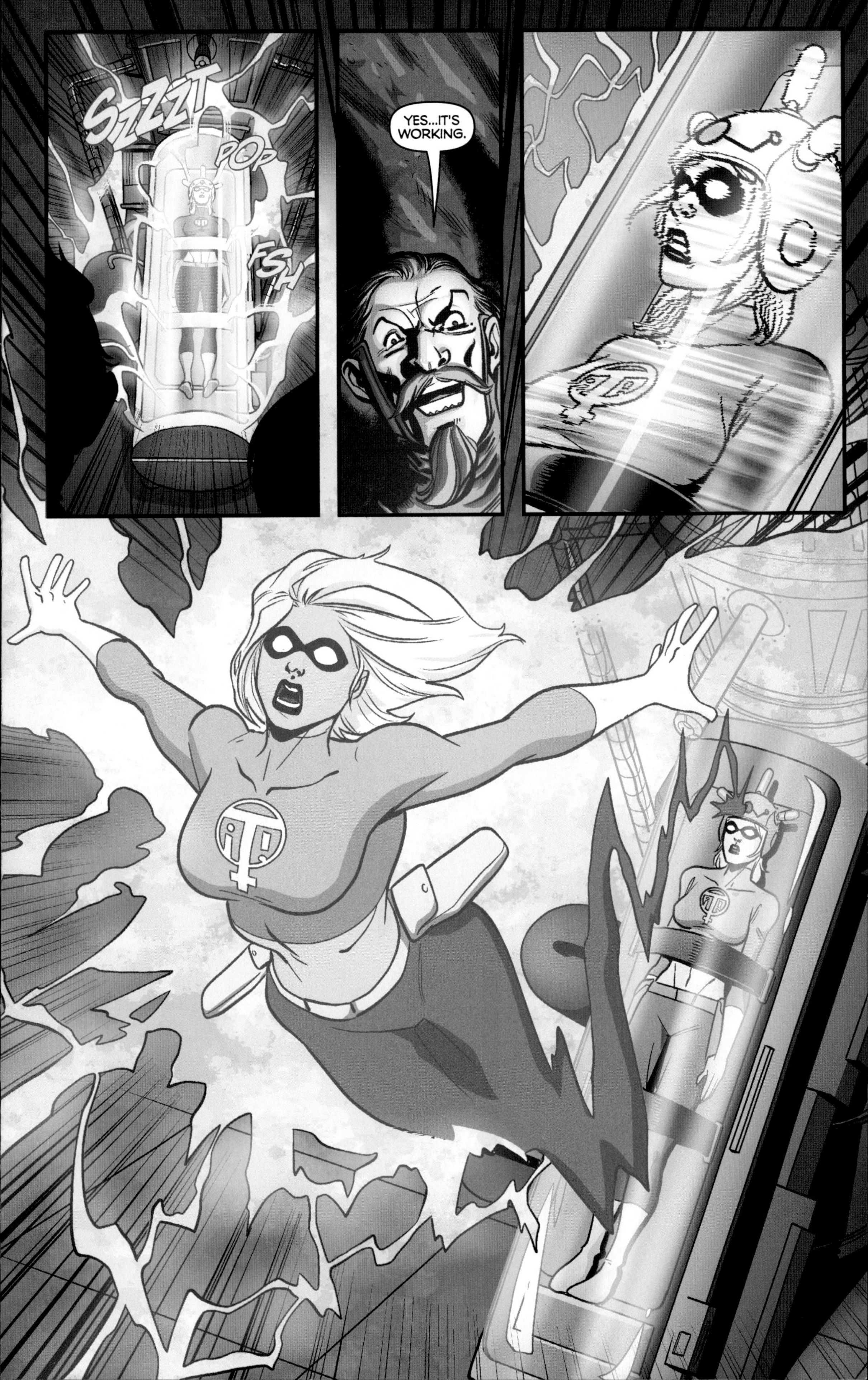
SzZZZT
POP
FSH
YES...IT'S WORKING.

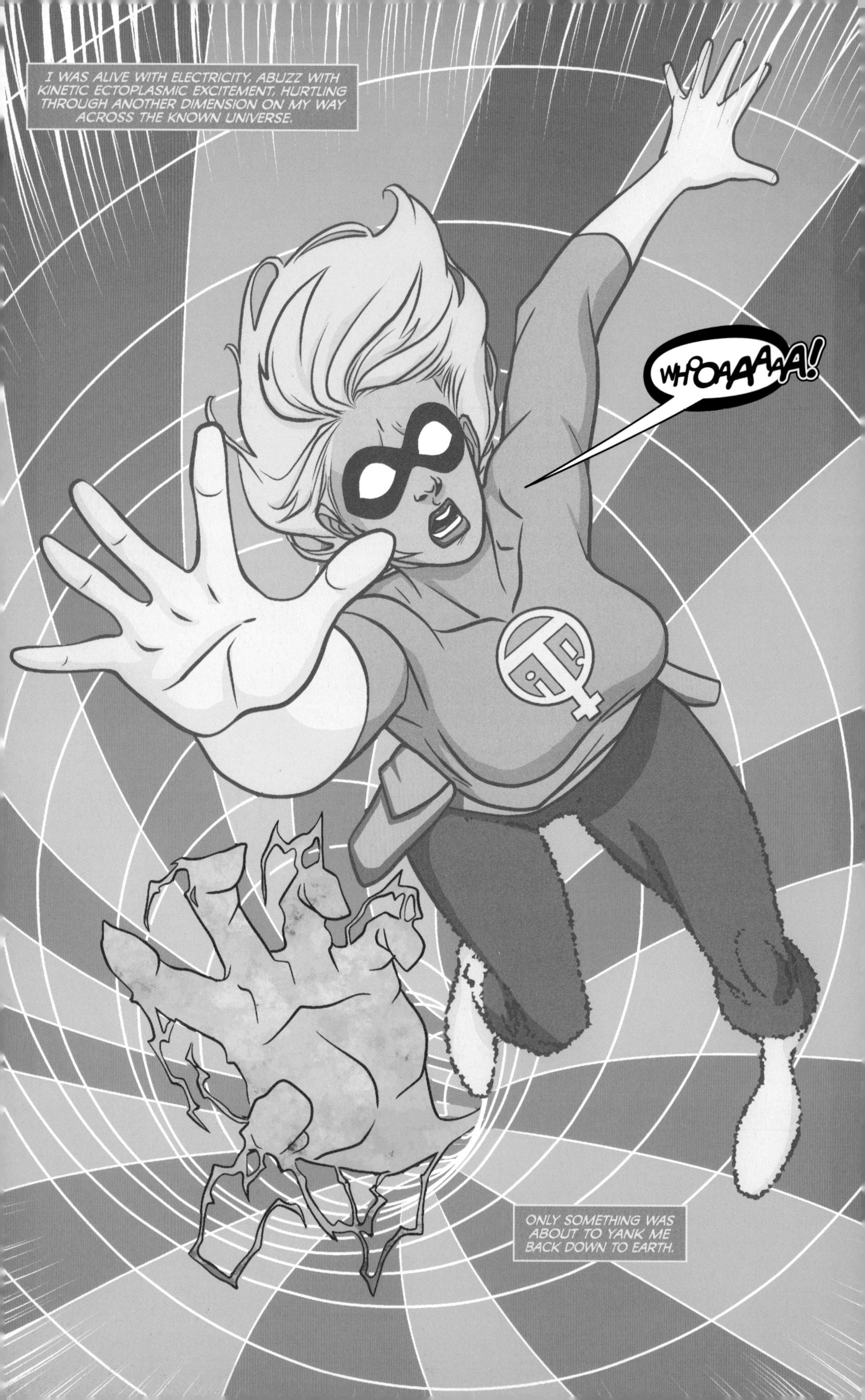
I WAS ALIVE WITH ELECTRICITY, ABUZZ WITH KINETIC ECTOPLASMIC EXCITEMENT, HURTLING THROUGH ANOTHER DIMENSION ON MY WAY ACROSS THE KNOWN UNIVERSE.
WHOAAAAA!
ONLY SOMETHING WAS ABOUT TO YANK ME BACK DOWN TO EARTH.

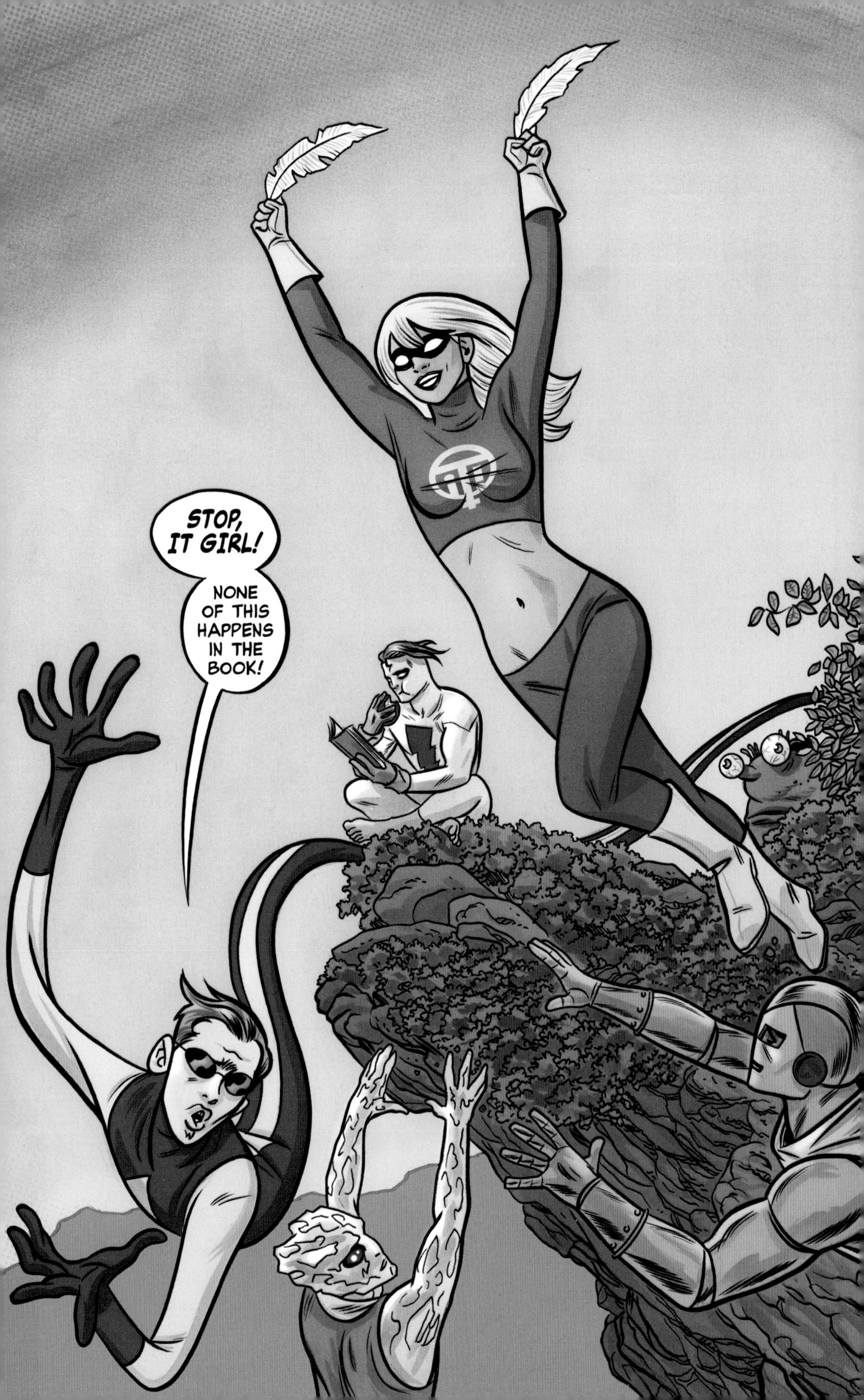
STOP, IT GIRL!
NONE OF THIS HAPPENS IN THE BOOK!

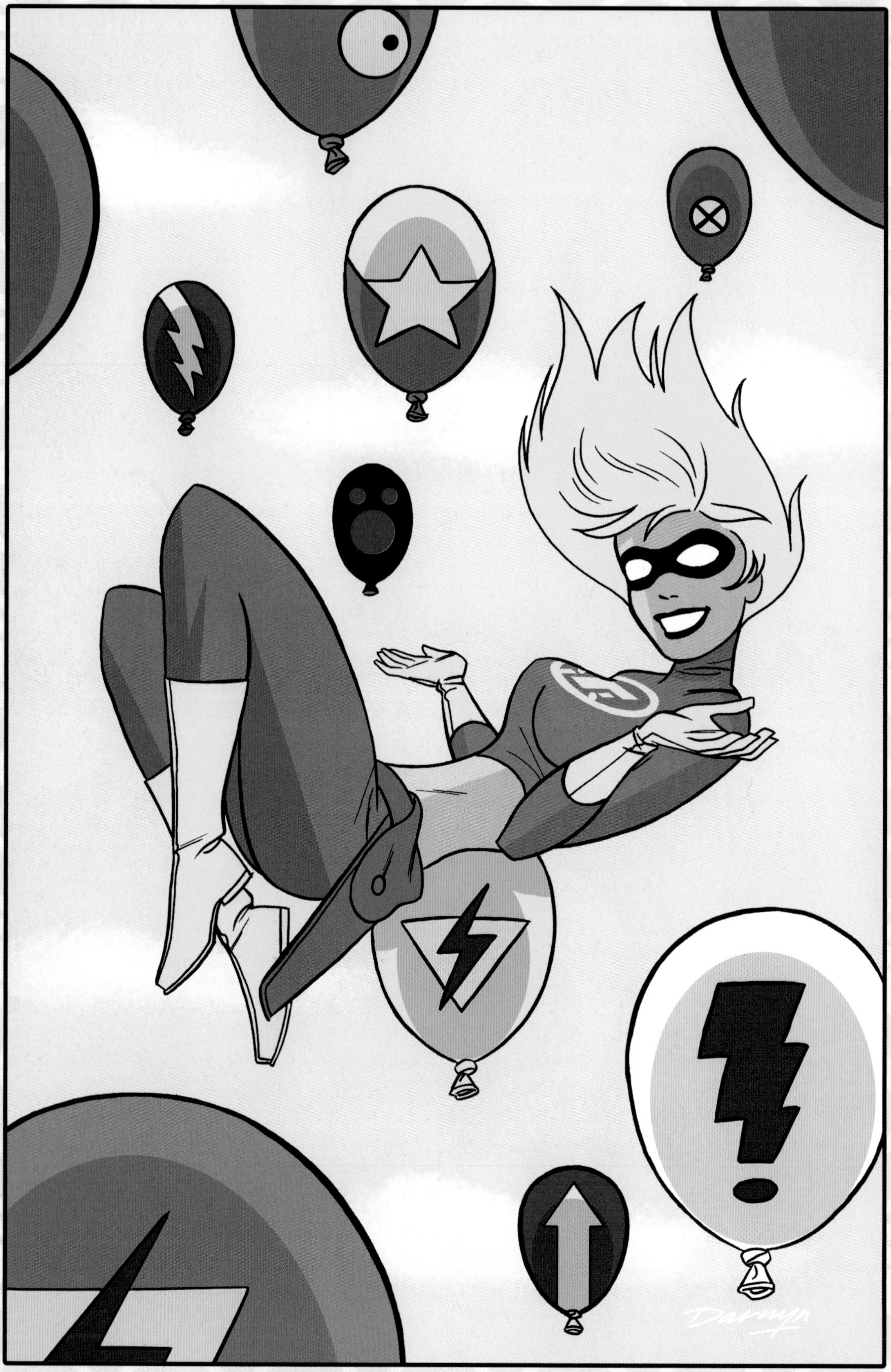
Darwyn

Illustration by Darwyn Cooke

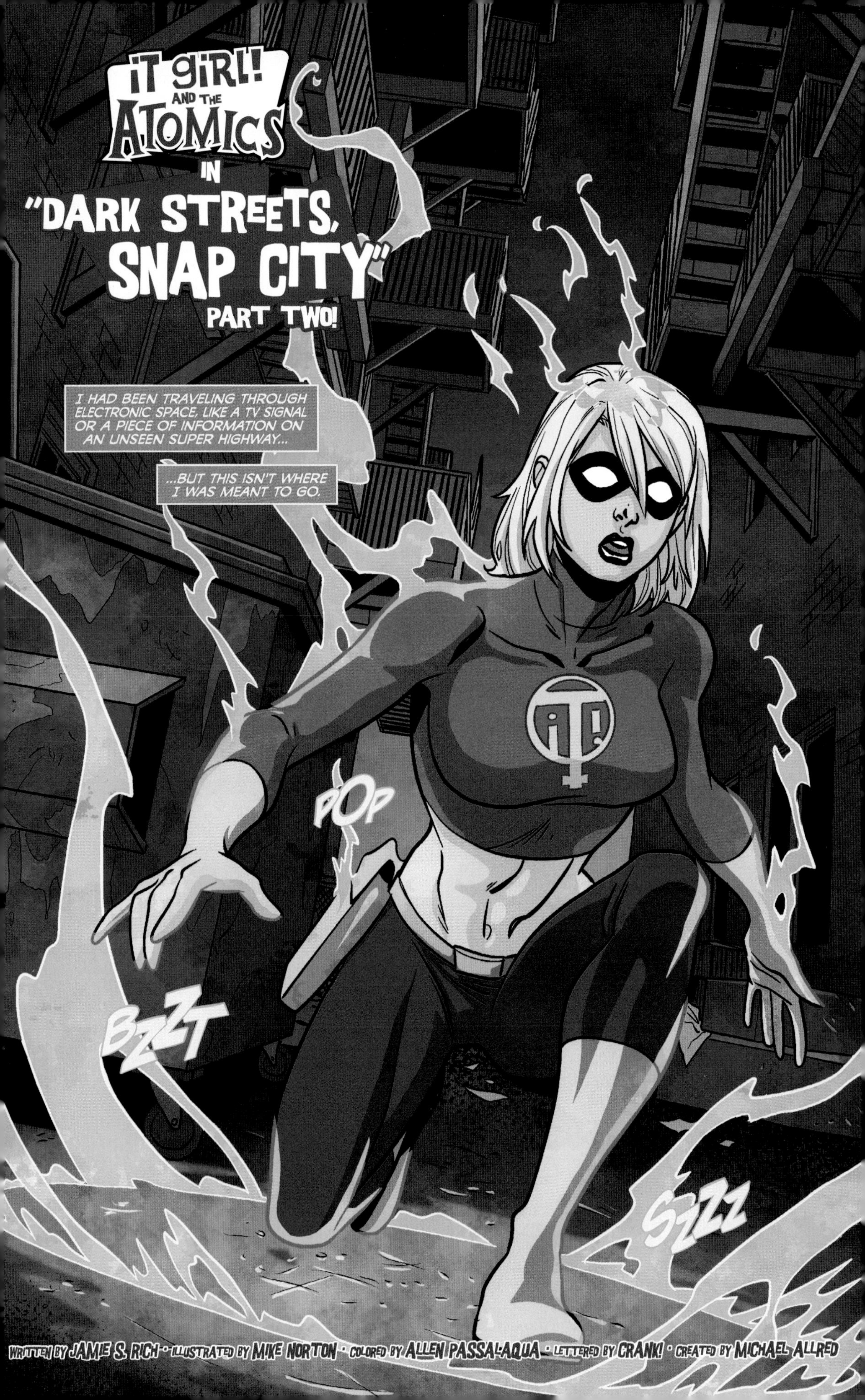
iT giRL! AND THE ATOMICS
IN
"DARK STREETS, SNAP CITY"
PART TWO!
I HAD BEEN TRAVELING THROUGH ELECTRONIC SPACE, LIKE A TV SIGNAL OR A PIECE OF INFORMATION ON AN UNSEEN SUPER HIGHWAY...
...BUT THIS ISN'T WHERE I WAS MEANT TO GO.
POP
BZZT
SZZZ
WRITTEN BY JAMIE S. RICH · ILLUSTRATED BY MIKE NORTON · COLORED BY ALLEN PASSALAQUA · LETTERED BY CRANK! · CREATED BY MICHAEL ALLRED

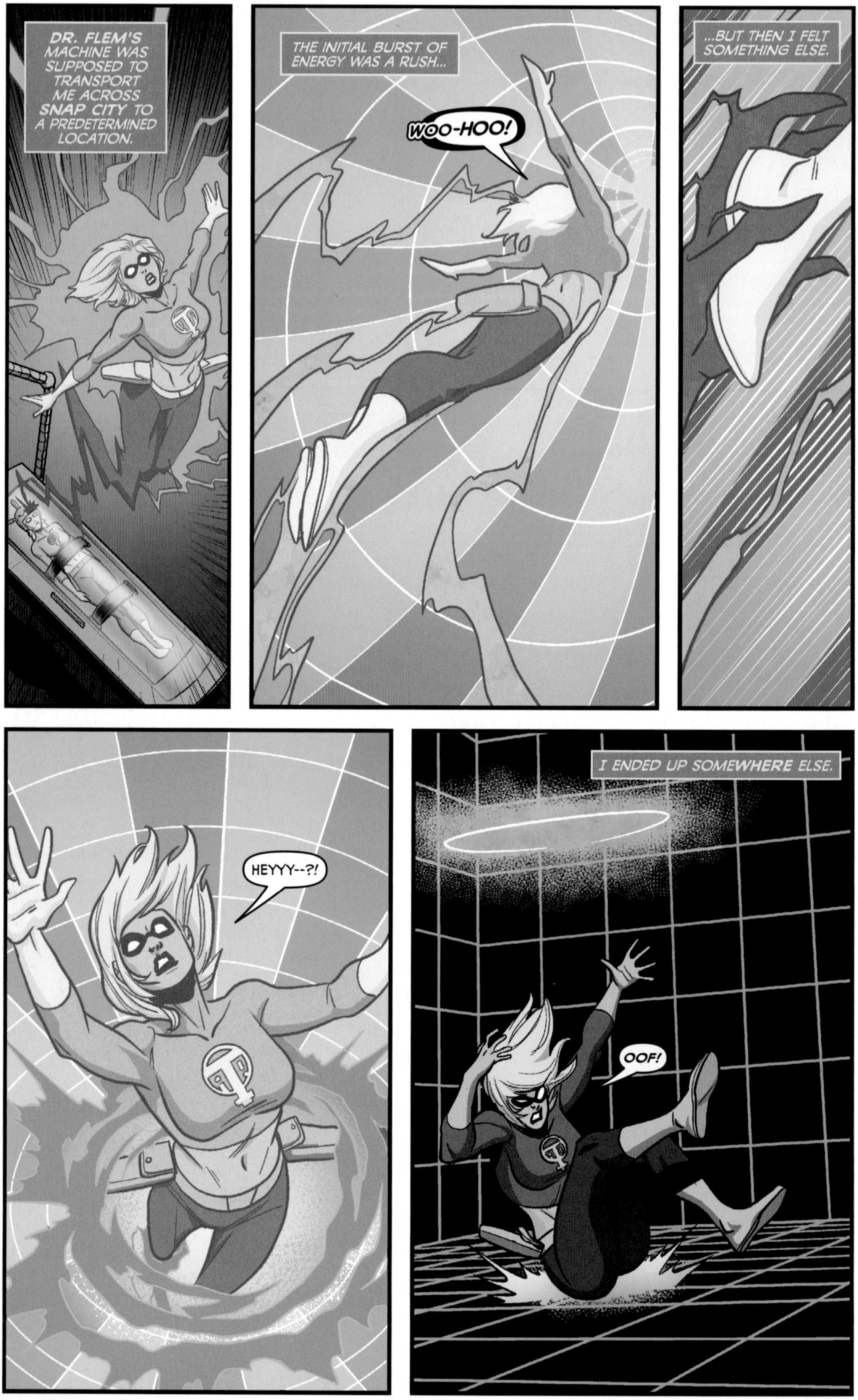
DR. FLEM'S MACHINE WAS SUPPOSED TO TRANSPORT ME ACROSS SNAP CITY TO A PREDETERMINED LOCATION.
THE INITIAL BURST OF ENERGY WAS A RUSH...
WOO-HOO!
...BUT THEN I FELT SOMETHING ELSE.
HEYYY--?!
I ENDED UP SOMEWHERE ELSE.
OOF!

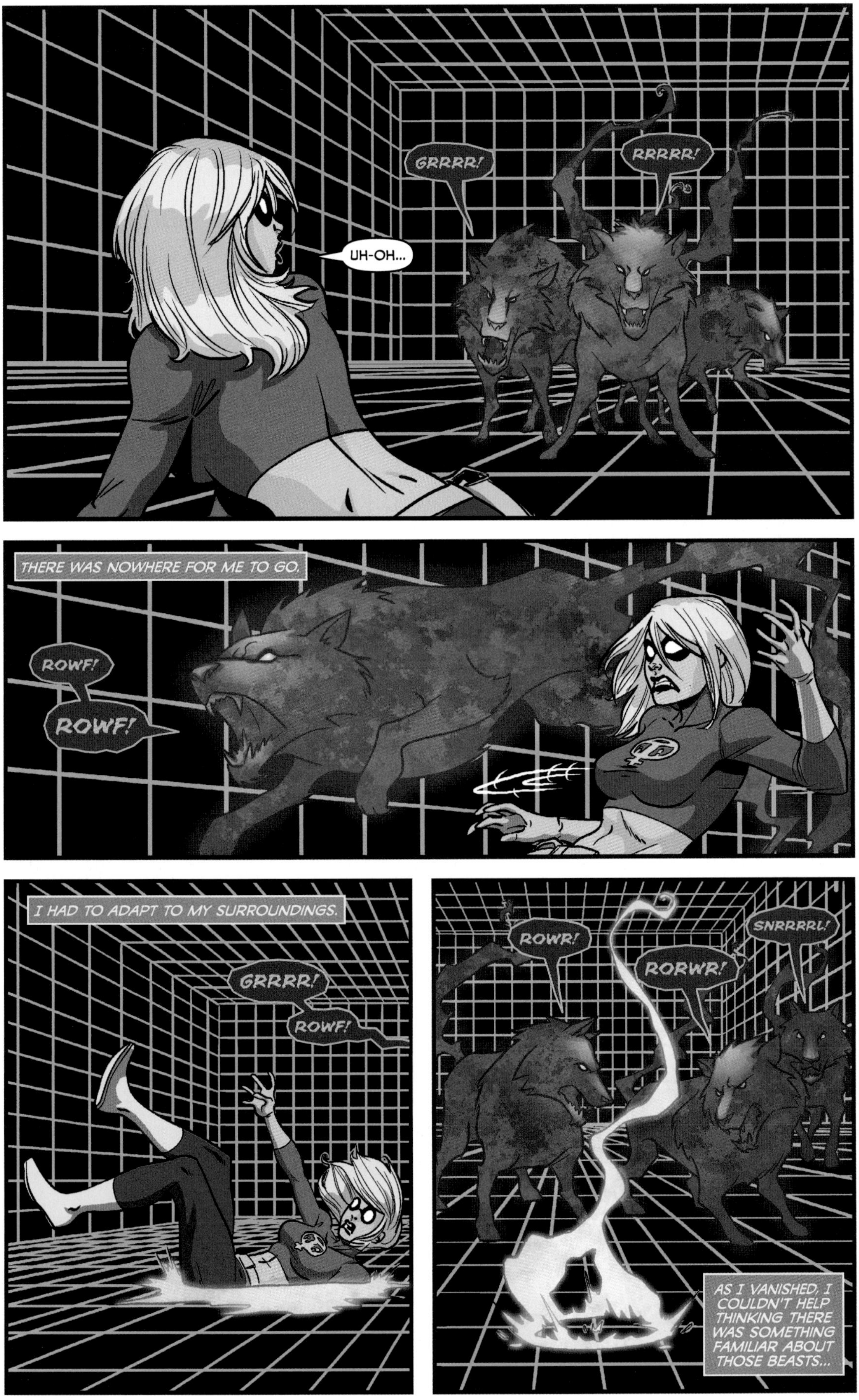
UH-OH...
GRRRR!
RRRRR!
THERE WAS NOWHERE FOR ME TO GO.
ROWF!
ROWF!
I HAD TO ADAPT TO MY SURROUNDINGS.
GRRRR!
ROWF!
ROWR!
RORWR!
SNRRRRL!
AS I VANISHED, I COULDN'T HELP THINKING THERE WAS SOMETHING FAMILIAR ABOUT THOSE BEASTS...

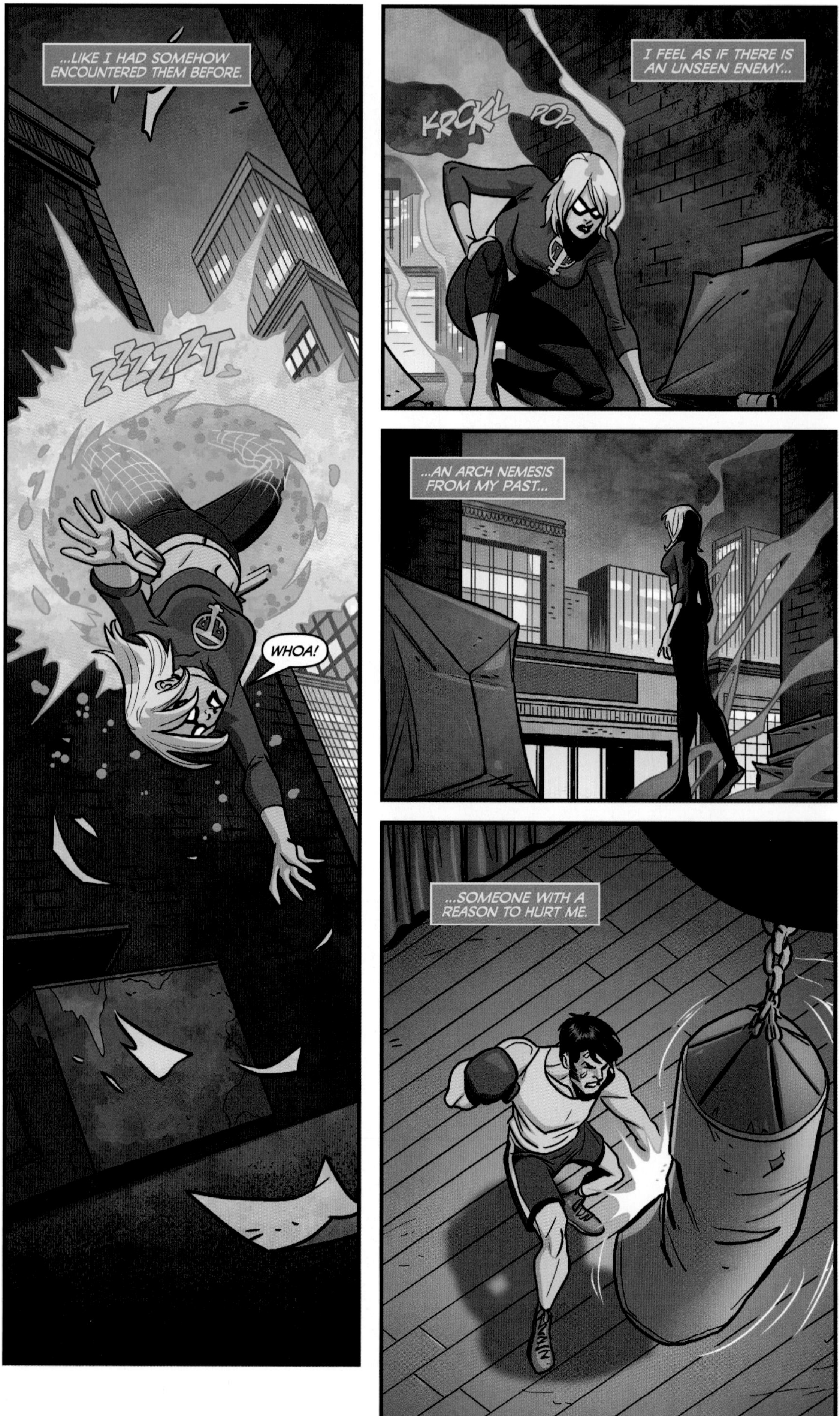

...LIKE I HAD SOMEHOW ENCOUNTERED THEM BEFORE.
ZZZZZT
WHOA!
I FEEL AS IF THERE IS AN UNSEEN ENEMY...
KRCKL
POP
...AN ARCH NEMESIS FROM MY PAST...
...SOMEONE WITH A REASON TO HURT ME.

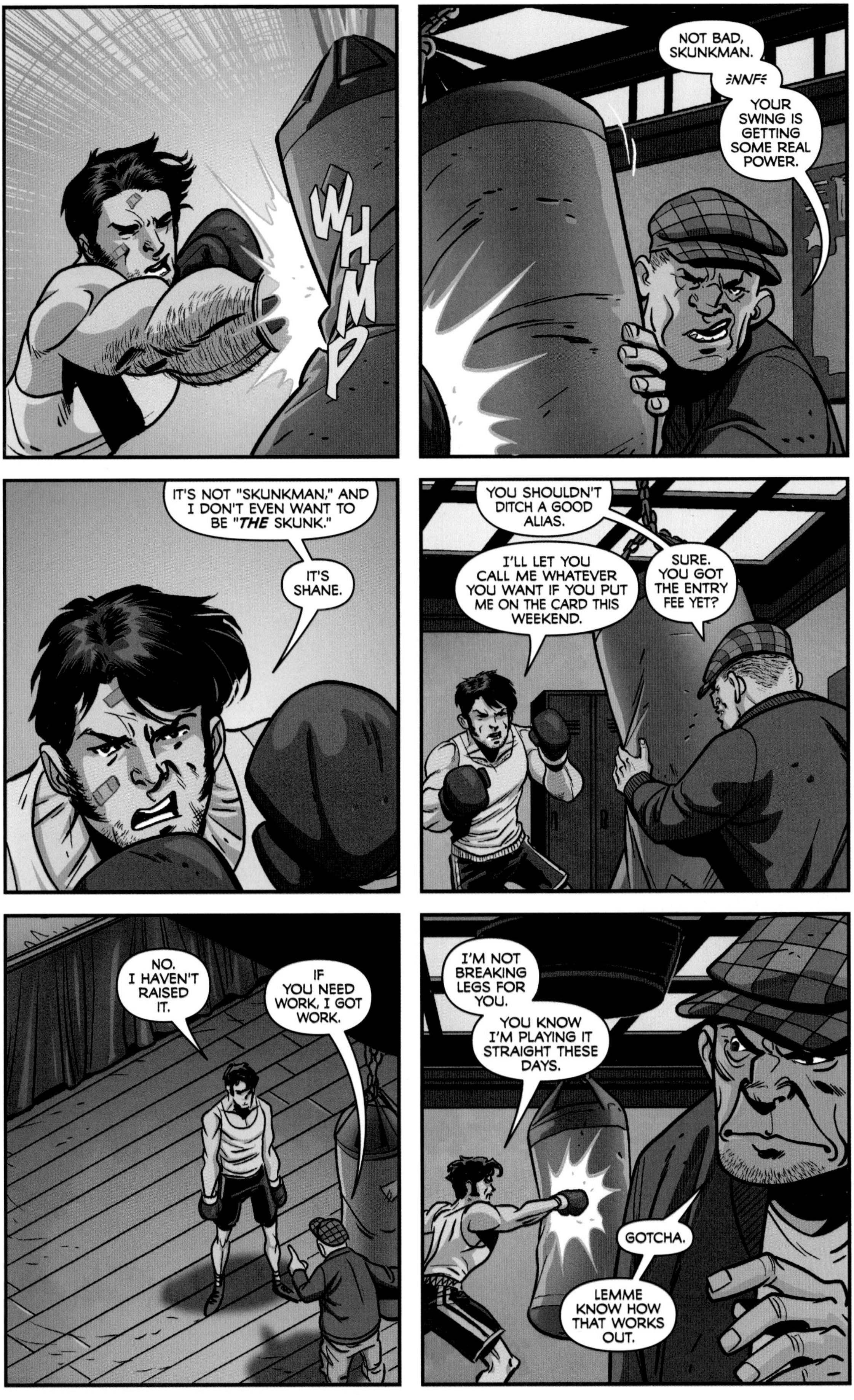
WHMP
NOT BAD, SKUNKMAN.
NNF
YOUR SWING IS GETTING SOME REAL POWER.
IT'S NOT "SKUNKMAN," AND I DON'T EVEN WANT TO BE "THE SKUNK."
IT'S SHANE.
YOU SHOULDN'T DITCH A GOOD ALIAS.
I'LL LET YOU CALL ME WHATEVER YOU WANT IF YOU PUT ME ON THE CARD THIS WEEKEND.
SURE. YOU GOT THE ENTRY FEE YET?
NO. I HAVEN'T RAISED IT.
IF YOU NEED WORK, I GOT WORK.
I'M NOT BREAKING LEGS FOR YOU.
YOU KNOW I'M PLAYING IT STRAIGHT THESE DAYS.
GOTCHA.
LEMME KNOW HOW THAT WORKS OUT.

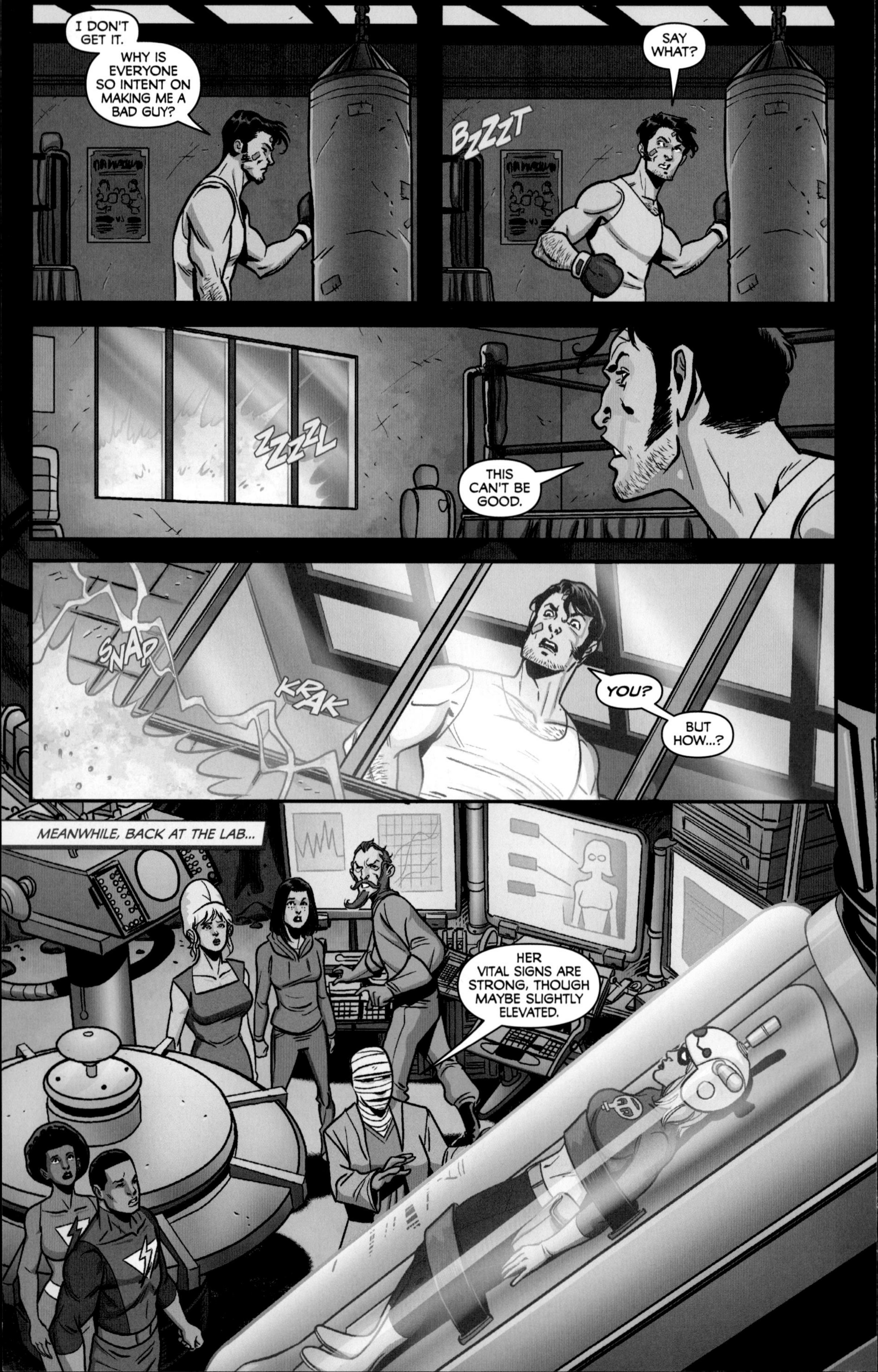
I DON'T GET IT.
WHY IS EVERYONE SO INTENT ON MAKING ME A BAD GUY?
BZZZT
SAY WHAT?
ZZZZL
THIS CAN'T BE GOOD.
SNAP
KRAK
YOU?
BUT HOW...?
MEANWHILE, BACK AT THE LAB...
HER VITAL SIGNS ARE STRONG, THOUGH MAYBE SLIGHTLY ELEVATED.

EXCELLENT.

WHAT DO YOU MEAN, "EXCELLENT"? YOU LOST TRACK OF HER PROJECTION!

PERHAPS. BUT SHE HAS SURVIVED REGARDLESS. SCHRODINGER'S CAT MAY BE IN THE BOX, BUT IN THIS CASE, WE KNOW IT IS ALIVE.

WHICH PROVES THE SYSTEM WORKS. A HUMAN *CAN* BE TRANSPORTED THROUGH THE ATMOSPHERE IN THIS FASHION.

IT PROVES NOTHING! YOU HAVE NO IDEA WHERE SHE ENDED UP!

IMMATERIAL. AS LONG AS *IT GIRL* IS STILL KICKING...

...SHE CAN FIND HER WAY HOME.

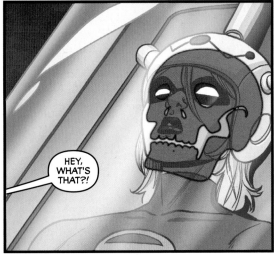

HEY, WHAT'S THAT?!

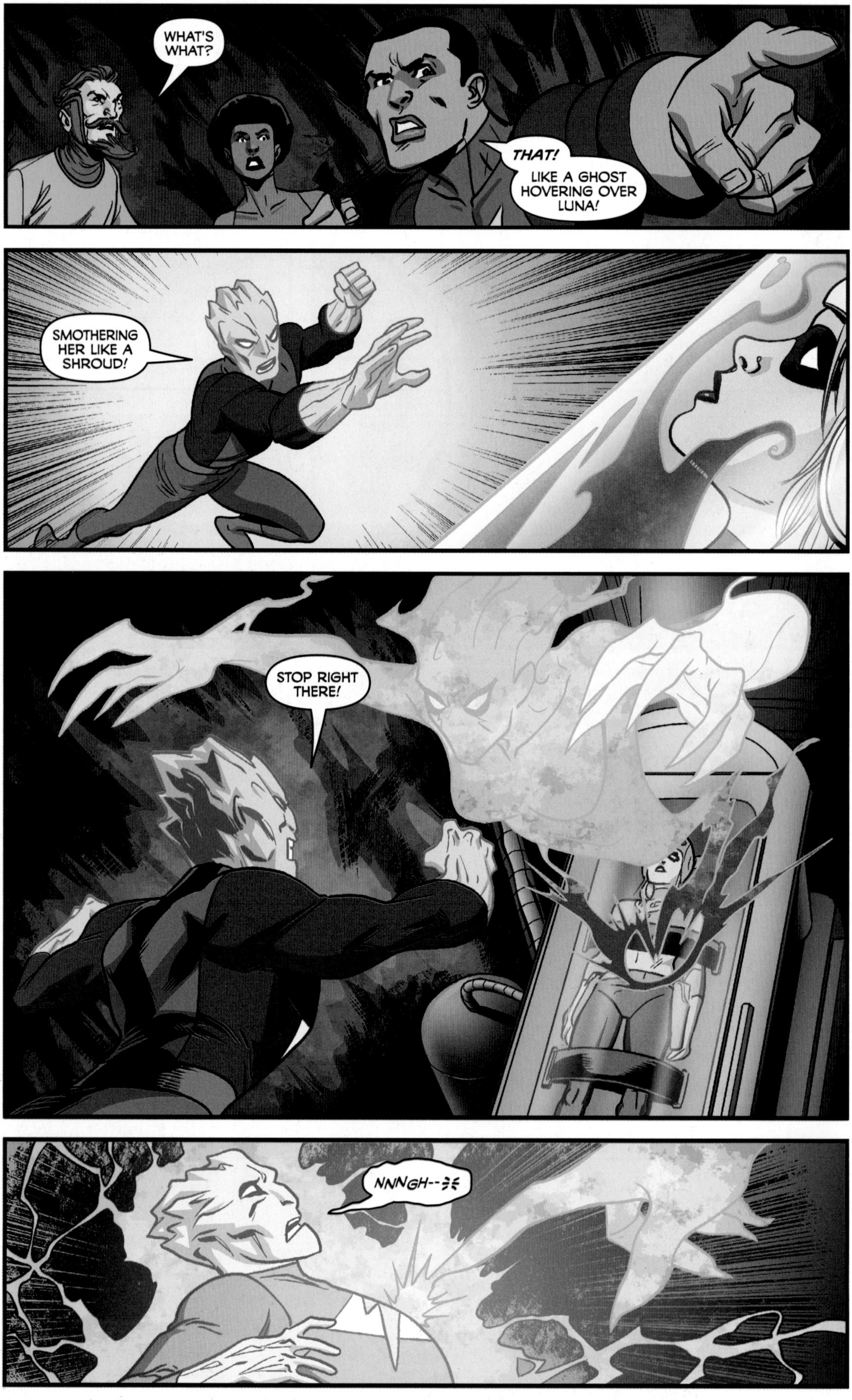
WHAT'S WHAT?
THAT! LIKE A GHOST HOVERING OVER LUNA!
SMOTHERING HER LIKE A SHROUD!
STOP RIGHT THERE!
NNNGH--

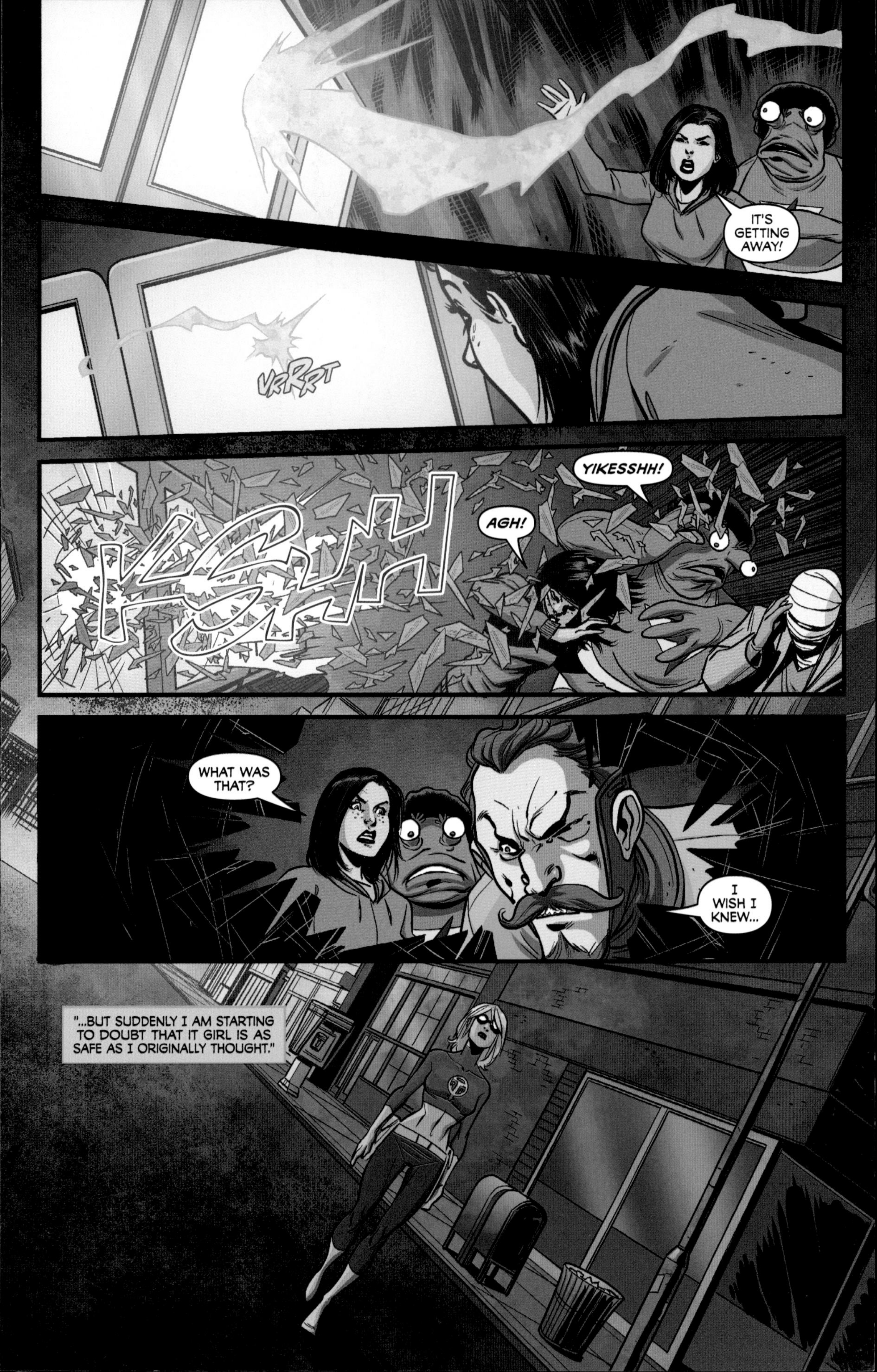
IT'S GETTING AWAY!
VRRRT
KSSHH
YIKESSHH!
AGH!
WHAT WAS THAT?
I WISH I KNEW...
"...BUT SUDDENLY I AM STARTING TO DOUBT THAT IT GIRL IS AS SAFE AS I ORIGINALLY THOUGHT."

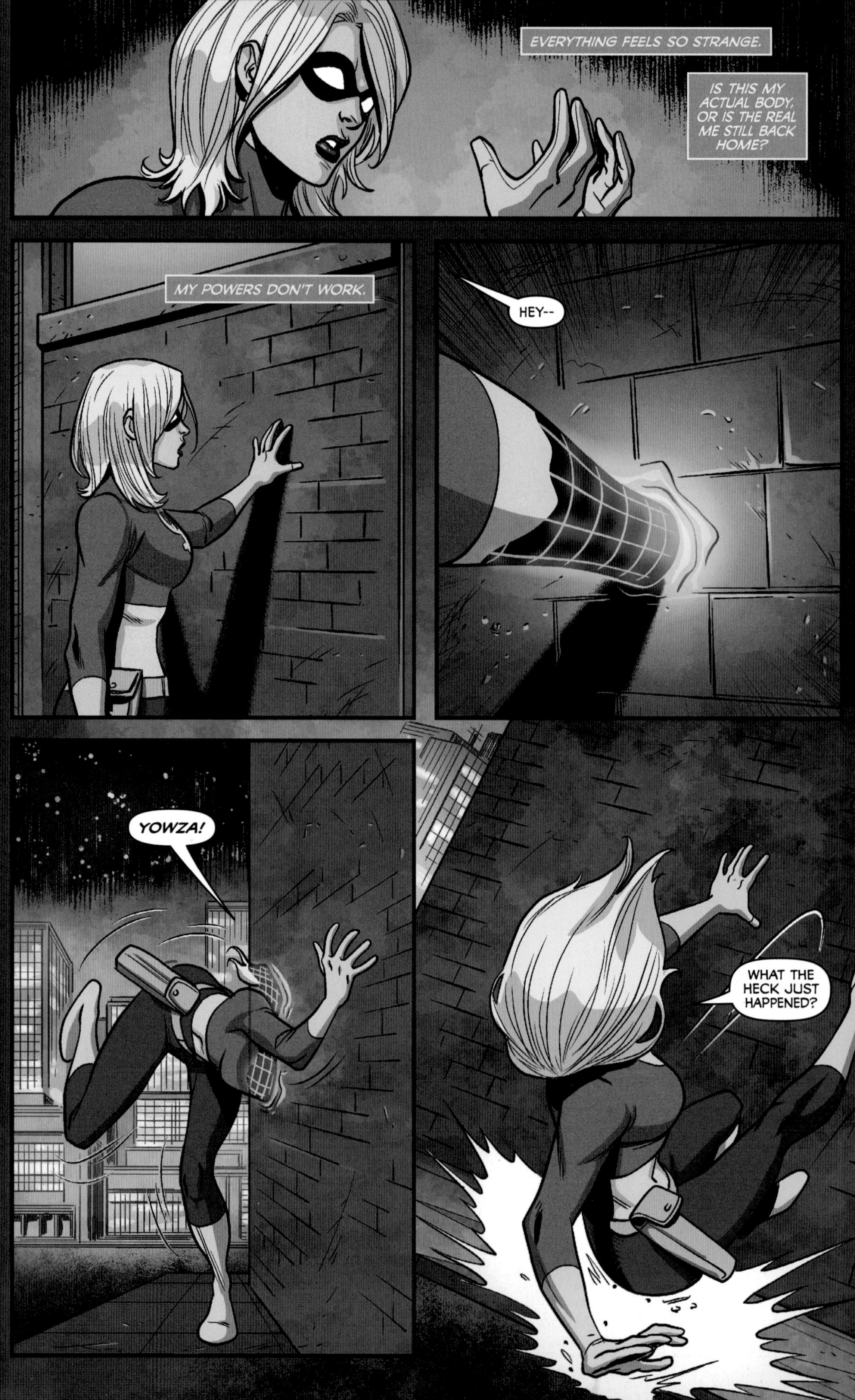
EVERYTHING FEELS SO STRANGE.
IS THIS MY ACTUAL BODY, OR IS THE REAL ME STILL BACK HOME?
MY POWERS DON'T WORK.
HEY--
YOWZA!
WHAT THE HECK JUST HAPPENED?

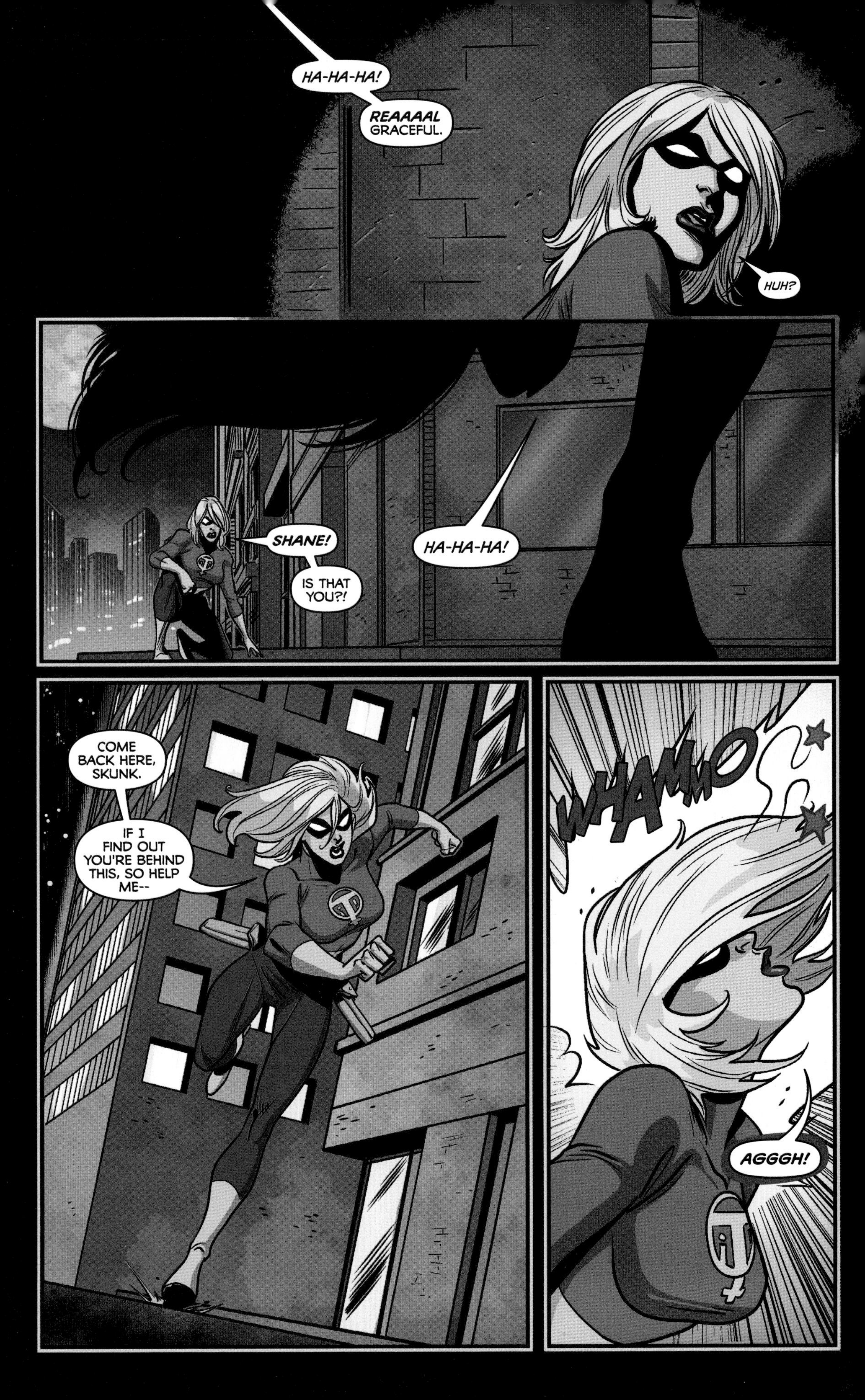

HA-HA-HA!
REAAAAL GRACEFUL.
HUH?
SHANE! IS THAT YOU?!
HA-HA-HA!
COME BACK HERE, SKUNK.
IF I FIND OUT YOU'RE BEHIND THIS, SO HELP ME--
WHAMMO
AGGGH!

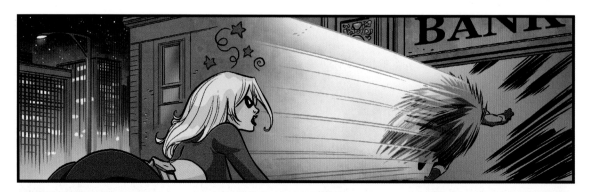

KER-ASH!

CLANG

CLANG

NGH!

CLANG

NICE WORK, HEDGEHOG. NOW KEEP THE DAME BUSY WHILE I WORK ON THAT SAFE.

CLANG

WSSSHOOM!

CLANG

CLANG

GLADLY.

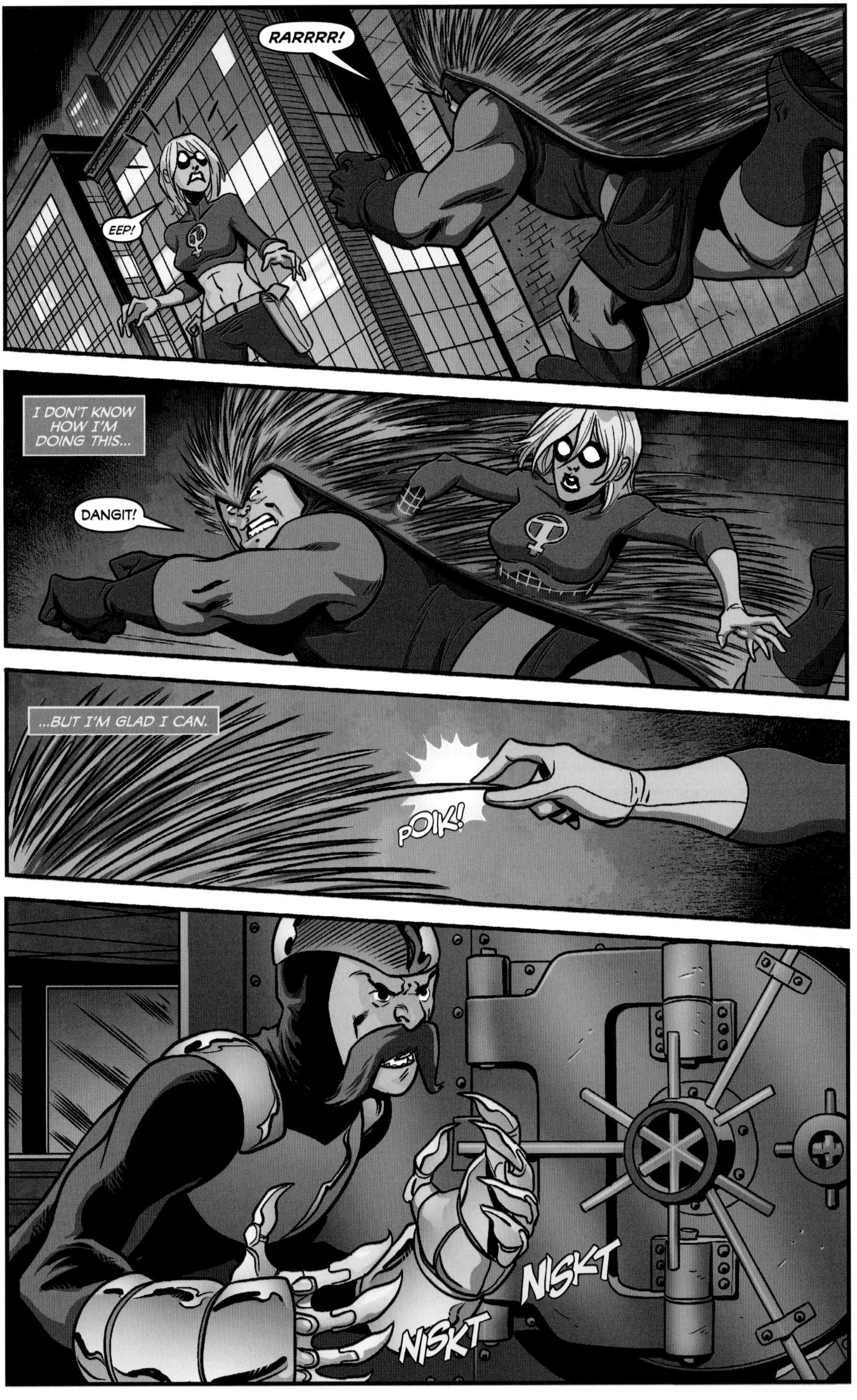
RARRRR!
EEP!
I DON'T KNOW HOW I'M DOING THIS...
DANGIT!
...BUT I'M GLAD I CAN.
POIK!
NISKT
NISKT

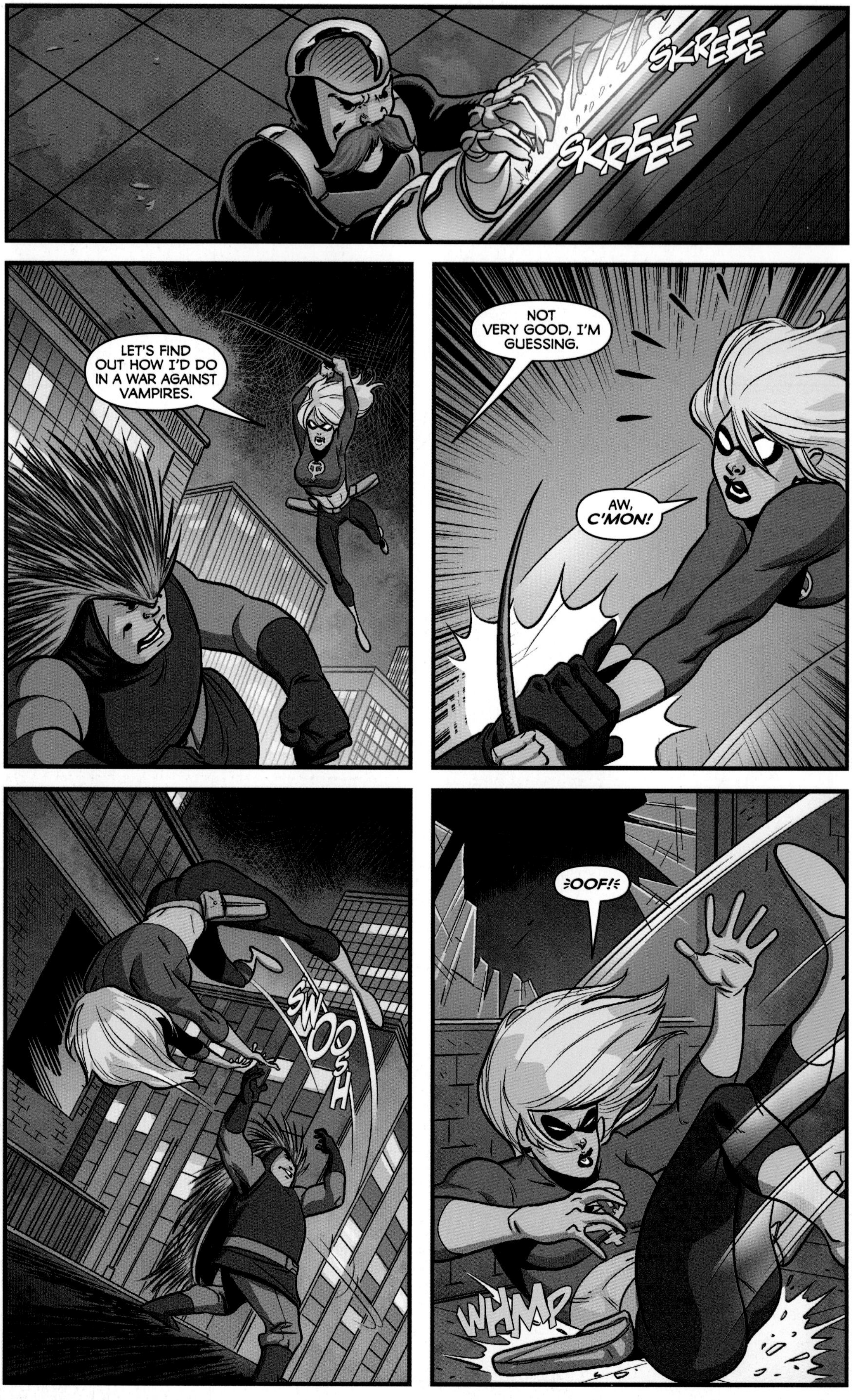
SKREEEE
SKREEEE
LET'S FIND OUT HOW I'D DO IN A WAR AGAINST VAMPIRES.
NOT VERY GOOD, I'M GUESSING.
AW, C'MON!
SWOOSH
OOF!
WHMP

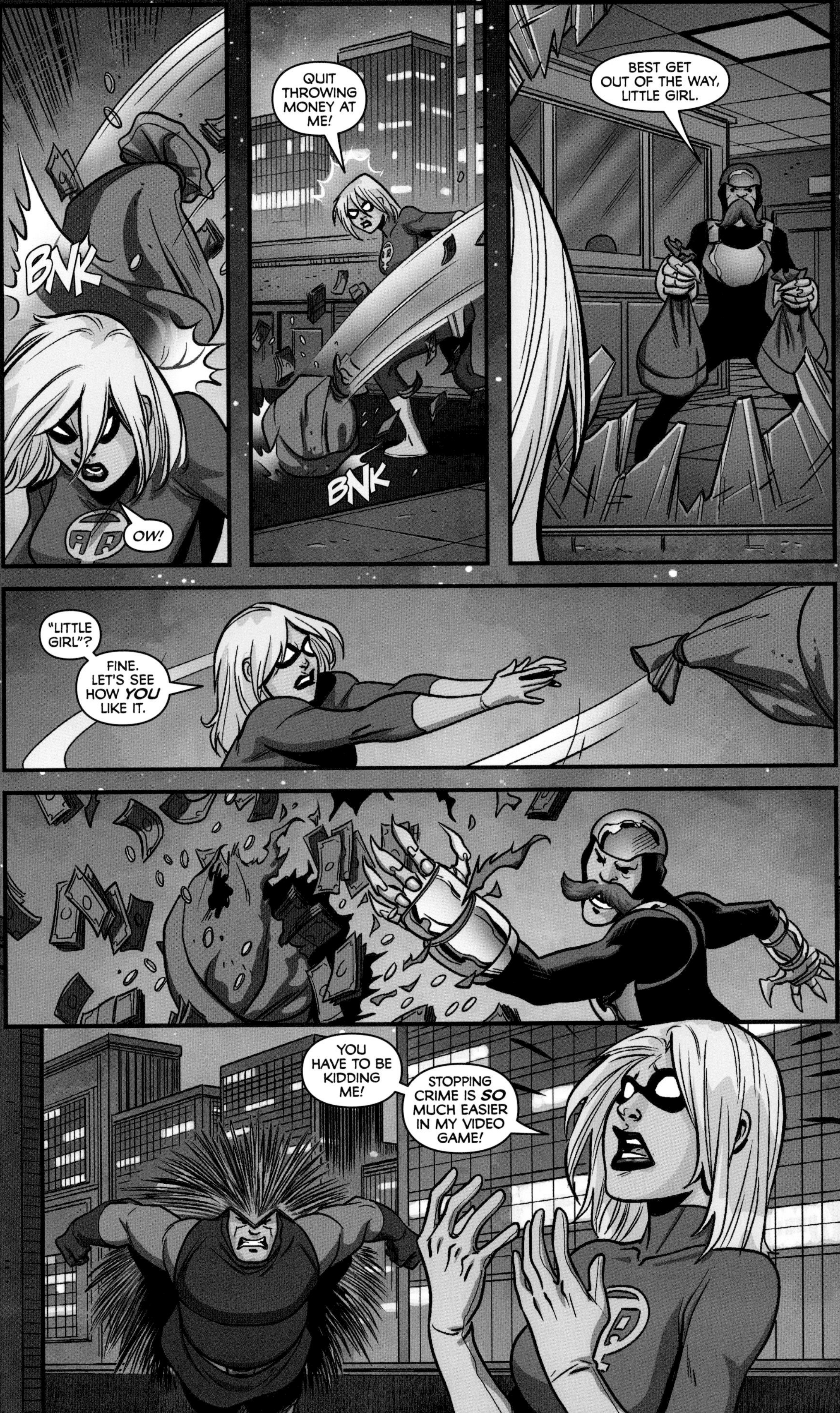
BNK
OW!
QUIT THROWING MONEY AT ME!
BNK
BEST GET OUT OF THE WAY, LITTLE GIRL.
"LITTLE GIRL"?
FINE. LET'S SEE HOW *YOU* LIKE IT.
YOU HAVE TO BE KIDDING ME!
STOPPING CRIME IS *SO* MUCH EASIER IN MY VIDEO GAME!

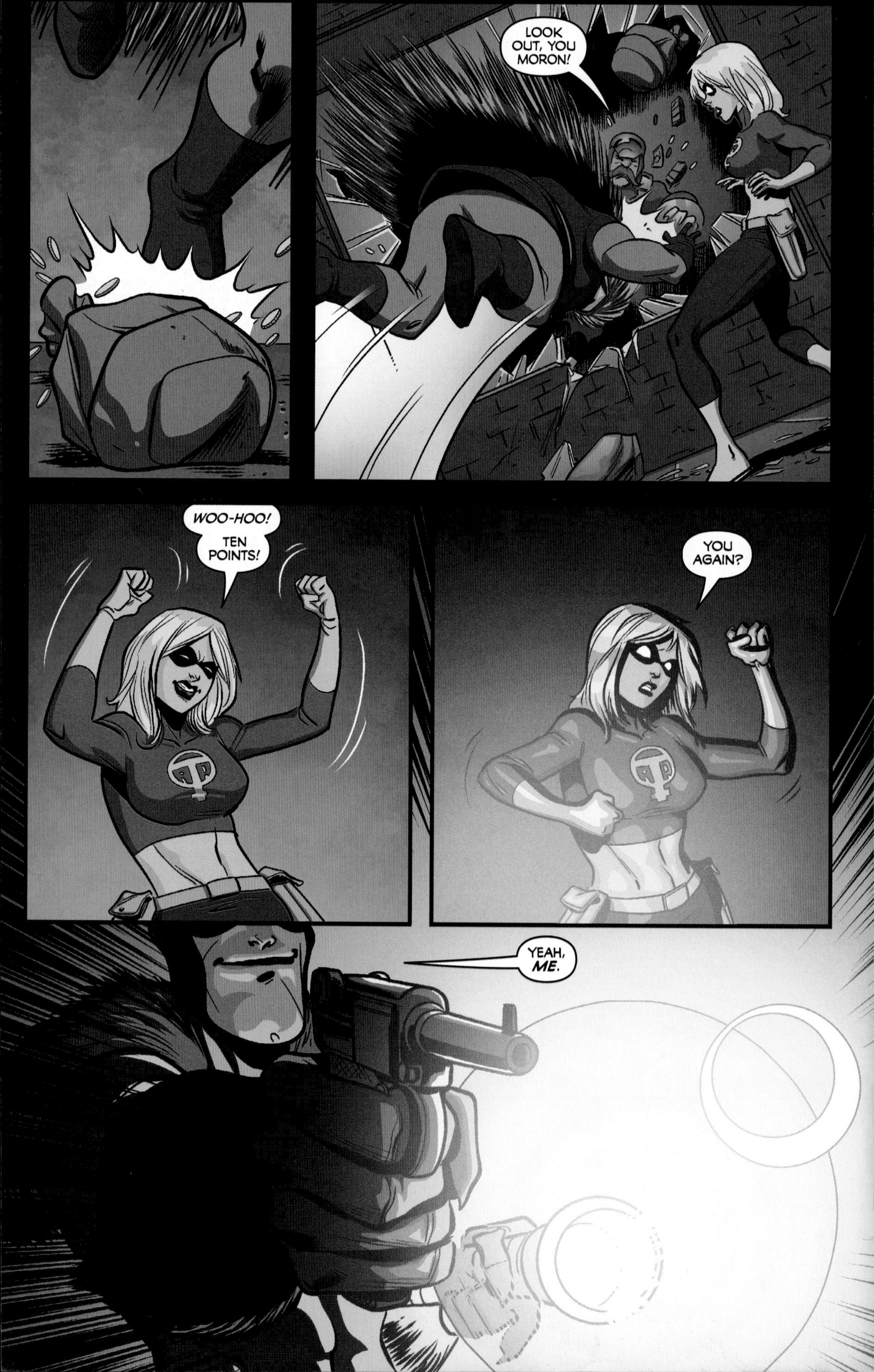
LOOK OUT, YOU MORON!
WOO-HOO! TEN POINTS!
YOU AGAIN?
YEAH, *ME*.

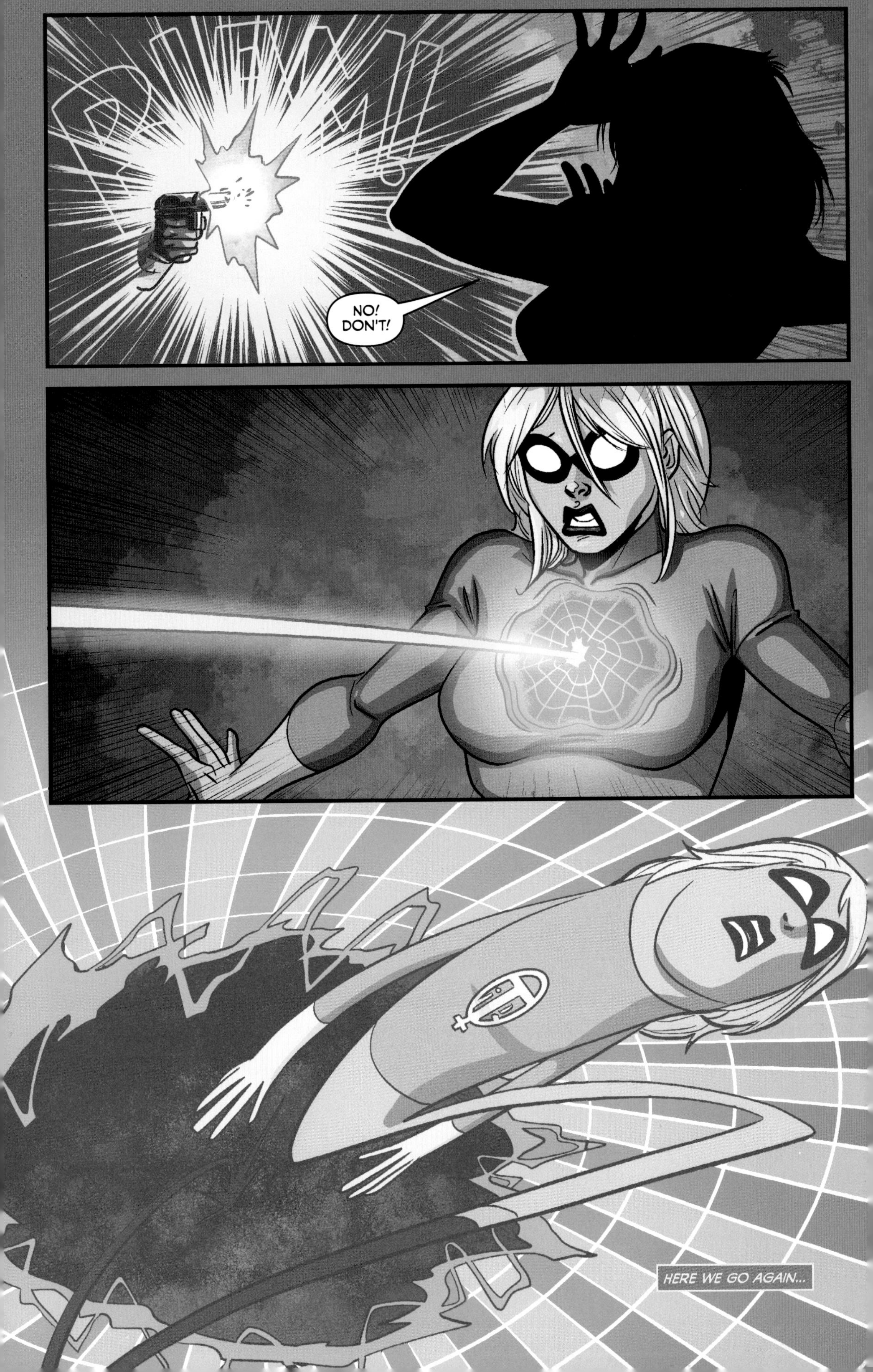
NO! DON'T!
HERE WE GO AGAIN...

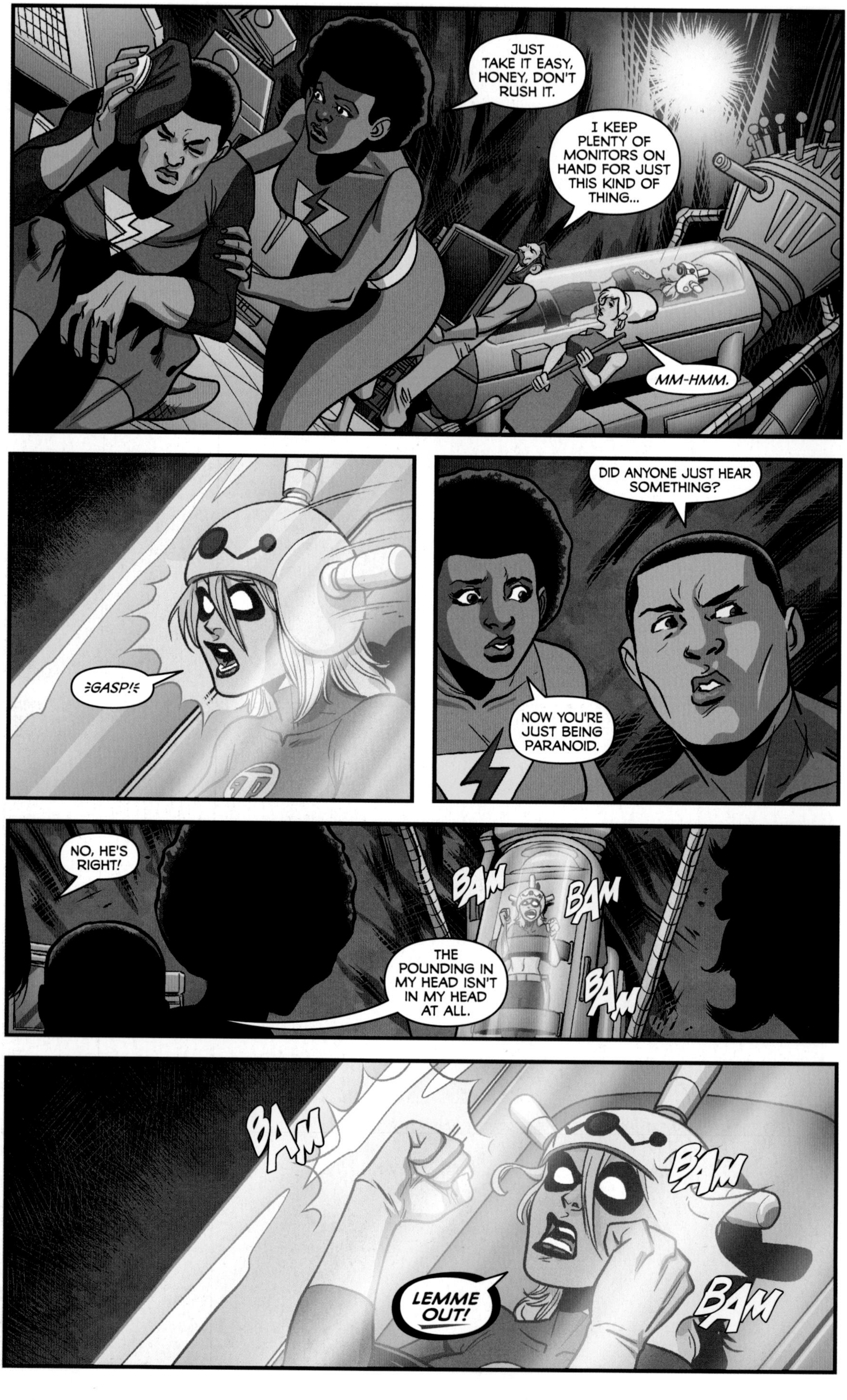
JUST TAKE IT EASY, HONEY, DON'T RUSH IT.
I KEEP PLENTY OF MONITORS ON HAND FOR JUST THIS KIND OF THING...
MM-HMM.
⪡GASP!⪢
DID ANYONE JUST HEAR SOMETHING?
NOW YOU'RE JUST BEING PARANOID.
NO, HE'S RIGHT!
BAM
BAM
BAM
THE POUNDING IN MY HEAD ISN'T IN MY HEAD AT ALL.
BAM
BAM
BAM
LEMME OUT!

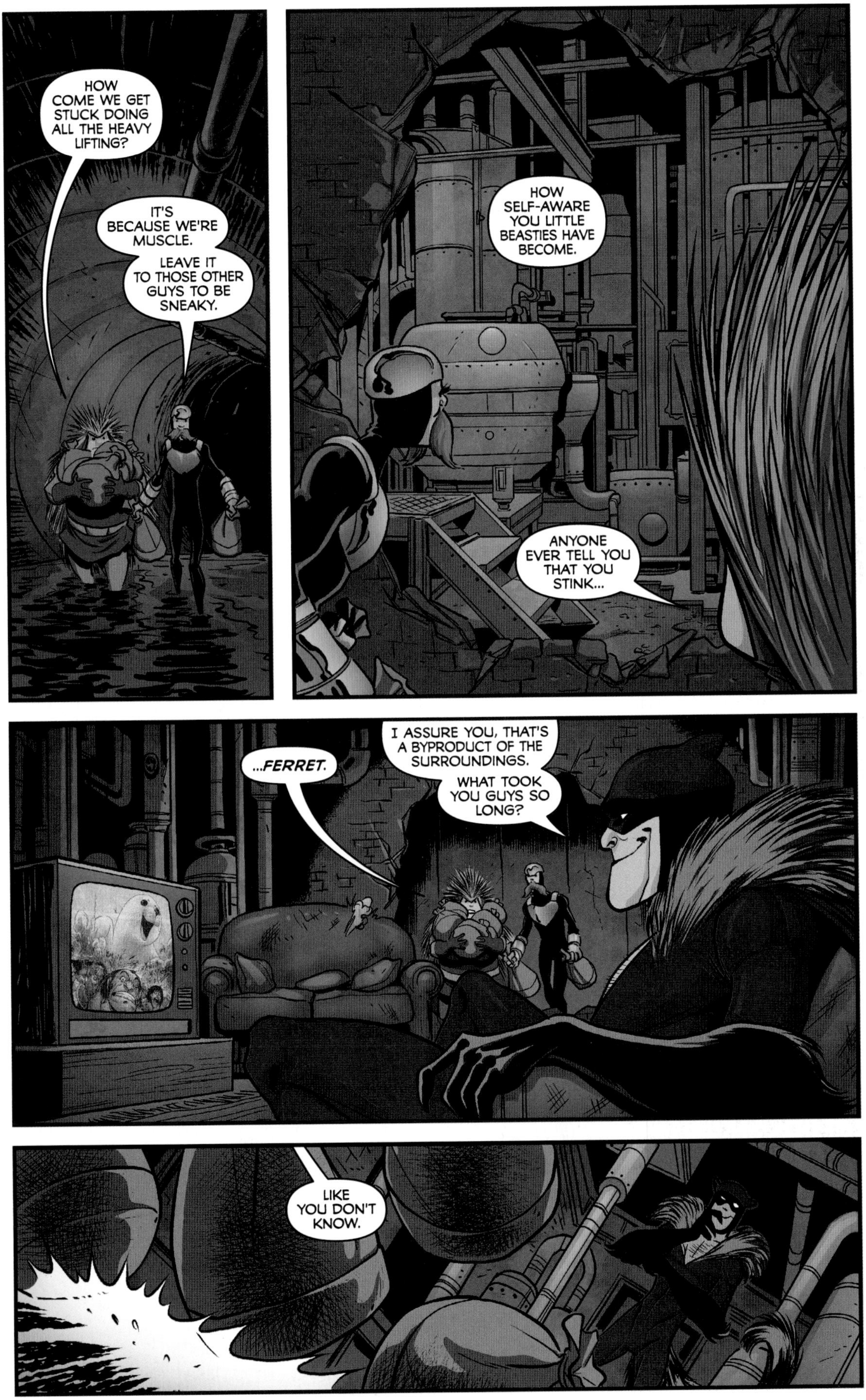
HOW COME WE GET STUCK DOING ALL THE HEAVY LIFTING?
IT'S BECAUSE WE'RE MUSCLE.
LEAVE IT TO THOSE OTHER GUYS TO BE SNEAKY.
HOW SELF-AWARE YOU LITTLE BEASTIES HAVE BECOME.
ANYONE EVER TELL YOU THAT YOU STINK...
...FERRET.
I ASSURE YOU, THAT'S A BYPRODUCT OF THE SURROUNDINGS.
WHAT TOOK YOU GUYS SO LONG?
LIKE YOU DON'T KNOW.

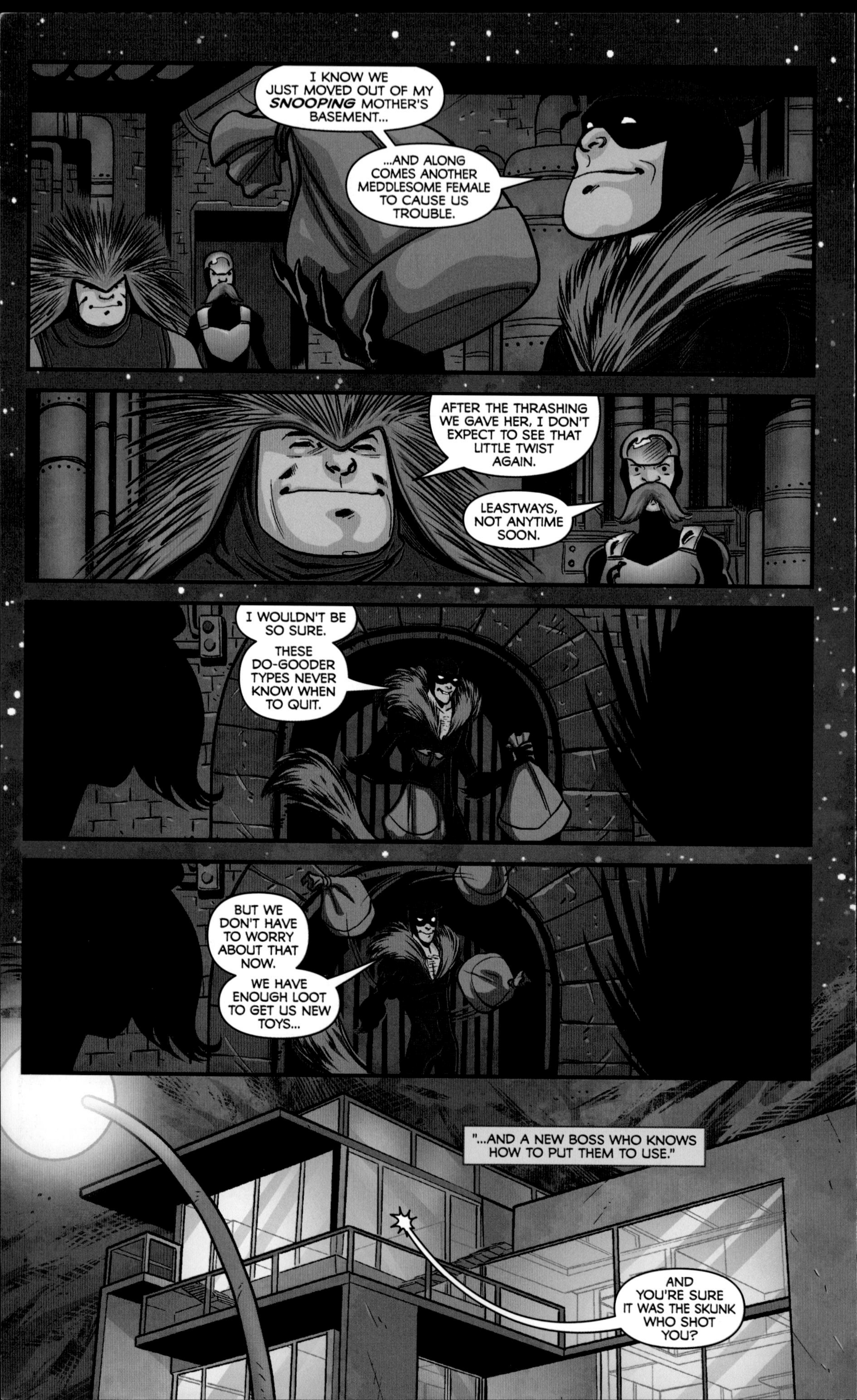
I KNOW WE JUST MOVED OUT OF MY SNOOPING MOTHER'S BASEMENT...
...AND ALONG COMES ANOTHER MEDDLESOME FEMALE TO CAUSE US TROUBLE.
AFTER THE THRASHING WE GAVE HER, I DON'T EXPECT TO SEE THAT LITTLE TWIST AGAIN.
LEASTWAYS, NOT ANYTIME SOON.
I WOULDN'T BE SO SURE.
THESE DO-GOODER TYPES NEVER KNOW WHEN TO QUIT.
BUT WE DON'T HAVE TO WORRY ABOUT THAT NOW.
WE HAVE ENOUGH LOOT TO GET US NEW TOYS...
"...AND A NEW BOSS WHO KNOWS HOW TO PUT THEM TO USE."
AND YOU'RE SURE IT WAS THE SKUNK WHO SHOT YOU?

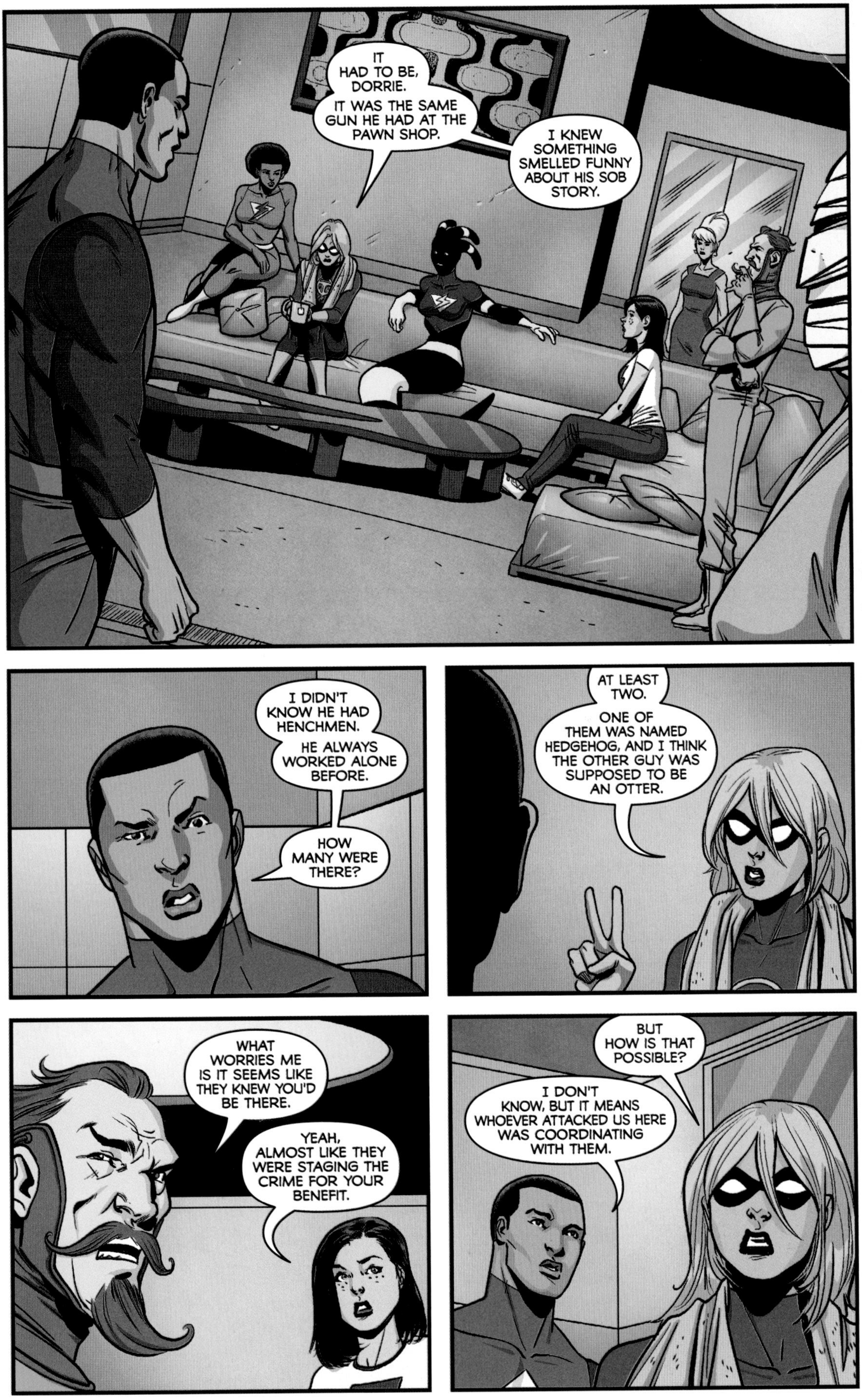
IT HAD TO BE, DORRIE.
IT WAS THE SAME GUN HE HAD AT THE PAWN SHOP.
I KNEW SOMETHING SMELLED FUNNY ABOUT HIS SOB STORY.
I DIDN'T KNOW HE HAD HENCHMEN.
HE ALWAYS WORKED ALONE BEFORE.
HOW MANY WERE THERE?
AT LEAST TWO.
ONE OF THEM WAS NAMED HEDGEHOG, AND I THINK THE OTHER GUY WAS SUPPOSED TO BE AN OTTER.
WHAT WORRIES ME IS IT SEEMS LIKE THEY KNEW YOU'D BE THERE.
YEAH, ALMOST LIKE THEY WERE STAGING THE CRIME FOR YOUR BENEFIT.
BUT HOW IS THAT POSSIBLE?
I DON'T KNOW, BUT IT MEANS WHOEVER ATTACKED US HERE WAS COORDINATING WITH THEM.

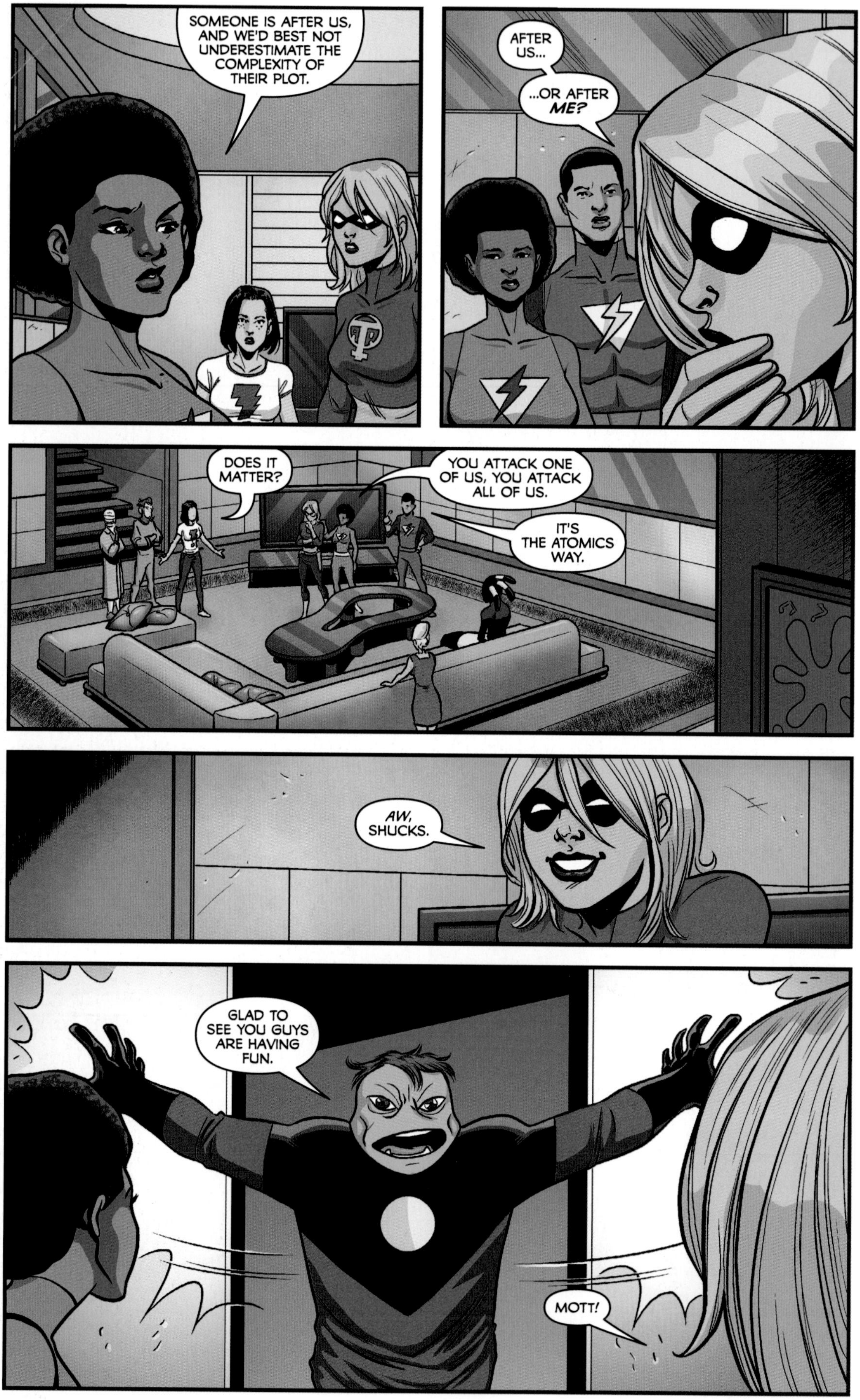
SOMEONE IS AFTER US, AND WE'D BEST NOT UNDERESTIMATE THE COMPLEXITY OF THEIR PLOT.
AFTER US...
...OR AFTER *ME?*
DOES IT MATTER?
YOU ATTACK ONE OF US, YOU ATTACK ALL OF US.
IT'S THE ATOMICS WAY.
AW, SHUCKS.
GLAD TO SEE YOU GUYS ARE HAVING FUN.
MOTT!

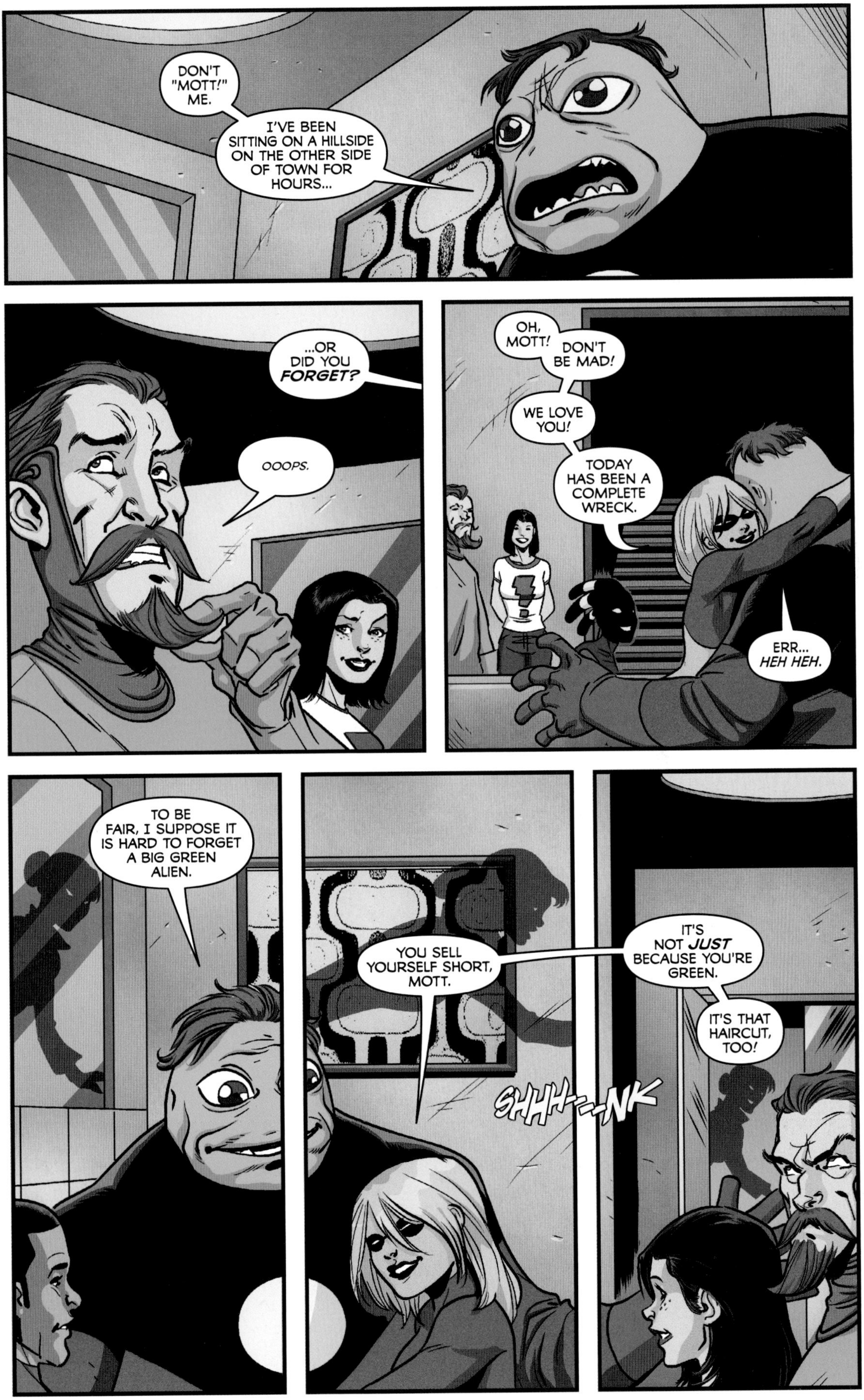
DON'T "MOTT!" ME.
I'VE BEEN SITTING ON A HILLSIDE ON THE OTHER SIDE OF TOWN FOR HOURS...
...OR DID YOU *FORGET?*
OOOPS.
OH, MOTT!
DON'T BE MAD!
WE LOVE YOU!
TODAY HAS BEEN A COMPLETE WRECK.
ERR... *HEH HEH.*
TO BE FAIR, I SUPPOSE IT IS HARD TO FORGET A BIG GREEN ALIEN.
YOU SELL YOURSELF SHORT, MOTT.
IT'S NOT *JUST* BECAUSE YOU'RE GREEN.
IT'S THAT HAIRCUT, TOO!
SHHH--NK

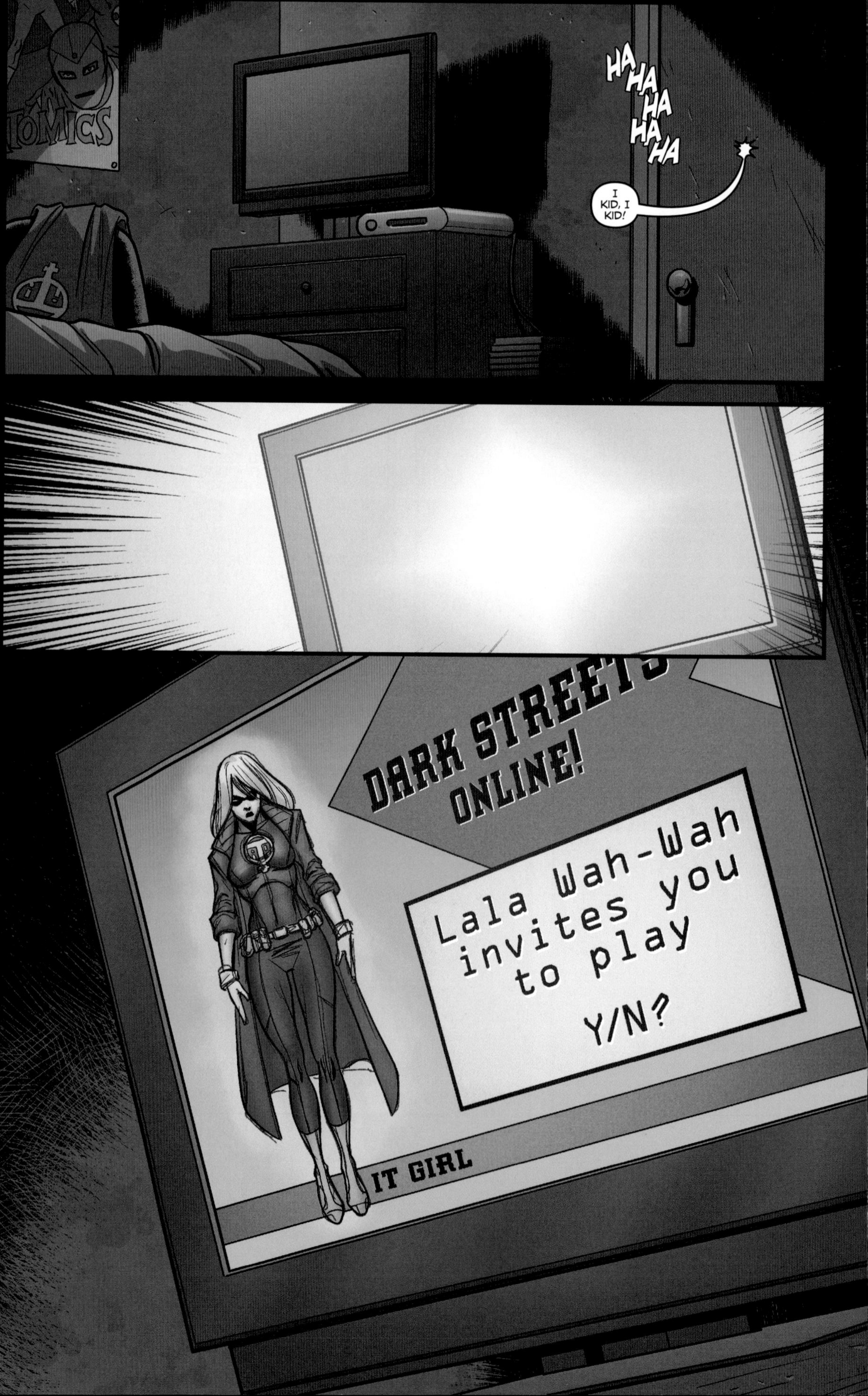
ATOMICS
HA HA HA HA HA
I KID, I KID!
DARK STREETS ONLINE!
Lala Wah-Wah invites you to play
Y/N?
IT GIRL

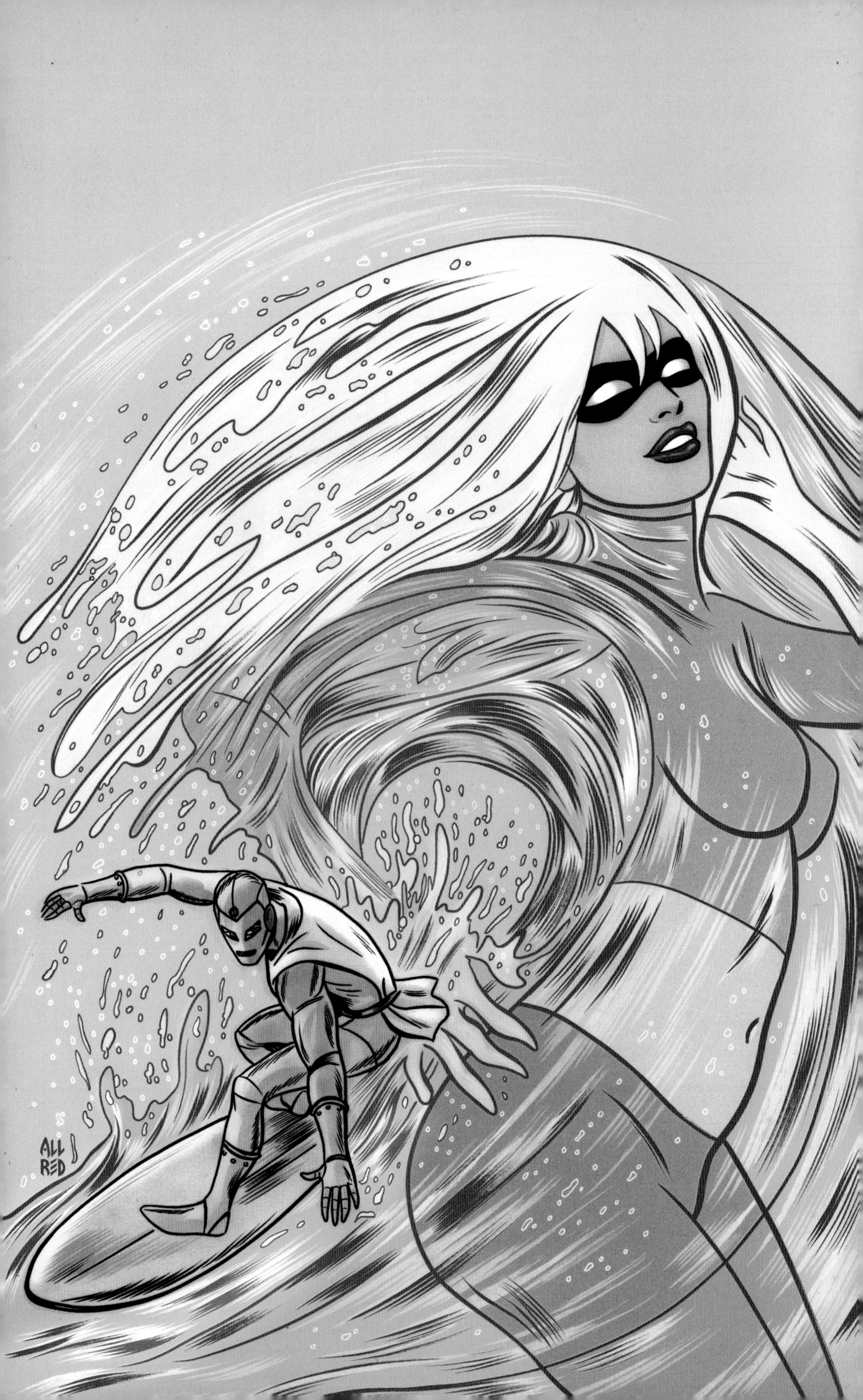
ALL
RED

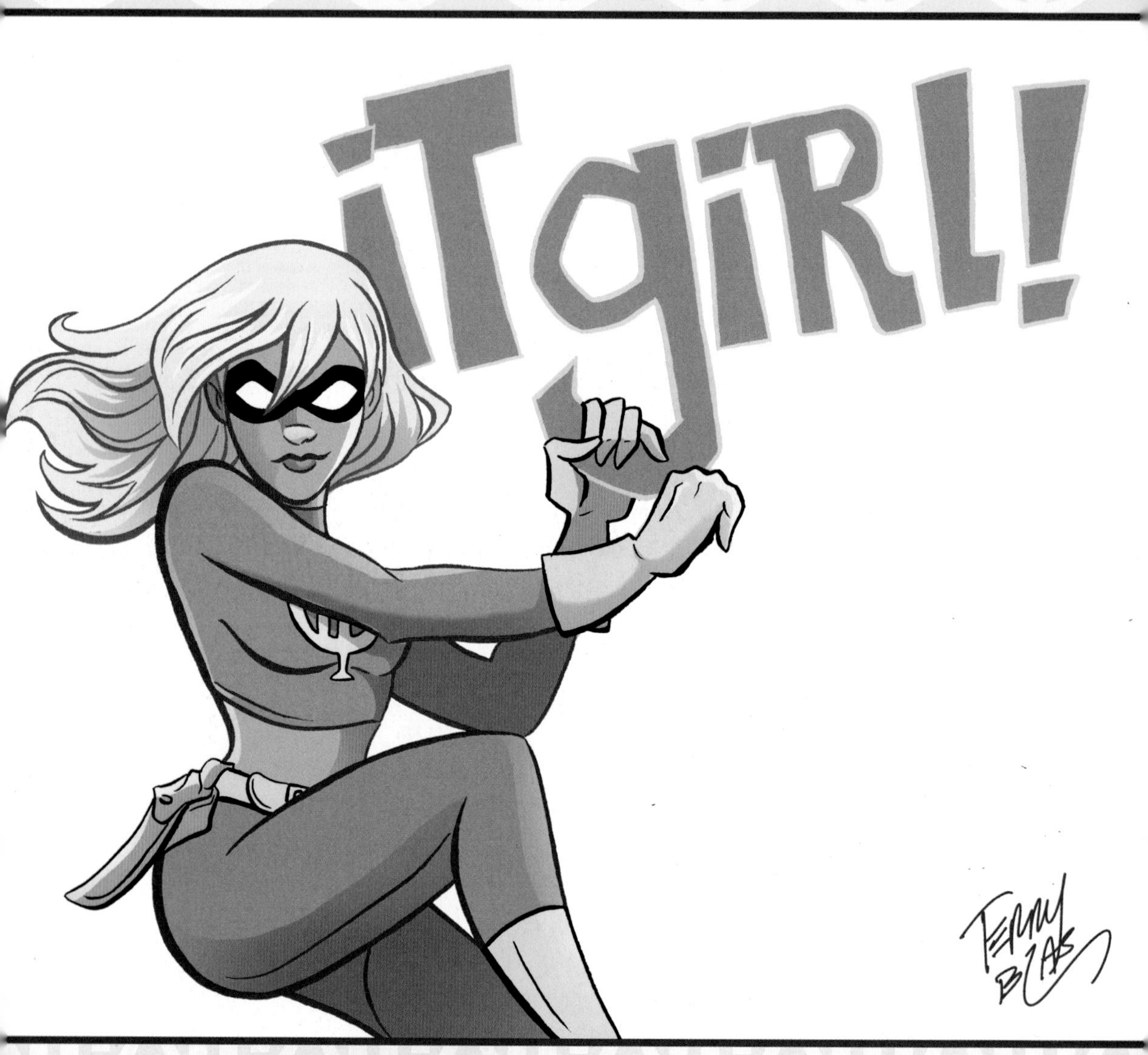
iT giRL!
Terry Blas

Illustration by Terry Blas

www.terryblas.com

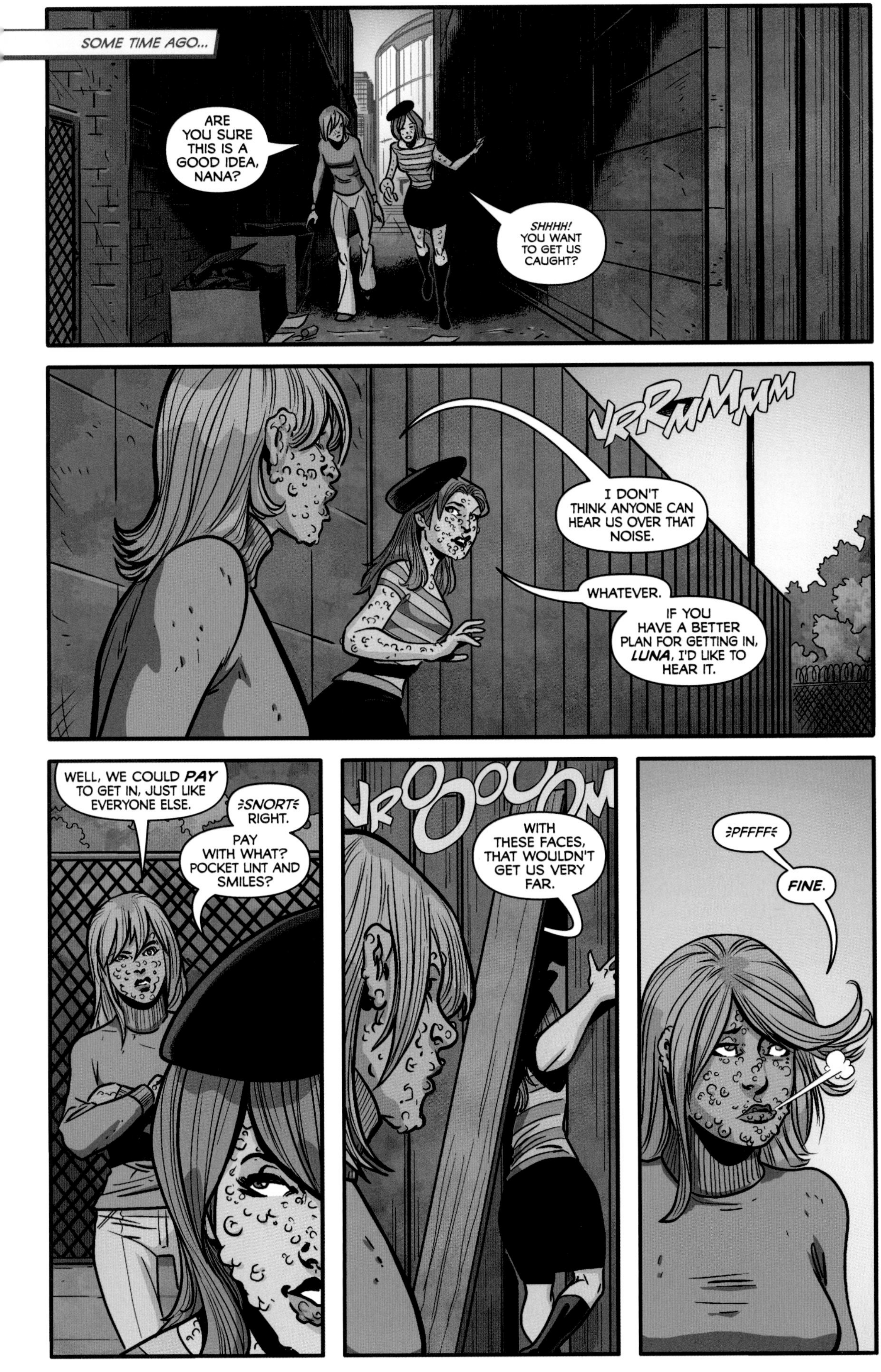
SOME TIME AGO...
ARE YOU SURE THIS IS A GOOD IDEA, NANA?
SHHHH! YOU WANT TO GET US CAUGHT?
VRRMMMMM
I DON'T THINK ANYONE CAN HEAR US OVER THAT NOISE.
WHATEVER.
IF YOU HAVE A BETTER PLAN FOR GETTING IN, LUNA, I'D LIKE TO HEAR IT.
WELL, WE COULD PAY TO GET IN, JUST LIKE EVERYONE ELSE.
SNORT RIGHT.
PAY WITH WHAT? POCKET LINT AND SMILES?
VROOOOOOM
WITH THESE FACES, THAT WOULDN'T GET US VERY FAR.
PFFFFF
FINE.

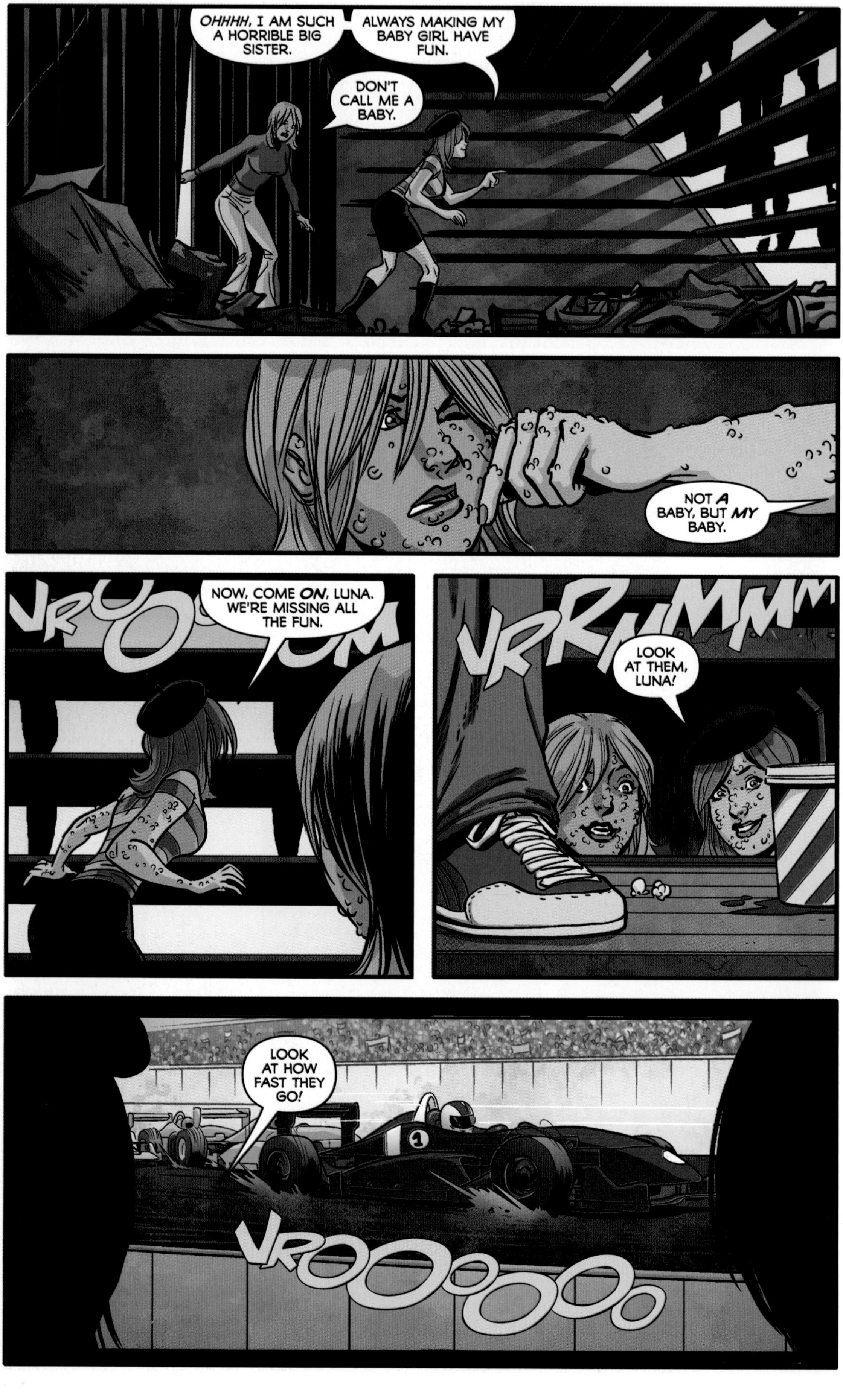
OHHHH, I AM SUCH A HORRIBLE BIG SISTER.
ALWAYS MAKING MY BABY GIRL HAVE FUN.
DON'T CALL ME A BABY.
NOT A BABY, BUT MY BABY.
VROOOOM
NOW, COME ON, LUNA. WE'RE MISSING ALL THE FUN.
VRRUMMM
LOOK AT THEM, LUNA!
LOOK AT HOW FAST THEY GO!
VROOOOOOO

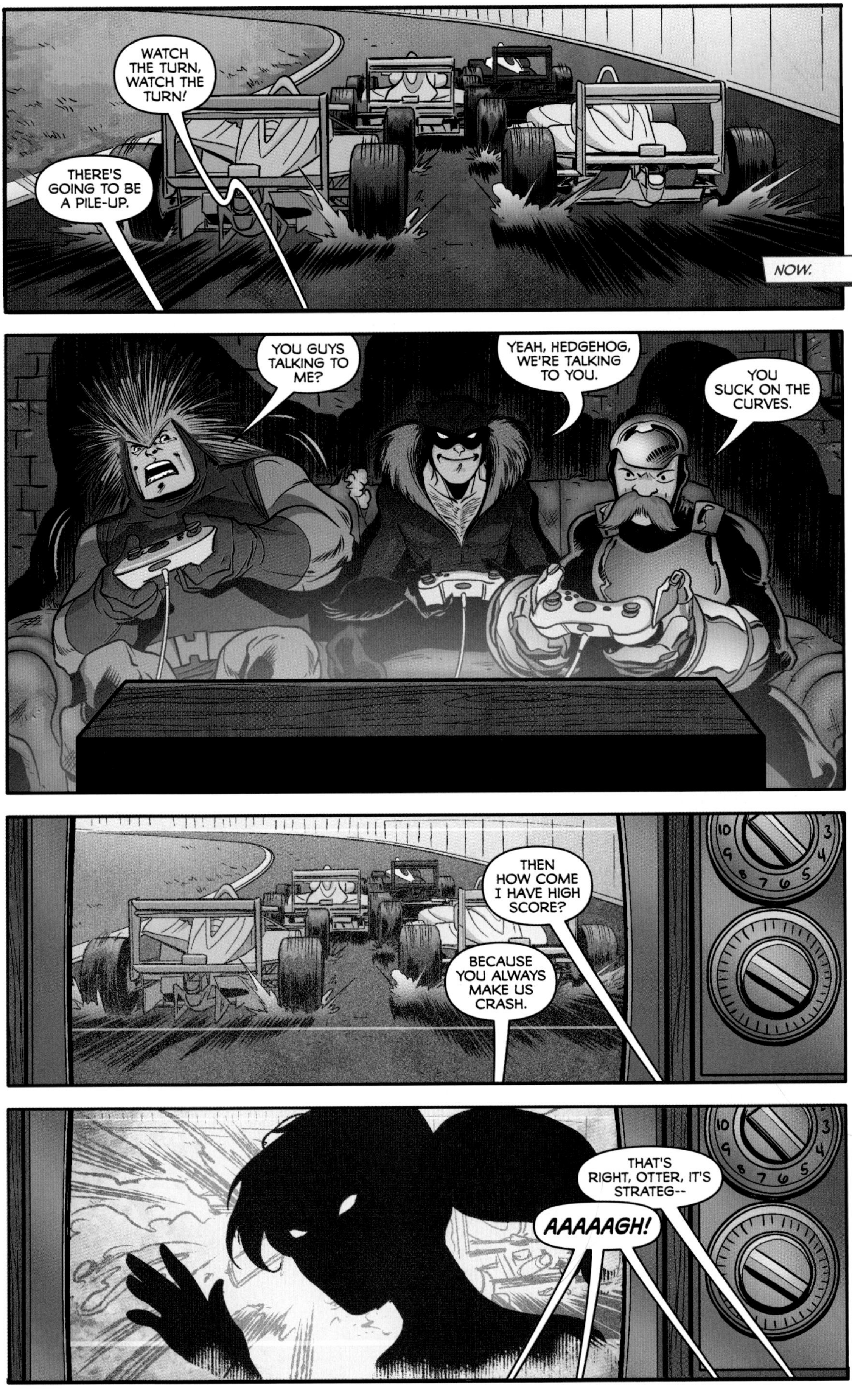
WATCH THE TURN, WATCH THE TURN!
THERE'S GOING TO BE A PILE-UP.
NOW.
YOU GUYS TALKING TO ME?
YEAH, HEDGEHOG, WE'RE TALKING TO YOU.
YOU SUCK ON THE CURVES.
THEN HOW COME I HAVE HIGH SCORE?
BECAUSE YOU ALWAYS MAKE US CRASH.
THAT'S RIGHT, OTTER, IT'S STRATEG--
AAAAAGH!

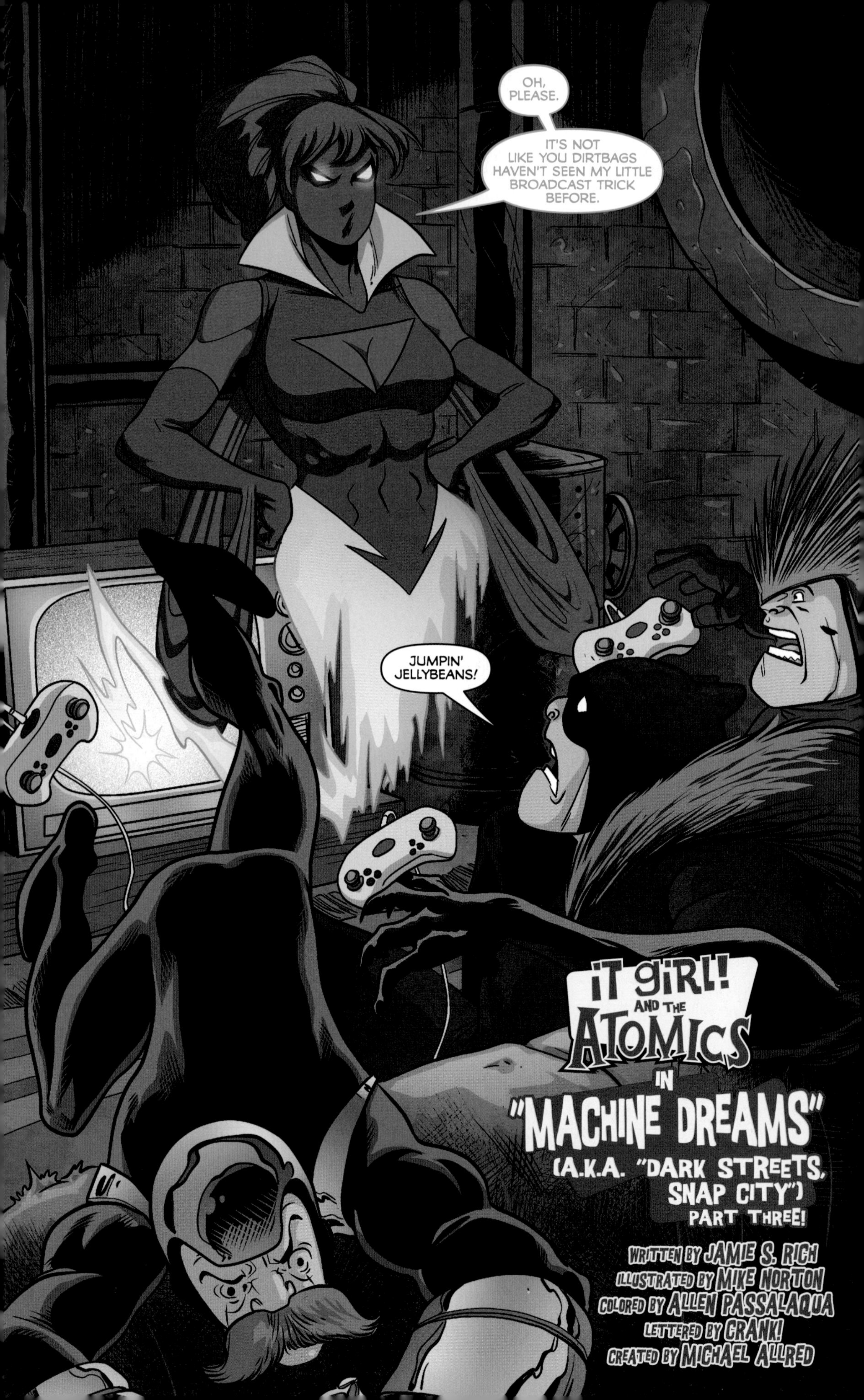
OH, PLEASE.
IT'S NOT LIKE YOU DIRTBAGS HAVEN'T SEEN MY LITTLE BROADCAST TRICK BEFORE.
JUMPIN' JELLYBEANS!
IT GIRL! AND THE ATOMICS
IN
"MACHINE DREAMS"
(A.K.A. "DARK STREETS, SNAP CITY")
PART THREE!
WRITTEN BY JAMIE S. RICH
ILLUSTRATED BY MIKE NORTON
COLORED BY ALLEN PASSALAQUA
LETTERED BY CRANK!
CREATED BY MICHAEL ALLRED

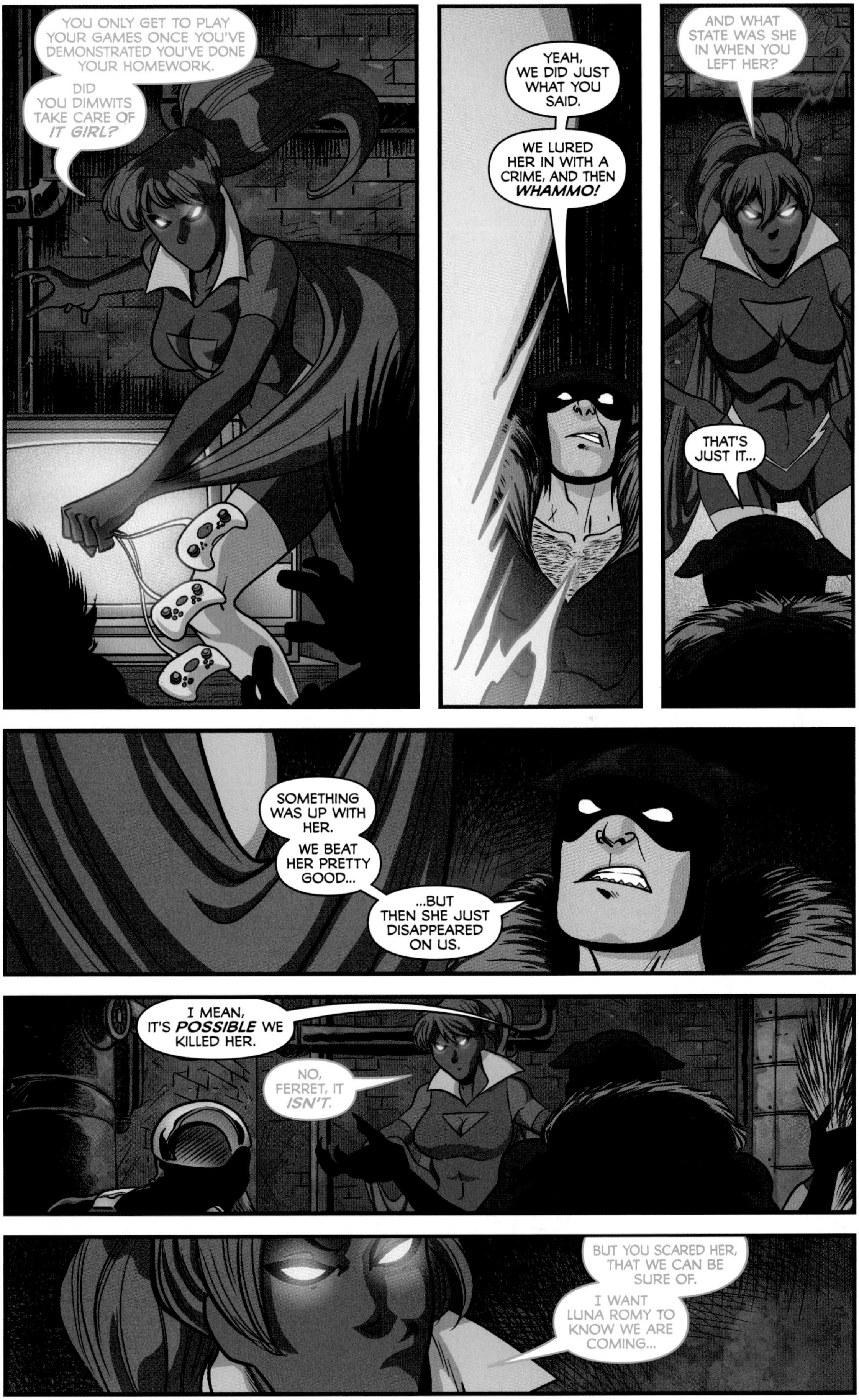
YOU ONLY GET TO PLAY YOUR GAMES ONCE YOU'VE DEMONSTRATED YOU'VE DONE YOUR HOMEWORK.
DID YOU DIMWITS TAKE CARE OF *IT GIRL?*
YEAH, WE DID JUST WHAT YOU SAID.
WE LURED HER IN WITH A CRIME, AND THEN ***WHAMMO!***
AND WHAT STATE WAS SHE IN WHEN YOU LEFT HER?
THAT'S JUST IT...
SOMETHING WAS UP WITH HER.
WE BEAT HER PRETTY GOOD...
...BUT THEN SHE JUST DISAPPEARED ON US.
I MEAN, IT'S ***POSSIBLE*** WE KILLED HER.
NO, FERRET, IT *ISN'T.*
BUT YOU SCARED HER, THAT WE CAN BE SURE OF.
I WANT LUNA ROMY TO KNOW WE ARE COMING...

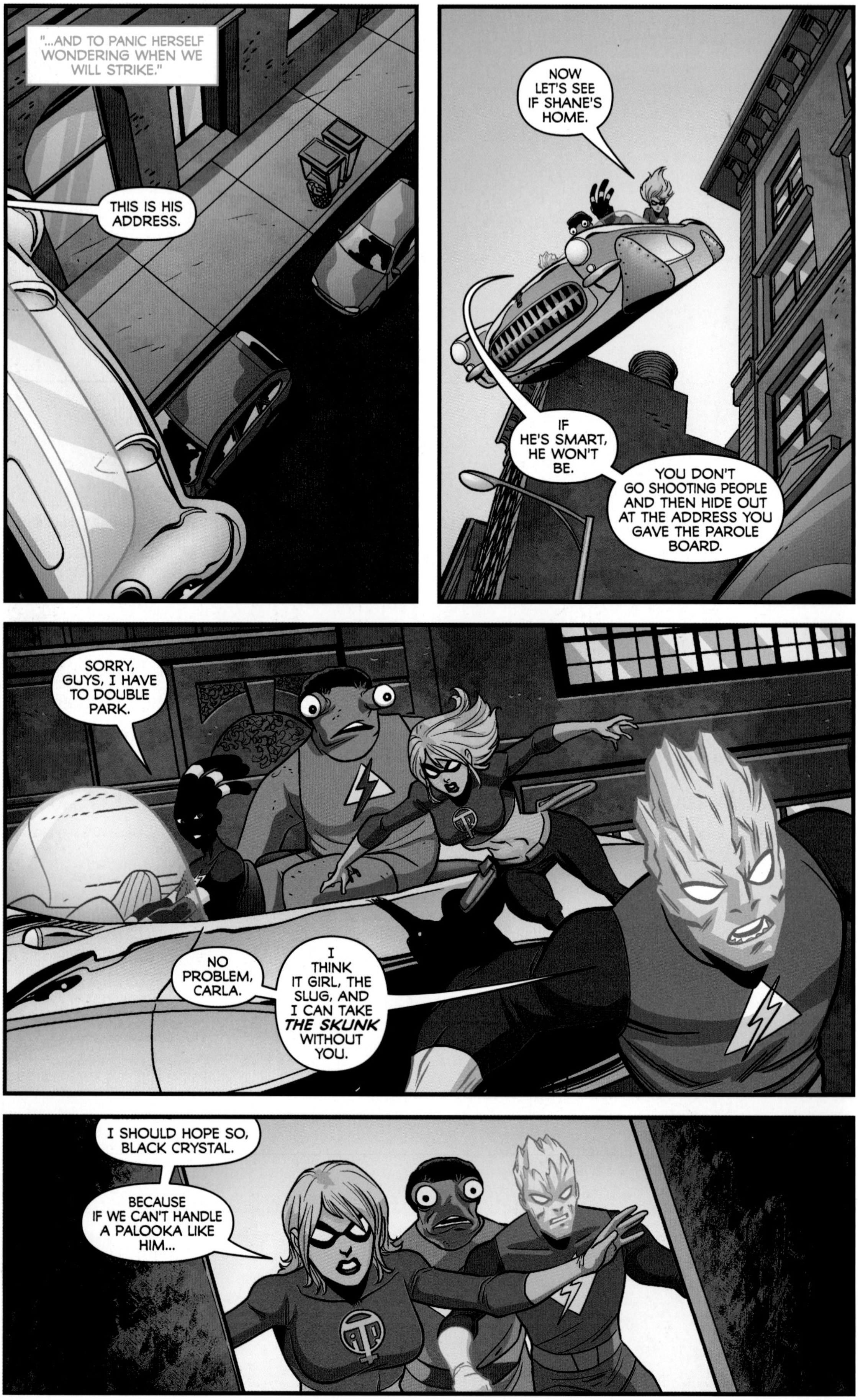
"...AND TO PANIC HERSELF WONDERING WHEN WE WILL STRIKE."
THIS IS HIS ADDRESS.
NOW LET'S SEE IF SHANE'S HOME.
IF HE'S SMART, HE WON'T BE.
YOU DON'T GO SHOOTING PEOPLE AND THEN HIDE OUT AT THE ADDRESS YOU GAVE THE PAROLE BOARD.
SORRY, GUYS, I HAVE TO DOUBLE PARK.
NO PROBLEM, CARLA.
I THINK IT GIRL, THE SLUG, AND I CAN TAKE *THE SKUNK* WITHOUT YOU.
I SHOULD HOPE SO, BLACK CRYSTAL.
BECAUSE IF WE CAN'T HANDLE A PALOOKA LIKE HIM...

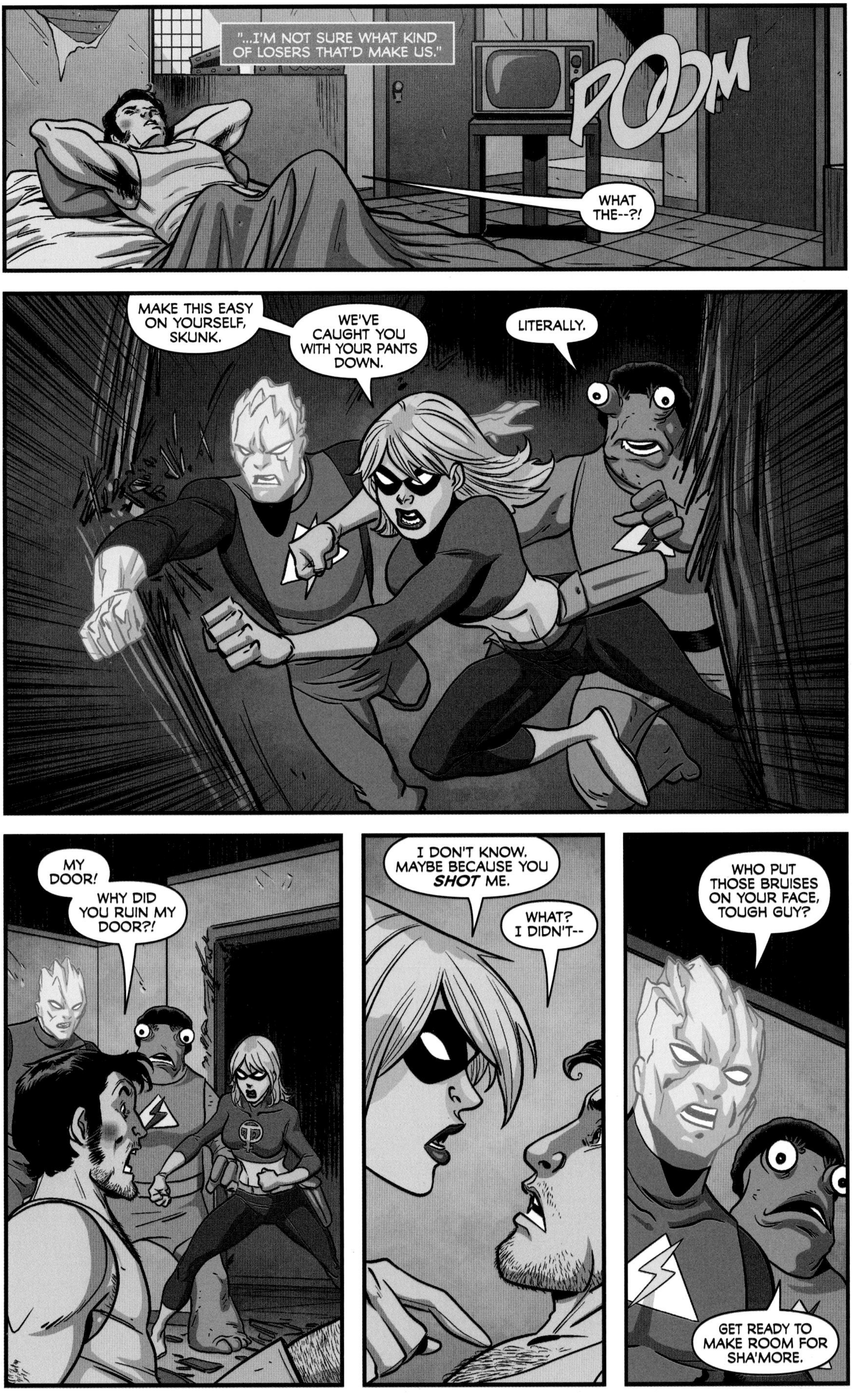
"...I'M NOT SURE WHAT KIND OF LOSERS THAT'D MAKE US."
POOM
WHAT THE--?!
MAKE THIS EASY ON YOURSELF, SKUNK.
WE'VE CAUGHT YOU WITH YOUR PANTS DOWN.
LITERALLY.
MY DOOR!
WHY DID YOU RUIN MY DOOR?!
I DON'T KNOW. MAYBE BECAUSE YOU *SHOT* ME.
WHAT? I DIDN'T--
WHO PUT THOSE BRUISES ON YOUR FACE, TOUGH GUY?
GET READY TO MAKE ROOM FOR SHA'MORE.

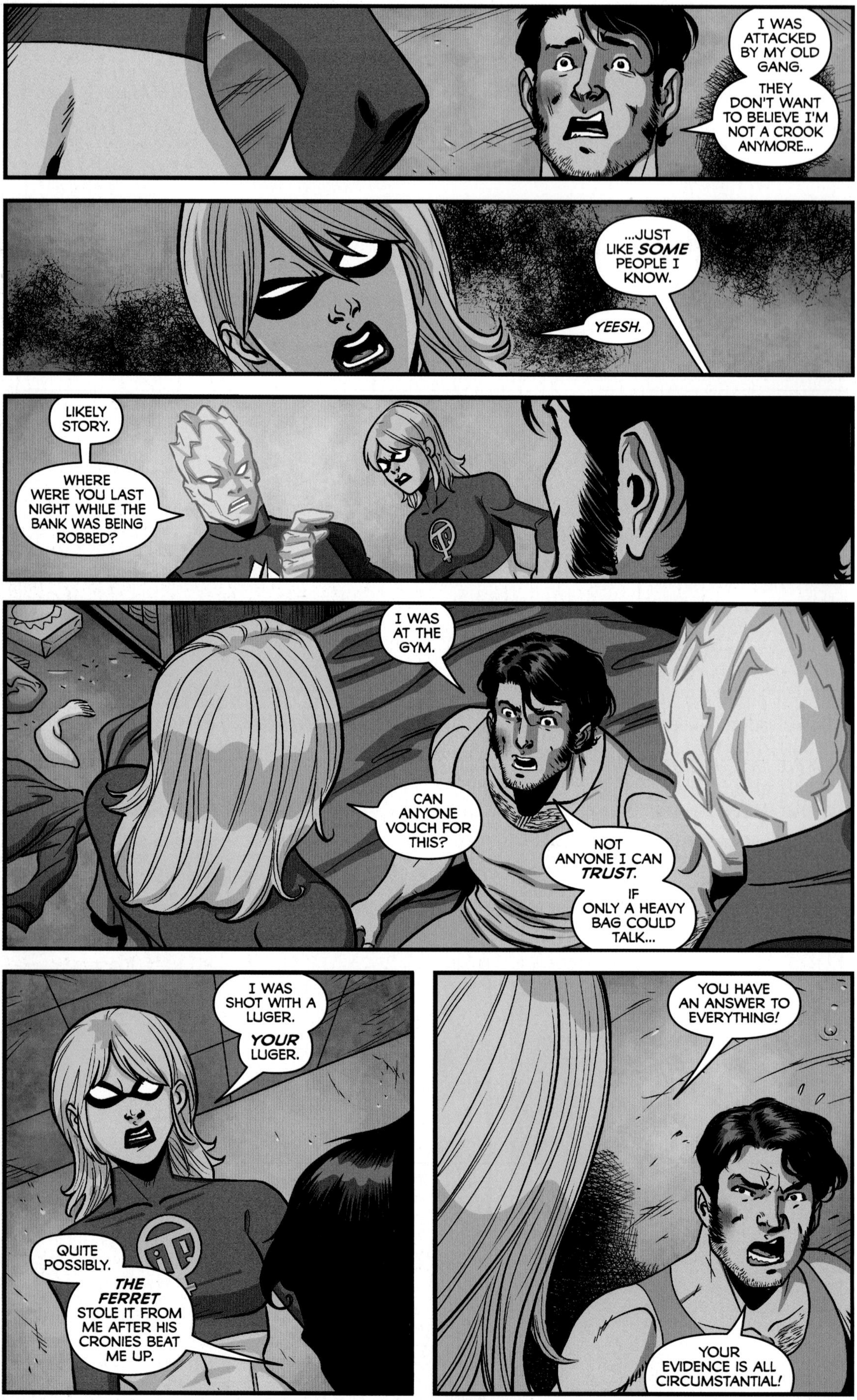
I WAS ATTACKED BY MY OLD GANG.
THEY DON'T WANT TO BELIEVE I'M NOT A CROOK ANYMORE...
...JUST LIKE SOME PEOPLE I KNOW.
YEESH.
LIKELY STORY.
WHERE WERE YOU LAST NIGHT WHILE THE BANK WAS BEING ROBBED?
I WAS AT THE GYM.
CAN ANYONE VOUCH FOR THIS?
NOT ANYONE I CAN TRUST.
IF ONLY A HEAVY BAG COULD TALK...
I WAS SHOT WITH A LUGER.
YOUR LUGER.
QUITE POSSIBLY.
THE FERRET STOLE IT FROM ME AFTER HIS CRONIES BEAT ME UP.
YOU HAVE AN ANSWER TO EVERYTHING!
YOUR EVIDENCE IS ALL CIRCUMSTANTIAL!

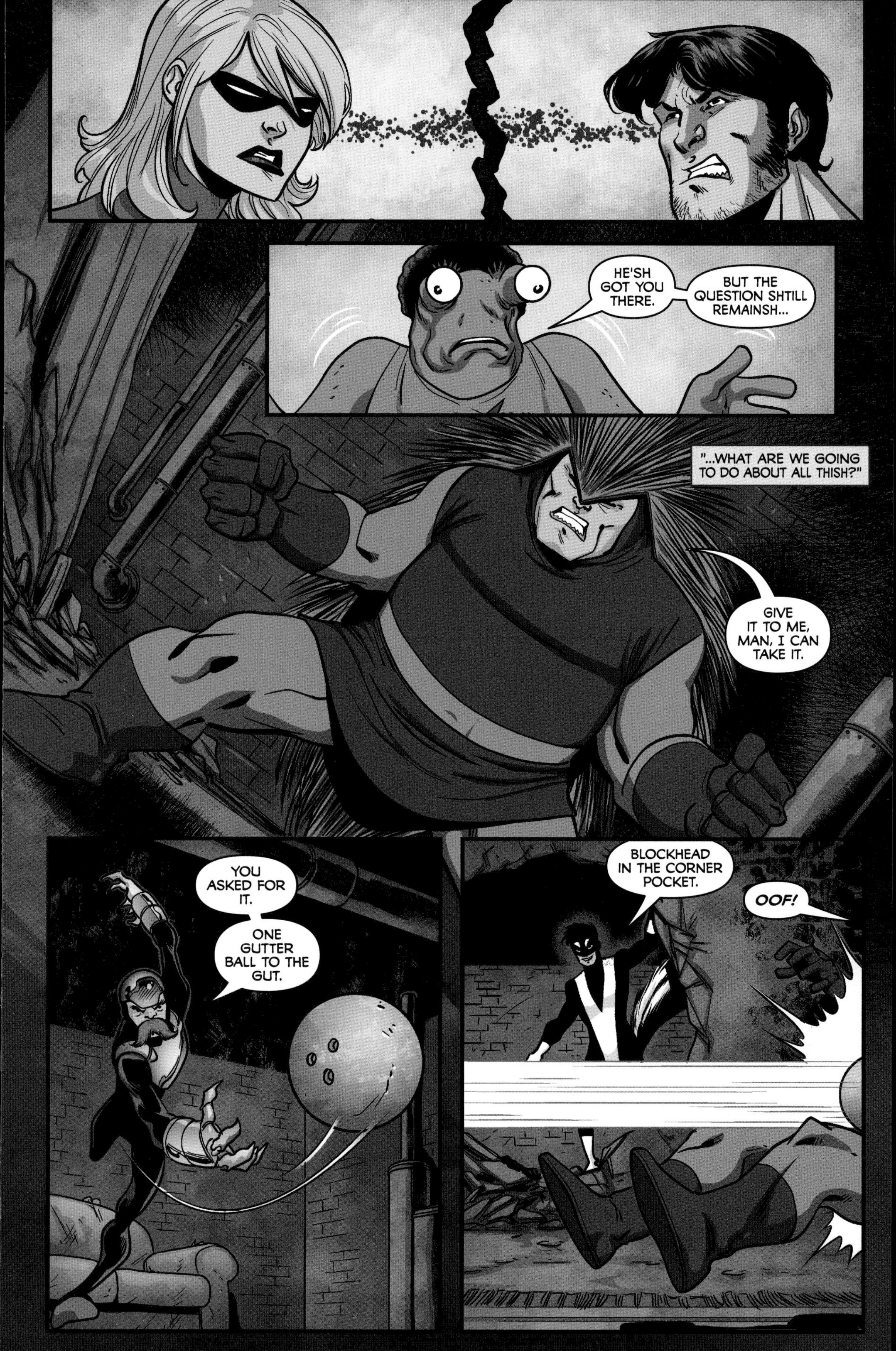
HE'SH GOT YOU THERE.
BUT THE QUESTION SHTILL REMAINSH...
"...WHAT ARE WE GOING TO DO ABOUT ALL THISH?"
GIVE IT TO ME, MAN, I CAN TAKE IT.
YOU ASKED FOR IT.
ONE GUTTER BALL TO THE GUT.
BLOCKHEAD IN THE CORNER POCKET.
OOF!

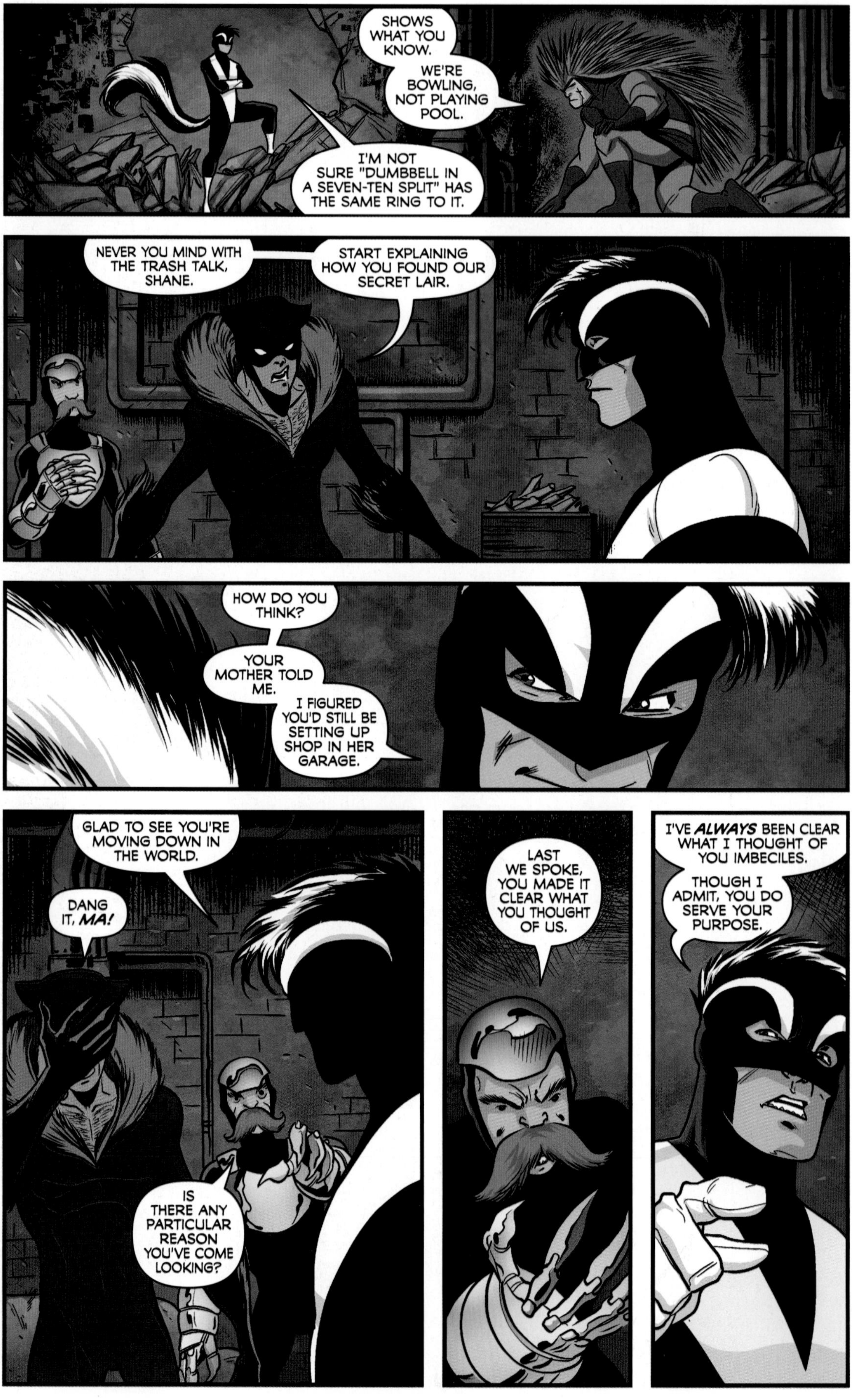
SHOWS WHAT YOU KNOW.
WE'RE BOWLING, NOT PLAYING POOL.
I'M NOT SURE "DUMBBELL IN A SEVEN-TEN SPLIT" HAS THE SAME RING TO IT.
NEVER YOU MIND WITH THE TRASH TALK, SHANE.
START EXPLAINING HOW YOU FOUND OUR SECRET LAIR.
HOW DO YOU THINK?
YOUR MOTHER TOLD ME.
I FIGURED YOU'D STILL BE SETTING UP SHOP IN HER GARAGE.
GLAD TO SEE YOU'RE MOVING DOWN IN THE WORLD.
DANG IT, MA!
IS THERE ANY PARTICULAR REASON YOU'VE COME LOOKING?
LAST WE SPOKE, YOU MADE IT CLEAR WHAT YOU THOUGHT OF US.
I'VE ALWAYS BEEN CLEAR WHAT I THOUGHT OF YOU IMBECILES.
THOUGH I ADMIT, YOU DO SERVE YOUR PURPOSE.

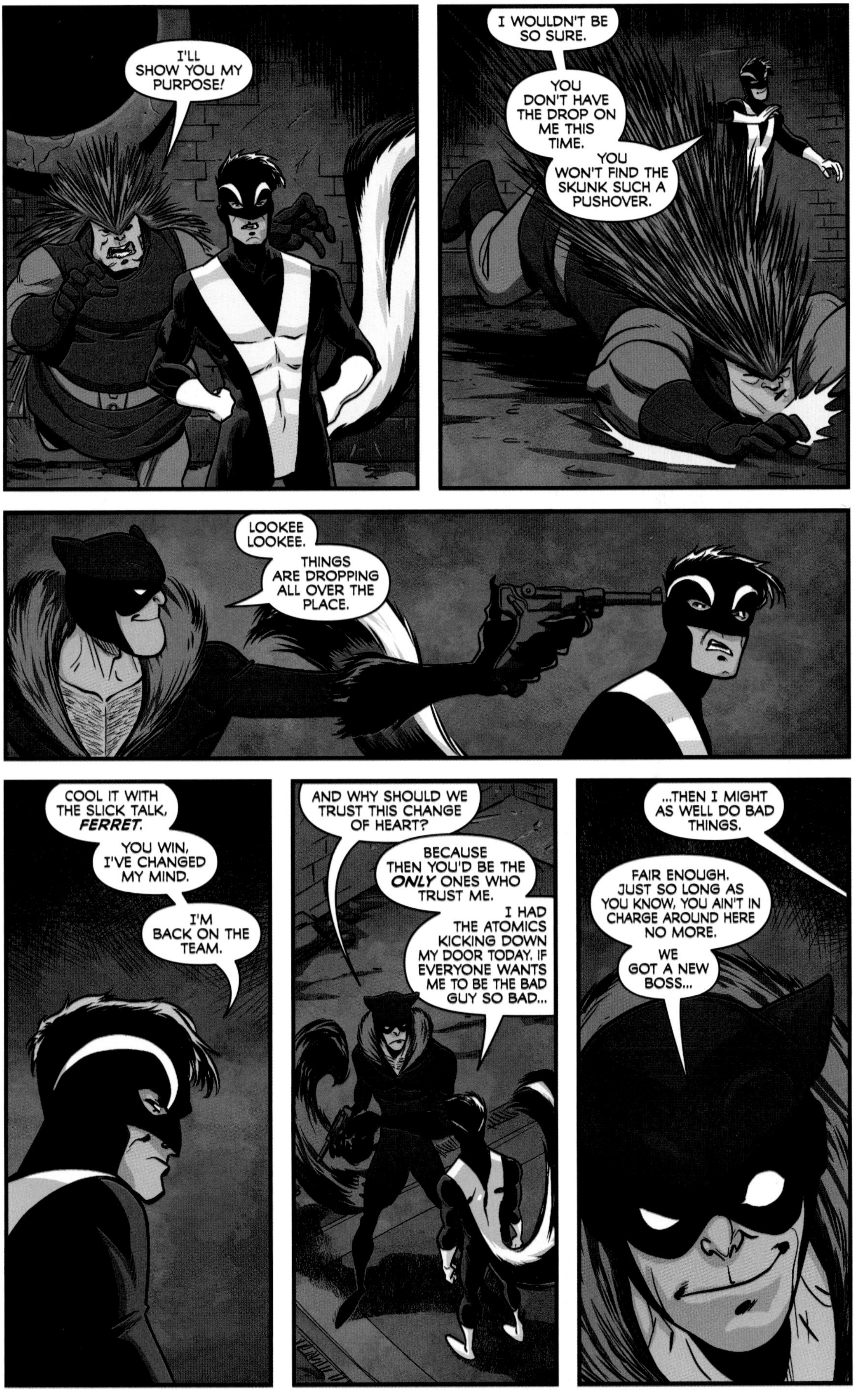
I'LL SHOW YOU MY PURPOSE!
I WOULDN'T BE SO SURE.
YOU DON'T HAVE THE DROP ON ME THIS TIME.
YOU WON'T FIND THE SKUNK SUCH A PUSHOVER.
LOOKEE LOOKEE.
THINGS ARE DROPPING ALL OVER THE PLACE.
COOL IT WITH THE SLICK TALK, FERRET.
YOU WIN, I'VE CHANGED MY MIND.
I'M BACK ON THE TEAM.
AND WHY SHOULD WE TRUST THIS CHANGE OF HEART?
BECAUSE THEN YOU'D BE THE ONLY ONES WHO TRUST ME.
I HAD THE ATOMICS KICKING DOWN MY DOOR TODAY. IF EVERYONE WANTS ME TO BE THE BAD GUY SO BAD...
...THEN I MIGHT AS WELL DO BAD THINGS.
FAIR ENOUGH. JUST SO LONG AS YOU KNOW, YOU AIN'T IN CHARGE AROUND HERE NO MORE.
WE GOT A NEW BOSS...

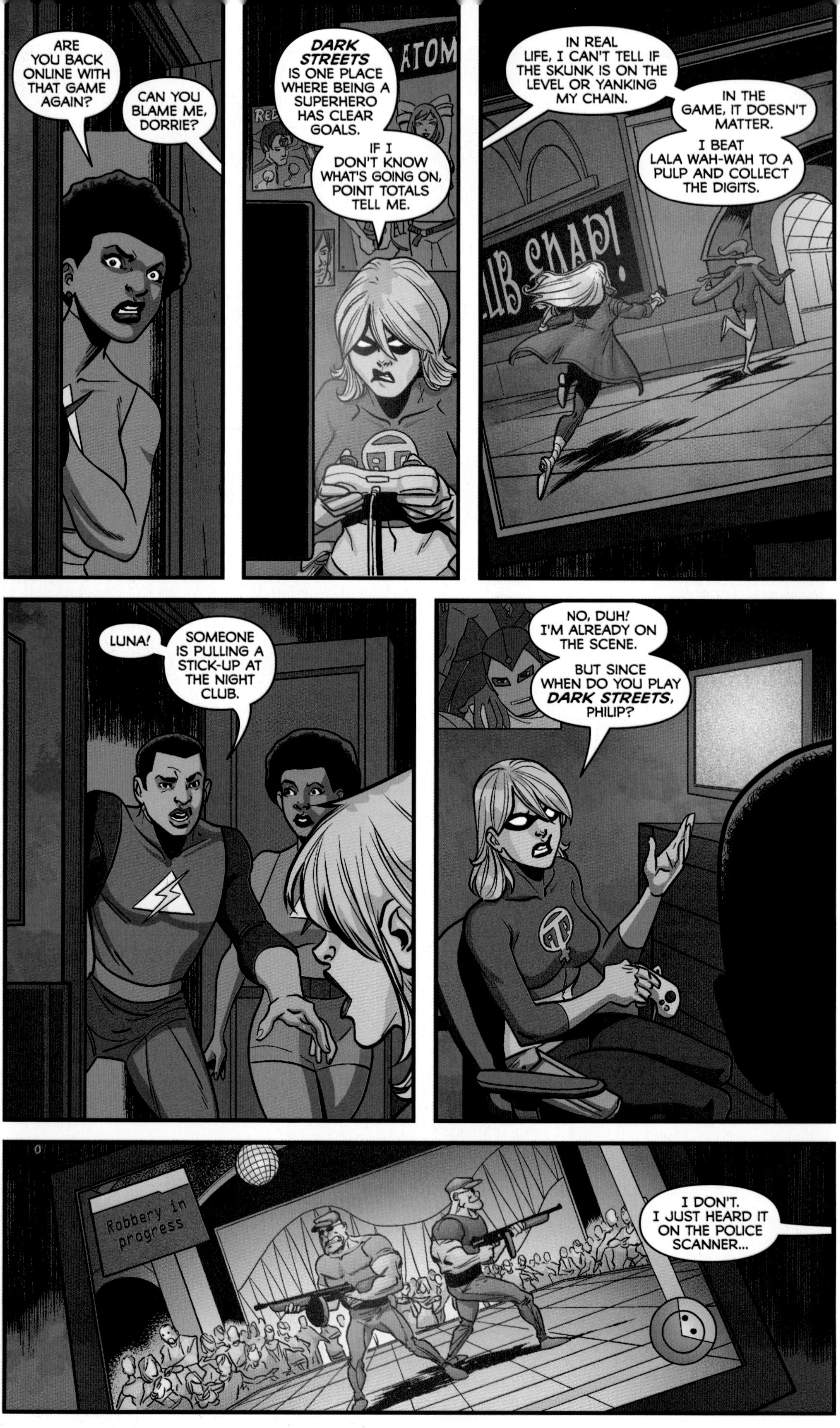
ARE YOU BACK ONLINE WITH THAT GAME AGAIN?
CAN YOU BLAME ME, DORRIE?
DARK STREETS IS ONE PLACE WHERE BEING A SUPERHERO HAS CLEAR GOALS.
IF I DON'T KNOW WHAT'S GOING ON, POINT TOTALS TELL ME.
IN REAL LIFE, I CAN'T TELL IF THE SKUNK IS ON THE LEVEL OR YANKING MY CHAIN.
IN THE GAME, IT DOESN'T MATTER.
I BEAT LALA WAH-WAH TO A PULP AND COLLECT THE DIGITS.
LUNA!
SOMEONE IS PULLING A STICK-UP AT THE NIGHT CLUB.
NO, DUH! I'M ALREADY ON THE SCENE.
BUT SINCE WHEN DO YOU PLAY DARK STREETS, PHILIP?
Robbery in progress
I DON'T. I JUST HEARD IT ON THE POLICE SCANNER...

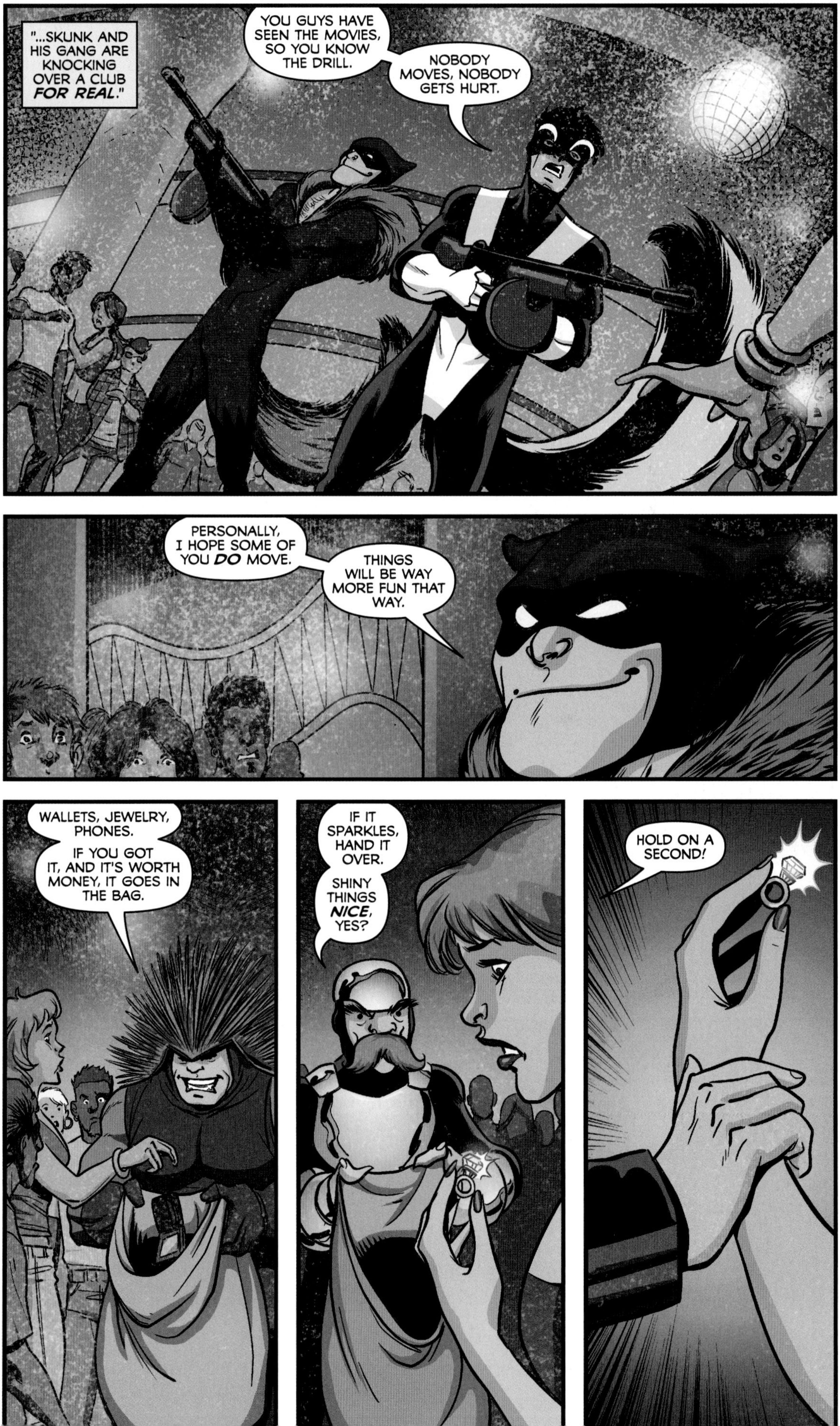
"...SKUNK AND HIS GANG ARE KNOCKING OVER A CLUB *FOR REAL*."
YOU GUYS HAVE SEEN THE MOVIES, SO YOU KNOW THE DRILL.
NOBODY MOVES, NOBODY GETS HURT.
PERSONALLY, I HOPE SOME OF YOU *DO* MOVE.
THINGS WILL BE WAY MORE FUN THAT WAY.
WALLETS, JEWELRY, PHONES.
IF YOU GOT IT, AND IT'S WORTH MONEY, IT GOES IN THE BAG.
IF IT SPARKLES, HAND IT OVER.
SHINY THINGS *NICE*, YES?
HOLD ON A SECOND!

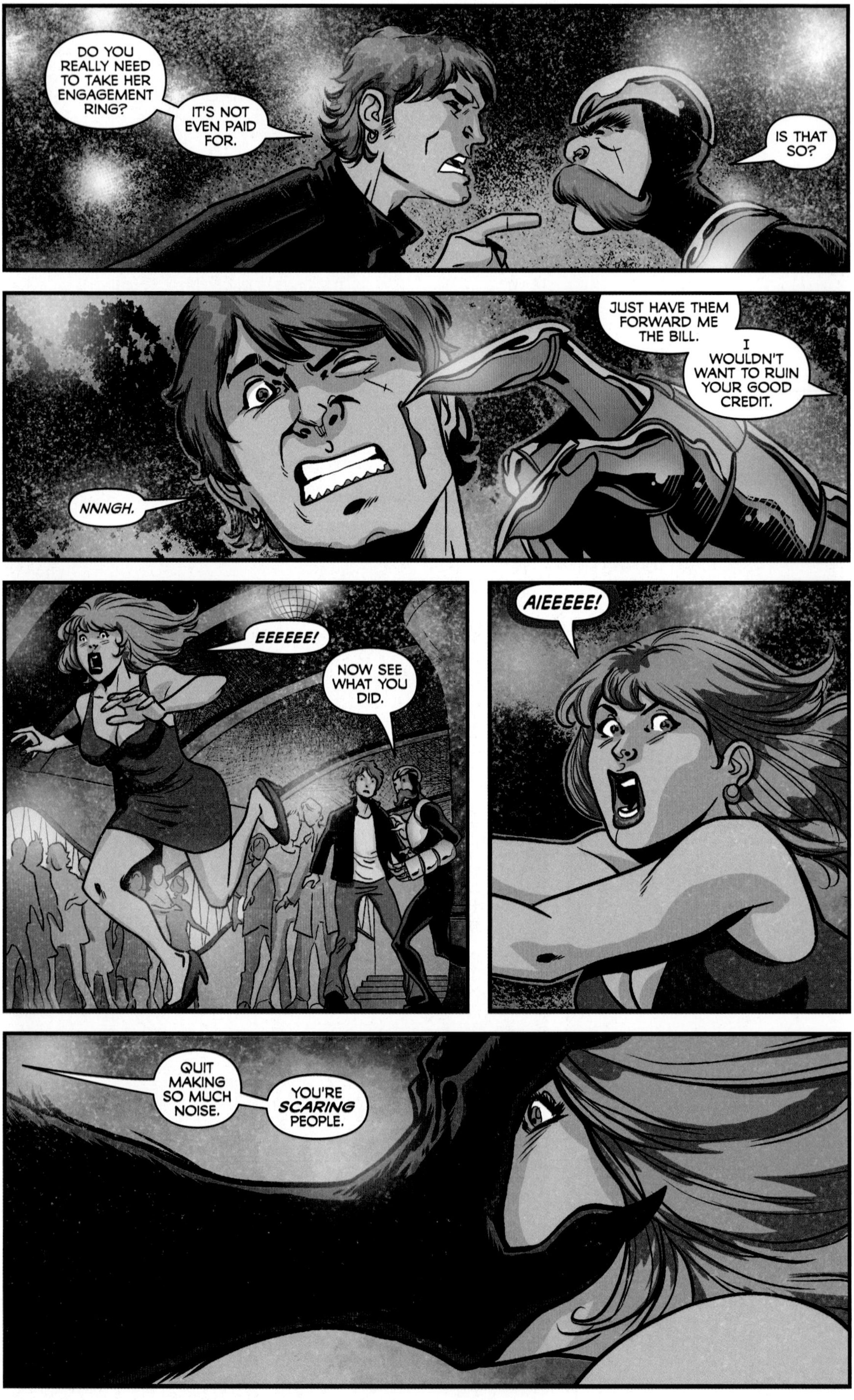
DO YOU REALLY NEED TO TAKE HER ENGAGEMENT RING?
IT'S NOT EVEN PAID FOR.
IS THAT SO?
JUST HAVE THEM FORWARD ME THE BILL.
I WOULDN'T WANT TO RUIN YOUR GOOD CREDIT.
NNNGH.
EEEEEE!
NOW SEE WHAT YOU DID.
AIEEEEE!
QUIT MAKING SO MUCH NOISE.
YOU'RE SCARING PEOPLE.

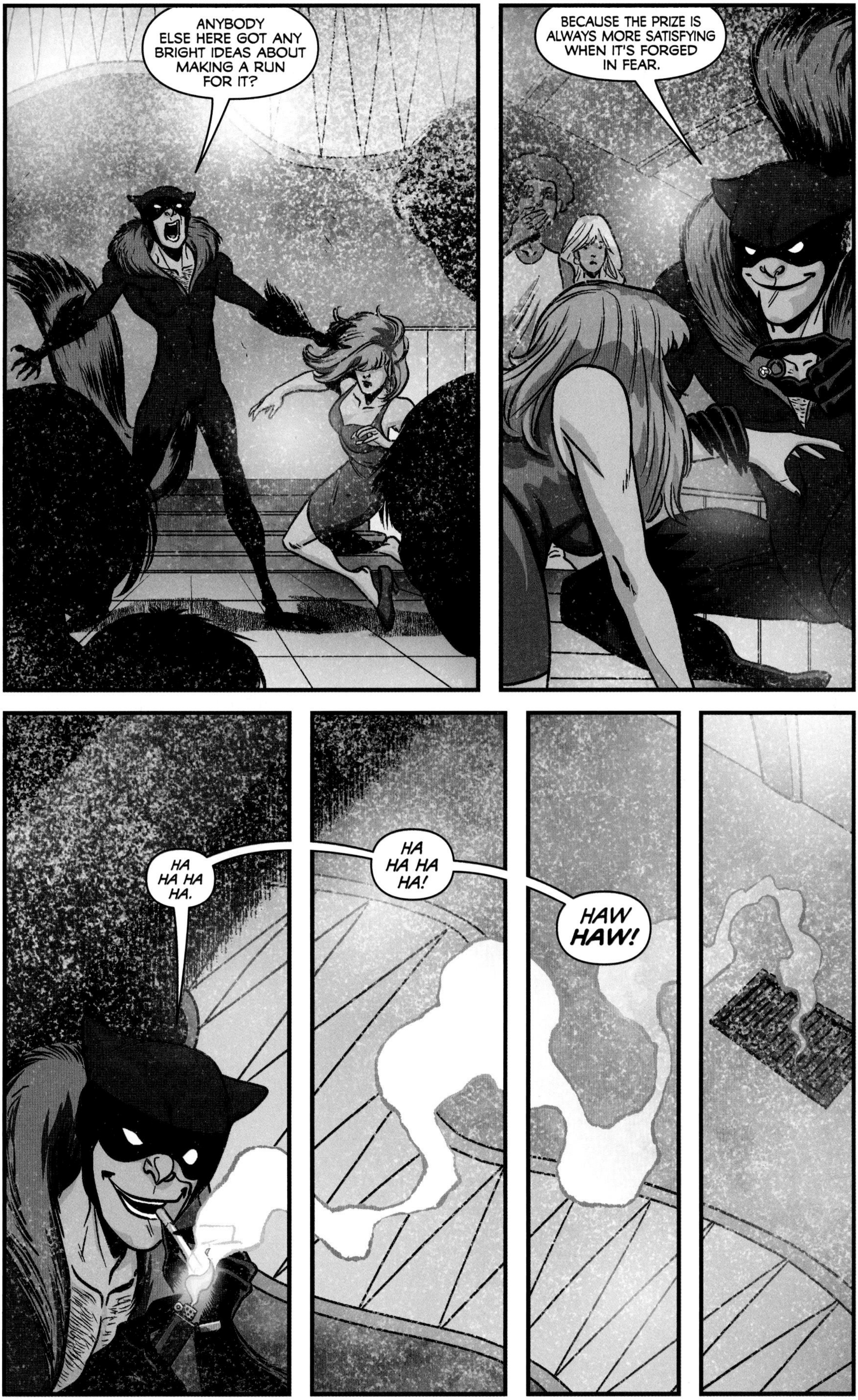
ANYBODY ELSE HERE GOT ANY BRIGHT IDEAS ABOUT MAKING A RUN FOR IT?
BECAUSE THE PRIZE IS ALWAYS MORE SATISFYING WHEN IT'S FORGED IN FEAR.
HA HA HA HA.
HA HA HA HA!
HAW HAW!

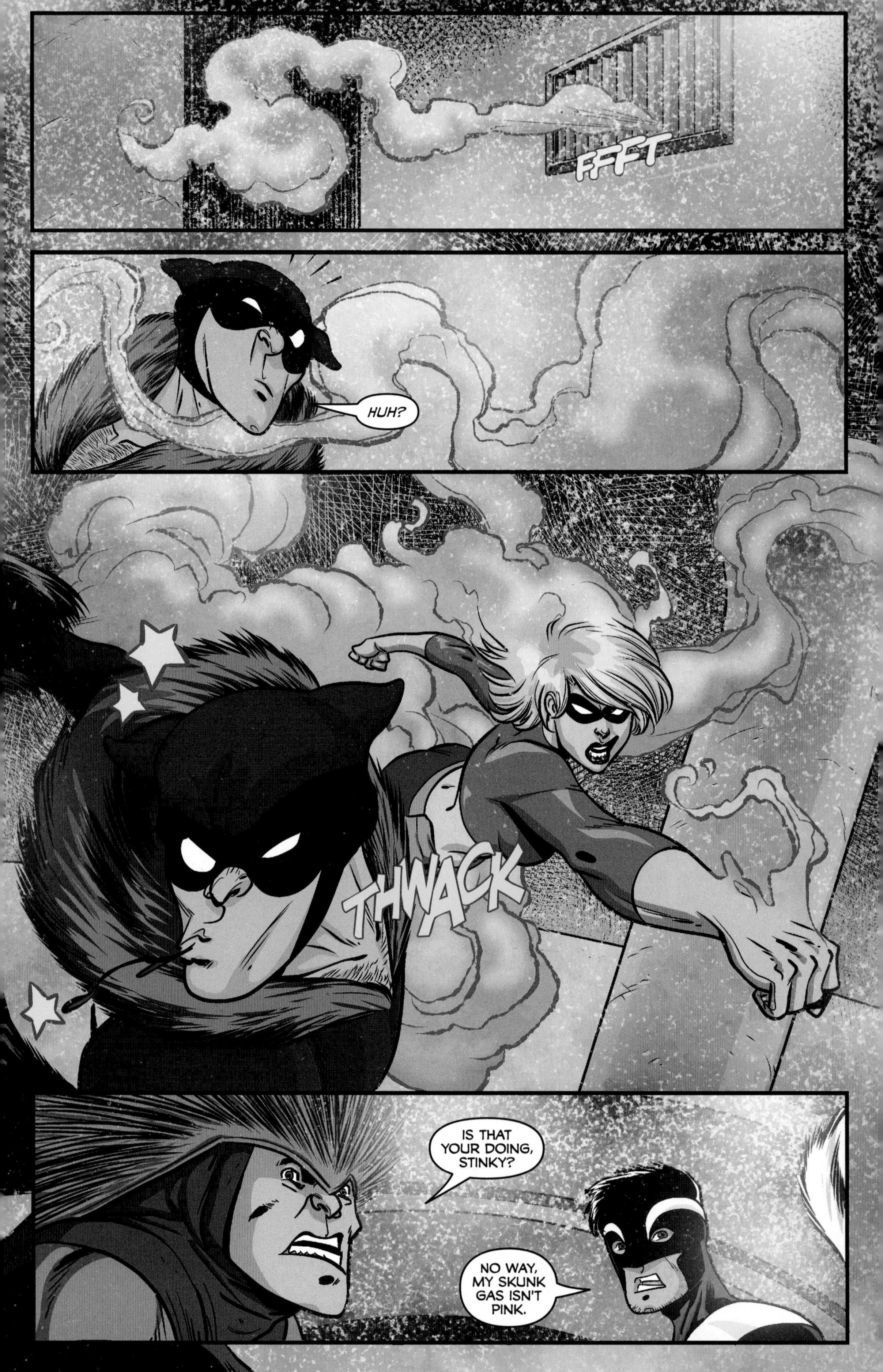
FFFT
HUH?
THWACK
IS THAT YOUR DOING, STINKY?
NO WAY, MY SKUNK GAS ISN'T PINK.

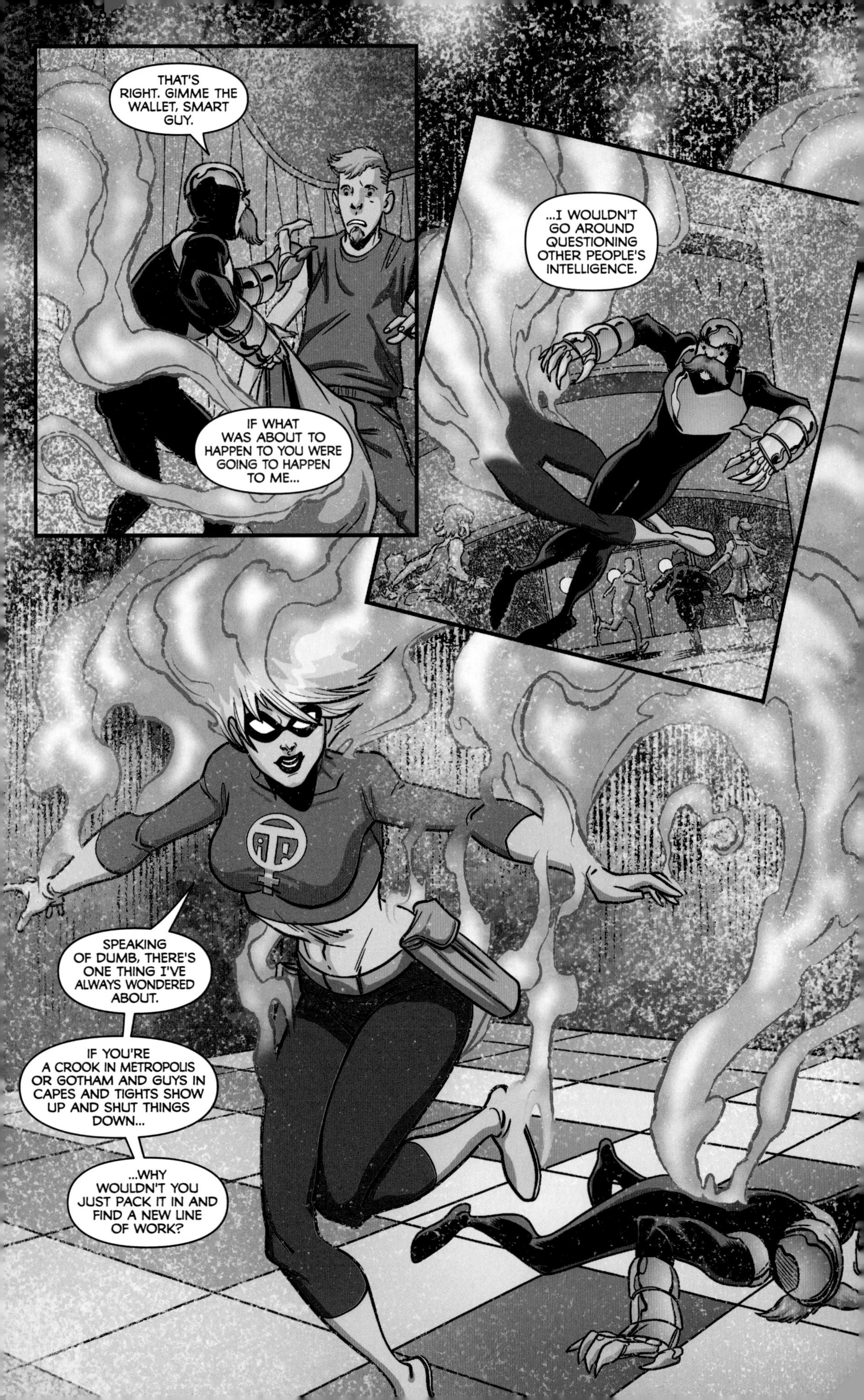
THAT'S RIGHT. GIMME THE WALLET, SMART GUY.
IF WHAT WAS ABOUT TO HAPPEN TO YOU WERE GOING TO HAPPEN TO ME...
...I WOULDN'T GO AROUND QUESTIONING OTHER PEOPLE'S INTELLIGENCE.
SPEAKING OF DUMB, THERE'S ONE THING I'VE ALWAYS WONDERED ABOUT.
IF YOU'RE A CROOK IN METROPOLIS OR GOTHAM AND GUYS IN CAPES AND TIGHTS SHOW UP AND SHUT THINGS DOWN...
...WHY WOULDN'T YOU JUST PACK IT IN AND FIND A NEW LINE OF WORK?

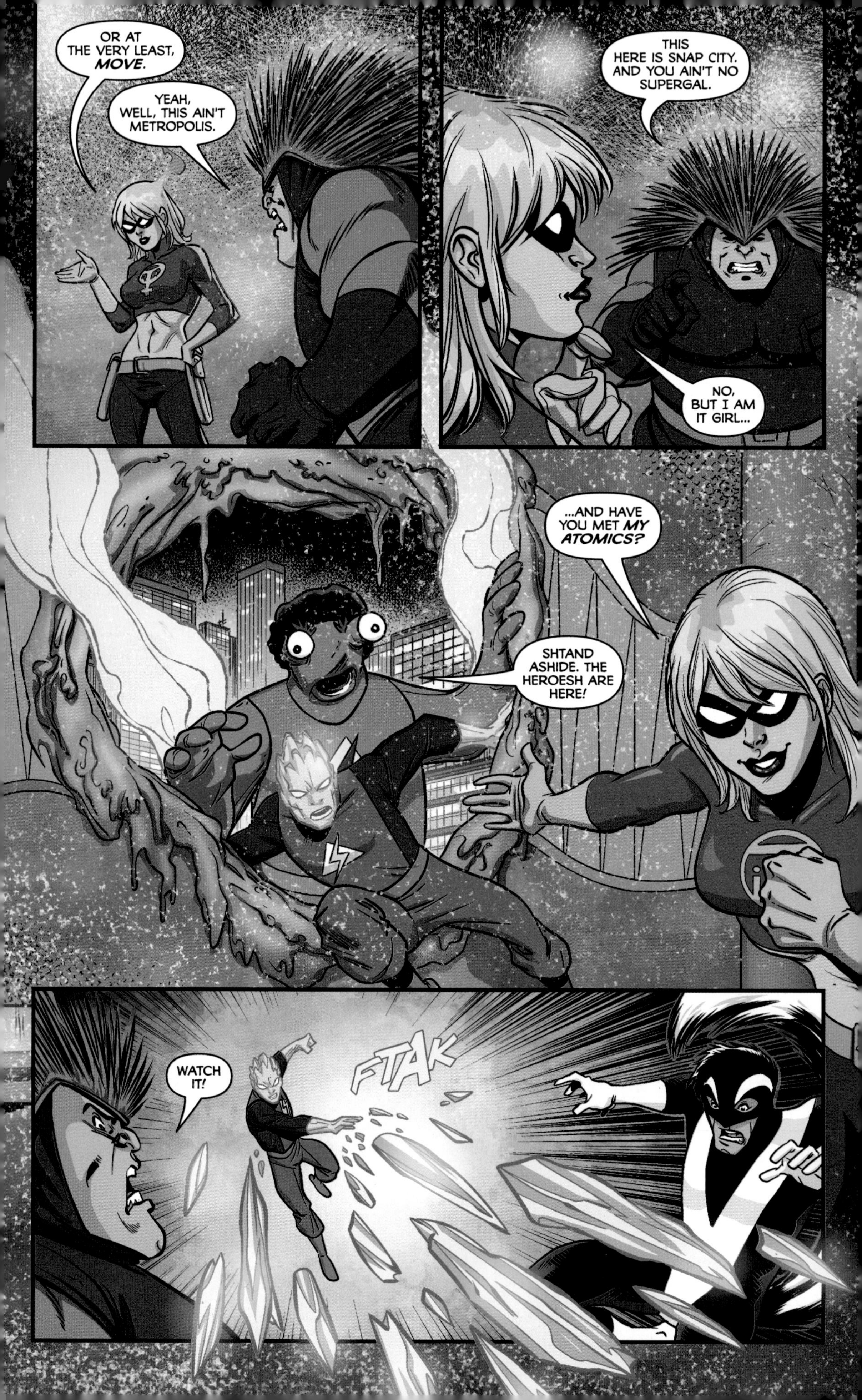
OR AT THE VERY LEAST, MOVE.
YEAH, WELL, THIS AIN'T METROPOLIS.
THIS HERE IS SNAP CITY. AND YOU AIN'T NO SUPERGAL.
NO, BUT I AM IT GIRL...
...AND HAVE YOU MET MY ATOMICS?
SHTAND ASHIDE. THE HEROESH ARE HERE!
WATCH IT!
FTAK

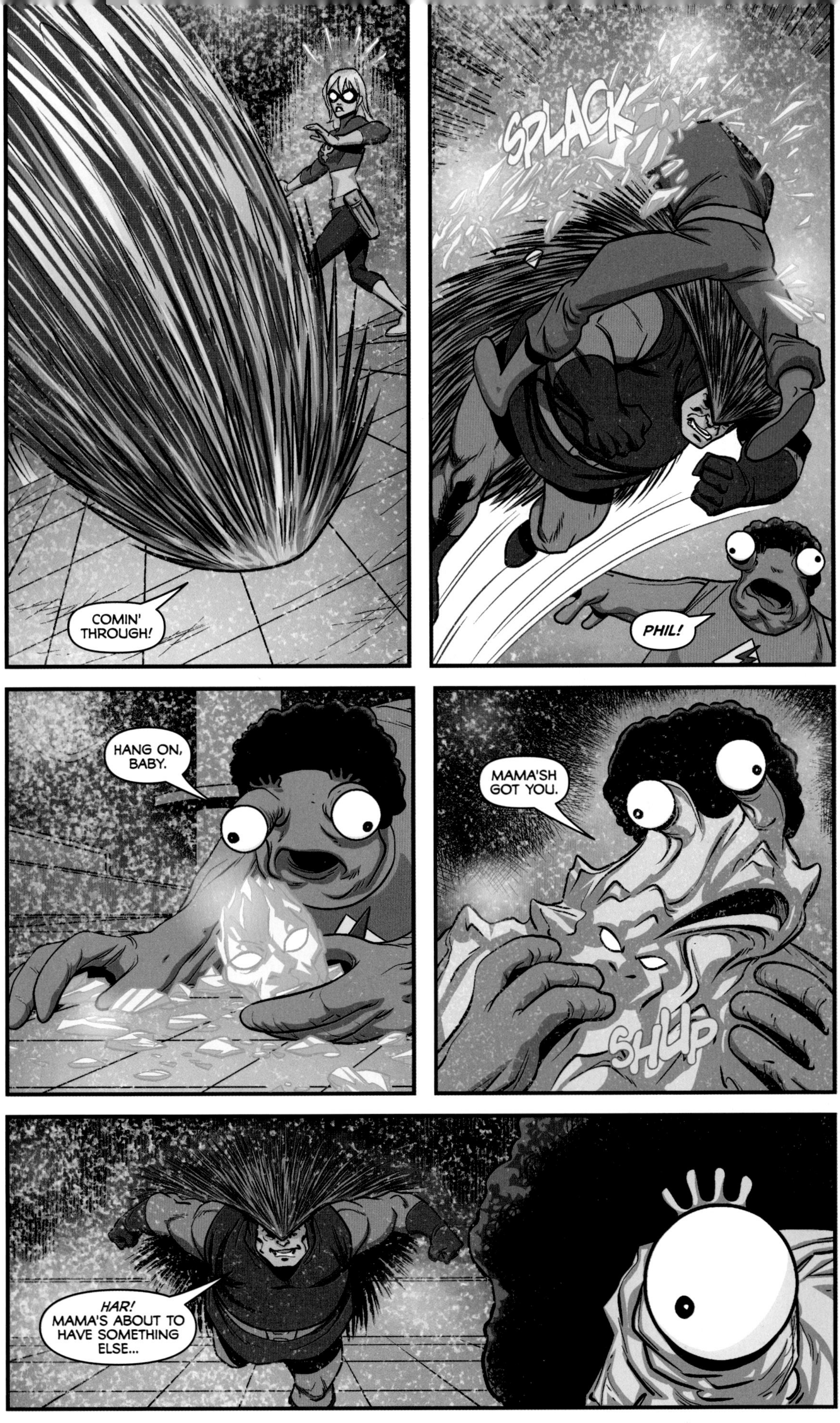
SPLACK
COMIN' THROUGH!
PHIL!
HANG ON, BABY.
MAMA'SH GOT YOU.
SHLUP
HAR! MAMA'S ABOUT TO HAVE SOMETHING ELSE...

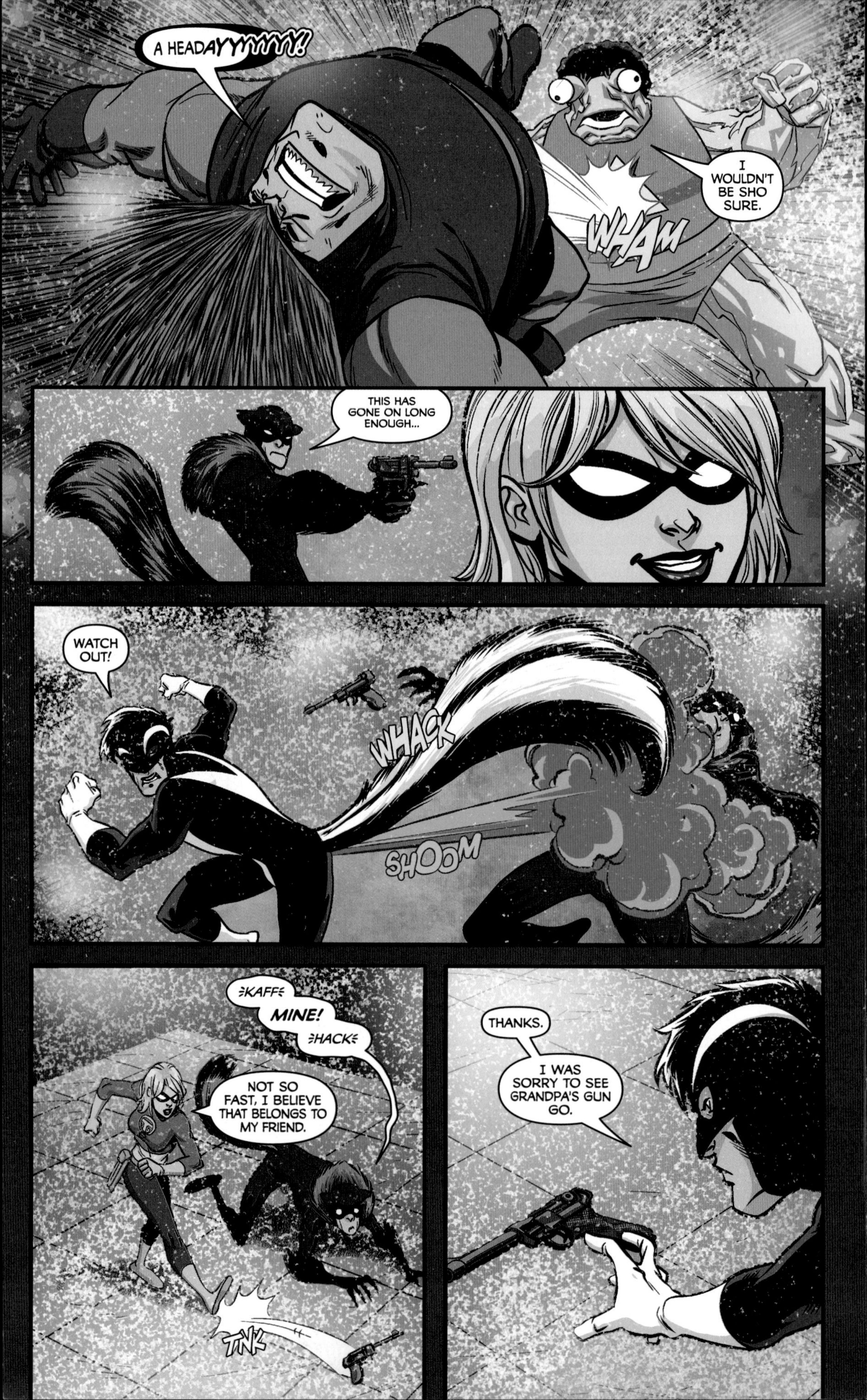
A HEADAYYYYYYY!
I WOULDN'T BE SHO SURE.
WHAM
THIS HAS GONE ON LONG ENOUGH...
WATCH OUT!
WHACK
SHOOM
KAFF
MINE!
HACK
NOT SO FAST, I BELIEVE THAT BELONGS TO MY FRIEND.
TNK
THANKS.
I WAS SORRY TO SEE GRANDPA'S GUN GO.

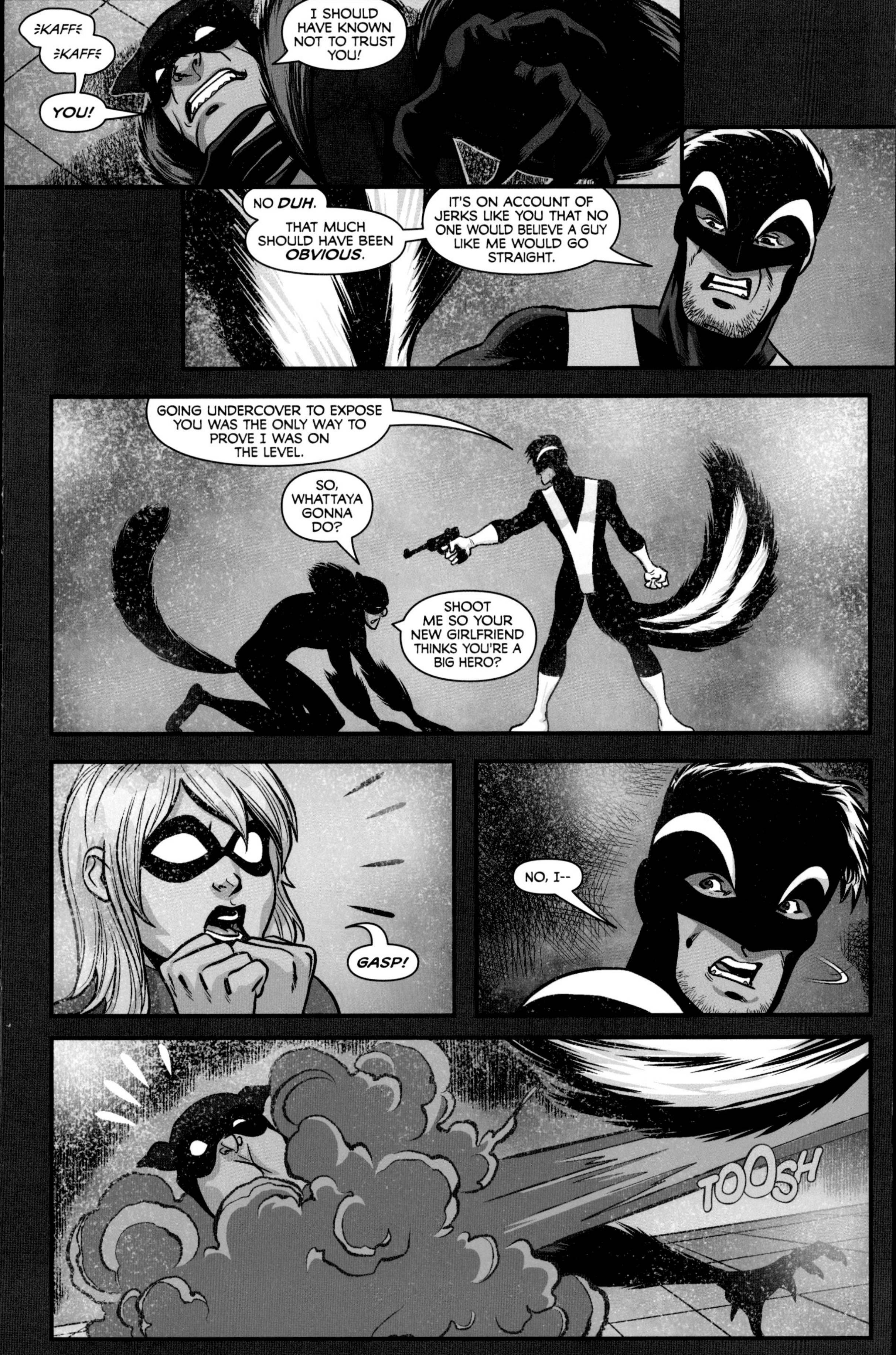
KAFF
KAFF
YOU!
I SHOULD HAVE KNOWN NOT TO TRUST YOU!
NO DUH.
THAT MUCH SHOULD HAVE BEEN OBVIOUS.
IT'S ON ACCOUNT OF JERKS LIKE YOU THAT NO ONE WOULD BELIEVE A GUY LIKE ME WOULD GO STRAIGHT.
GOING UNDERCOVER TO EXPOSE YOU WAS THE ONLY WAY TO PROVE I WAS ON THE LEVEL.
SO, WHATTAYA GONNA DO?
SHOOT ME SO YOUR NEW GIRLFRIEND THINKS YOU'RE A BIG HERO?
GASP!
NO, I--
TOOSH

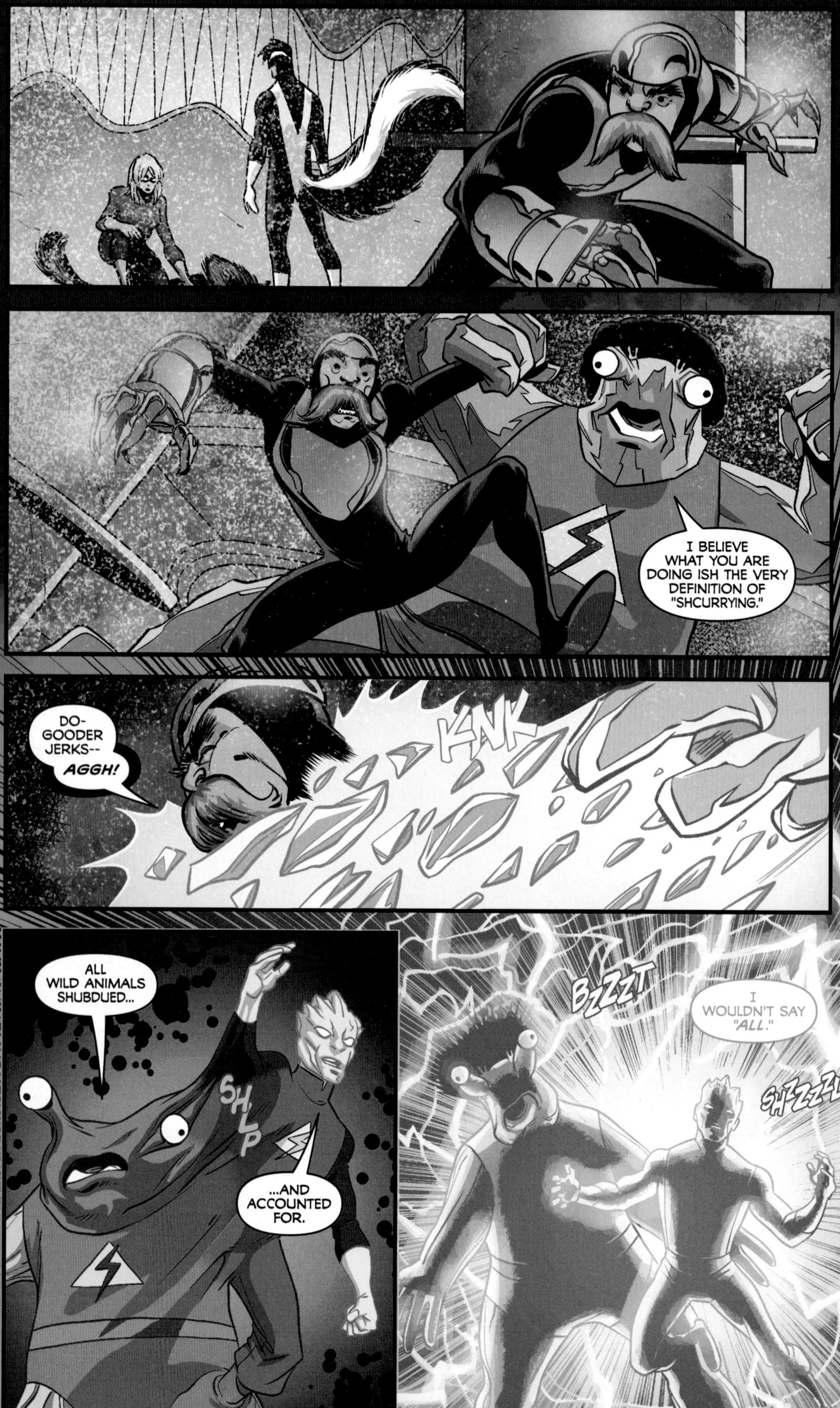
I BELIEVE WHAT YOU ARE DOING ISH THE VERY DEFINITION OF "SHCURRYING."
DO-GOODER JERKS-- AGGH!
KNK
ALL WILD ANIMALS SHUBDUED...
SHLP
...AND ACCOUNTED FOR.
BZZZT
I WOULDN'T SAY "ALL."
SHZZZZL

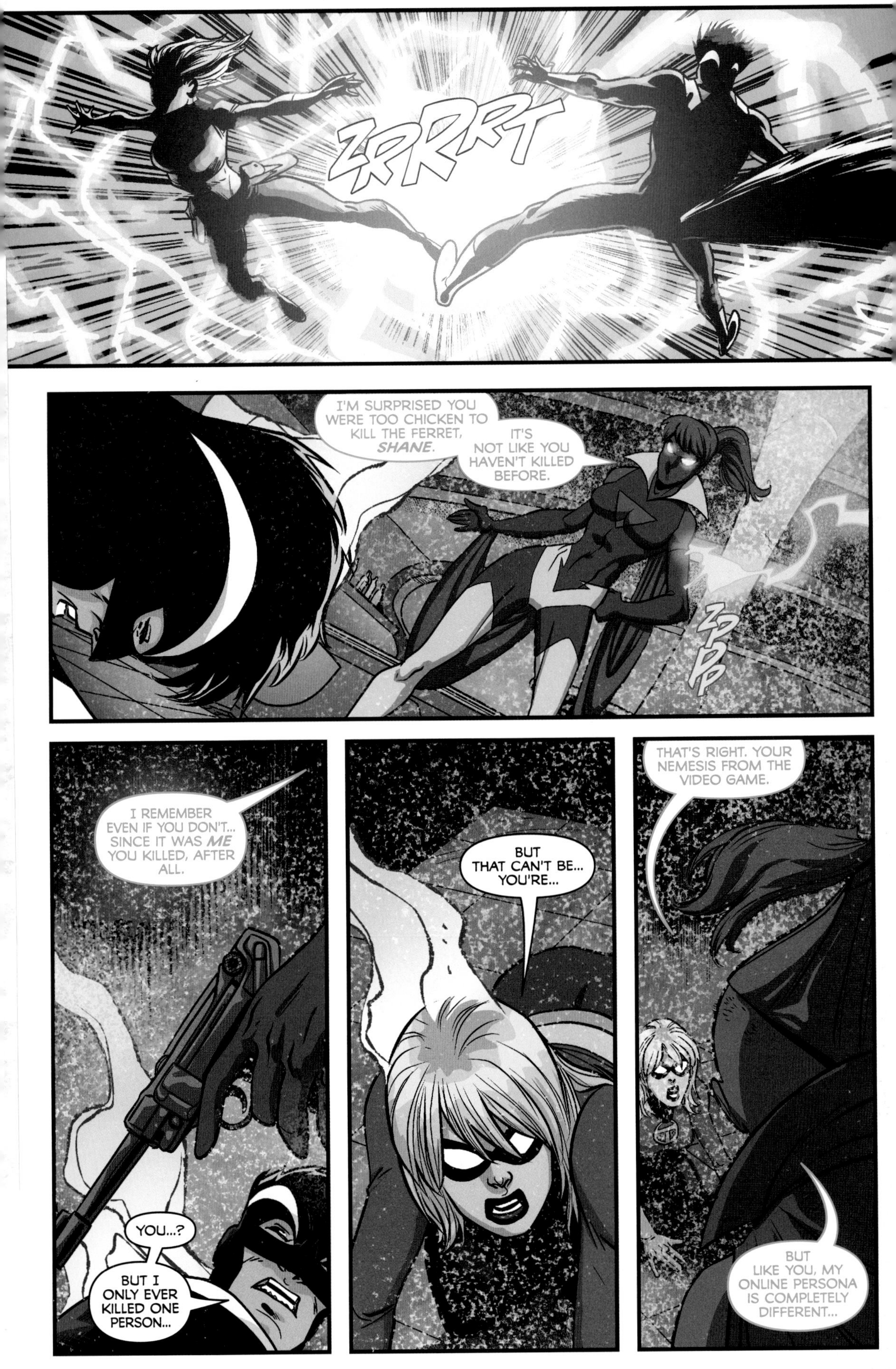
ZRRRT
I'M SURPRISED YOU WERE TOO CHICKEN TO KILL THE FERRET, SHANE.
IT'S NOT LIKE YOU HAVEN'T KILLED BEFORE.
ZPPP
I REMEMBER EVEN IF YOU DON'T... SINCE IT WAS ME YOU KILLED, AFTER ALL.
YOU...?
BUT I ONLY EVER KILLED ONE PERSON...
BUT THAT CAN'T BE... YOU'RE...
THAT'S RIGHT. YOUR NEMESIS FROM THE VIDEO GAME.
BUT LIKE YOU, MY ONLINE PERSONA IS COMPLETELY DIFFERENT...

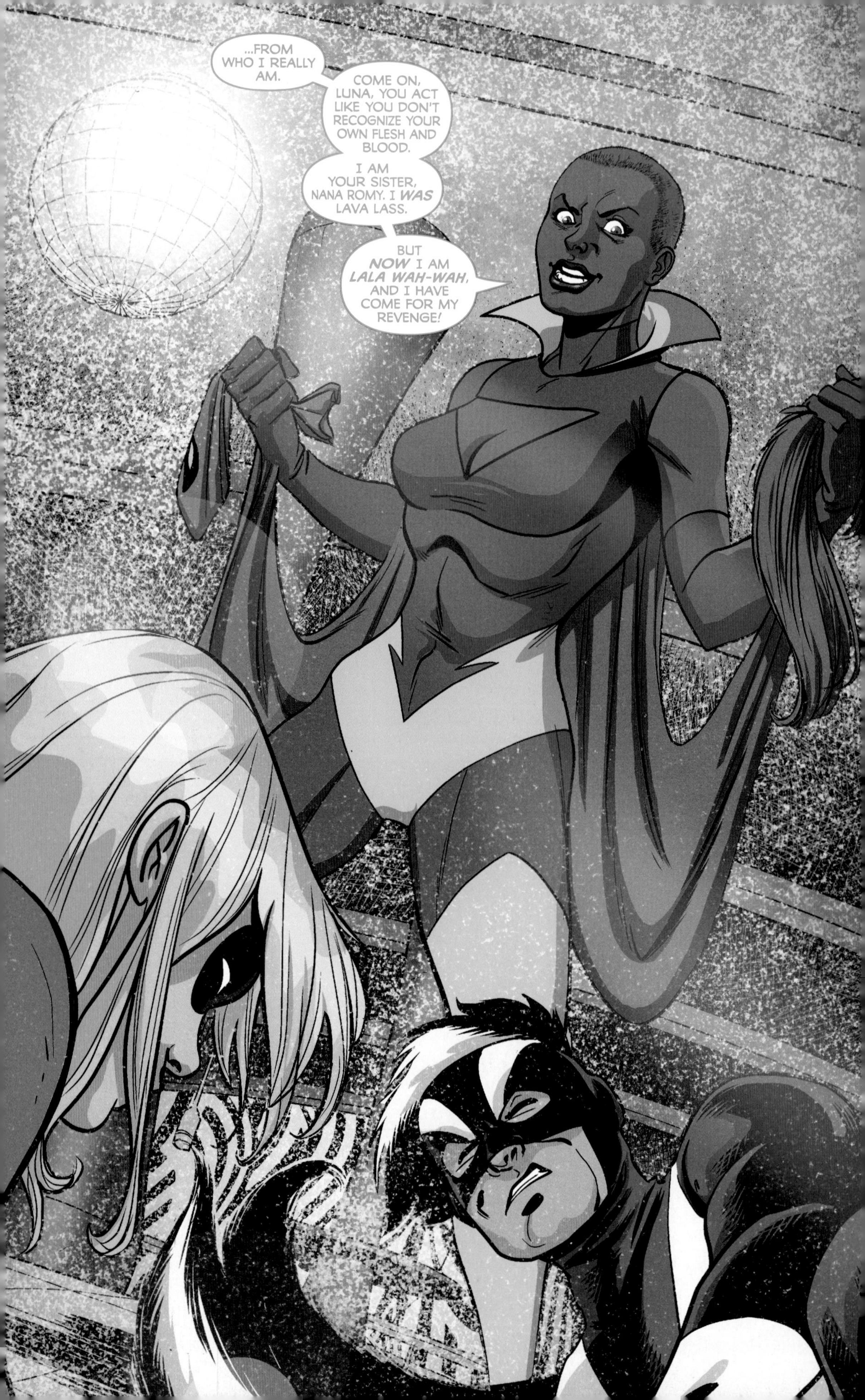
...FROM WHO I REALLY AM.
COME ON, LUNA, YOU ACT LIKE YOU DON'T RECOGNIZE YOUR OWN FLESH AND BLOOD.
I AM YOUR SISTER, NANA ROMY. I *WAS* LAVA LASS.
BUT *NOW* I AM *LALA WAH-WAH*, AND I HAVE COME FOR MY REVENGE!

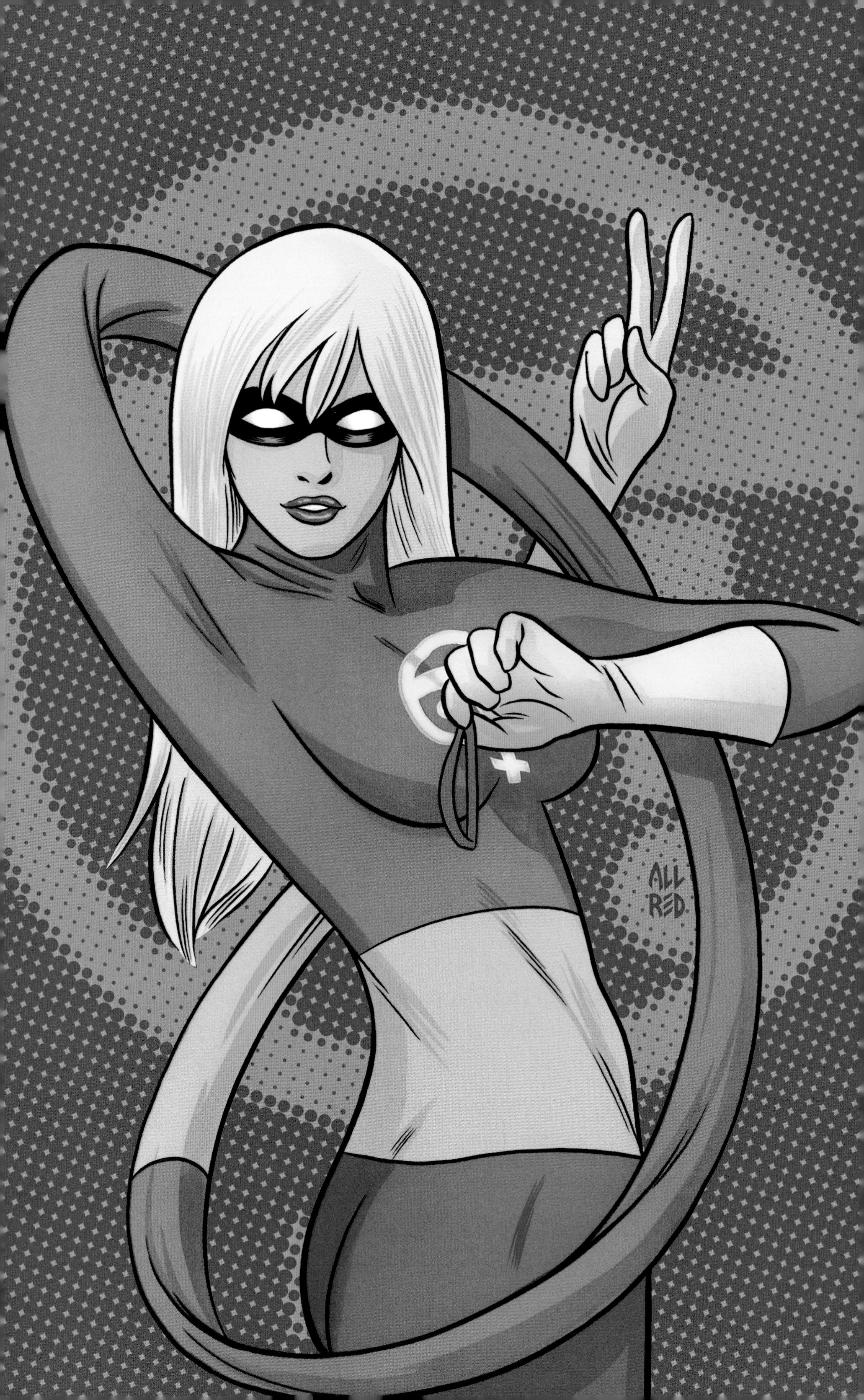
ALL
RED.

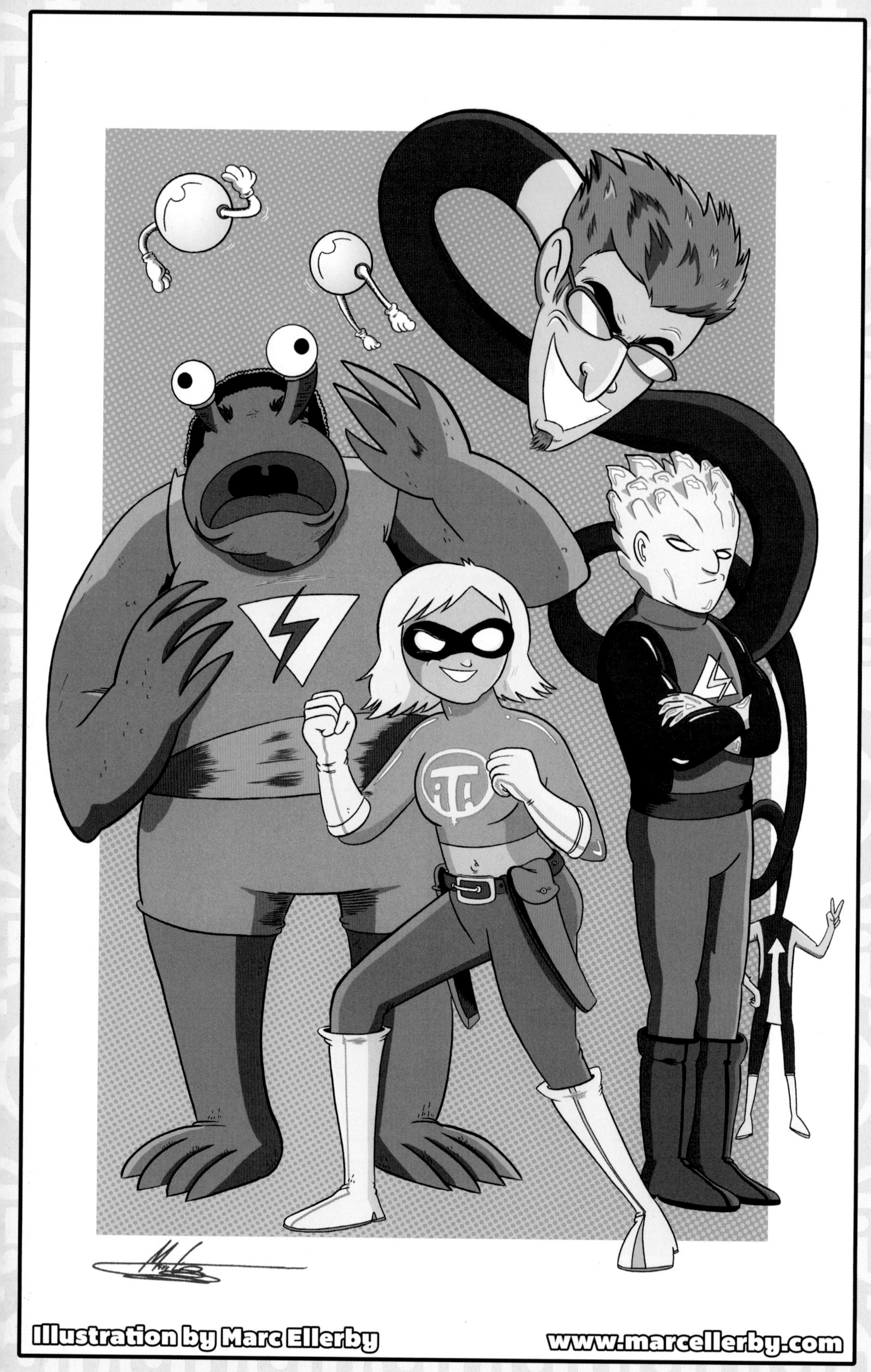

Illustration by Marc Ellerby www.marcellerby.com

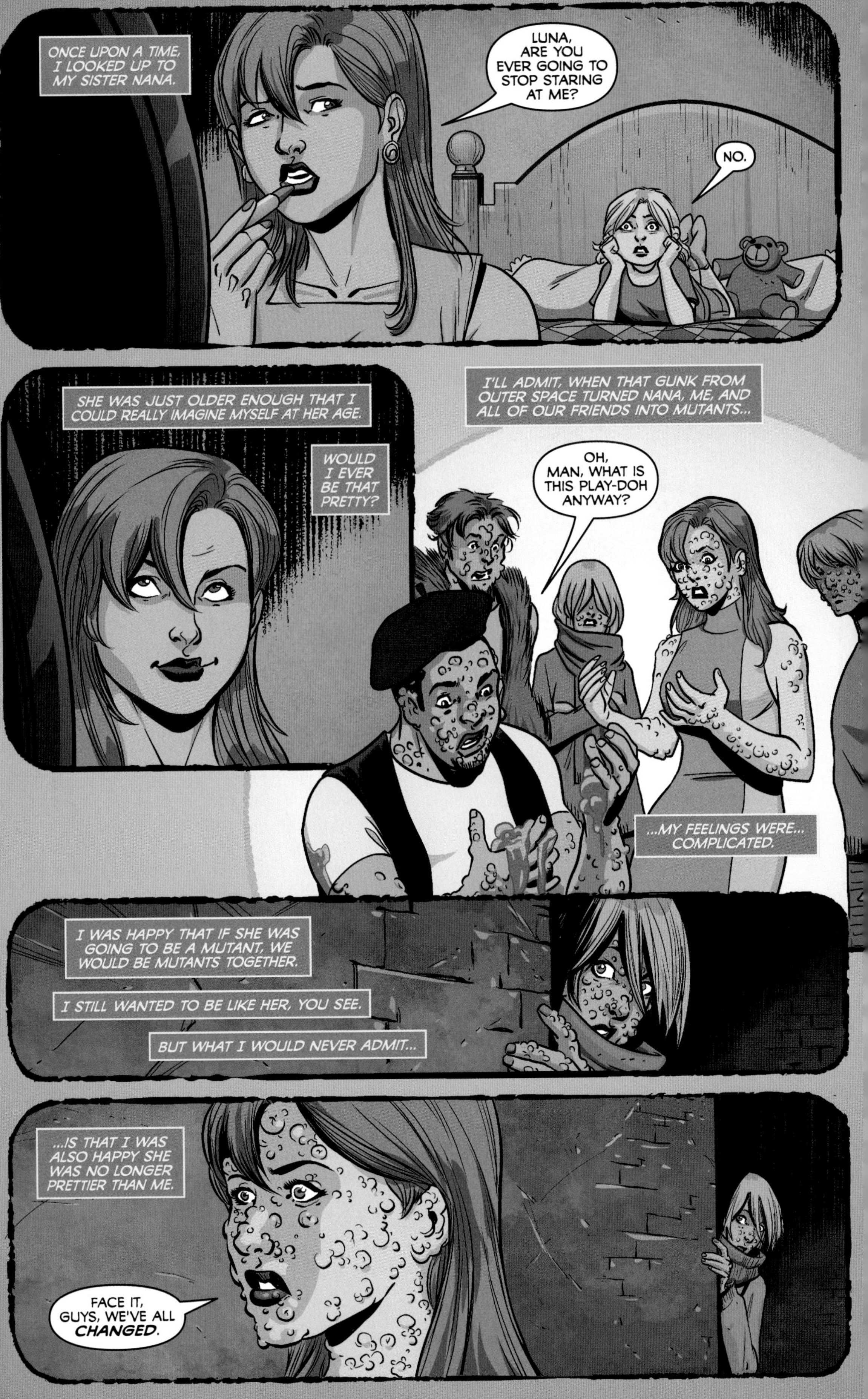
ONCE UPON A TIME, I LOOKED UP TO MY SISTER NANA.
LUNA, ARE YOU EVER GOING TO STOP STARING AT ME?
NO.
SHE WAS JUST OLDER ENOUGH THAT I COULD REALLY IMAGINE MYSELF AT HER AGE.
WOULD I EVER BE THAT PRETTY?
I'LL ADMIT, WHEN THAT GUNK FROM OUTER SPACE TURNED NANA, ME, AND ALL OF OUR FRIENDS INTO MUTANTS...
OH, MAN, WHAT IS THIS PLAY-DOH ANYWAY?
...MY FEELINGS WERE... COMPLICATED.
I WAS HAPPY THAT IF SHE WAS GOING TO BE A MUTANT, WE WOULD BE MUTANTS TOGETHER.
I STILL WANTED TO BE LIKE HER, YOU SEE.
BUT WHAT I WOULD NEVER ADMIT...
...IS THAT I WAS ALSO HAPPY SHE WAS NO LONGER PRETTIER THAN ME.
FACE IT, GUYS, WE'VE ALL CHANGED.

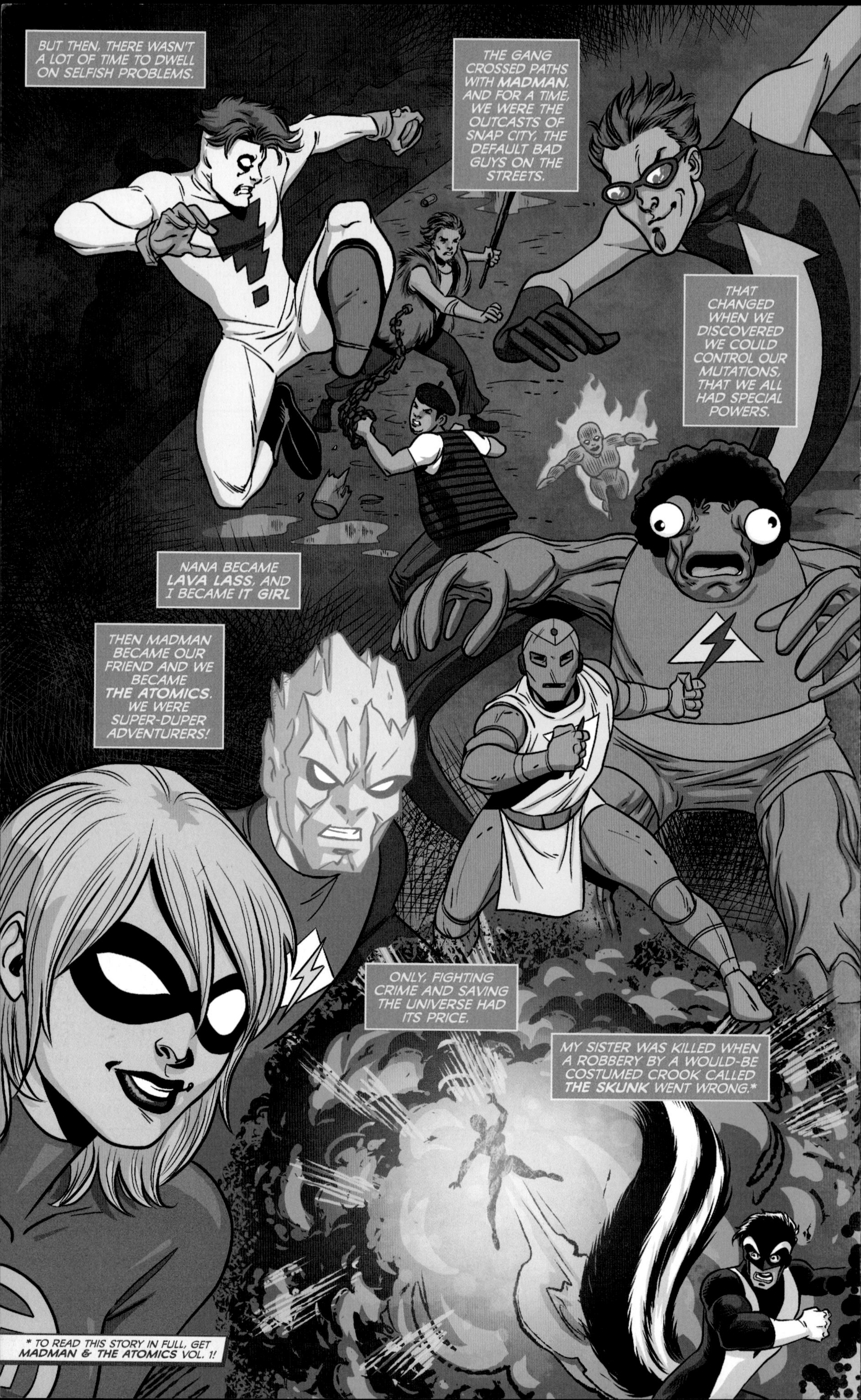
BUT THEN, THERE WASN'T A LOT OF TIME TO DWELL ON SELFISH PROBLEMS.
THE GANG CROSSED PATHS WITH MADMAN, AND FOR A TIME, WE WERE THE OUTCASTS OF SNAP CITY, THE DEFAULT BAD GUYS ON THE STREETS.
THAT CHANGED WHEN WE DISCOVERED WE COULD CONTROL OUR MUTATIONS, THAT WE ALL HAD SPECIAL POWERS.
NANA BECAME LAVA LASS, AND I BECAME IT GIRL
THEN MADMAN BECAME OUR FRIEND AND WE BECAME THE ATOMICS. WE WERE SUPER-DUPER ADVENTURERS!
ONLY, FIGHTING CRIME AND SAVING THE UNIVERSE HAD ITS PRICE.
MY SISTER WAS KILLED WHEN A ROBBERY BY A WOULD-BE COSTUMED CROOK CALLED THE SKUNK WENT WRONG.*
* TO READ THIS STORY IN FULL, GET MADMAN & THE ATOMICS VOL. 1!

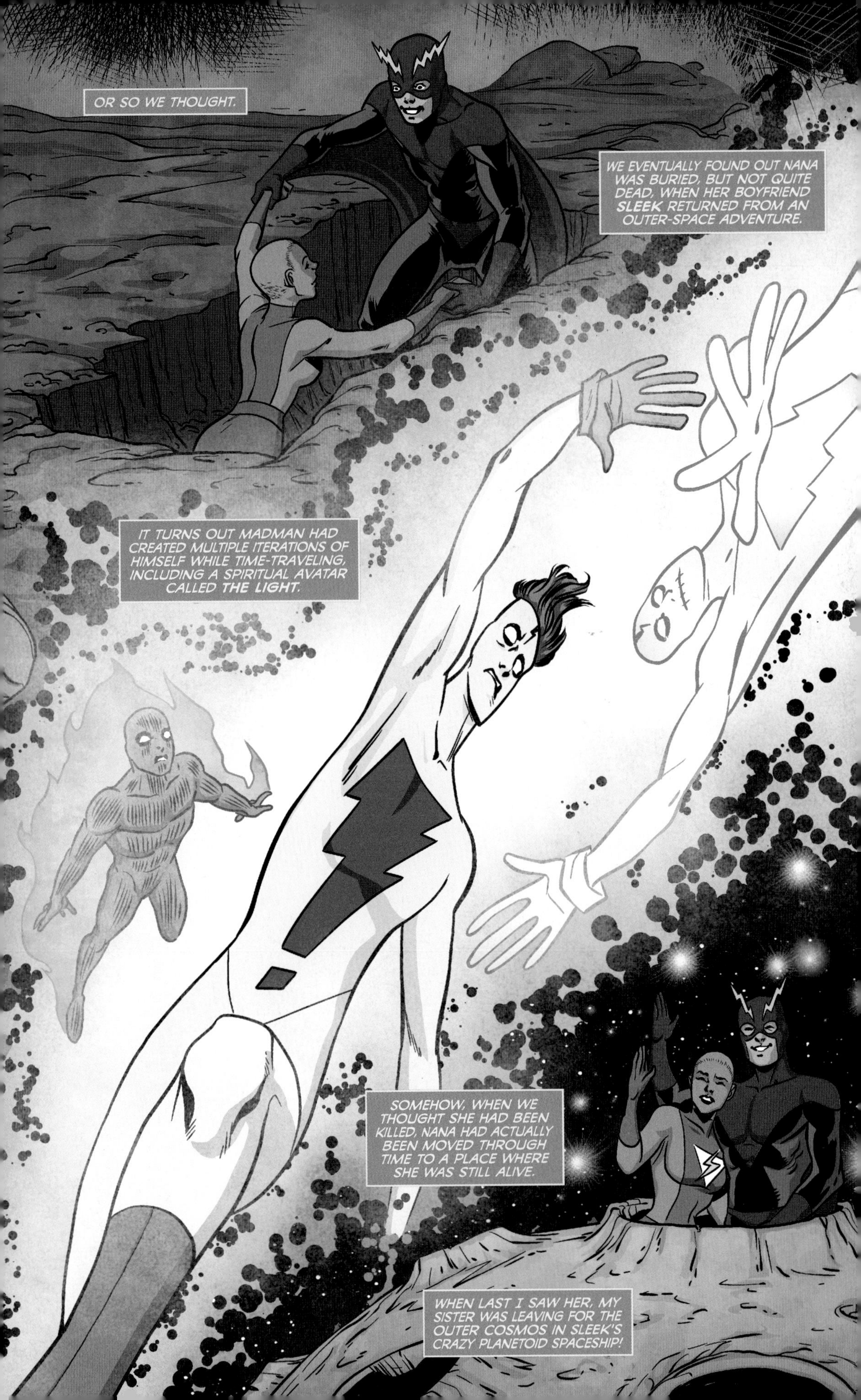
OR SO WE THOUGHT.
WE EVENTUALLY FOUND OUT NANA WAS BURIED, BUT NOT QUITE DEAD, WHEN HER BOYFRIEND SLEEK RETURNED FROM AN OUTER-SPACE ADVENTURE.
IT TURNS OUT MADMAN HAD CREATED MULTIPLE ITERATIONS OF HIMSELF WHILE TIME-TRAVELING, INCLUDING A SPIRITUAL AVATAR CALLED THE LIGHT.
SOMEHOW, WHEN WE THOUGHT SHE HAD BEEN KILLED, NANA HAD ACTUALLY BEEN MOVED THROUGH TIME TO A PLACE WHERE SHE WAS STILL ALIVE.
WHEN LAST I SAW HER, MY SISTER WAS LEAVING FOR THE OUTER COSMOS IN SLEEK'S CRAZY PLANETOID SPACESHIP!

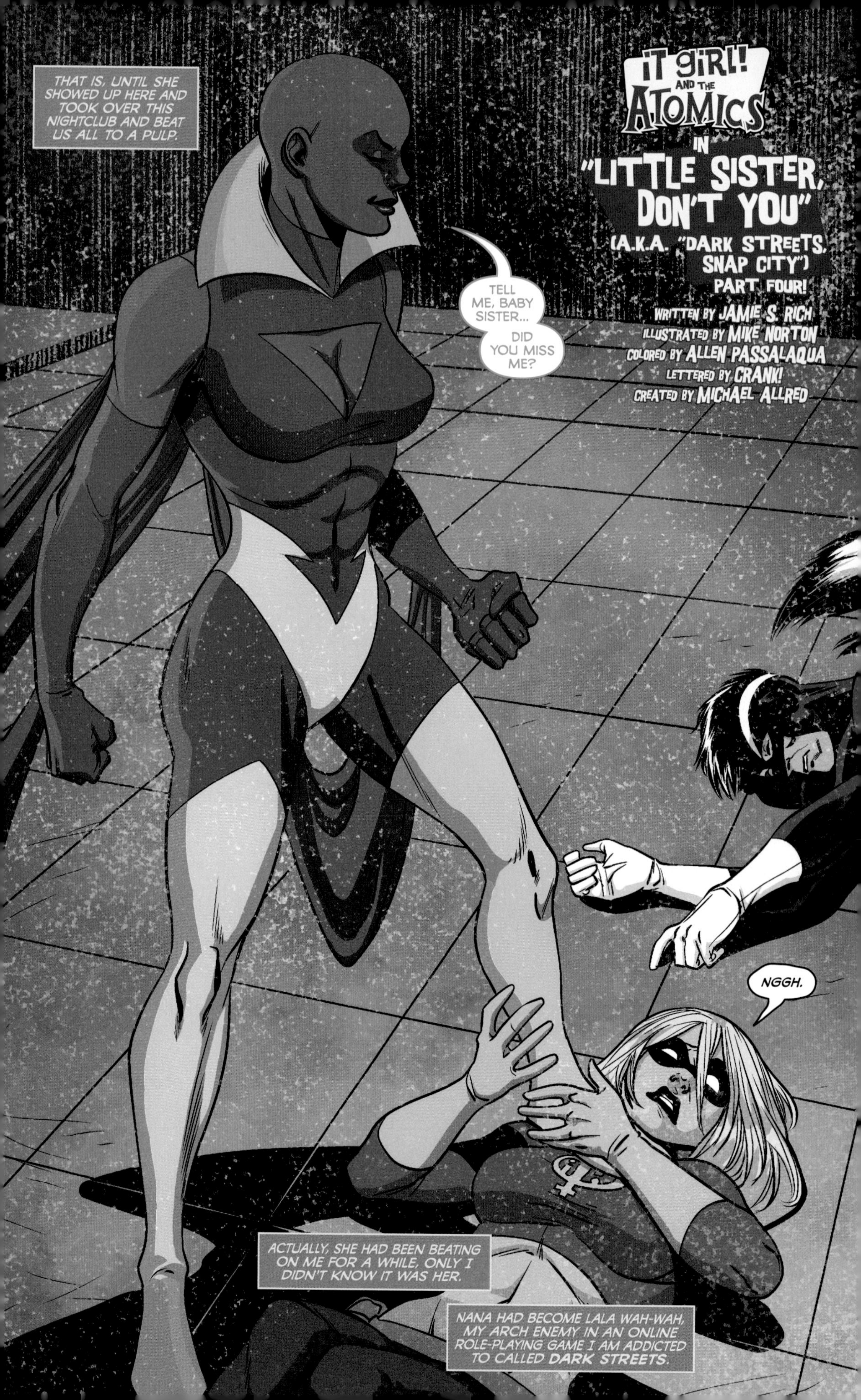
THAT IS, UNTIL SHE SHOWED UP HERE AND TOOK OVER THIS NIGHTCLUB AND BEAT US ALL TO A PULP.
IT GIRL! AND THE ATOMICS IN "LITTLE SISTER, DON'T YOU" (A.K.A. "DARK STREETS, SNAP CITY") PART FOUR!
WRITTEN BY JAMIE S. RICH
ILLUSTRATED BY MIKE NORTON
COLORED BY ALLEN PASSALAQUA
LETTERED BY CRANK!
CREATED BY MICHAEL ALLRED
TELL ME, BABY SISTER...
DID YOU MISS ME?
NGGH.
ACTUALLY, SHE HAD BEEN BEATING ON ME FOR A WHILE, ONLY I DIDN'T KNOW IT WAS HER.
NANA HAD BECOME LALA WAH-WAH, MY ARCH ENEMY IN AN ONLINE ROLE-PLAYING GAME I AM ADDICTED TO CALLED DARK STREETS.

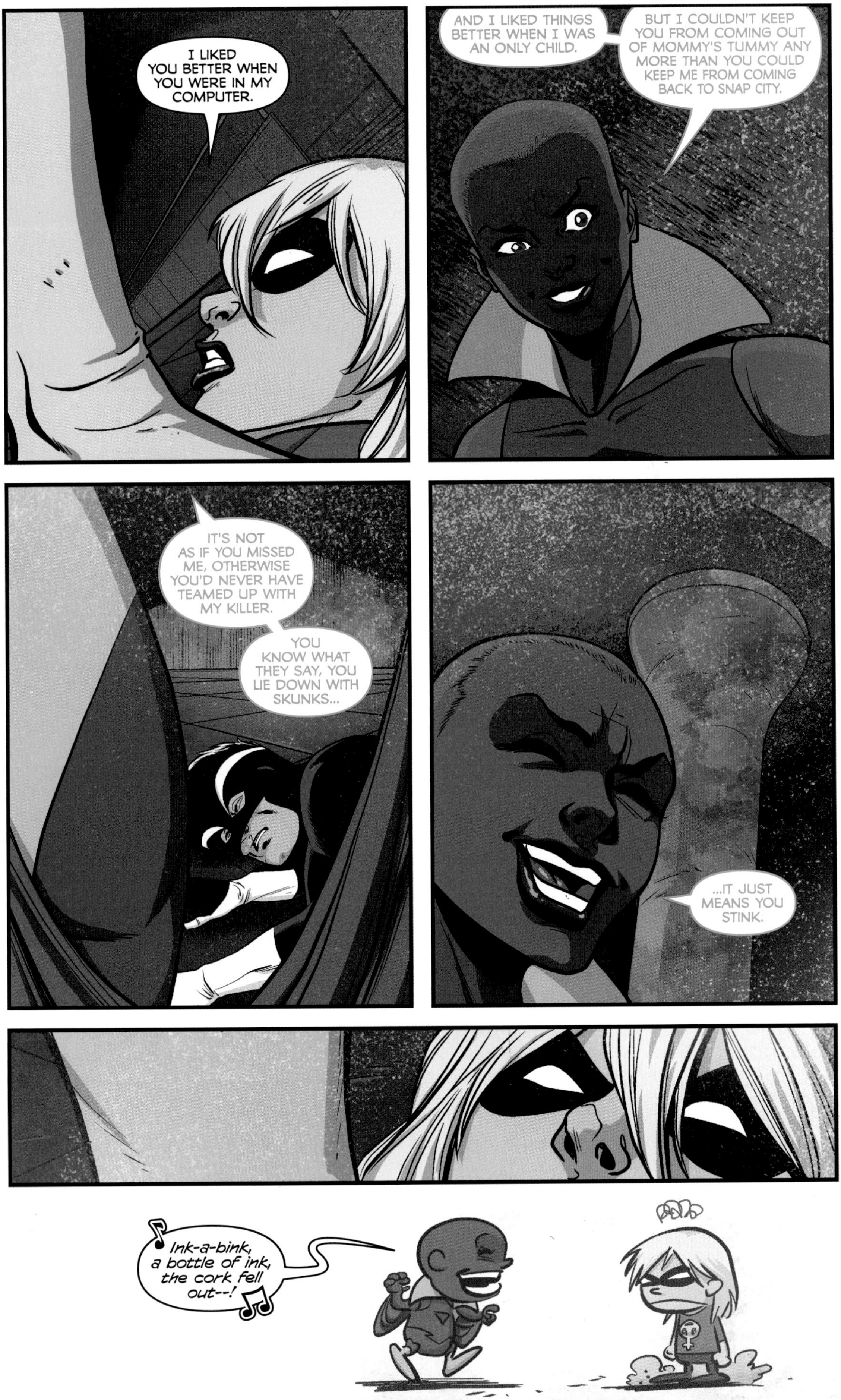
I LIKED YOU BETTER WHEN YOU WERE IN MY COMPUTER.
AND I LIKED THINGS BETTER WHEN I WAS AN ONLY CHILD.
BUT I COULDN'T KEEP YOU FROM COMING OUT OF MOMMY'S TUMMY ANY MORE THAN YOU COULD KEEP ME FROM COMING BACK TO SNAP CITY.
IT'S NOT AS IF YOU MISSED ME, OTHERWISE YOU'D NEVER HAVE TEAMED UP WITH MY KILLER.
YOU KNOW WHAT THEY SAY, YOU LIE DOWN WITH SKUNKS...
...IT JUST MEANS YOU STINK.
Ink-a-bink, a bottle of ink, the cork fell out--!

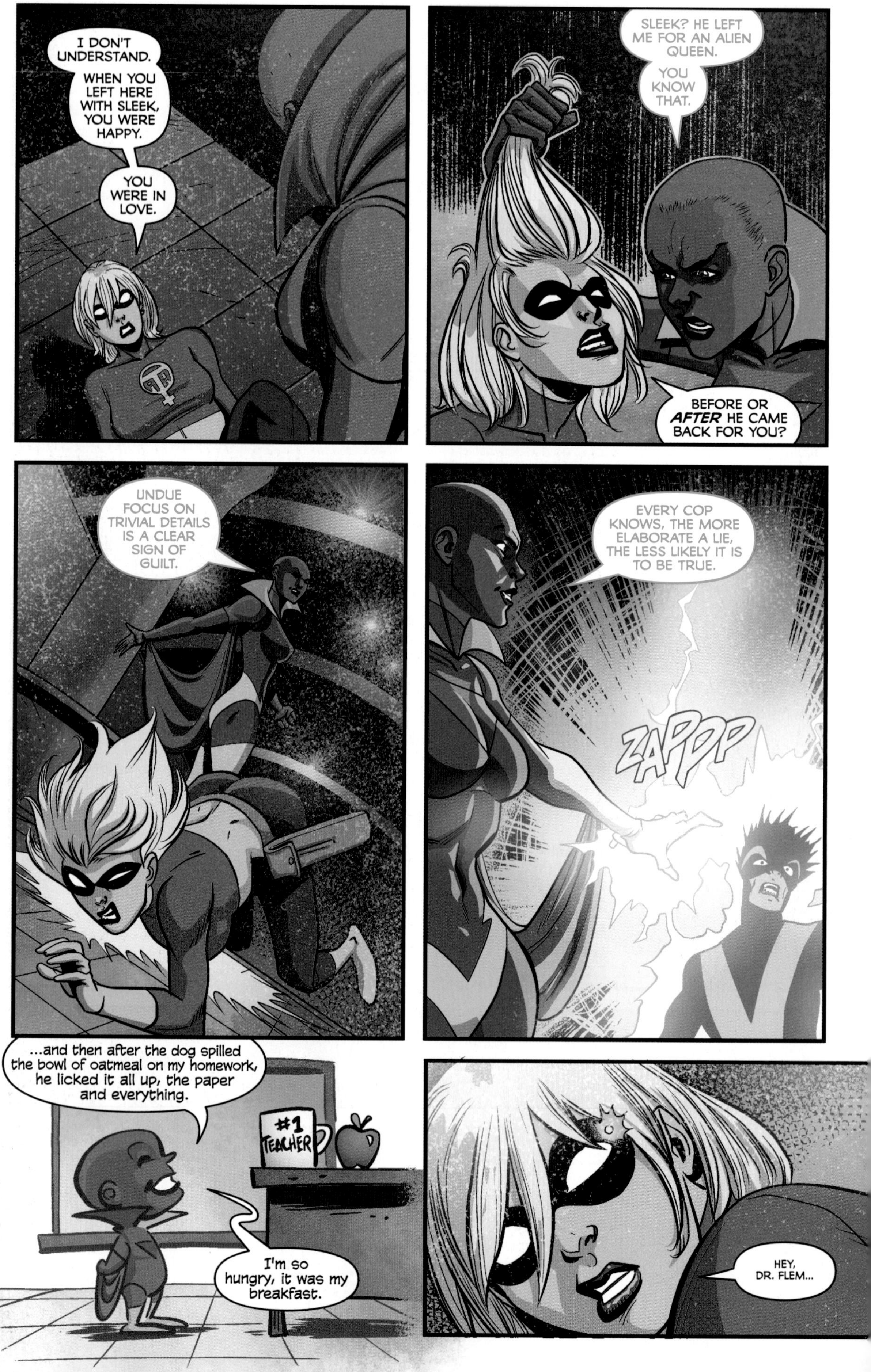
I DON'T UNDERSTAND.
WHEN YOU LEFT HERE WITH SLEEK, YOU WERE HAPPY.
YOU WERE IN LOVE.
SLEEK? HE LEFT ME FOR AN ALIEN QUEEN.
YOU KNOW THAT.
BEFORE OR AFTER HE CAME BACK FOR YOU?
UNDUE FOCUS ON TRIVIAL DETAILS IS A CLEAR SIGN OF GUILT.
EVERY COP KNOWS, THE MORE ELABORATE A LIE, THE LESS LIKELY IT IS TO BE TRUE.
ZAPPP
...and then after the dog spilled the bowl of oatmeal on my homework, he licked it all up, the paper and everything.
#1 TEACHER
I'm so hungry, it was my breakfast.
HEY, DR. FLEM...

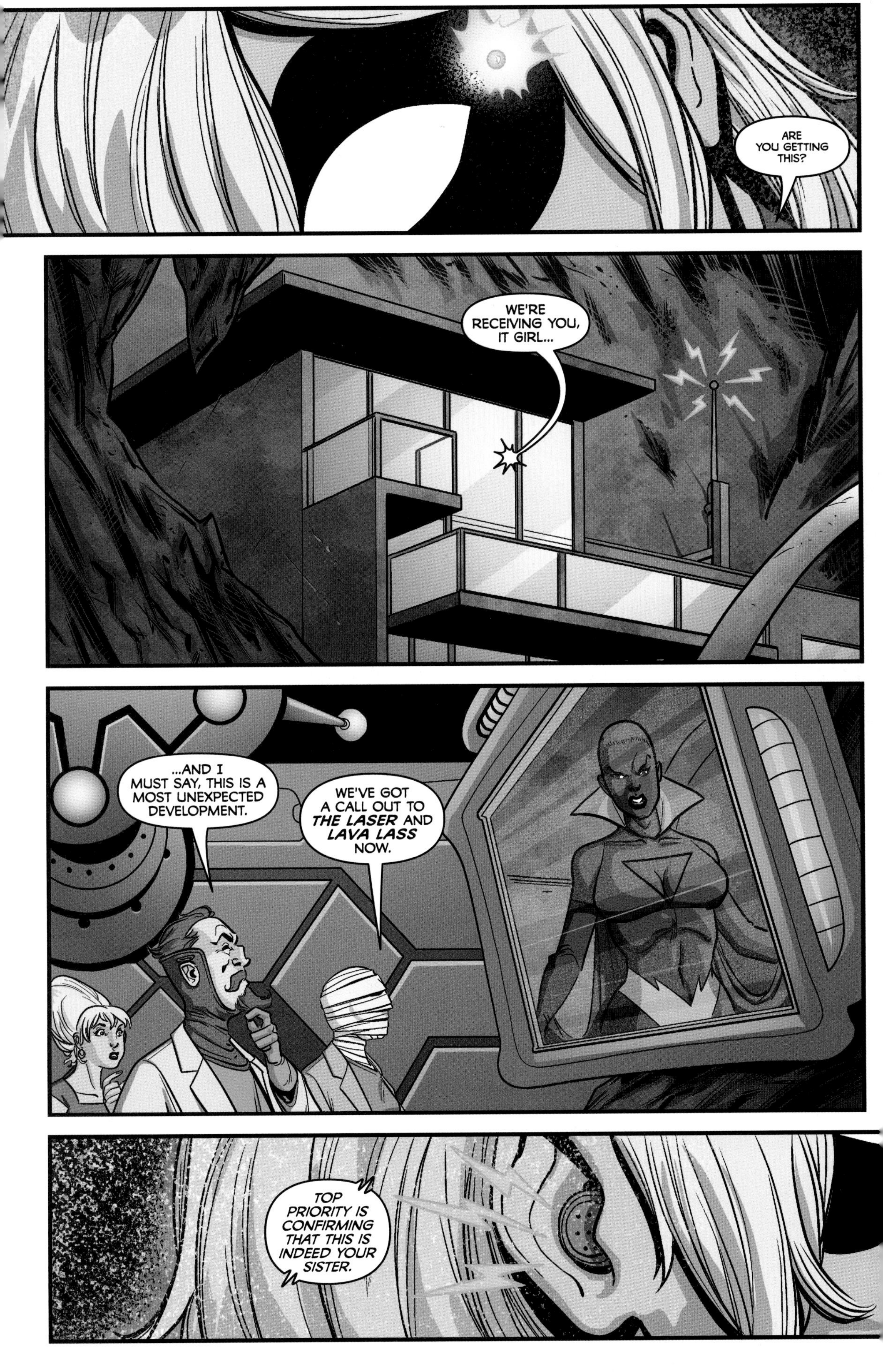
ARE YOU GETTING THIS?
WE'RE RECEIVING YOU, IT GIRL...
...AND I MUST SAY, THIS IS A MOST UNEXPECTED DEVELOPMENT.
WE'VE GOT A CALL OUT TO THE LASER AND LAVA LASS NOW.
TOP PRIORITY IS CONFIRMING THAT THIS IS INDEED YOUR SISTER.

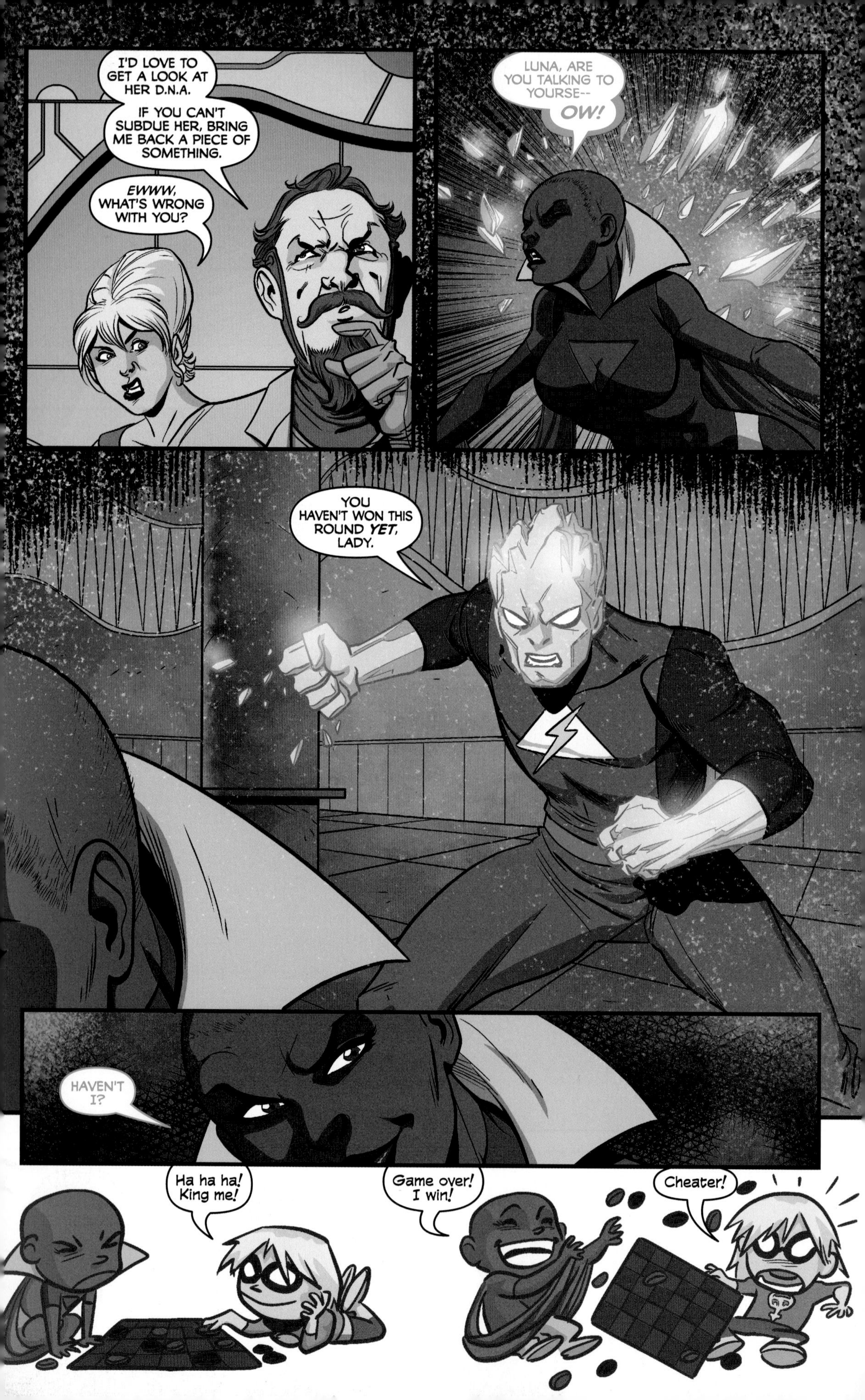
I'D LOVE TO GET A LOOK AT HER D.N.A.
IF YOU CAN'T SUBDUE HER, BRING ME BACK A PIECE OF SOMETHING.
EWWW, WHAT'S WRONG WITH YOU?
LUNA, ARE YOU TALKING TO YOURSE-- OW!
YOU HAVEN'T WON THIS ROUND YET, LADY.
HAVEN'T I?
Ha ha ha! King me!
Game over! I win!
Cheater!

ZZZSHH
I HAVE AN IDEA, DOC.
YOU READY TO TRY THAT NEW TOY OF YOURS AGAIN?
ZZZZZZZ
RAWRRR!!

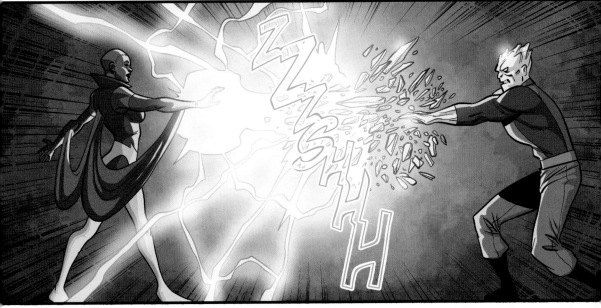

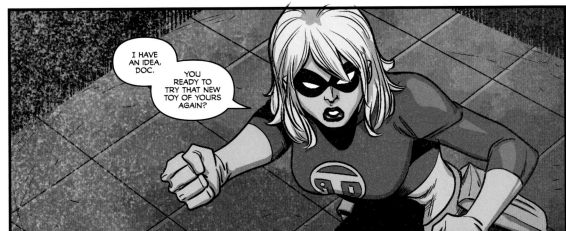

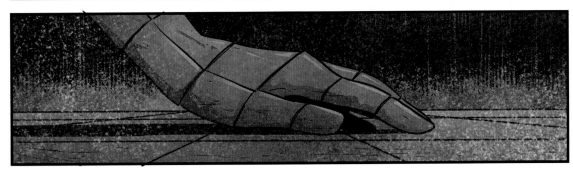

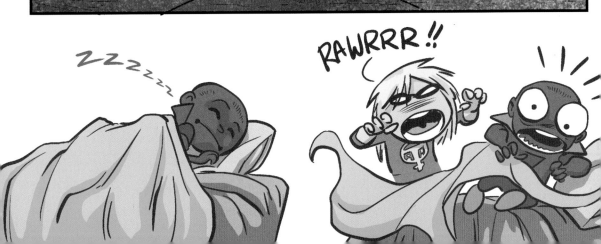

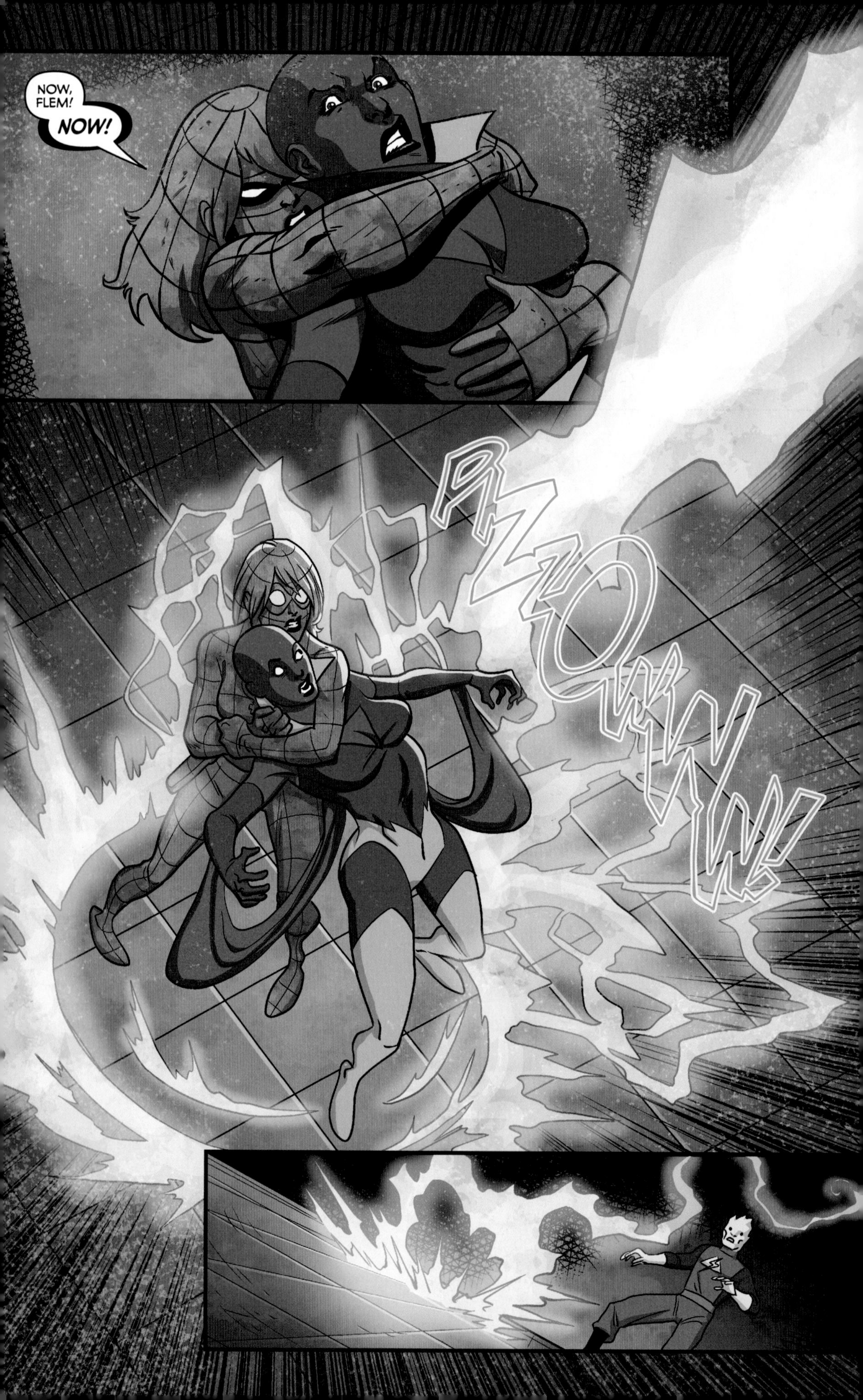
NOW, FLEM! NOW!
PZZOWWWW!

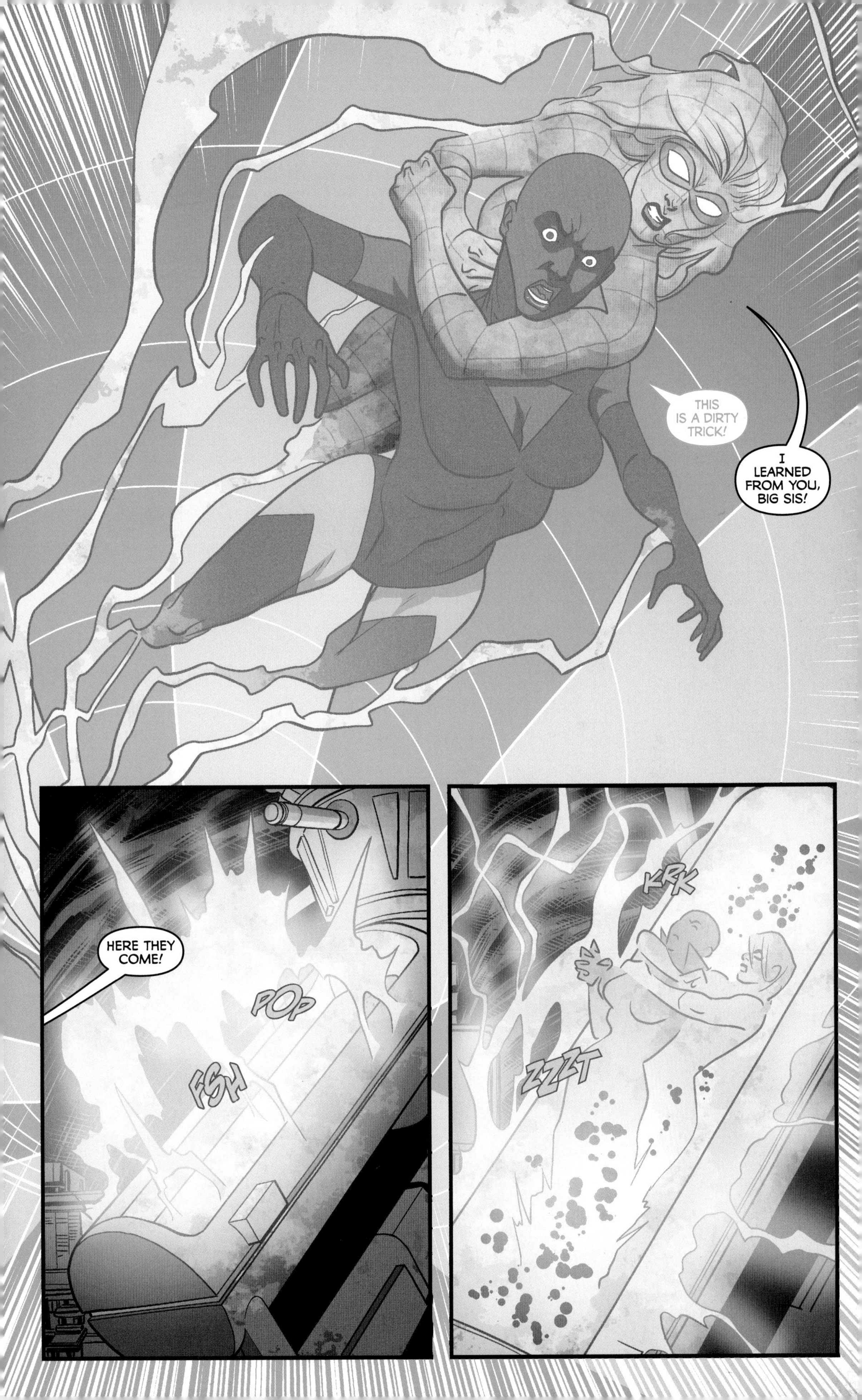
THIS IS A DIRTY TRICK!
I LEARNED FROM YOU, BIG SIS!
HERE THEY COME!
POP
FSH
KRK
ZZZT

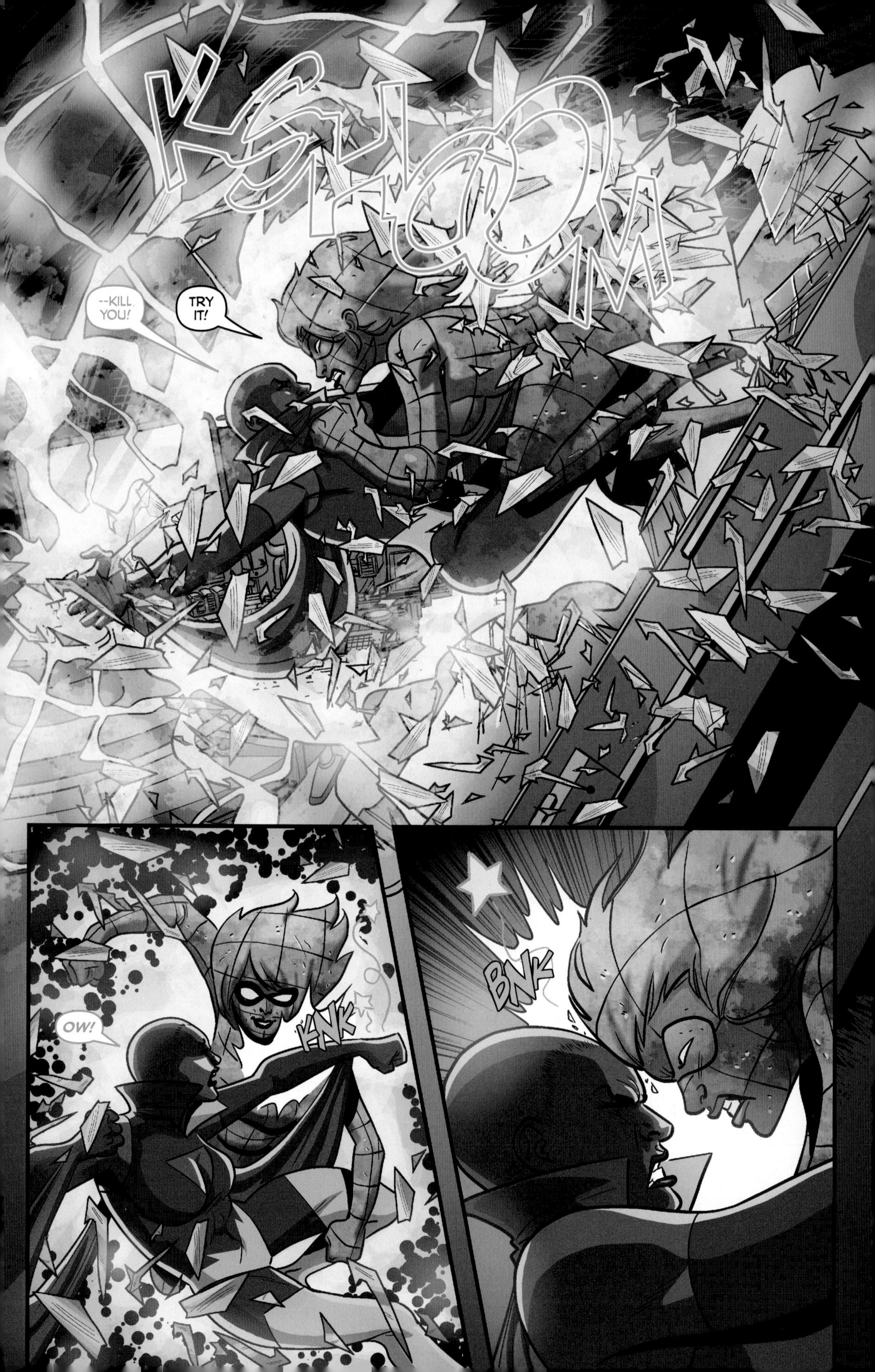
KSHOOM
--KILL YOU!
TRY IT!
OW!
KNK
BNK

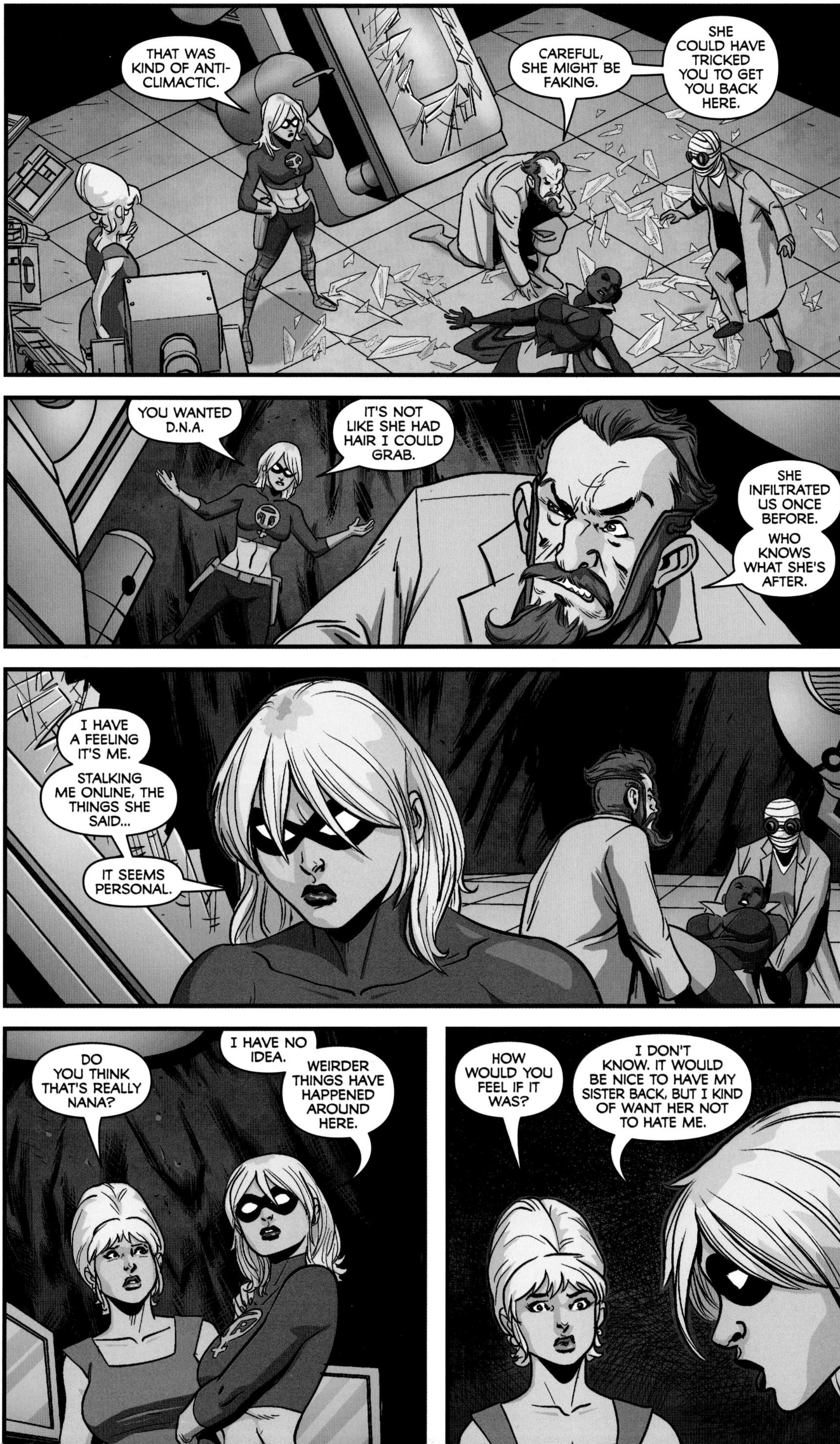

THAT WAS KIND OF ANTI-CLIMACTIC.
CAREFUL, SHE MIGHT BE FAKING.
SHE COULD HAVE TRICKED YOU TO GET YOU BACK HERE.
YOU WANTED D.N.A.
IT'S NOT LIKE SHE HAD HAIR I COULD GRAB.
SHE INFILTRATED US ONCE BEFORE.
WHO KNOWS WHAT SHE'S AFTER.
I HAVE A FEELING IT'S ME.
STALKING ME ONLINE, THE THINGS SHE SAID...
IT SEEMS PERSONAL.
DO YOU THINK THAT'S REALLY NANA?
I HAVE NO IDEA.
WEIRDER THINGS HAVE HAPPENED AROUND HERE.
HOW WOULD YOU FEEL IF IT WAS?
I DON'T KNOW. IT WOULD BE NICE TO HAVE MY SISTER BACK, BUT I KIND OF WANT HER NOT TO HATE ME.

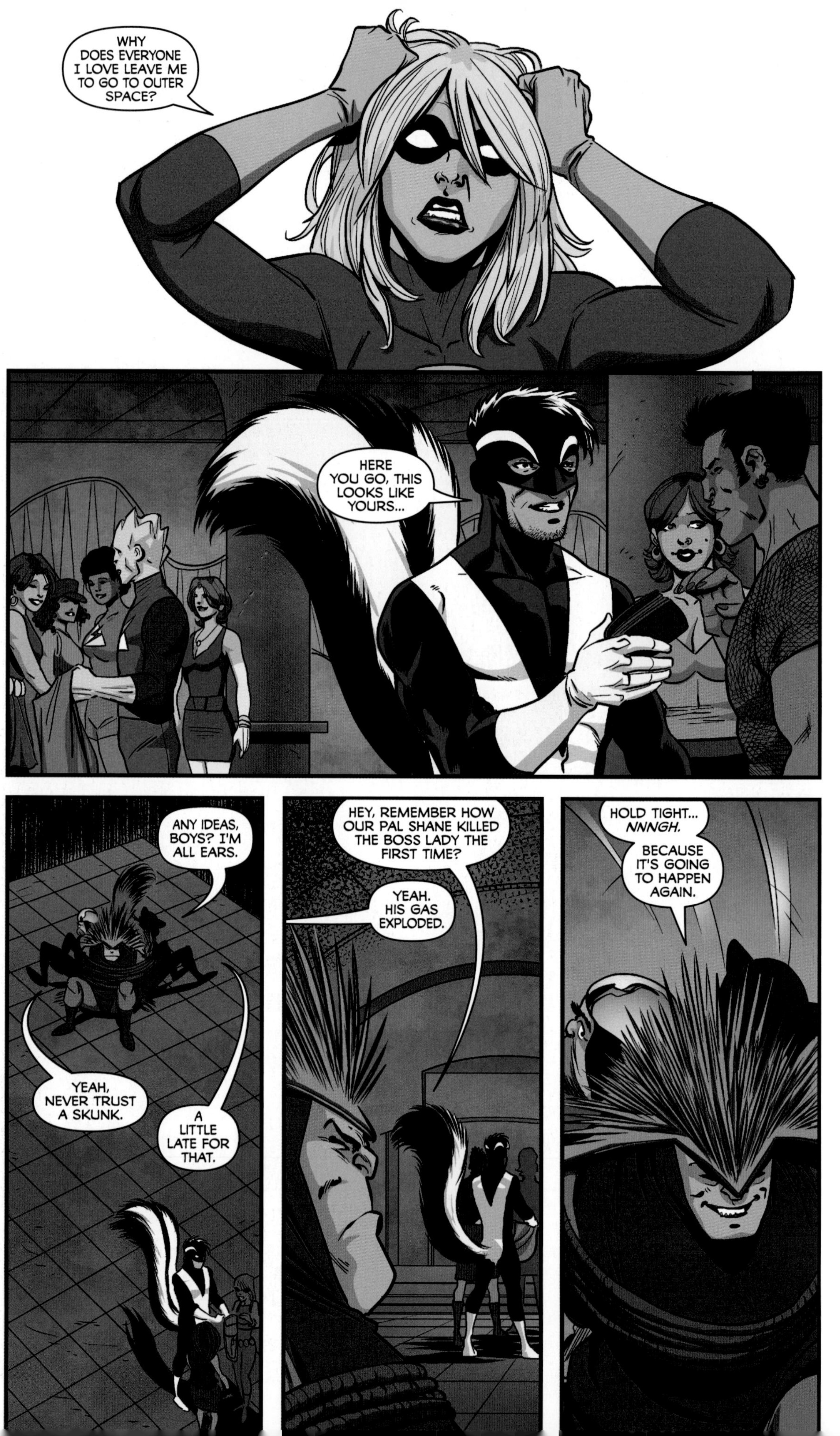
WHY DOES EVERYONE I LOVE LEAVE ME TO GO TO OUTER SPACE?
HERE YOU GO, THIS LOOKS LIKE YOURS...
ANY IDEAS, BOYS? I'M ALL EARS.
YEAH, NEVER TRUST A SKUNK.
A LITTLE LATE FOR THAT.
HEY, REMEMBER HOW OUR PAL SHANE KILLED THE BOSS LADY THE FIRST TIME?
YEAH. HIS GAS EXPLODED.
HOLD TIGHT... *NNNGH.*
BECAUSE IT'S GOING TO HAPPEN AGAIN.

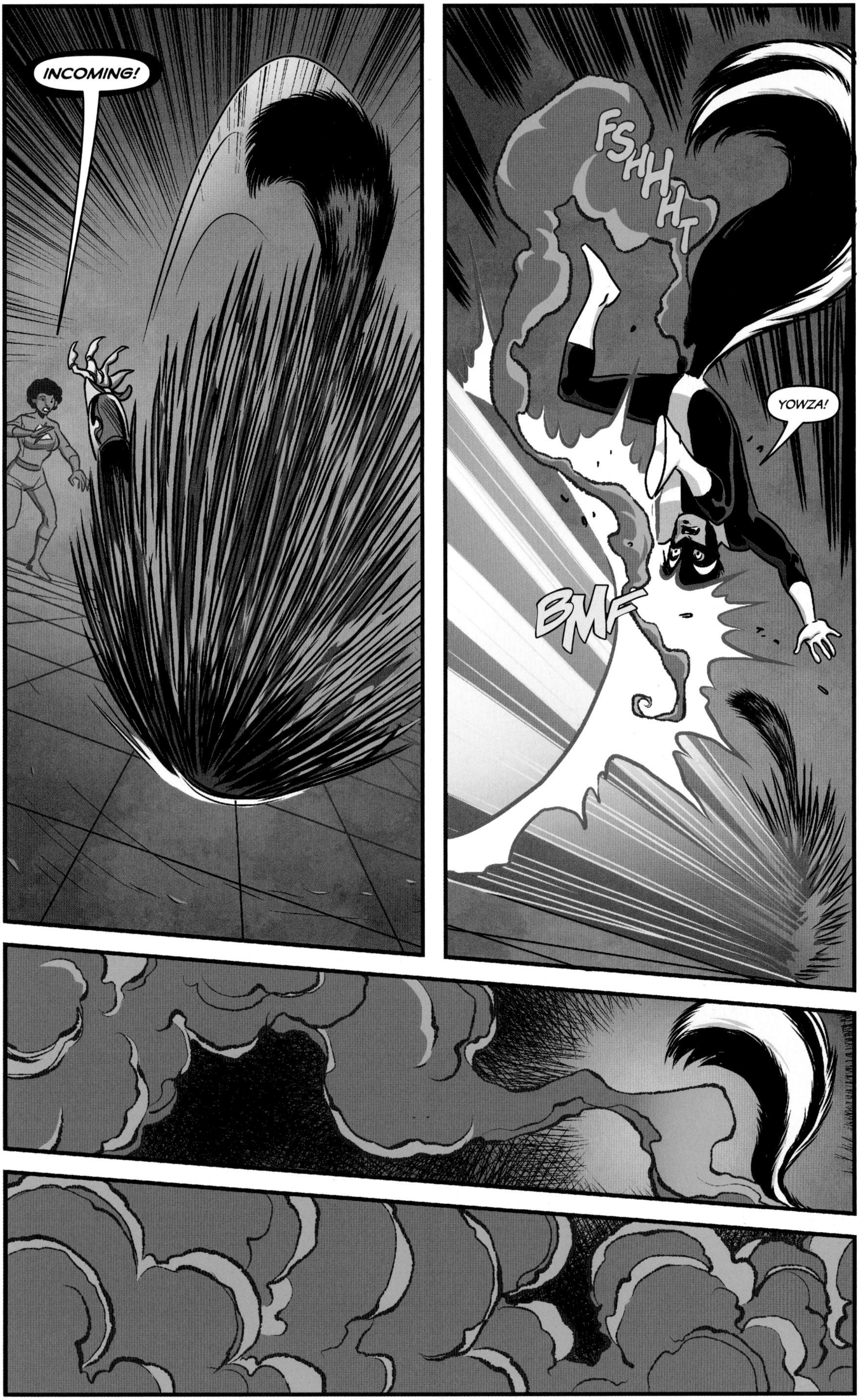
INCOMING!
FSHHHT
YOWZA!
BMF

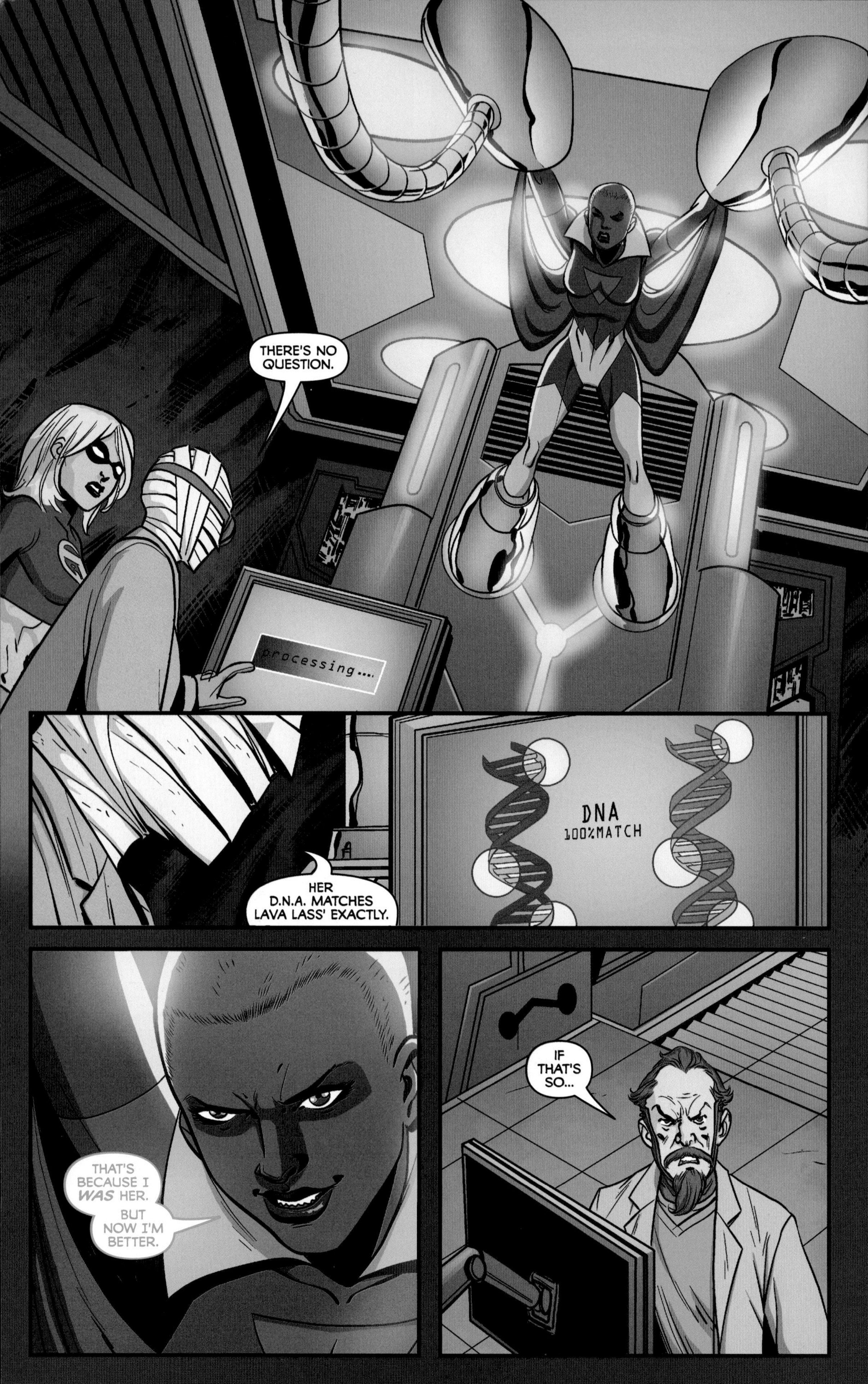
THERE'S NO QUESTION.
processing....
HER D.N.A. MATCHES LAVA LASS' EXACTLY.
DNA
100%MATCH
THAT'S BECAUSE I *WAS* HER.
BUT NOW I'M BETTER.
IF THAT'S SO...

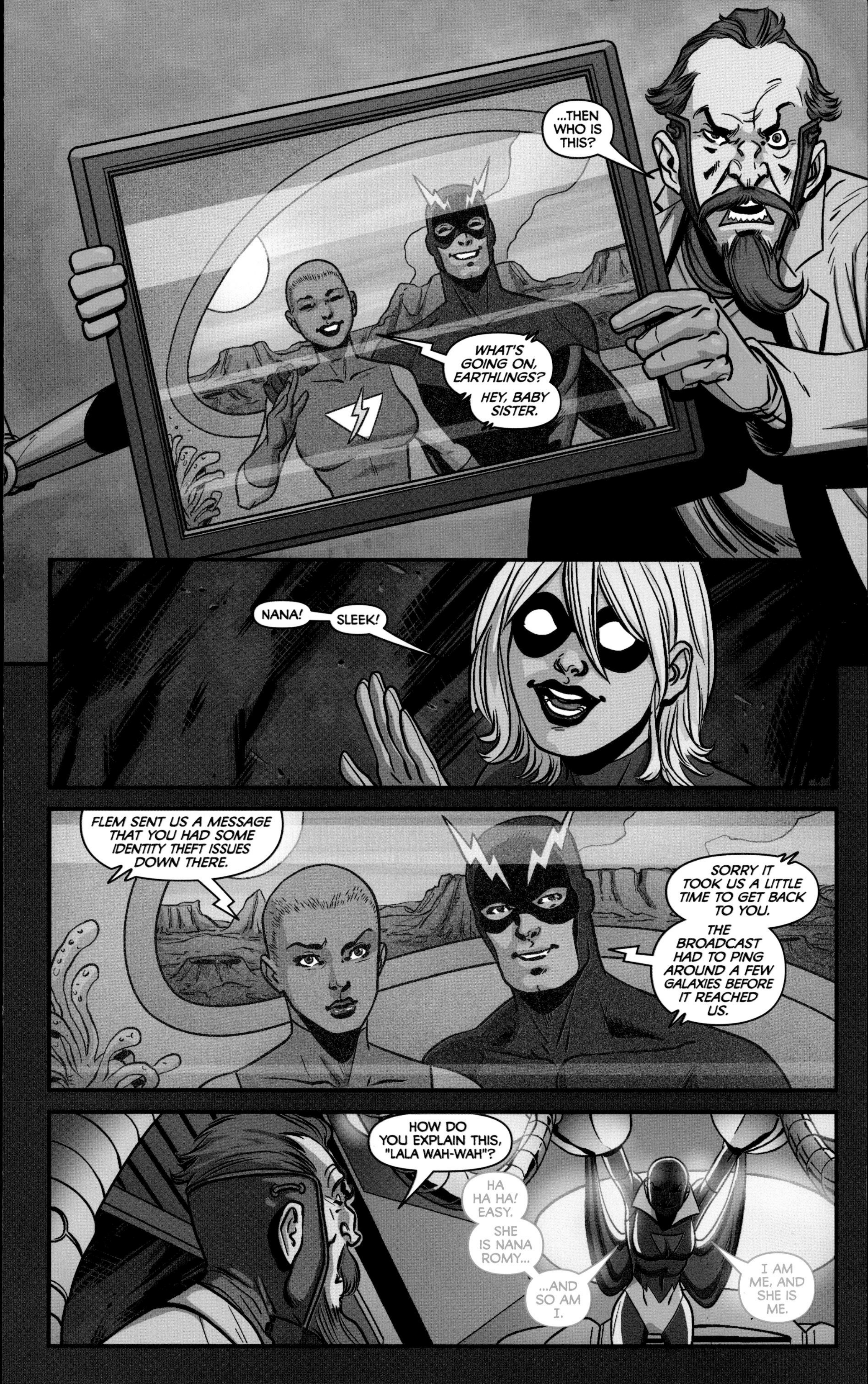
...THEN WHO IS THIS?
WHAT'S GOING ON, EARTHLINGS?
HEY, BABY SISTER.
NANA!
SLEEK!
FLEM SENT US A MESSAGE THAT YOU HAD SOME IDENTITY THEFT ISSUES DOWN THERE.
SORRY IT TOOK US A LITTLE TIME TO GET BACK TO YOU.
THE BROADCAST HAD TO PING AROUND A FEW GALAXIES BEFORE IT REACHED US.
HOW DO YOU EXPLAIN THIS, "LALA WAH-WAH"?
HA HA HA! EASY.
SHE IS NANA ROMY...
...AND SO AM I.
I AM ME, AND SHE IS ME.

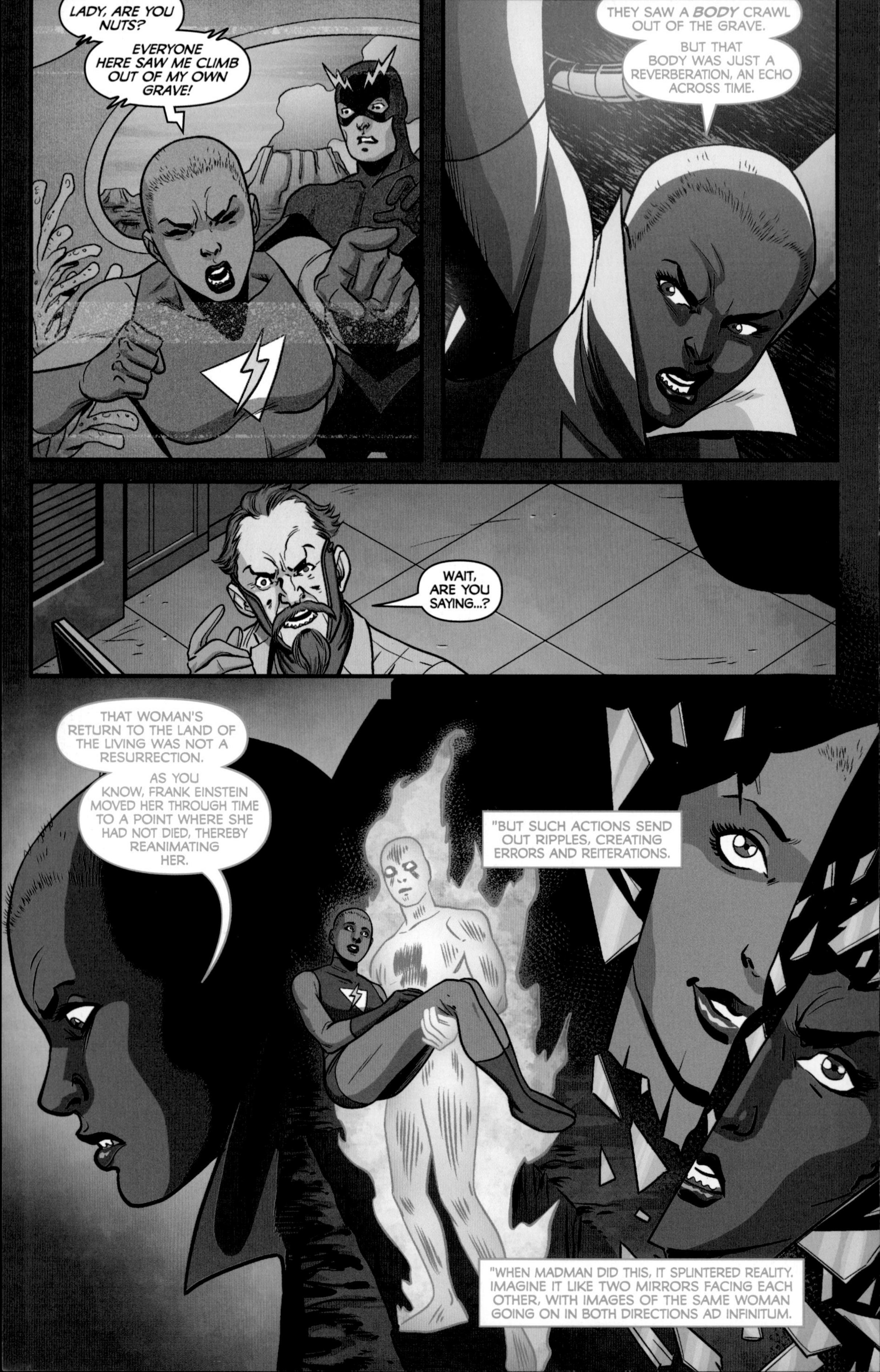
LADY, ARE YOU NUTS?
EVERYONE HERE SAW ME CLIMB OUT OF MY OWN GRAVE!
THEY SAW A BODY CRAWL OUT OF THE GRAVE.
BUT THAT BODY WAS JUST A REVERBERATION, AN ECHO ACROSS TIME.
WAIT, ARE YOU SAYING...?
THAT WOMAN'S RETURN TO THE LAND OF THE LIVING WAS NOT A RESURRECTION.
AS YOU KNOW, FRANK EINSTEIN MOVED HER THROUGH TIME TO A POINT WHERE SHE HAD NOT DIED, THEREBY REANIMATING HER.
"BUT SUCH ACTIONS SEND OUT RIPPLES, CREATING ERRORS AND REITERATIONS.
"WHEN MADMAN DID THIS, IT SPLINTERED REALITY. IMAGINE IT LIKE TWO MIRRORS FACING EACH OTHER, WITH IMAGES OF THE SAME WOMAN GOING ON IN BOTH DIRECTIONS AD INFINITUM.

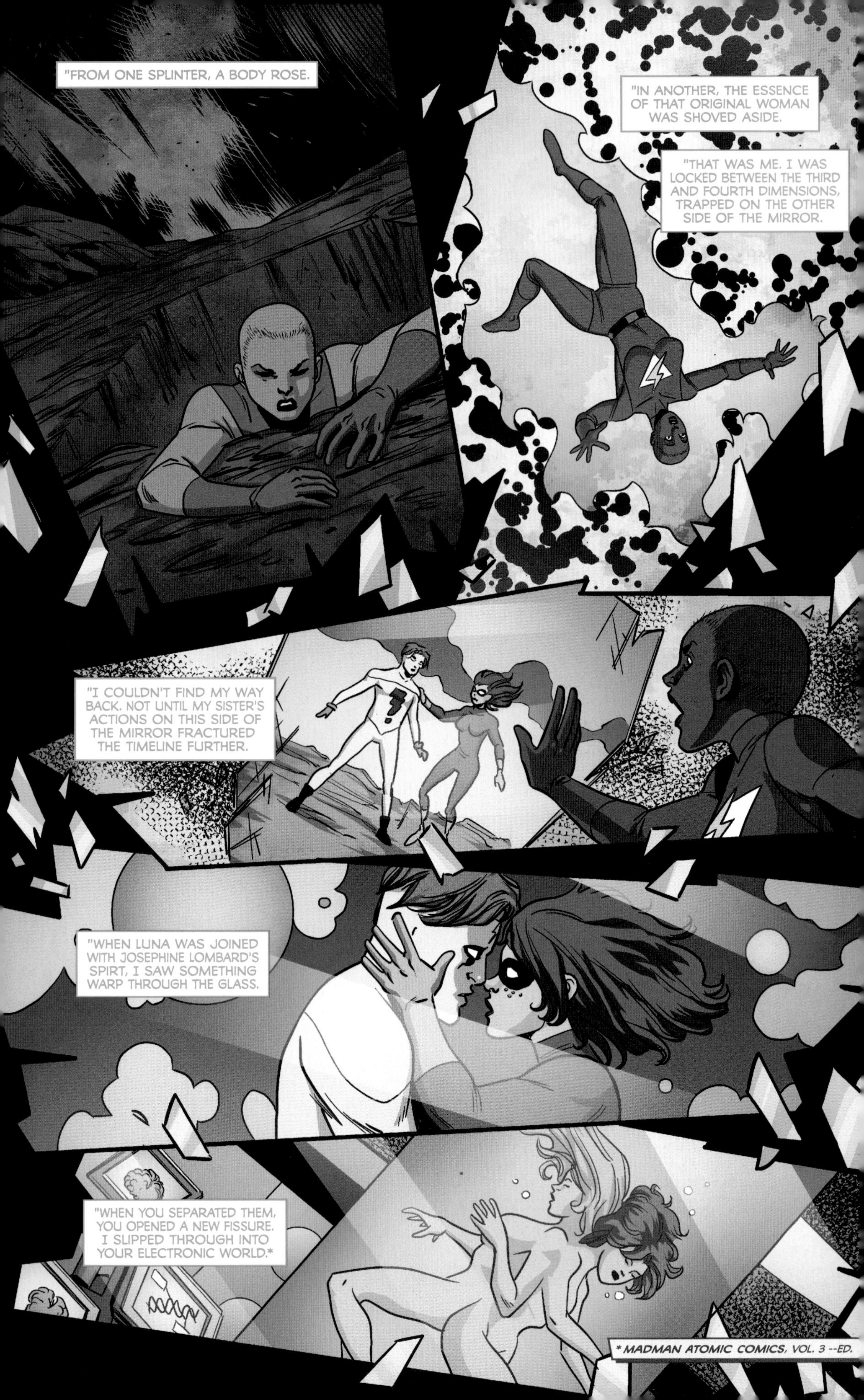
"FROM ONE SPLINTER, A BODY ROSE.
"IN ANOTHER, THE ESSENCE OF THAT ORIGINAL WOMAN WAS SHOVED ASIDE.
"THAT WAS ME. I WAS LOCKED BETWEEN THE THIRD AND FOURTH DIMENSIONS, TRAPPED ON THE OTHER SIDE OF THE MIRROR.
"I COULDN'T FIND MY WAY BACK. NOT UNTIL MY SISTER'S ACTIONS ON THIS SIDE OF THE MIRROR FRACTURED THE TIMELINE FURTHER.
"WHEN LUNA WAS JOINED WITH JOSEPHINE LOMBARD'S SPIRT, I SAW SOMETHING WARP THROUGH THE GLASS.
"WHEN YOU SEPARATED THEM, YOU OPENED A NEW FISSURE. I SLIPPED THROUGH INTO YOUR ELECTRONIC WORLD.*
*MADMAN ATOMIC COMICS, VOL. 3 --ED.

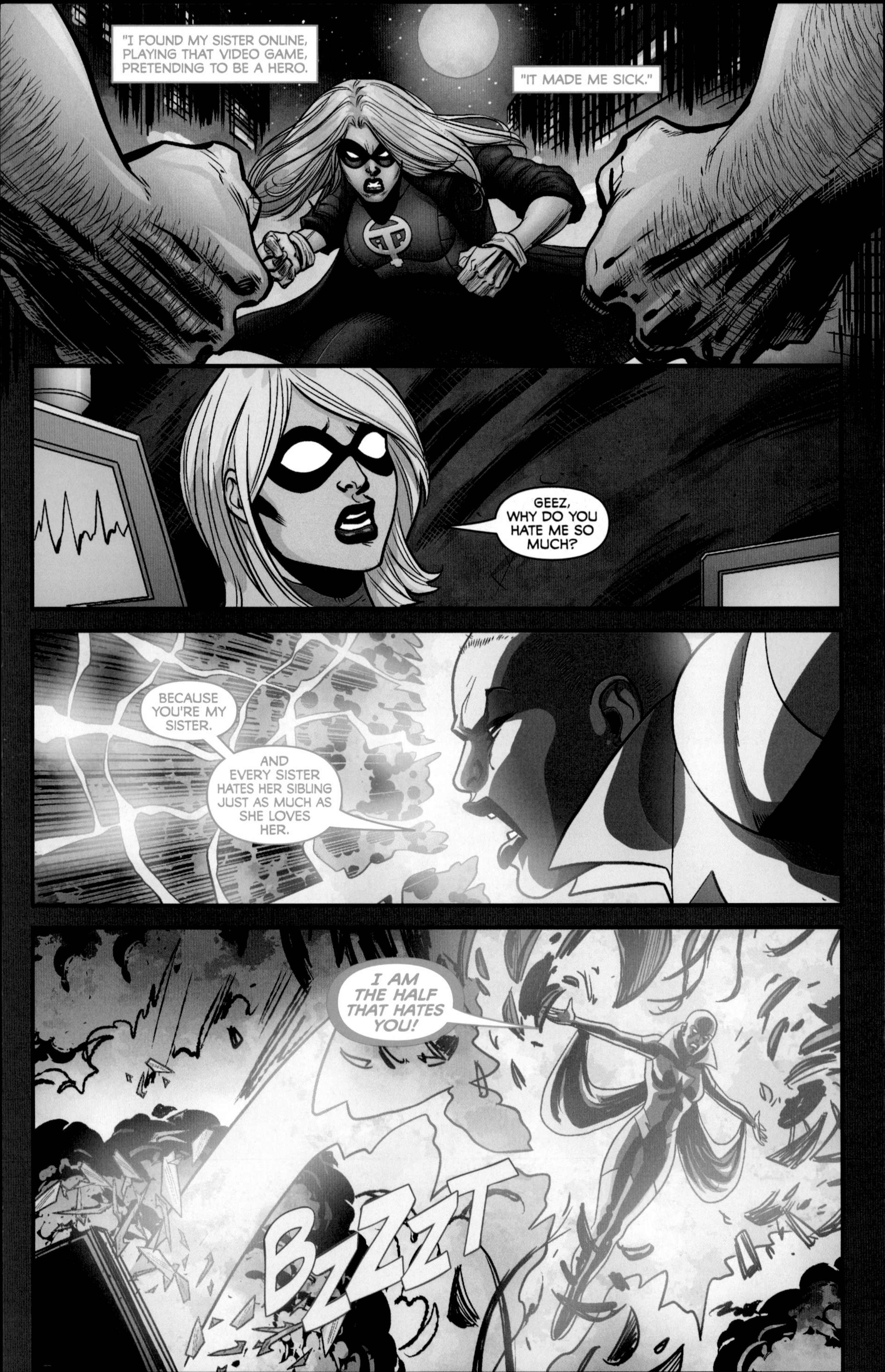
"I FOUND MY SISTER ONLINE, PLAYING THAT VIDEO GAME, PRETENDING TO BE A HERO.
"IT MADE ME SICK."
GEEZ, WHY DO YOU HATE ME SO MUCH?
BECAUSE YOU'RE MY SISTER.
AND EVERY SISTER HATES HER SIBLING JUST AS MUCH AS SHE LOVES HER.
I AM THE HALF THAT HATES YOU!
BZZZT

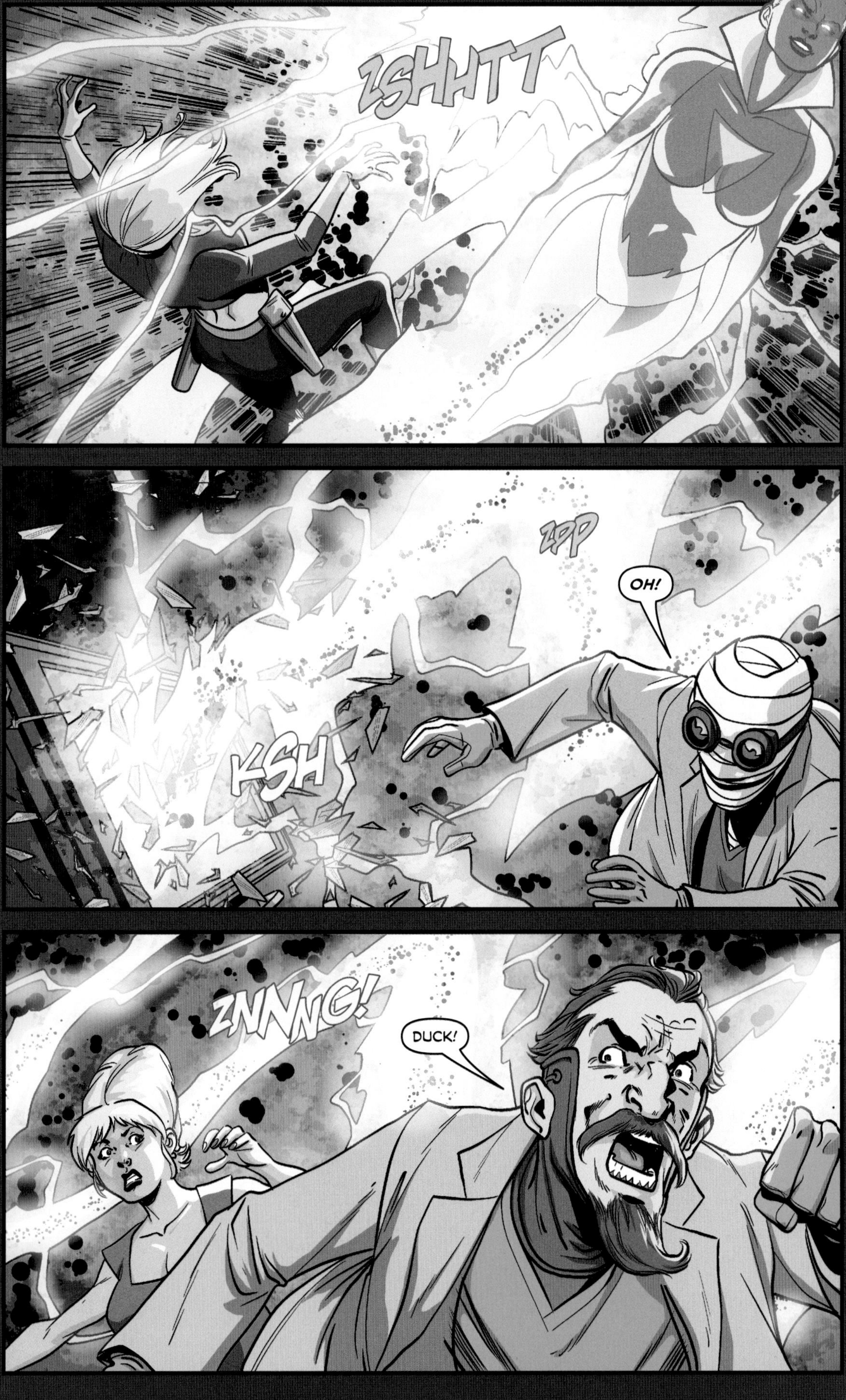
ZSHHTT
ZPP
OH!
KSH
ZNNNG!
DUCK!

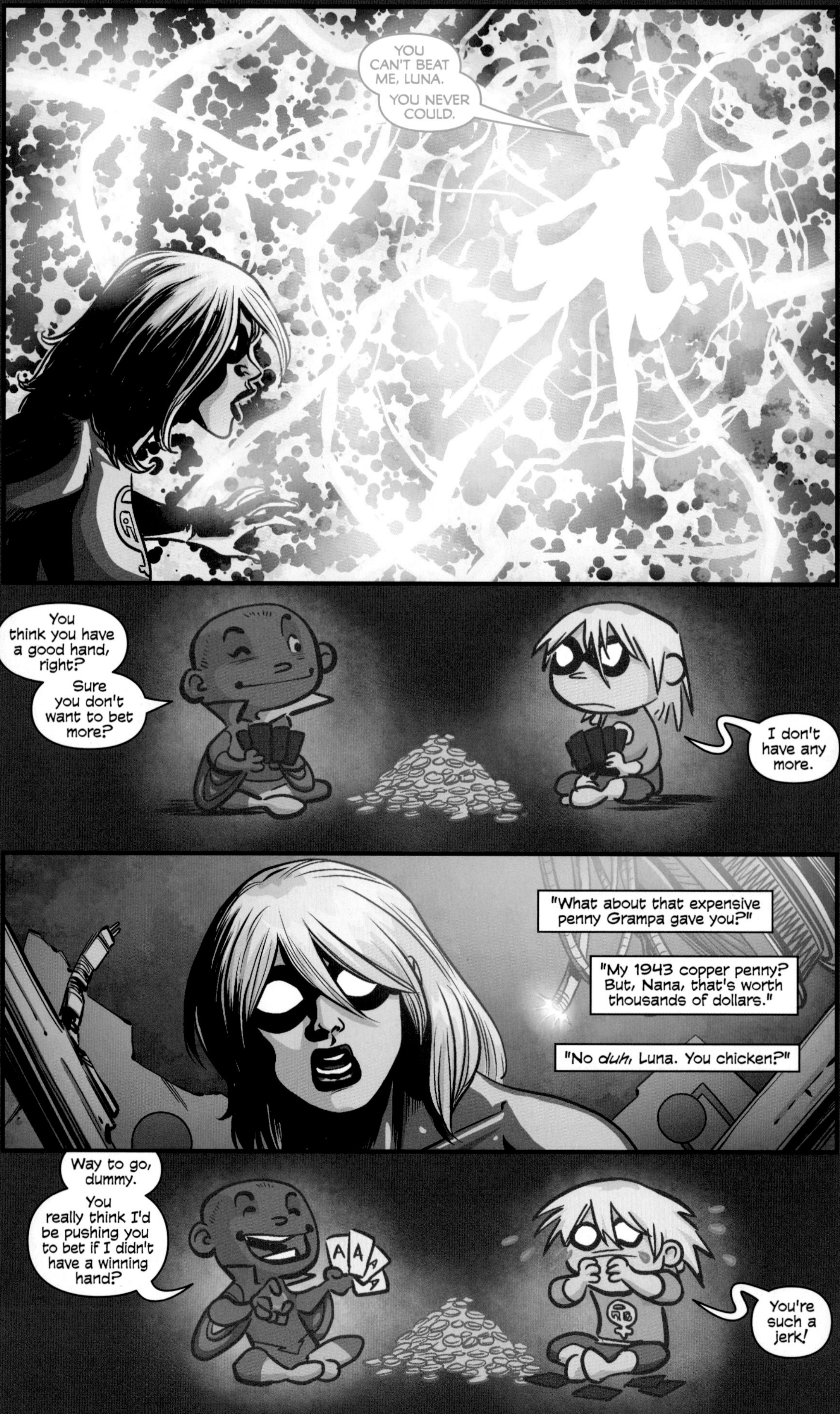
YOU CAN'T BEAT ME, LUNA.
YOU NEVER COULD.
You think you have a good hand, right?
Sure you don't want to bet more?
I don't have any more.
"What about that expensive penny Grampa gave you?"
"My 1943 copper penny? But, Nana, that's worth thousands of dollars."
"No *duh*, Luna. You chicken?"
Way to go, dummy.
You really think I'd be pushing you to bet if I didn't have a winning hand?
You're such a jerk!

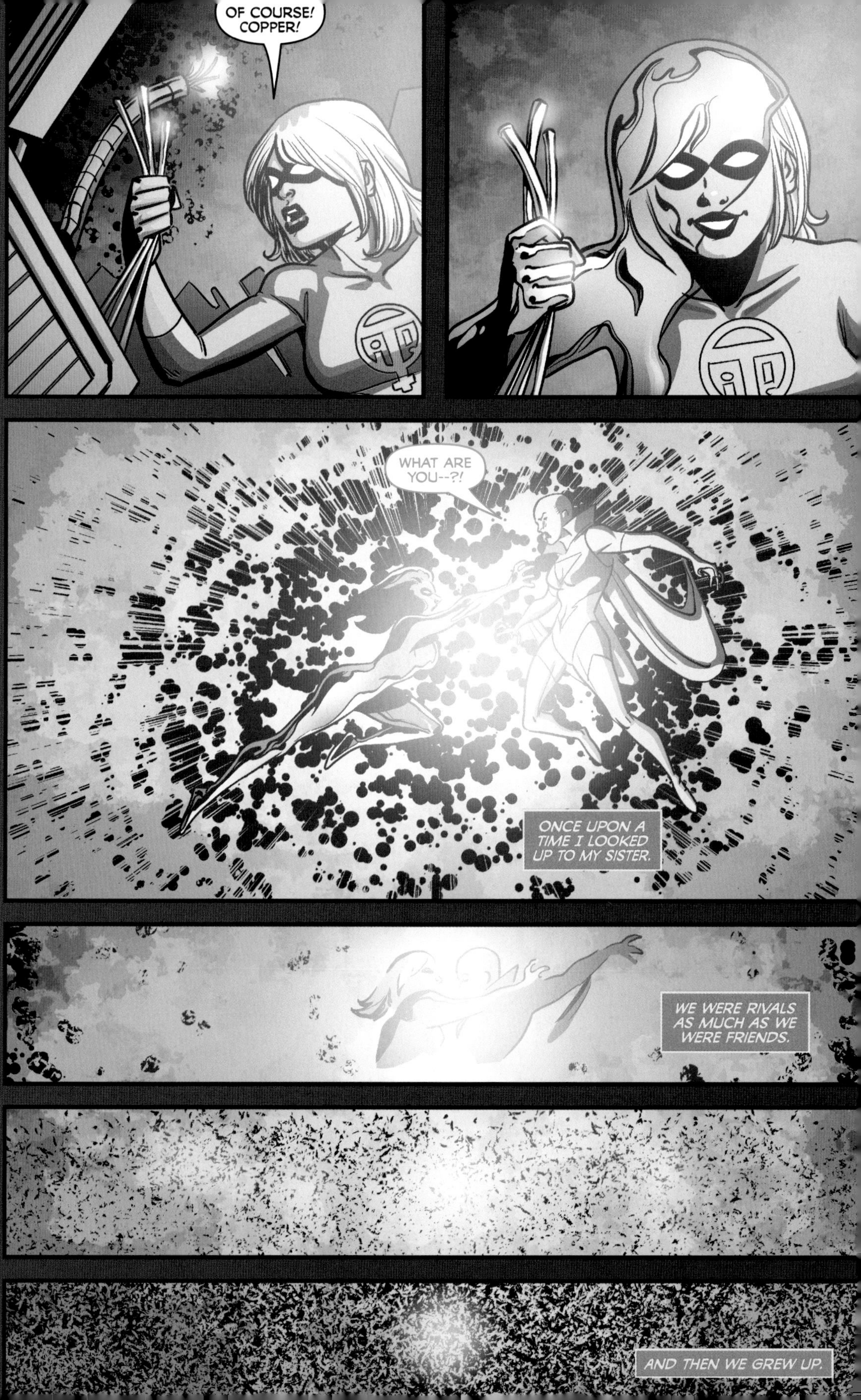
OF COURSE! COPPER!
WHAT ARE YOU--?!
ONCE UPON A TIME I LOOKED UP TO MY SISTER.
WE WERE RIVALS AS MUCH AS WE WERE FRIENDS.
AND THEN WE GREW UP.

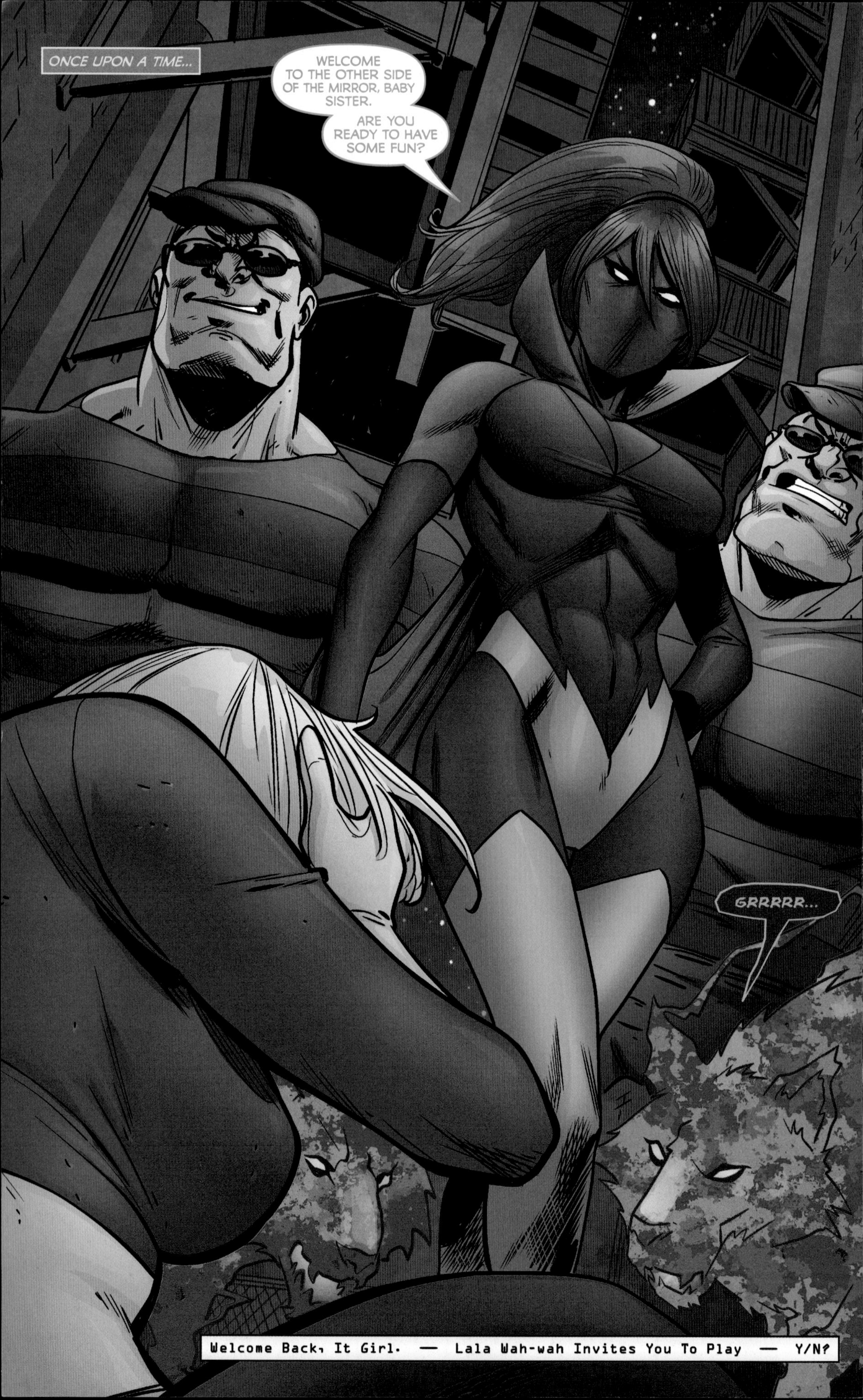
ONCE UPON A TIME...
WELCOME TO THE OTHER SIDE OF THE MIRROR, BABY SISTER.
ARE YOU READY TO HAVE SOME FUN?
GRRRRR...
Welcome Back, It Girl. — Lala Wah-wah Invites You To Play — Y/N?

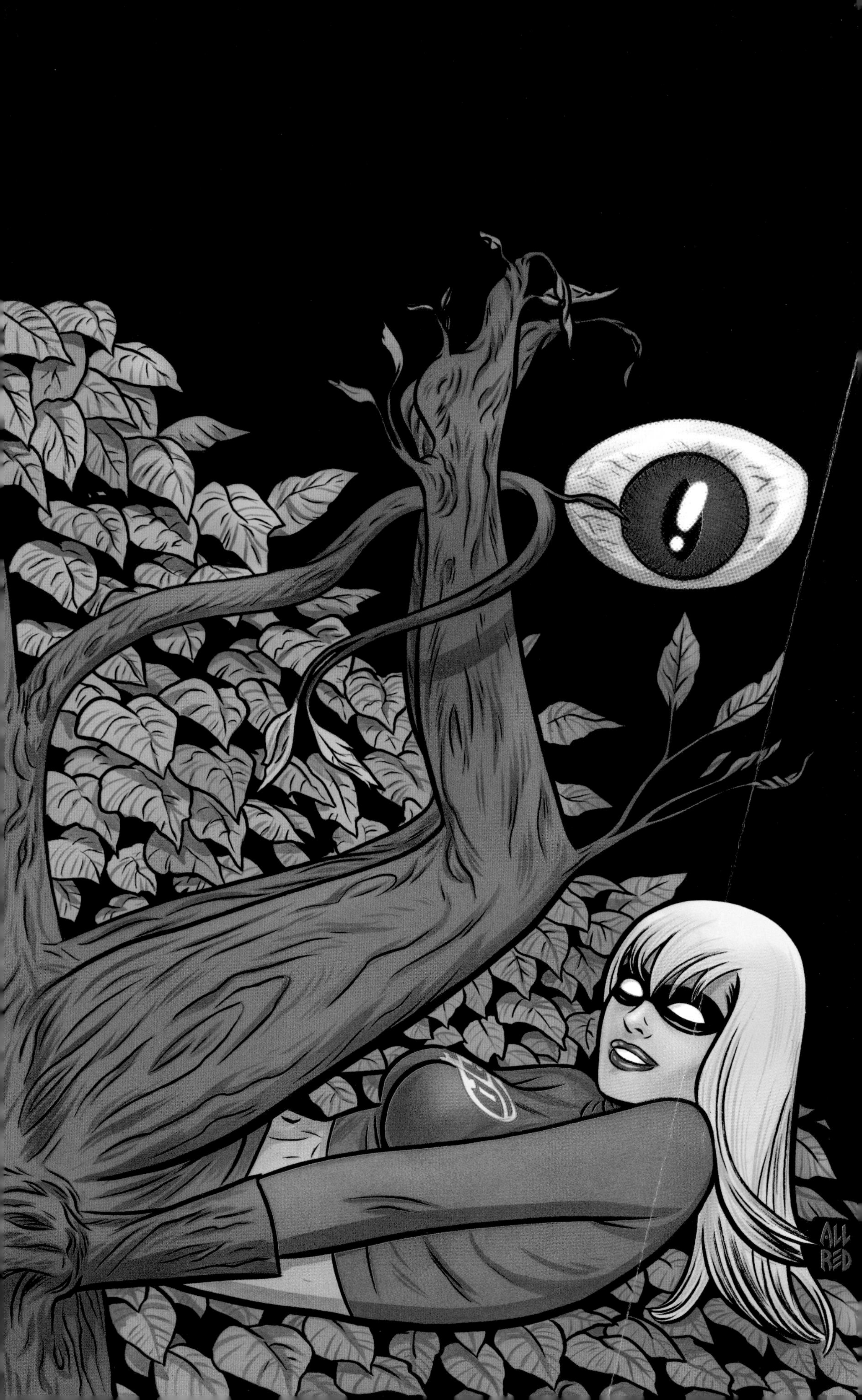
ALL
RED

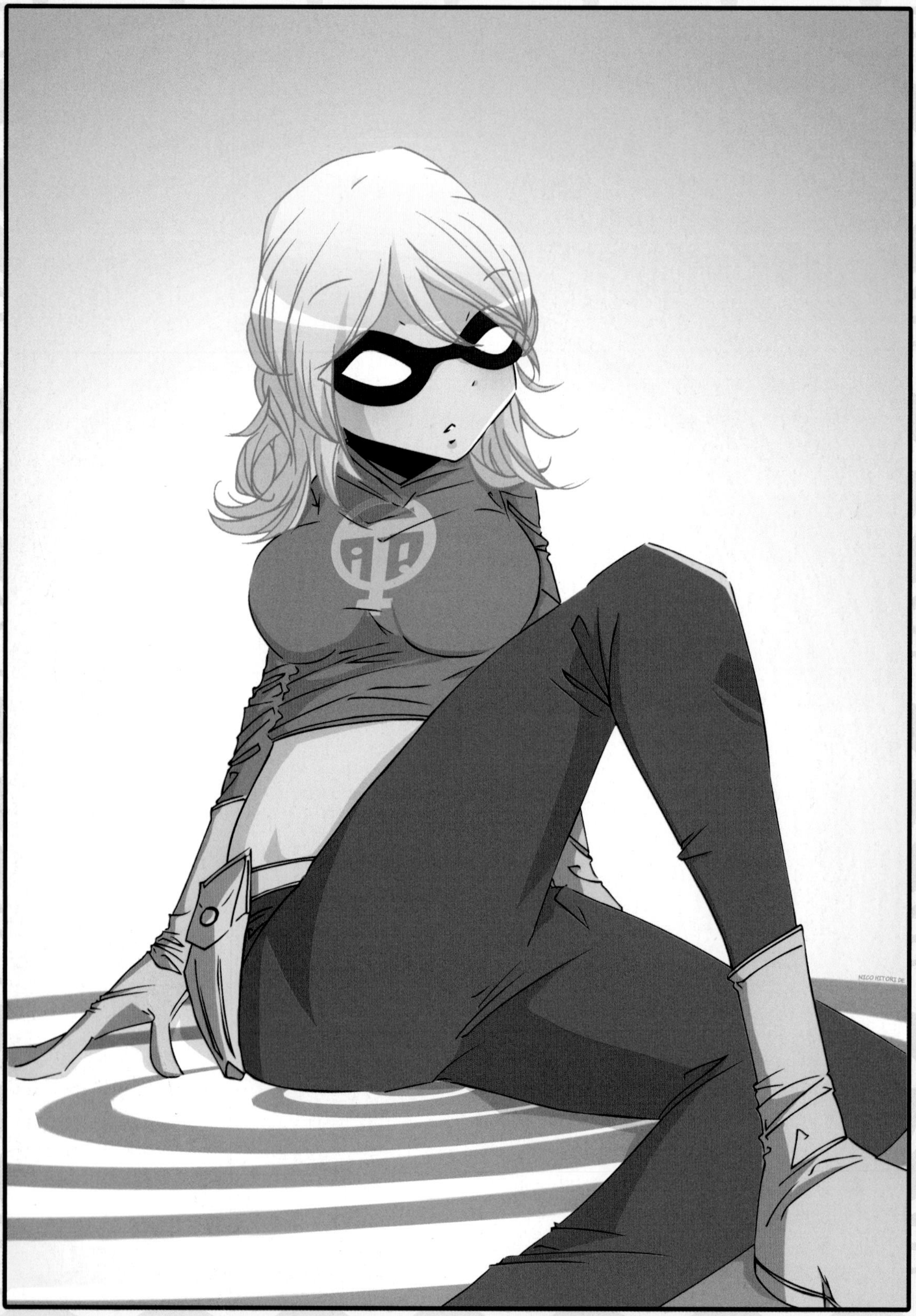
NICO HITORI DE

Illustration by Nicolas Hitori de

nicohitoride.com

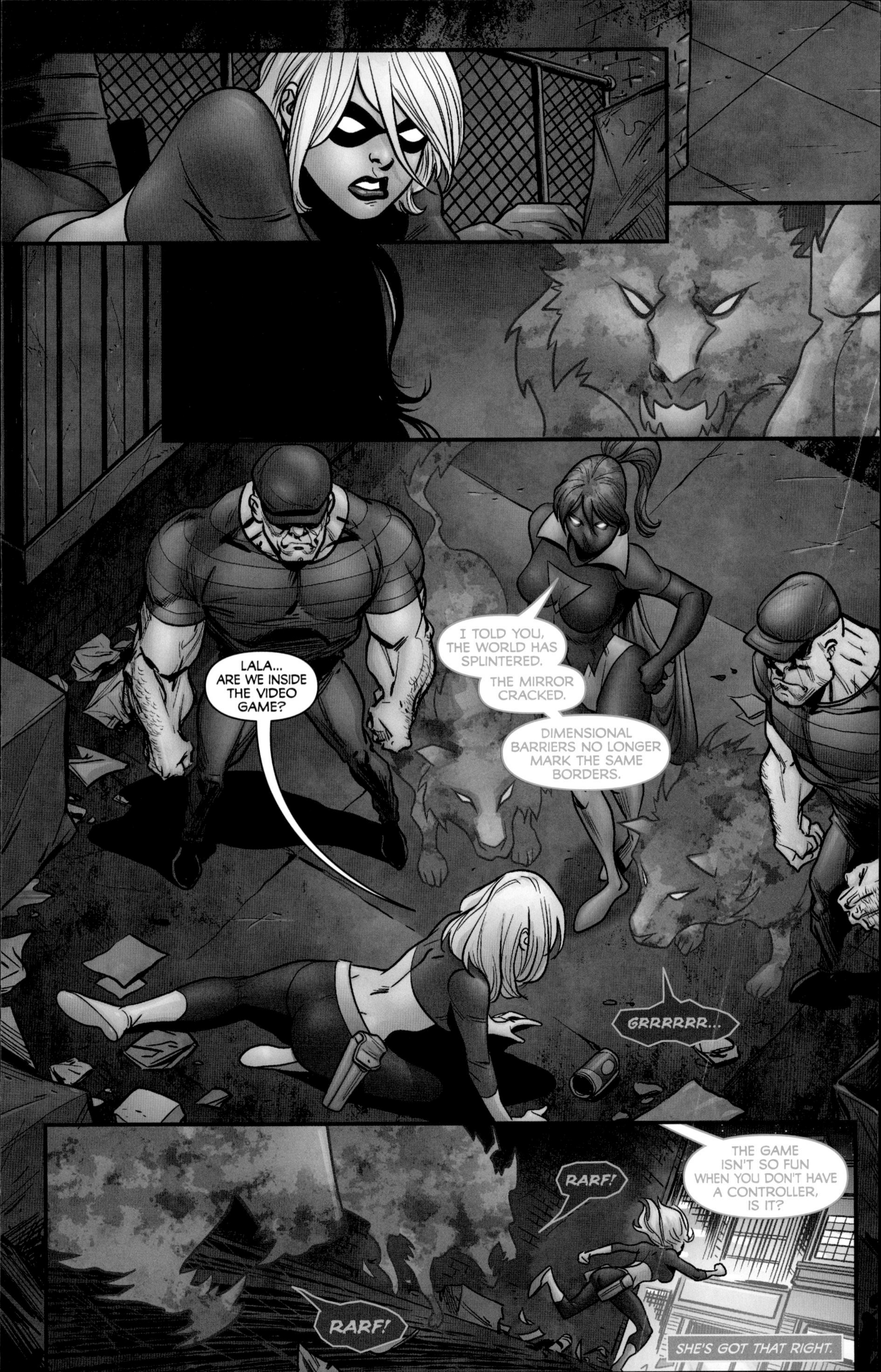

LALA... ARE WE INSIDE THE VIDEO GAME?
I TOLD YOU, THE WORLD HAS SPLINTERED.
THE MIRROR CRACKED.
DIMENSIONAL BARRIERS NO LONGER MARK THE SAME BORDERS.
GRRRRRR...
THE GAME ISN'T SO FUN WHEN YOU DON'T HAVE A CONTROLLER, IS IT?
RARF!
RARF!
SHE'S GOT THAT RIGHT.

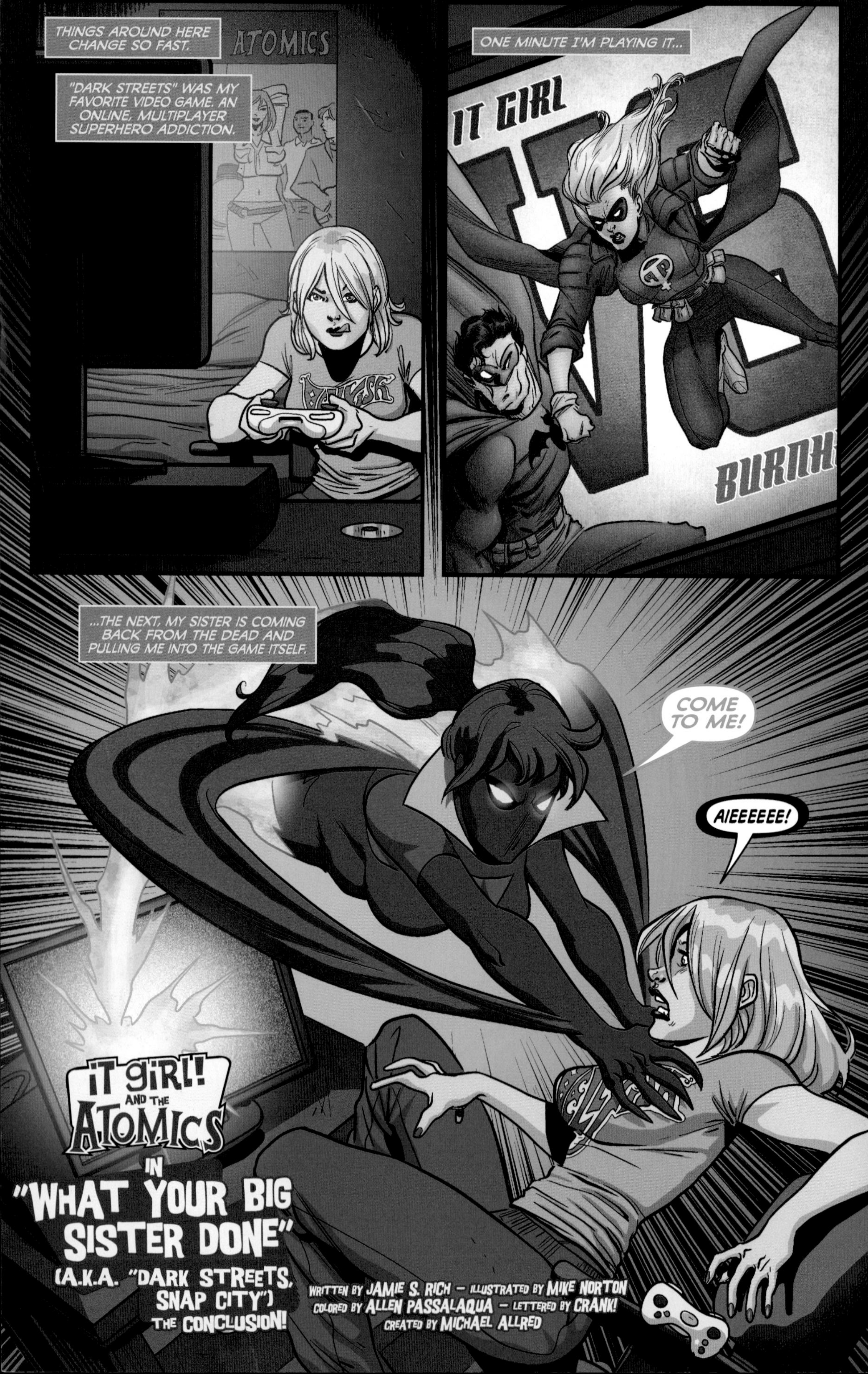
THINGS AROUND HERE CHANGE SO FAST.
ATOMICS
"DARK STREETS" WAS MY FAVORITE VIDEO GAME. AN ONLINE, MULTIPLAYER SUPERHERO ADDICTION.
ONE MINUTE I'M PLAYING IT...
IT GIRL
...THE NEXT, MY SISTER IS COMING BACK FROM THE DEAD AND PULLING ME INTO THE GAME ITSELF.
COME TO ME!
AIEEEEEE!
IT GIRL! AND THE ATOMICS
IN
"WHAT YOUR BIG SISTER DONE"
(A.K.A. "DARK STREETS, SNAP CITY")
THE CONCLUSION!
WRITTEN BY JAMIE S. RICH – ILLUSTRATED BY MIKE NORTON
COLORED BY ALLEN PASSALAQUA – LETTERED BY CRANK!
CREATED BY MICHAEL ALLRED

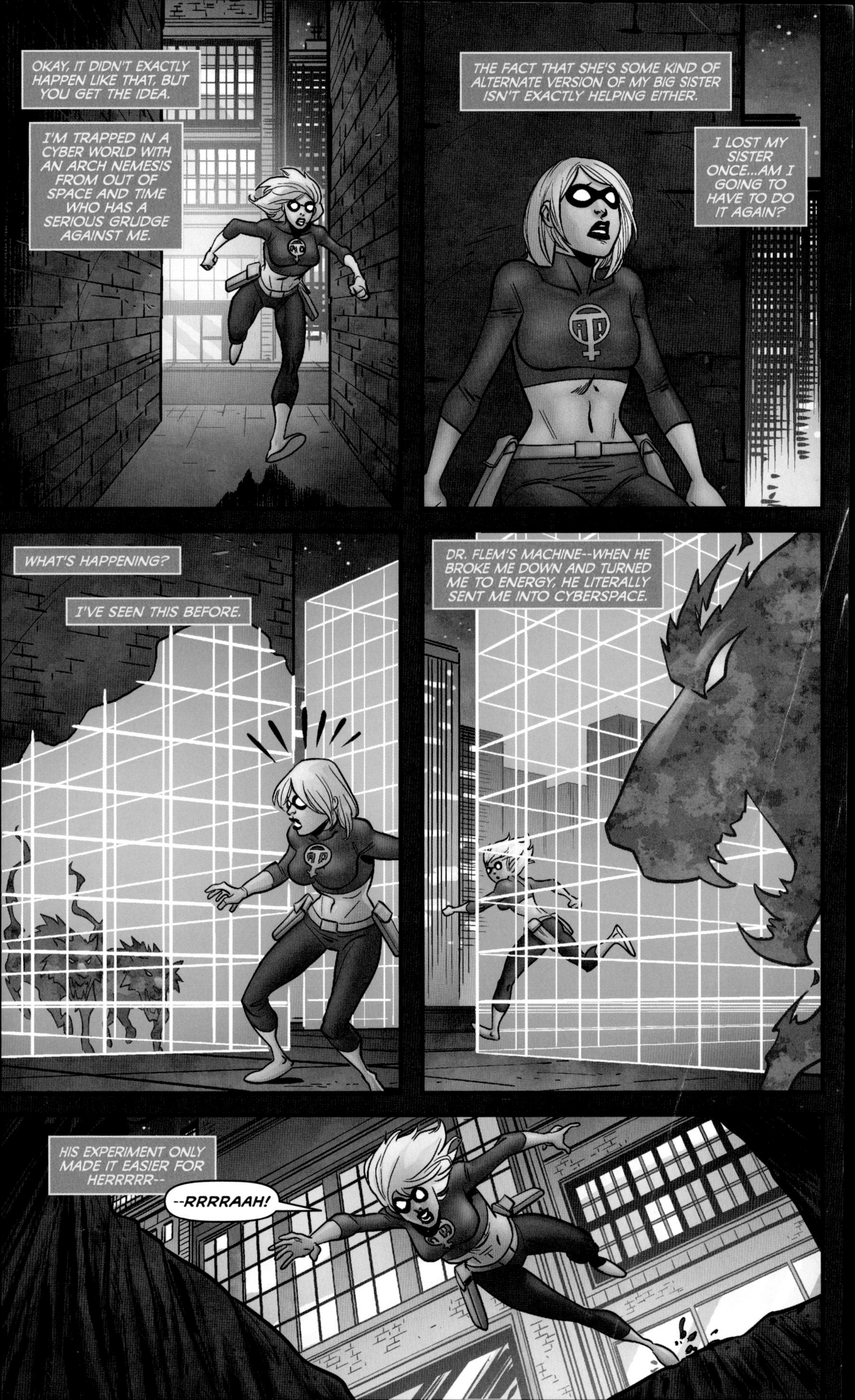
OKAY, IT DIDN'T EXACTLY HAPPEN LIKE THAT, BUT YOU GET THE IDEA.
I'M TRAPPED IN A CYBER WORLD WITH AN ARCH NEMESIS FROM OUT OF SPACE AND TIME WHO HAS A SERIOUS GRUDGE AGAINST ME.
THE FACT THAT SHE'S SOME KIND OF ALTERNATE VERSION OF MY BIG SISTER ISN'T EXACTLY HELPING EITHER.
I LOST MY SISTER ONCE...AM I GOING TO HAVE TO DO IT AGAIN?
WHAT'S HAPPENING?
I'VE SEEN THIS BEFORE.
DR. FLEM'S MACHINE--WHEN HE BROKE ME DOWN AND TURNED ME TO ENERGY, HE LITERALLY SENT ME INTO CYBERSPACE.
HIS EXPERIMENT ONLY MADE IT EASIER FOR HERRRRR--
--RRRRAAH!

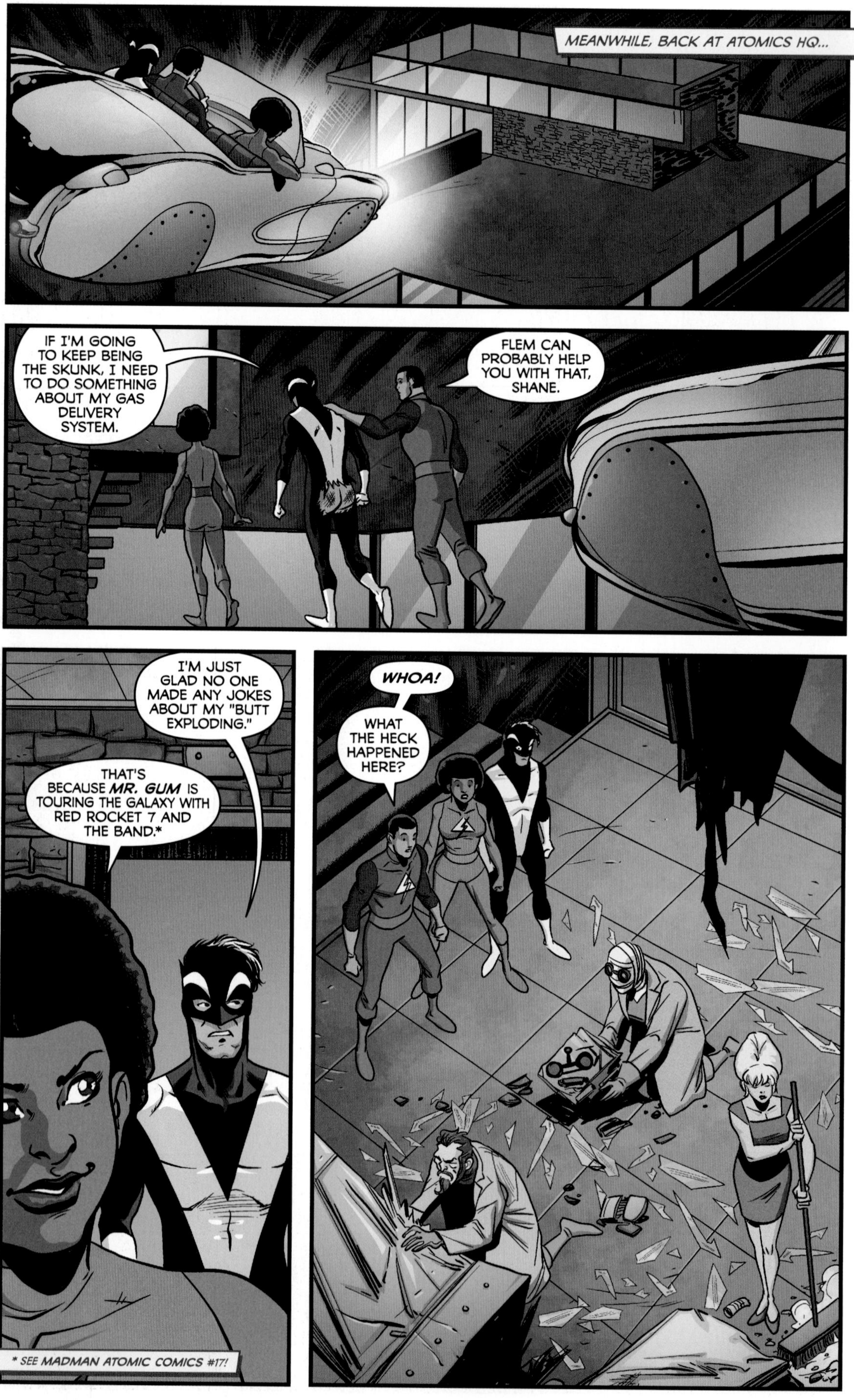
MEANWHILE, BACK AT ATOMICS HQ...
IF I'M GOING TO KEEP BEING THE SKUNK, I NEED TO DO SOMETHING ABOUT MY GAS DELIVERY SYSTEM.
FLEM CAN PROBABLY HELP YOU WITH THAT, SHANE.
I'M JUST GLAD NO ONE MADE ANY JOKES ABOUT MY "BUTT EXPLODING."
THAT'S BECAUSE MR. GUM IS TOURING THE GALAXY WITH RED ROCKET 7 AND THE BAND.*
* SEE MADMAN ATOMIC COMICS #17!
WHOA!
WHAT THE HECK HAPPENED HERE?

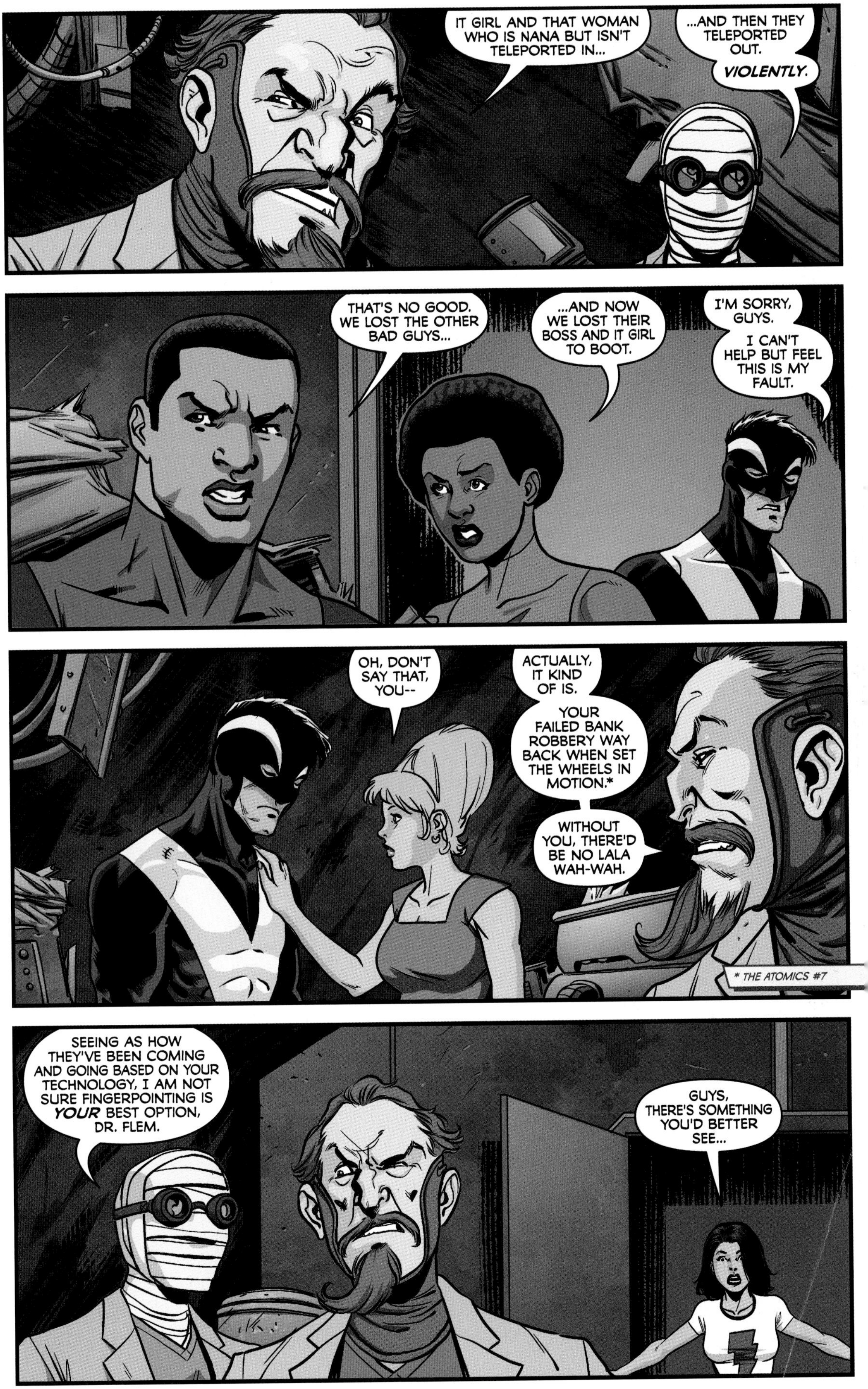
IT GIRL AND THAT WOMAN WHO IS NANA BUT ISN'T TELEPORTED IN...
...AND THEN THEY TELEPORTED OUT.
VIOLENTLY.
THAT'S NO GOOD. WE LOST THE OTHER BAD GUYS...
...AND NOW WE LOST THEIR BOSS AND IT GIRL TO BOOT.
I'M SORRY, GUYS.
I CAN'T HELP BUT FEEL THIS IS MY FAULT.
OH, DON'T SAY THAT, YOU--
ACTUALLY, IT KIND OF IS.
YOUR FAILED BANK ROBBERY WAY BACK WHEN SET THE WHEELS IN MOTION.*
WITHOUT YOU, THERE'D BE NO LALA WAH-WAH.
* THE ATOMICS #7
SEEING AS HOW THEY'VE BEEN COMING AND GOING BASED ON YOUR TECHNOLOGY, I AM NOT SURE FINGERPOINTING IS *YOUR* BEST OPTION, DR. FLEM.
GUYS, THERE'S SOMETHING YOU'D BETTER SEE...

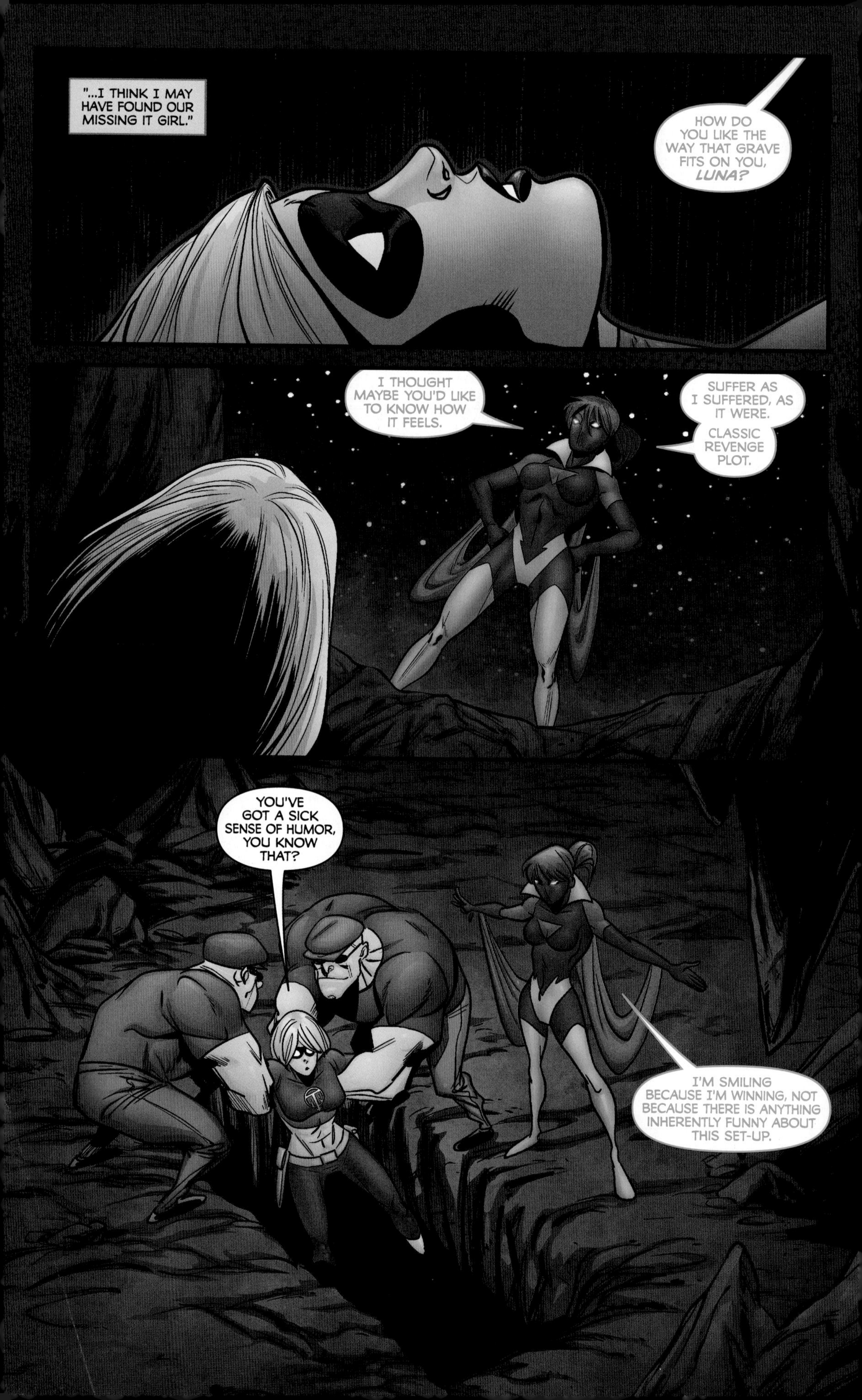
"...I THINK I MAY HAVE FOUND OUR MISSING IT GIRL."
HOW DO YOU LIKE THE WAY THAT GRAVE FITS ON YOU, *LUNA?*
I THOUGHT MAYBE YOU'D LIKE TO KNOW HOW IT FEELS.
SUFFER AS I SUFFERED, AS IT WERE.
CLASSIC REVENGE PLOT.
YOU'VE GOT A SICK SENSE OF HUMOR, YOU KNOW THAT?
I'M SMILING BECAUSE I'M WINNING, NOT BECAUSE THERE IS ANYTHING INHERENTLY FUNNY ABOUT THIS SET-UP.

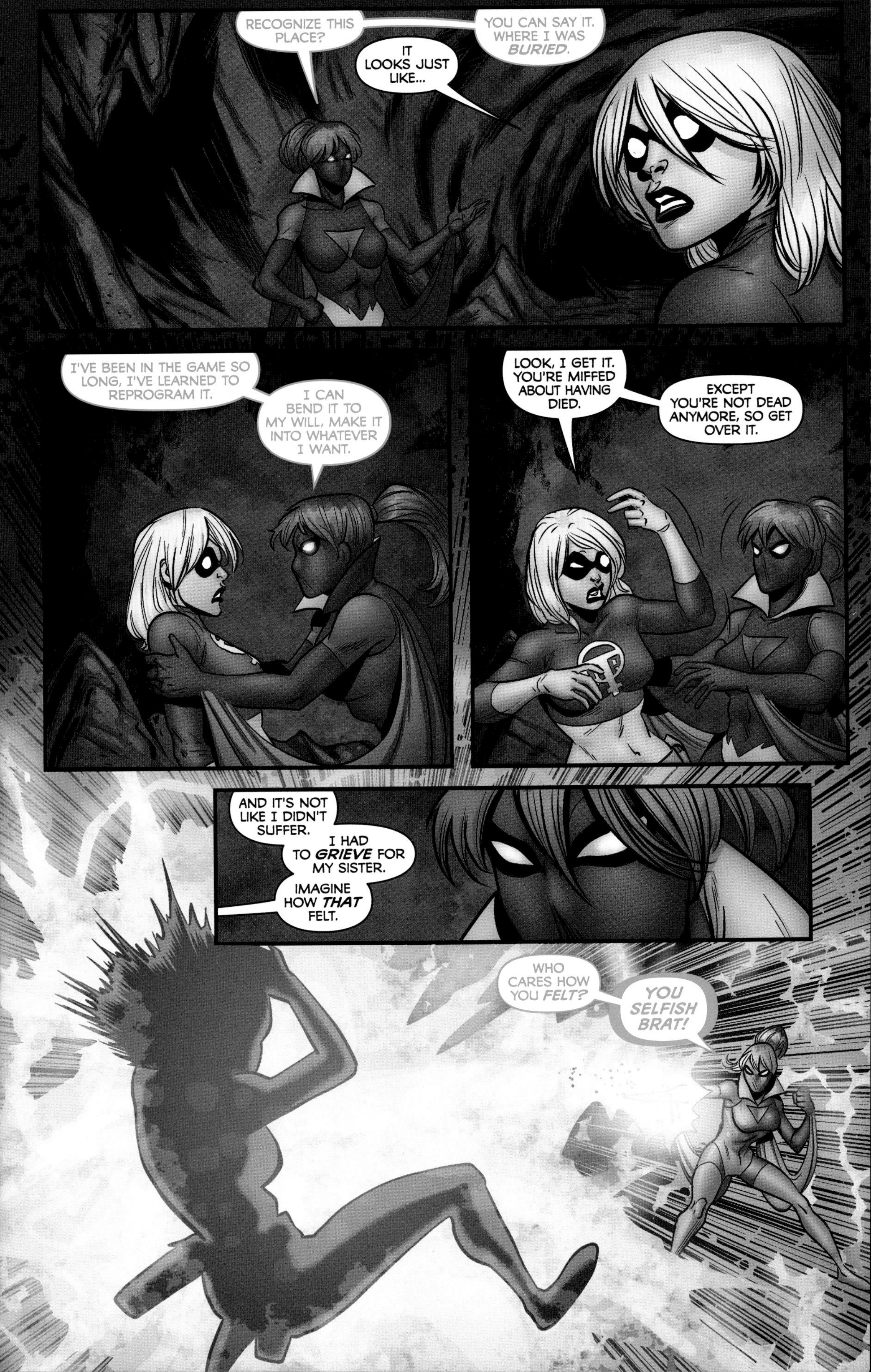
RECOGNIZE THIS PLACE?
IT LOOKS JUST LIKE...
YOU CAN SAY IT. WHERE I WAS BURIED.
I'VE BEEN IN THE GAME SO LONG, I'VE LEARNED TO REPROGRAM IT.
I CAN BEND IT TO MY WILL, MAKE IT INTO WHATEVER I WANT.
LOOK, I GET IT. YOU'RE MIFFED ABOUT HAVING DIED.
EXCEPT YOU'RE NOT DEAD ANYMORE, SO GET OVER IT.
AND IT'S NOT LIKE I DIDN'T SUFFER.
I HAD TO GRIEVE FOR MY SISTER.
IMAGINE HOW THAT FELT.
WHO CARES HOW YOU FELT?
YOU SELFISH BRAT!

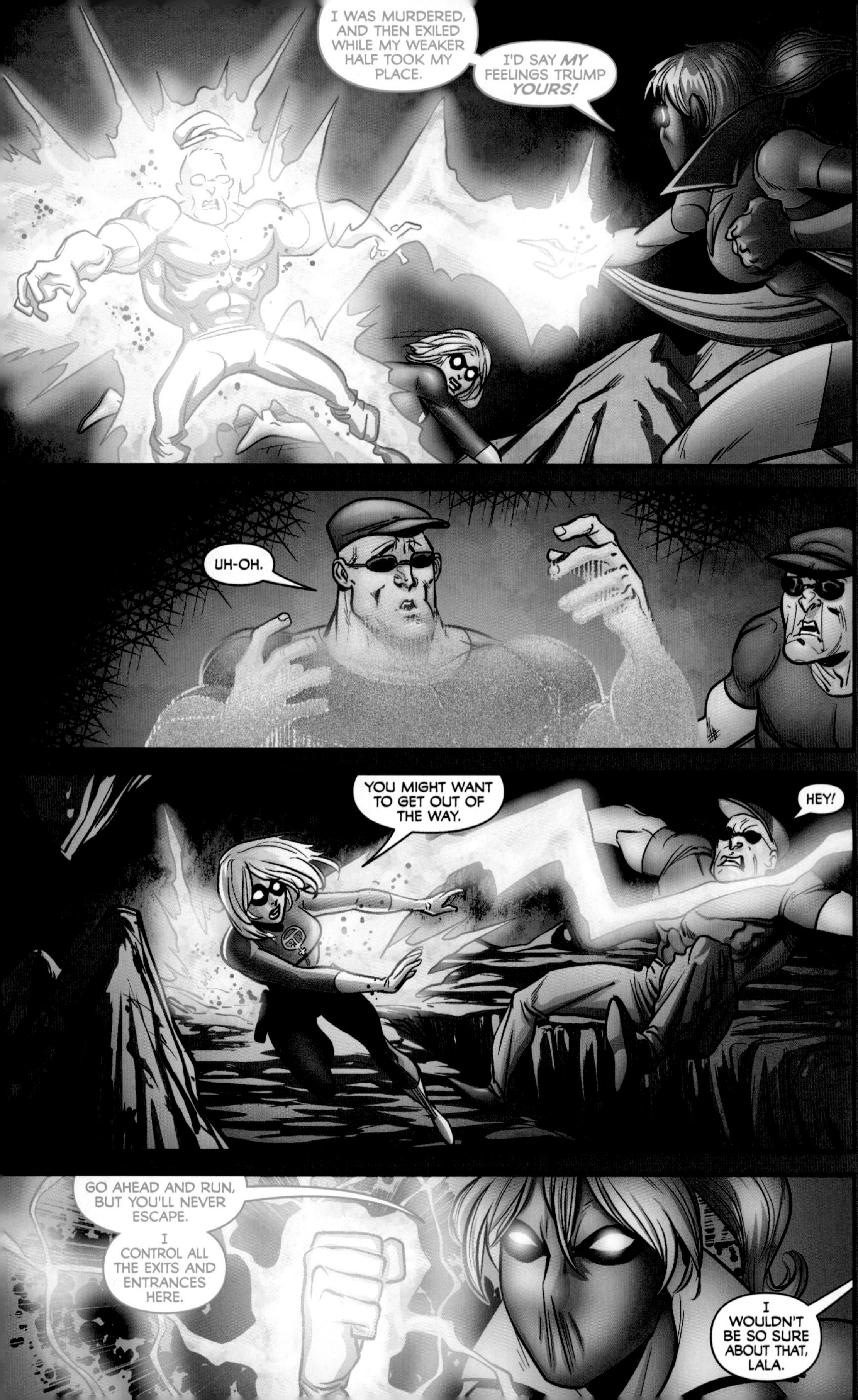
I WAS MURDERED, AND THEN EXILED WHILE MY WEAKER HALF TOOK MY PLACE.
I'D SAY *MY* FEELINGS TRUMP *YOURS!*
UH-OH.
YOU MIGHT WANT TO GET OUT OF THE WAY.
HEY!
GO AHEAD AND RUN, BUT YOU'LL NEVER ESCAPE.
I CONTROL ALL THE EXITS AND ENTRANCES HERE.
I WOULDN'T BE SO SURE ABOUT THAT, LALA.

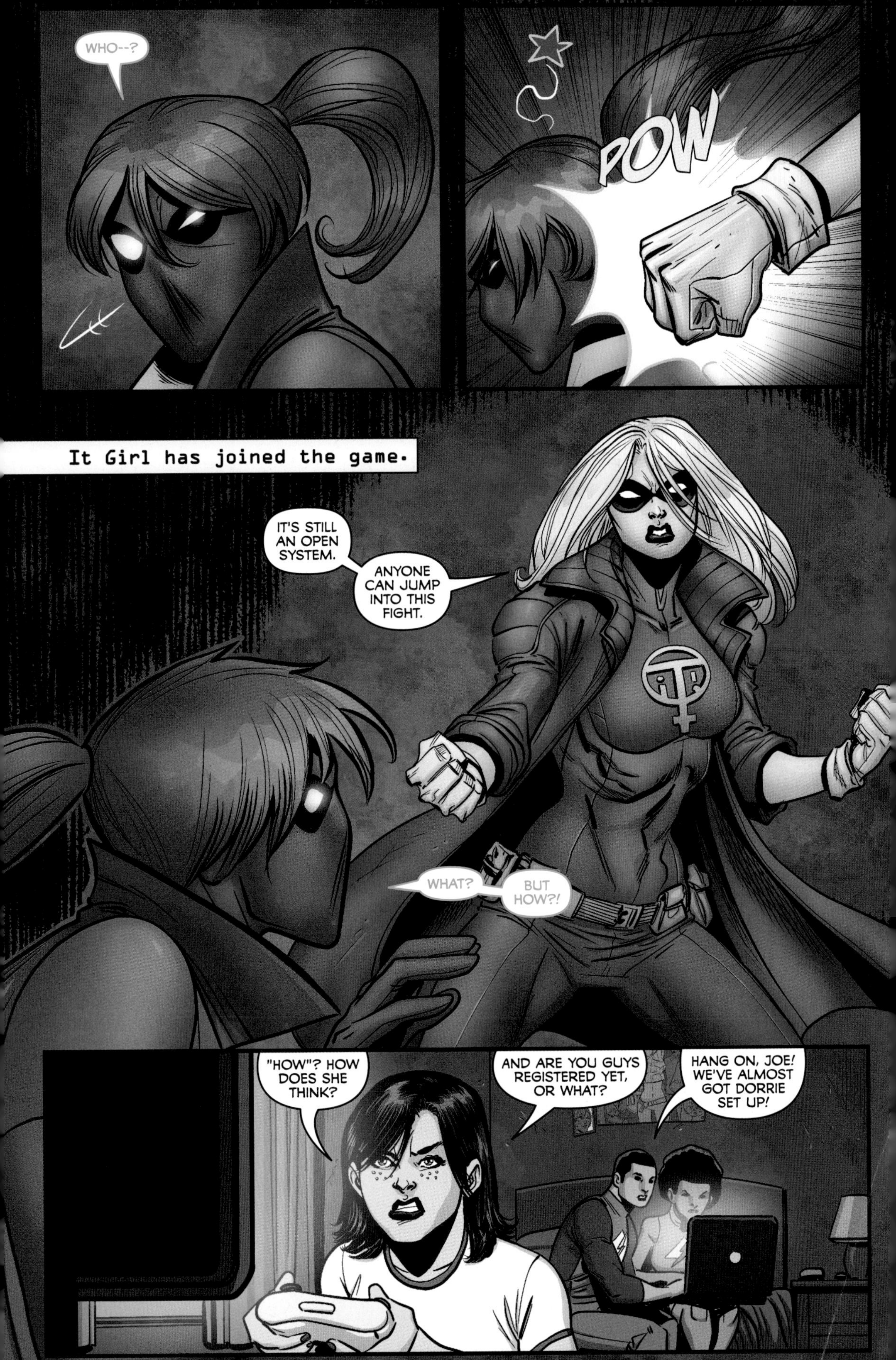
WHO--?
POW
It Girl has joined the game.
IT'S STILL AN OPEN SYSTEM.
ANYONE CAN JUMP INTO THIS FIGHT.
WHAT?
BUT HOW?!
"HOW"? HOW DOES SHE THINK?
AND ARE YOU GUYS REGISTERED YET, OR WHAT?
HANG ON, JOE! WE'VE ALMOST GOT DORRIE SET UP!

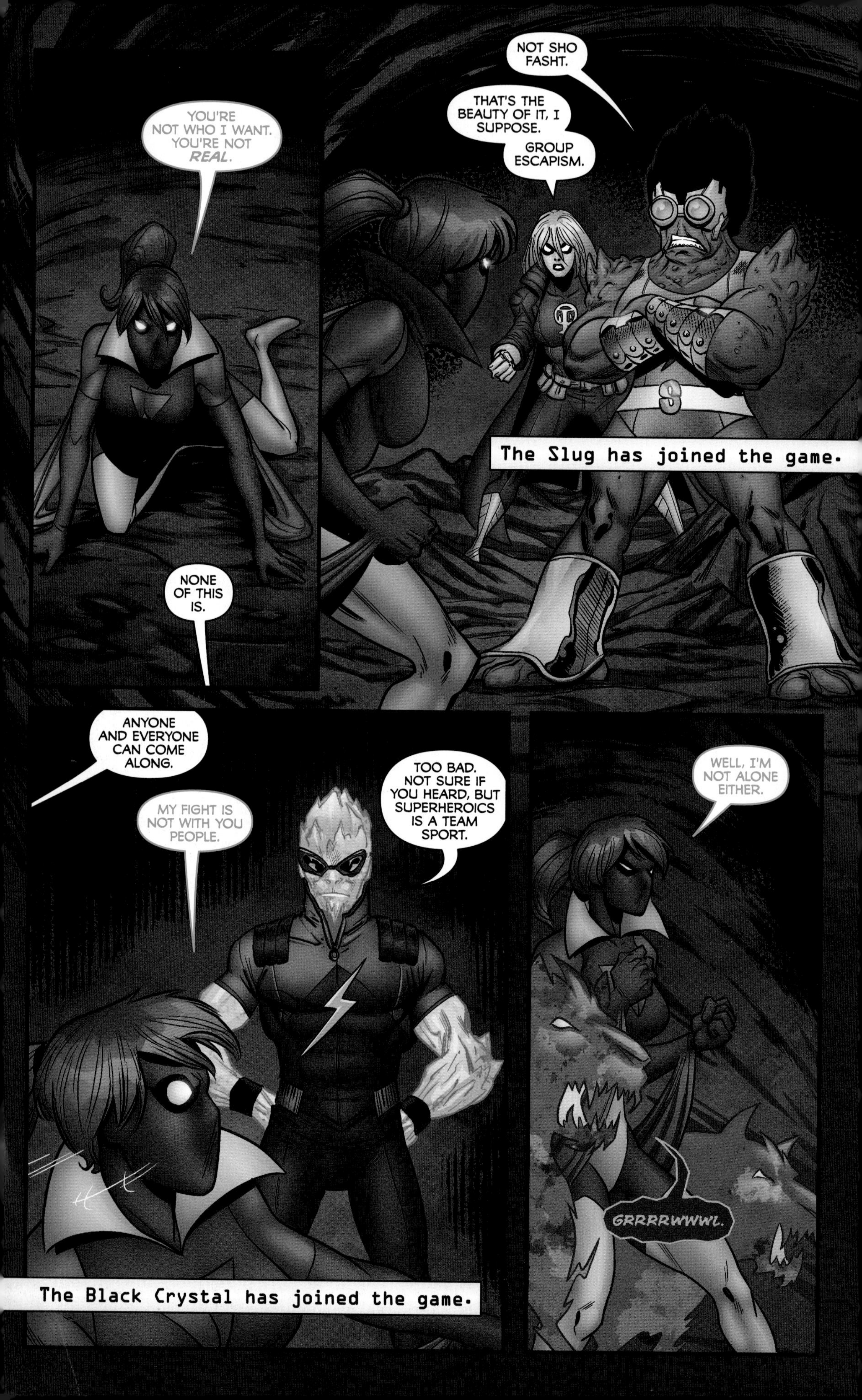
YOU'RE NOT WHO I WANT. YOU'RE NOT *REAL*.
NONE OF THIS IS.
NOT SHO FASHT.
THAT'S THE BEAUTY OF IT, I SUPPOSE.
GROUP ESCAPISM.
The Slug has joined the game.
ANYONE AND EVERYONE CAN COME ALONG.
MY FIGHT IS NOT WITH YOU PEOPLE.
TOO BAD. NOT SURE IF YOU HEARD, BUT SUPERHEROICS IS A TEAM SPORT.
The Black Crystal has joined the game.
WELL, I'M NOT ALONE EITHER.
GRRRRWWWL.

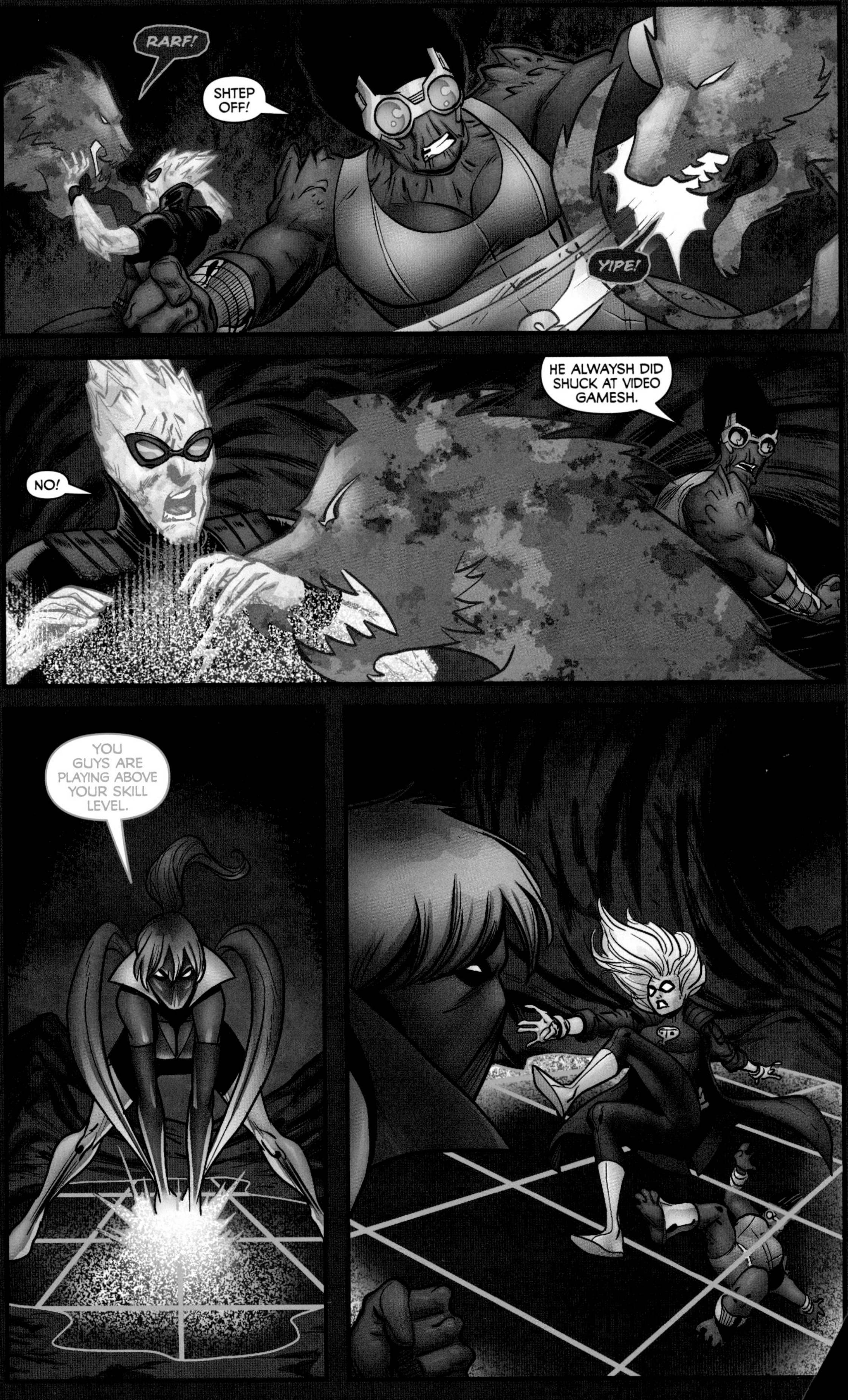
RARF!
SHTEP OFF!
YIPE!
HE ALWAYSH DID SHUCK AT VIDEO GAMESH.
NO!
YOU GUYS ARE PLAYING ABOVE YOUR SKILL LEVEL.

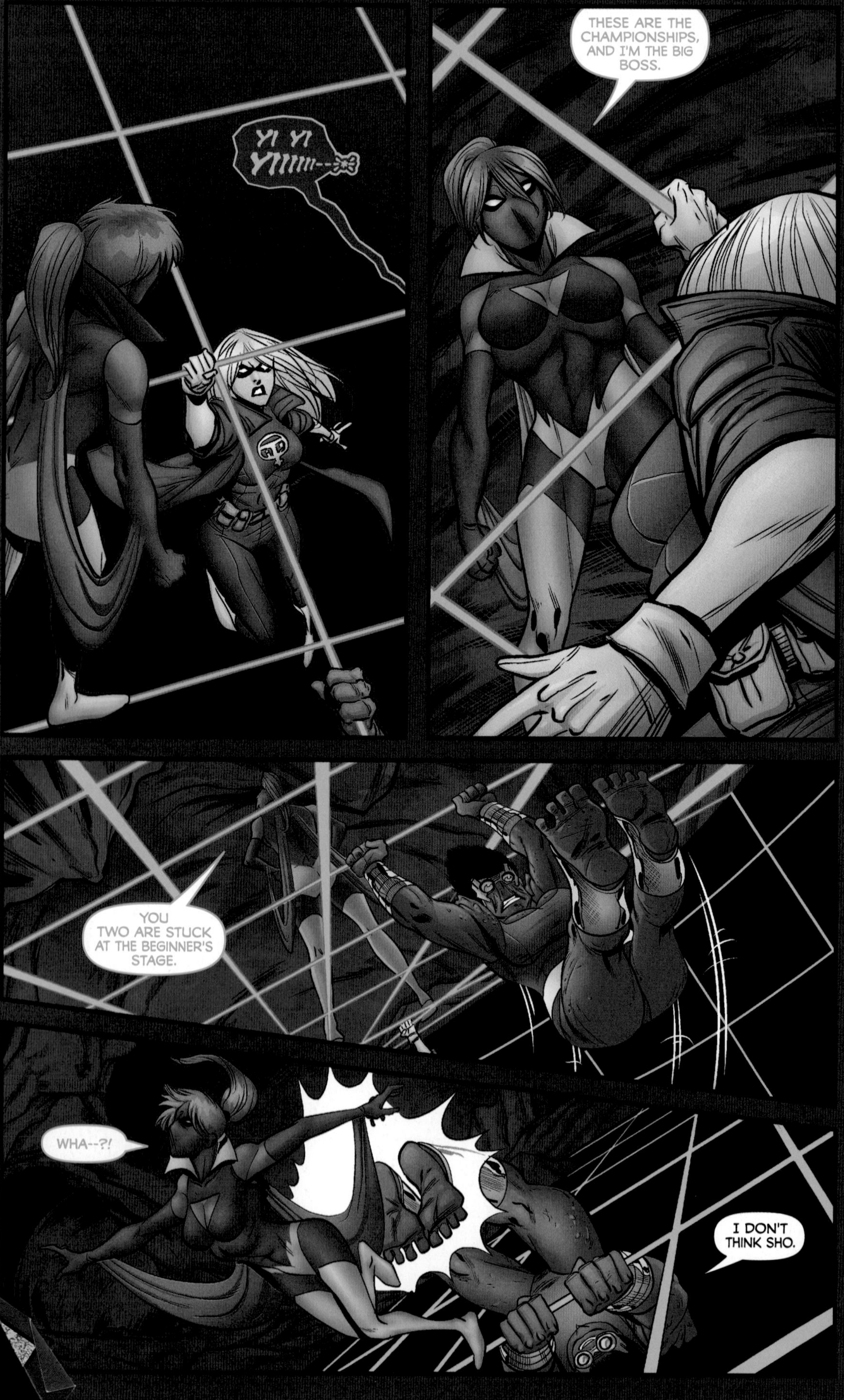

YI YI YIIIIII--
THESE ARE THE CHAMPIONSHIPS, AND I'M THE BIG BOSS.
YOU TWO ARE STUCK AT THE BEGINNER'S STAGE.
WHA--?!
I DON'T THINK SHO.

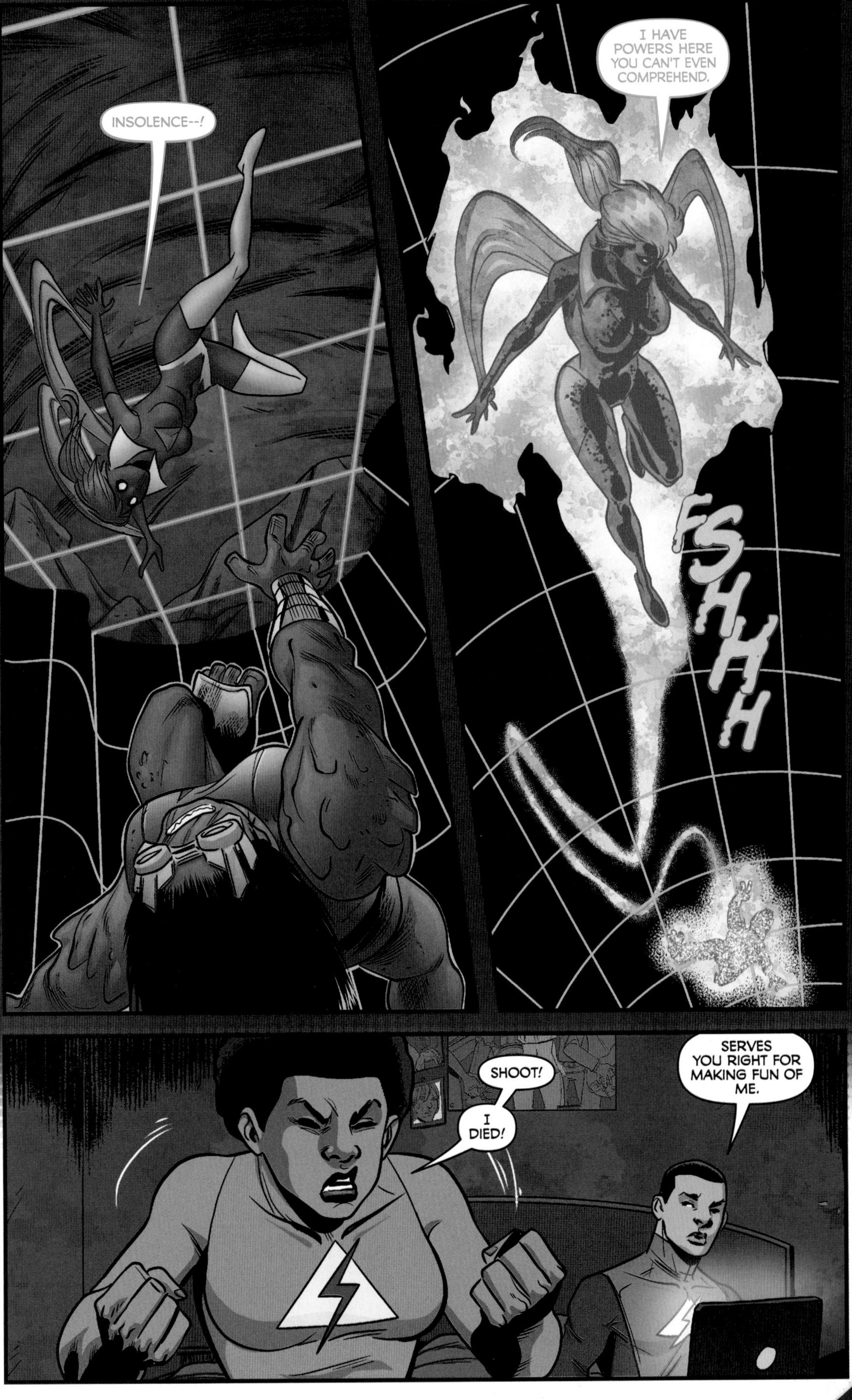
INSOLENCE--!
I HAVE POWERS HERE YOU CAN'T EVEN COMPREHEND.
FSHHHH
SHOOT!
I DIED!
SERVES YOU RIGHT FOR MAKING FUN OF ME.

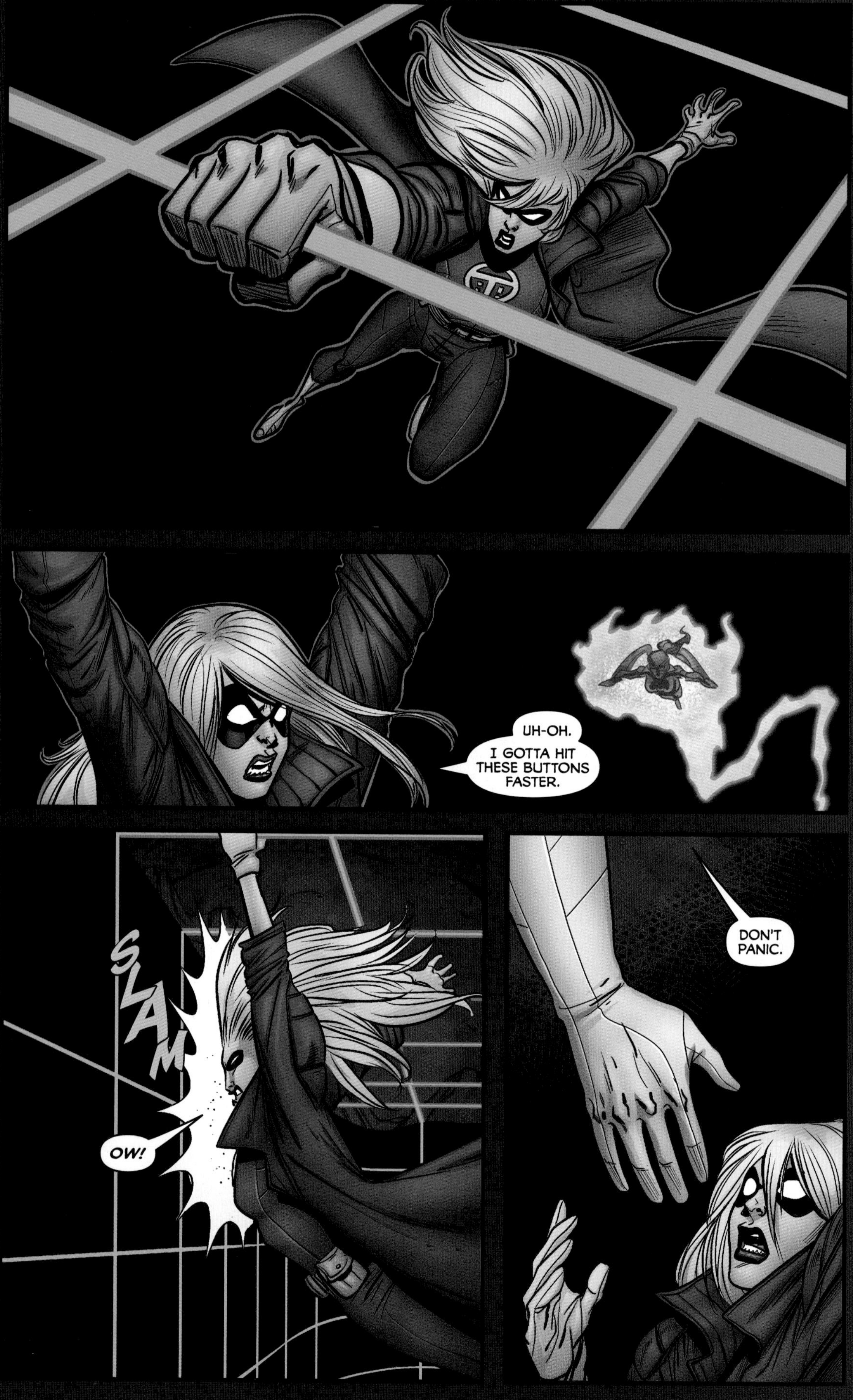
UH-OH.
I GOTTA HIT THESE BUTTONS FASTER.
SLAM
OW!
DON'T PANIC.

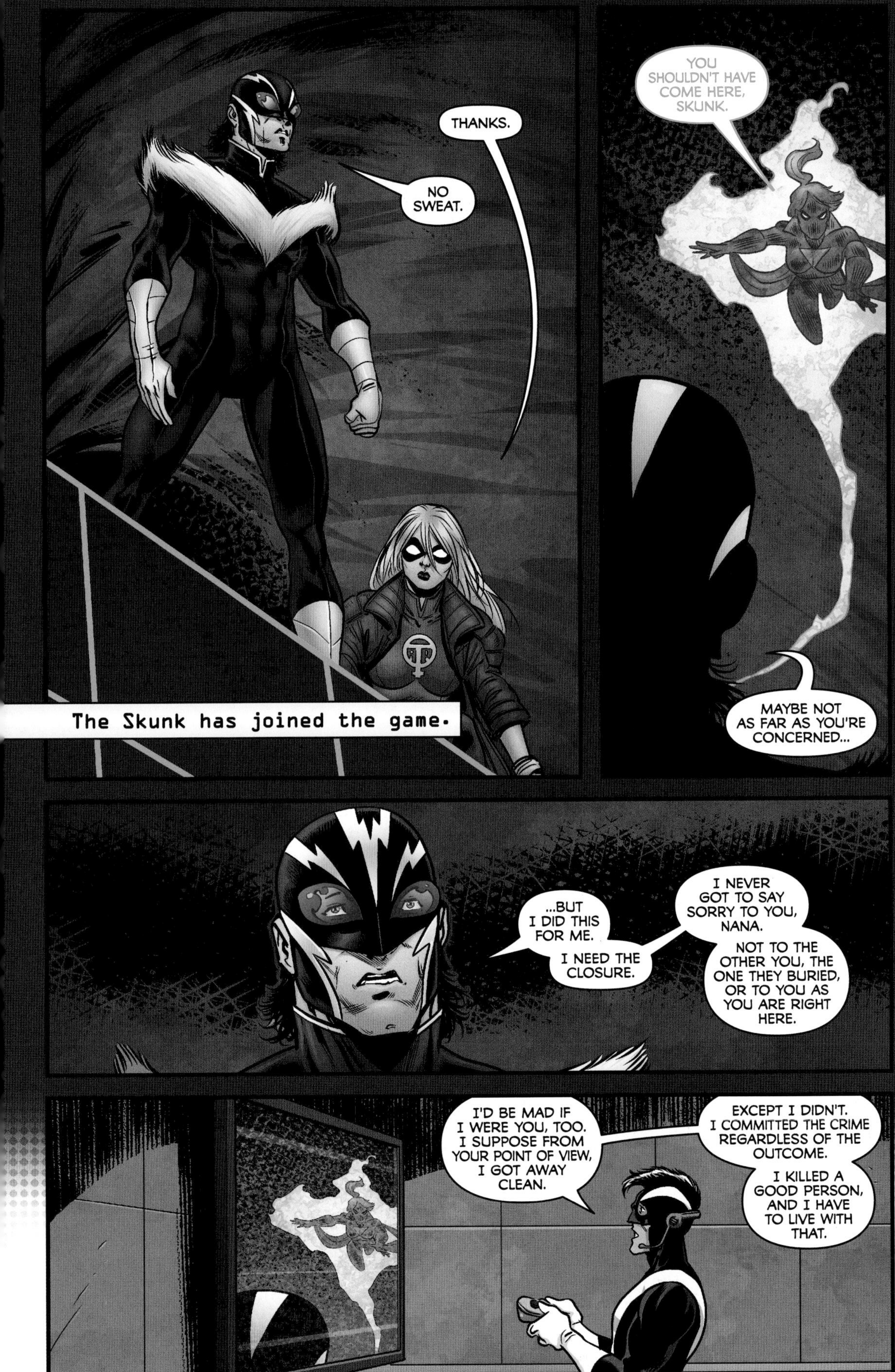
THANKS.
NO SWEAT.
The Skunk has joined the game.
YOU SHOULDN'T HAVE COME HERE, SKUNK.
MAYBE NOT AS FAR AS YOU'RE CONCERNED...
...BUT I DID THIS FOR ME.
I NEED THE CLOSURE.
I NEVER GOT TO SAY SORRY TO YOU, NANA.
NOT TO THE OTHER YOU, THE ONE THEY BURIED, OR TO YOU AS YOU ARE RIGHT HERE.
I'D BE MAD IF I WERE YOU, TOO. I SUPPOSE FROM YOUR POINT OF VIEW, I GOT AWAY CLEAN.
EXCEPT I DIDN'T. I COMMITTED THE CRIME REGARDLESS OF THE OUTCOME.
I KILLED A GOOD PERSON, AND I HAVE TO LIVE WITH THAT.

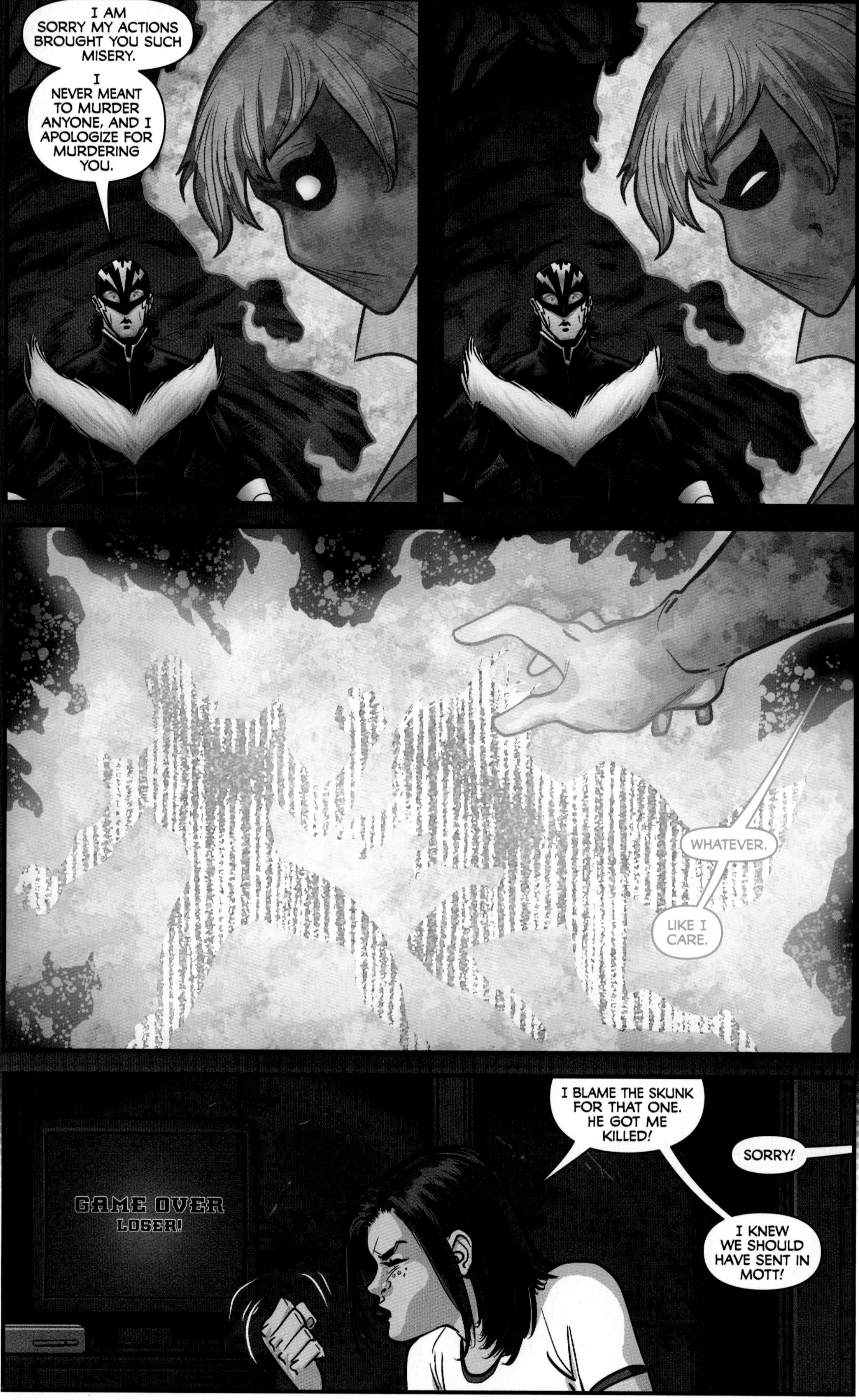
I AM SORRY MY ACTIONS BROUGHT YOU SUCH MISERY.
I NEVER MEANT TO MURDER ANYONE, AND I APOLOGIZE FOR MURDERING YOU.
WHATEVER.
LIKE I CARE.
GAME OVER
LOSER!
I BLAME THE SKUNK FOR THAT ONE. HE GOT ME KILLED!
SORRY!
I KNEW WE SHOULD HAVE SENT IN MOTT!

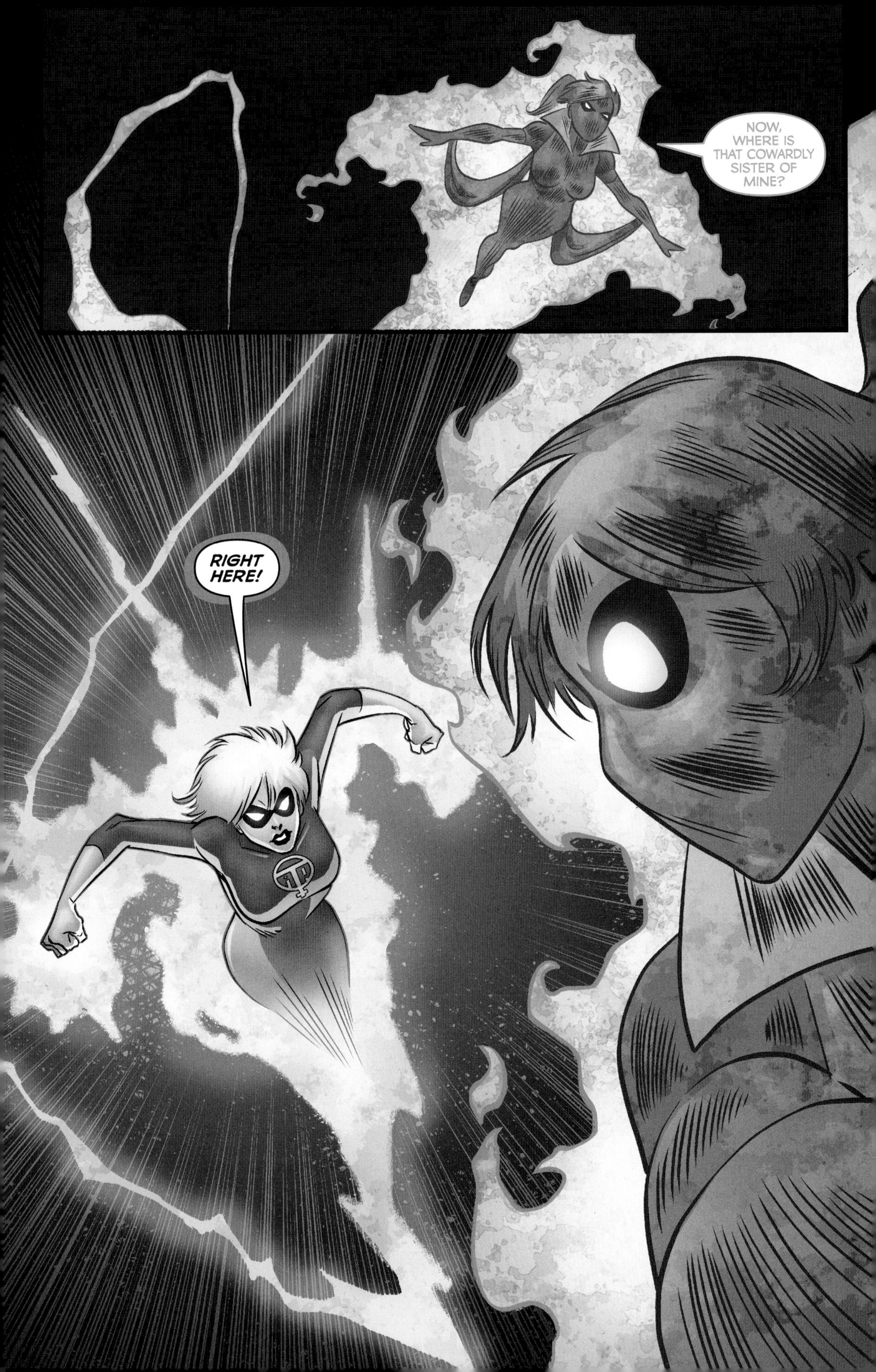
NOW, WHERE IS THAT COWARDLY SISTER OF MINE?
RIGHT HERE!

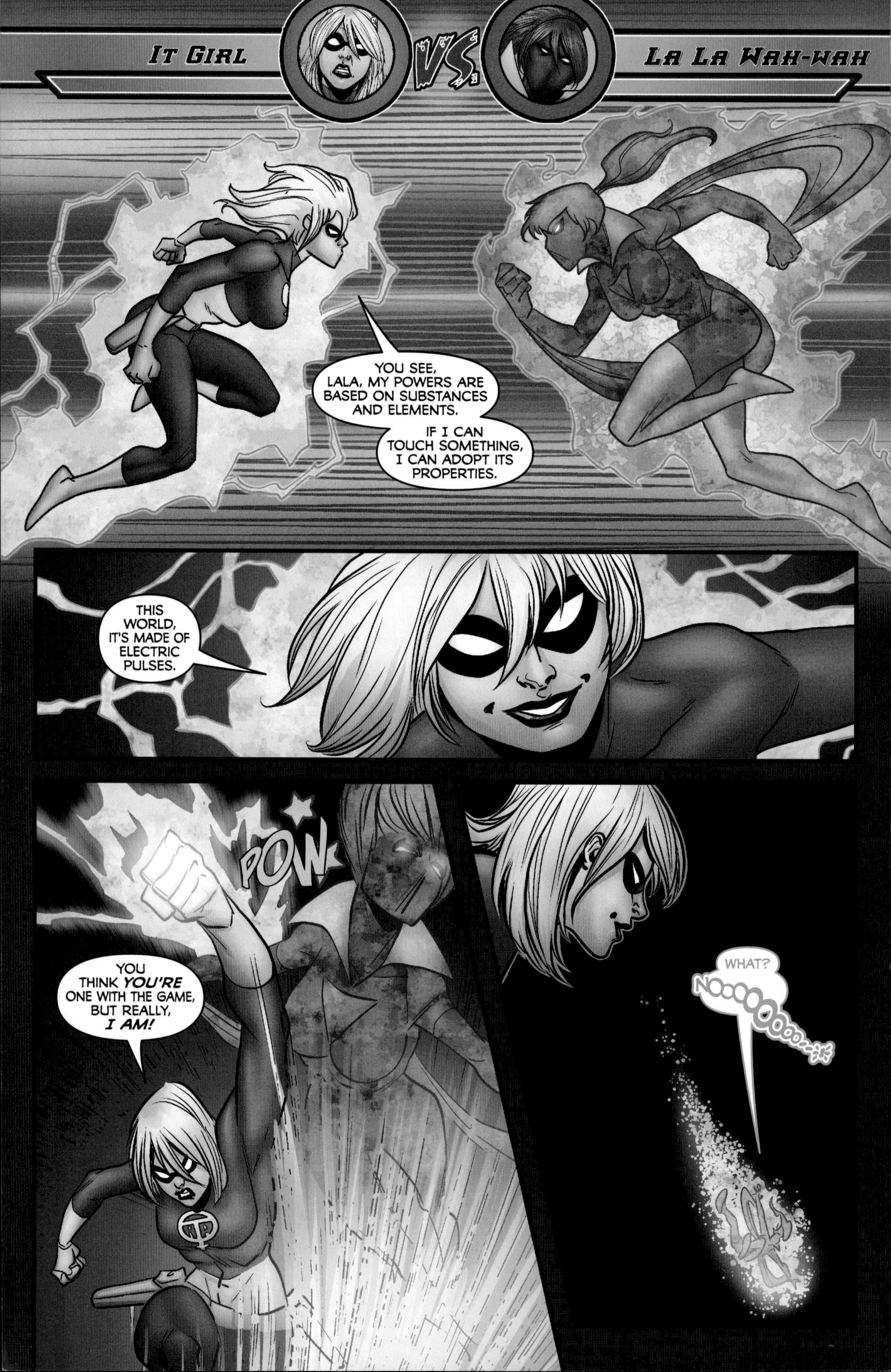
IT GIRL
VS.
LA LA WAH-WAH
YOU SEE, LALA, MY POWERS ARE BASED ON SUBSTANCES AND ELEMENTS.
IF I CAN TOUCH SOMETHING, I CAN ADOPT ITS PROPERTIES.
THIS WORLD, IT'S MADE OF ELECTRIC PULSES.
POW
YOU THINK *YOU'RE* ONE WITH THE GAME, BUT REALLY, ***I AM!***
WHAT?
NOOOOOOoo--

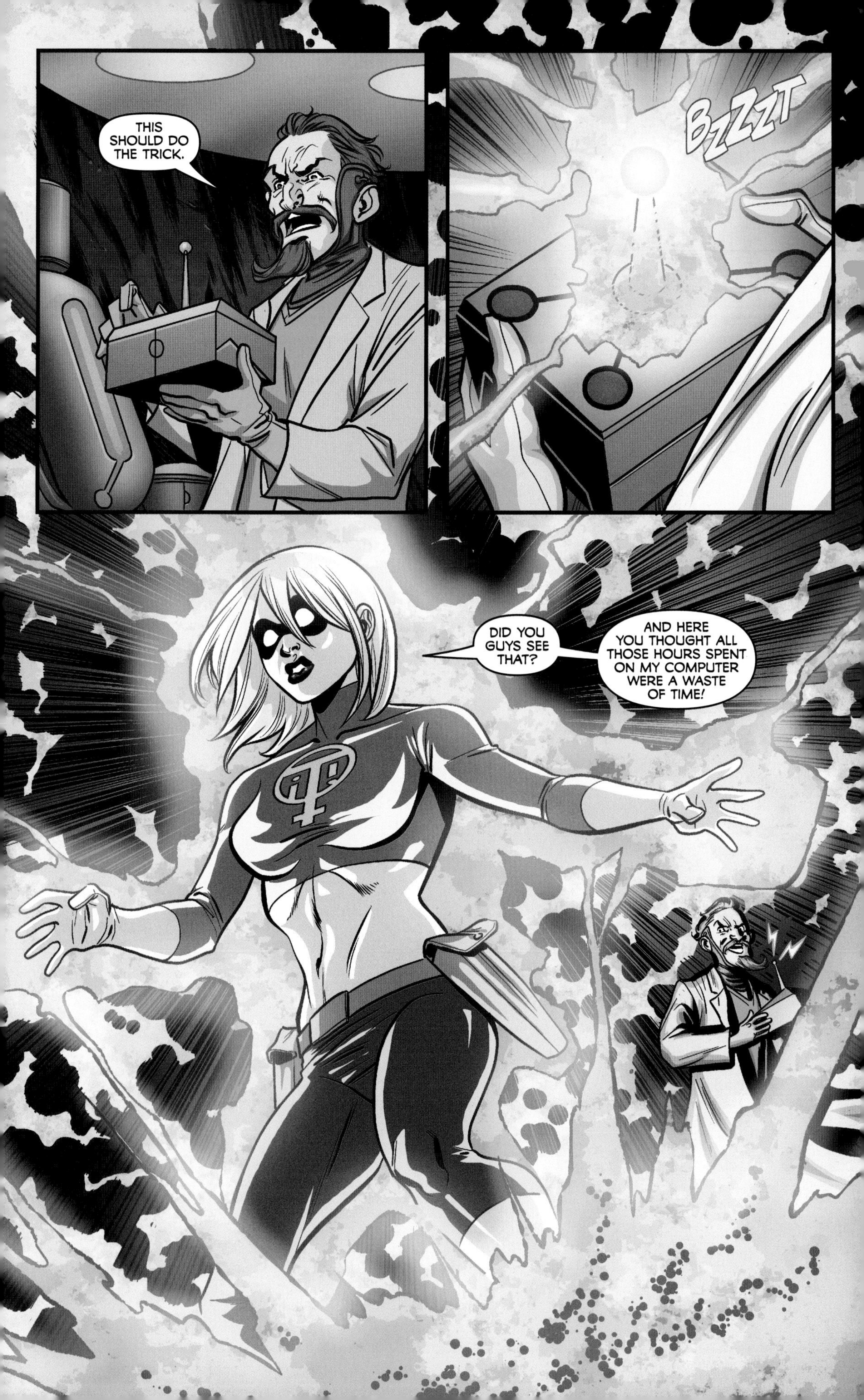
THIS SHOULD DO THE TRICK.
BZZZT
DID YOU GUYS SEE THAT?
AND HERE YOU THOUGHT ALL THOSE HOURS SPENT ON MY COMPUTER WERE A WASTE OF TIME!

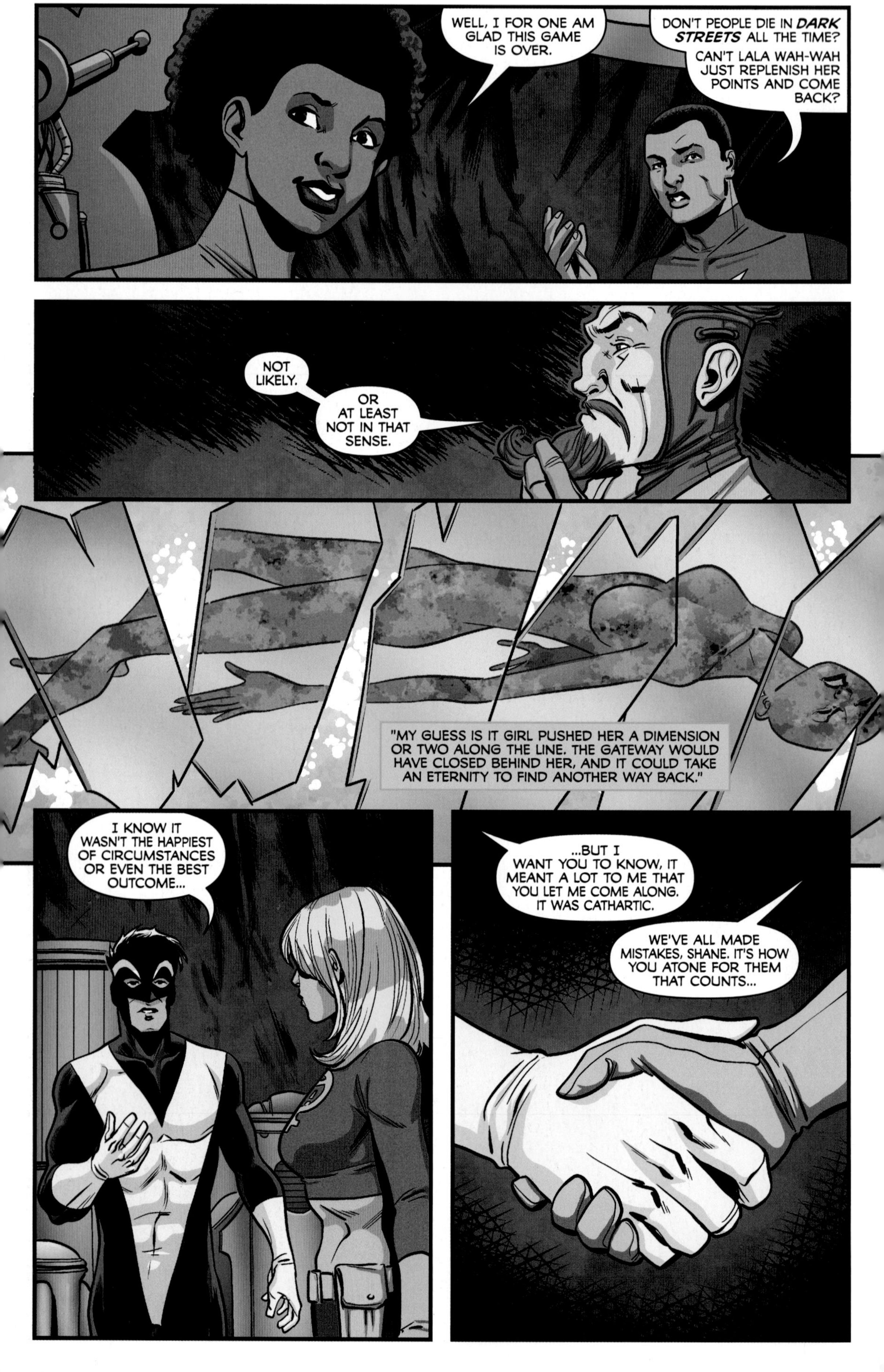
WELL, I FOR ONE AM GLAD THIS GAME IS OVER.
DON'T PEOPLE DIE IN DARK STREETS ALL THE TIME?
CAN'T LALA WAH-WAH JUST REPLENISH HER POINTS AND COME BACK?
NOT LIKELY.
OR AT LEAST NOT IN THAT SENSE.
"MY GUESS IS IT GIRL PUSHED HER A DIMENSION OR TWO ALONG THE LINE. THE GATEWAY WOULD HAVE CLOSED BEHIND HER, AND IT COULD TAKE AN ETERNITY TO FIND ANOTHER WAY BACK."
I KNOW IT WASN'T THE HAPPIEST OF CIRCUMSTANCES OR EVEN THE BEST OUTCOME...
...BUT I WANT YOU TO KNOW, IT MEANT A LOT TO ME THAT YOU LET ME COME ALONG. IT WAS CATHARTIC.
WE'VE ALL MADE MISTAKES, SHANE. IT'S HOW YOU ATONE FOR THEM THAT COUNTS...

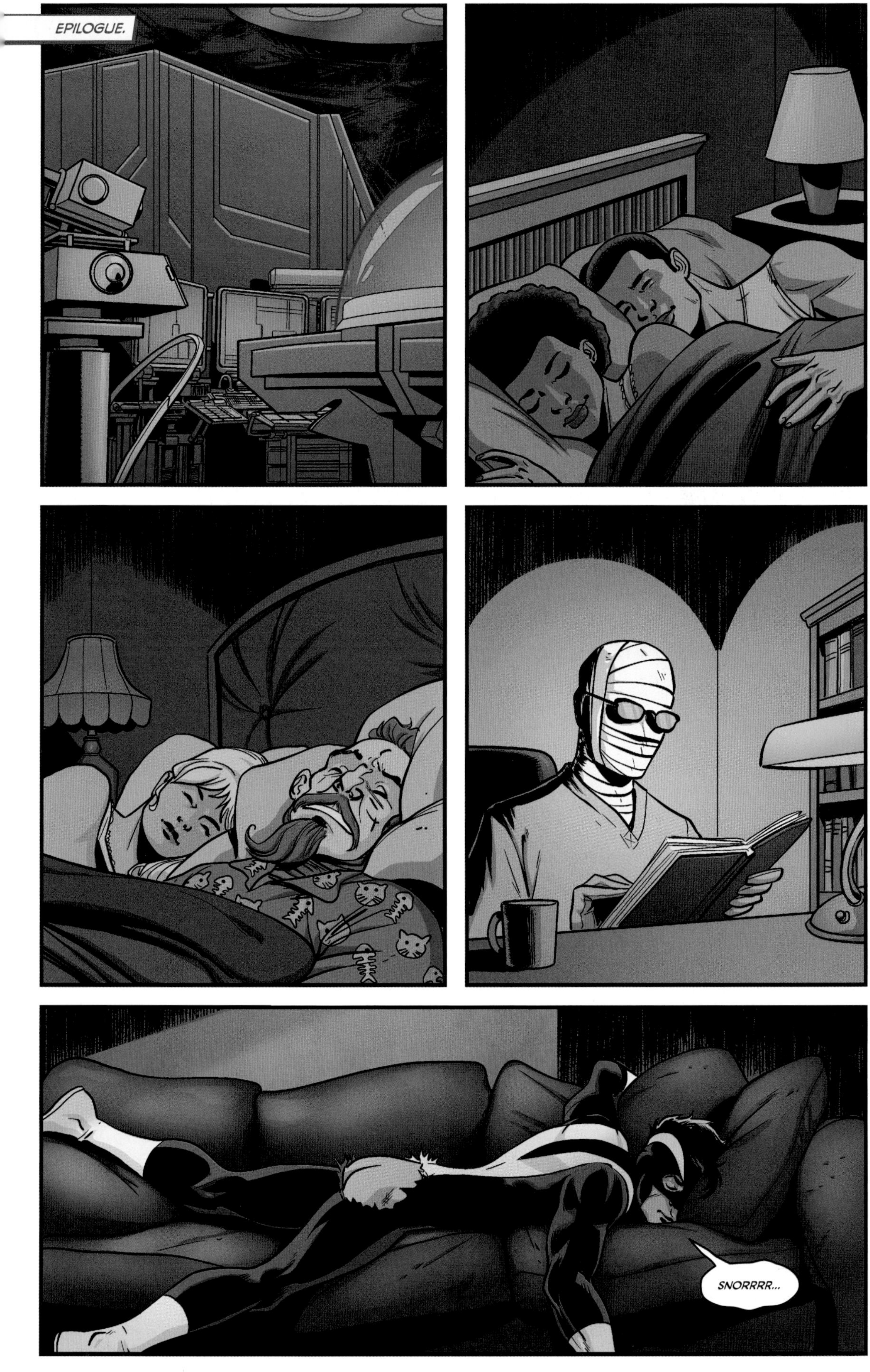
EPILOGUE.
SNORRRR...

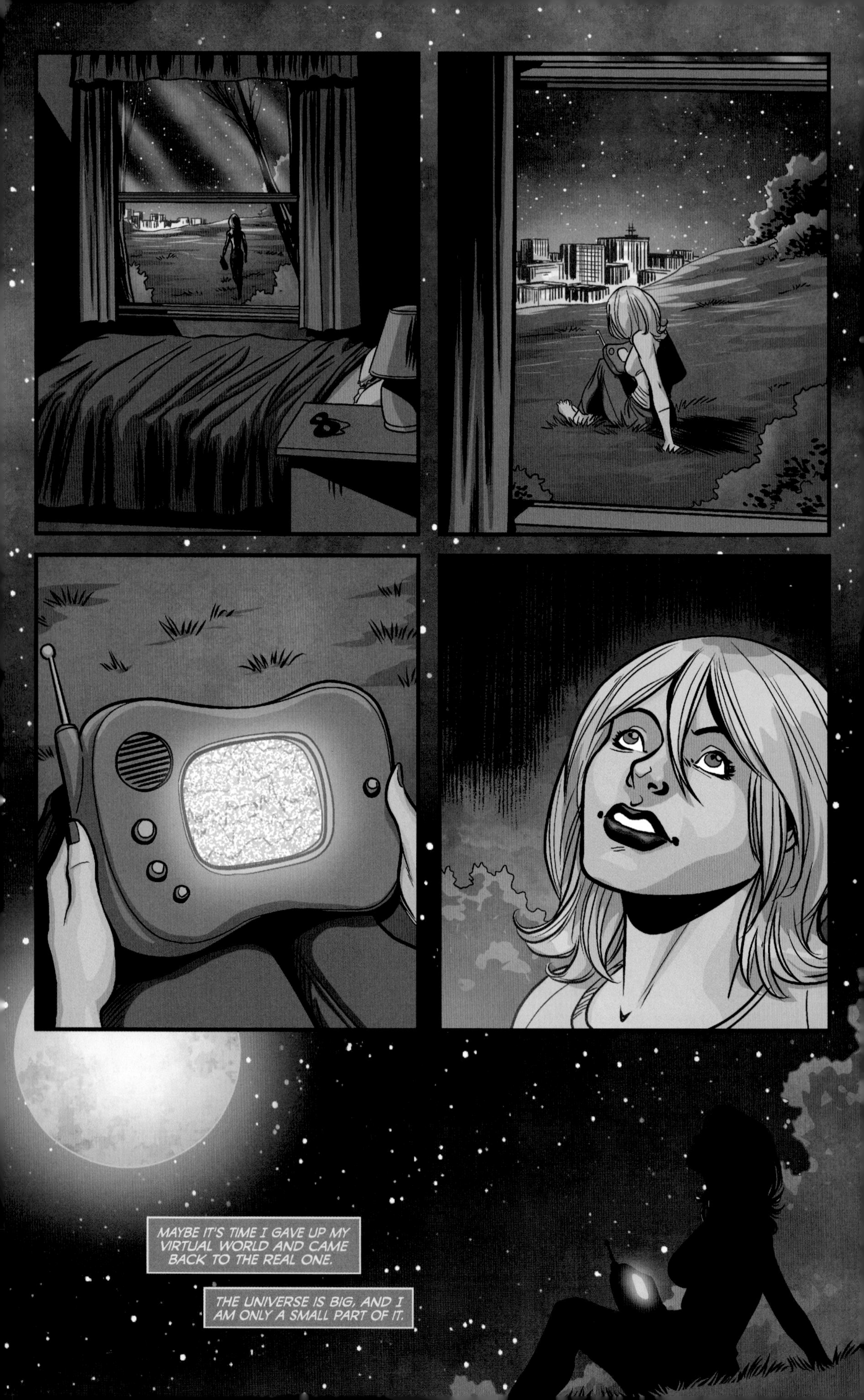
MAYBE IT'S TIME I GAVE UP MY VIRTUAL WORLD AND CAME BACK TO THE REAL ONE.
THE UNIVERSE IS BIG, AND I AM ONLY A SMALL PART OF IT.

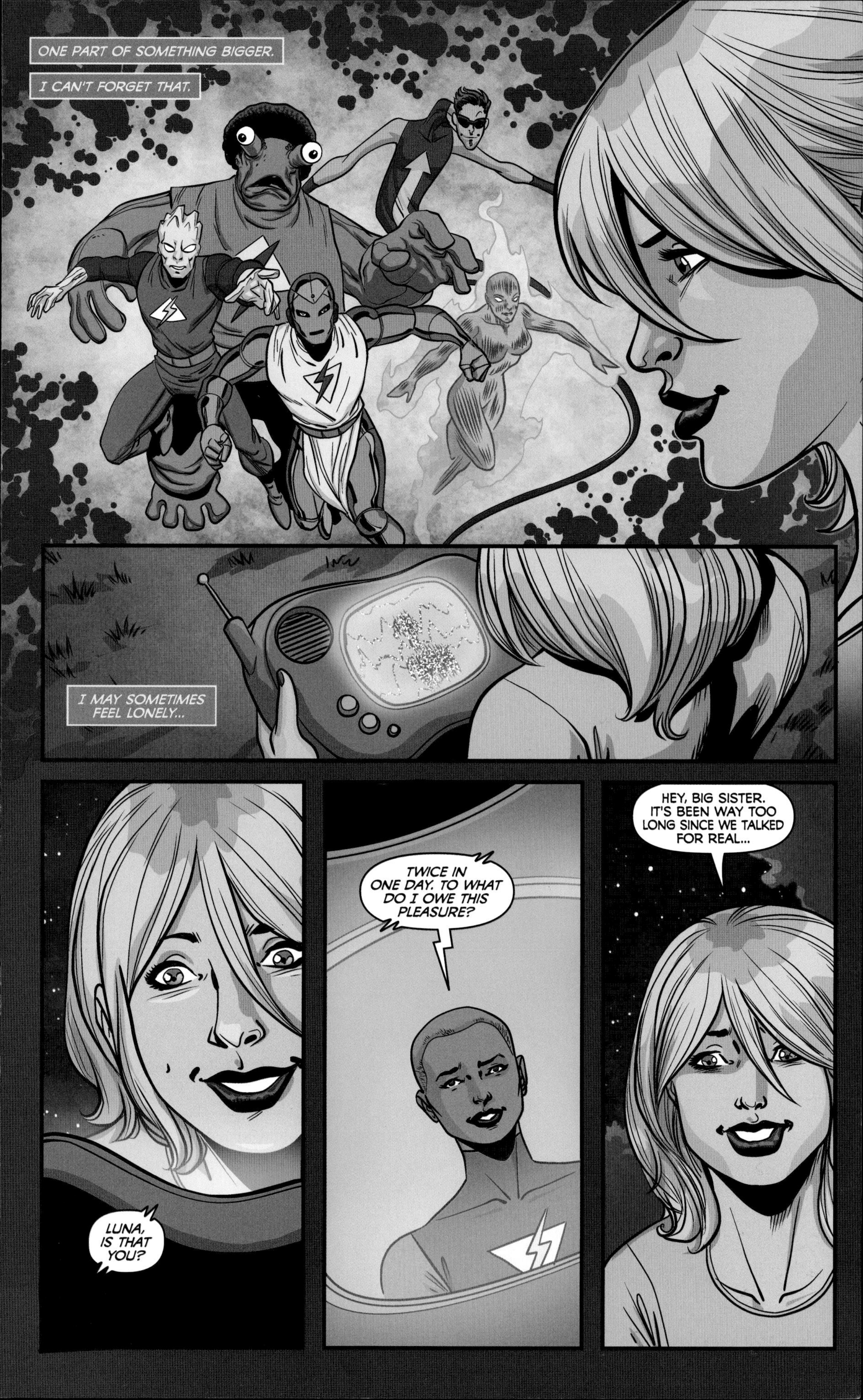
ONE PART OF SOMETHING BIGGER.
I CAN'T FORGET THAT.
I MAY SOMETIMES FEEL LONELY...
LUNA, IS THAT YOU?
TWICE IN ONE DAY. TO WHAT DO I OWE THIS PLEASURE?
HEY, BIG SISTER. IT'S BEEN WAY TOO LONG SINCE WE TALKED FOR REAL...

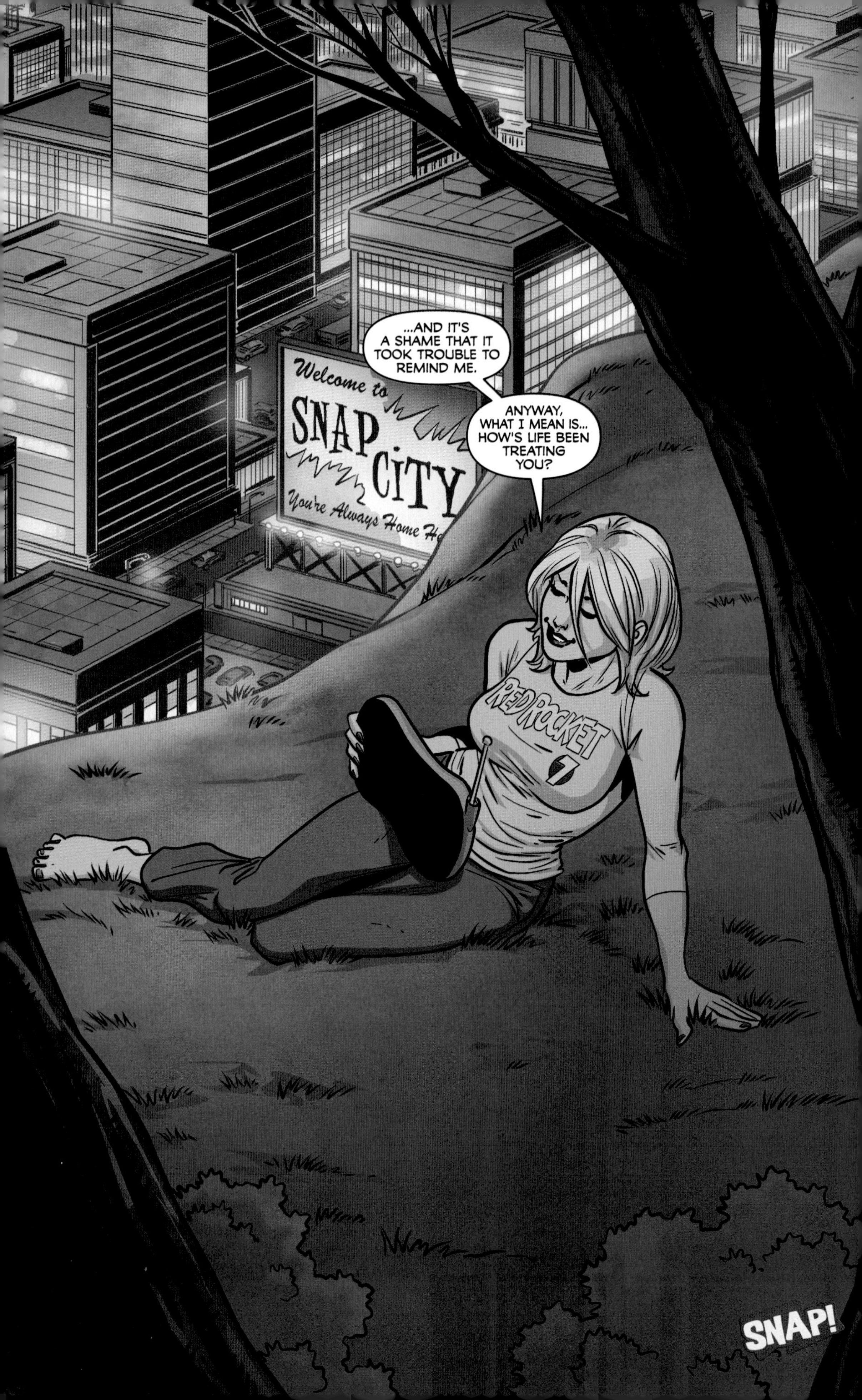
Welcome to SNAP CITY You're Always Home H
...AND IT'S A SHAME THAT IT TOOK TROUBLE TO REMIND ME.
ANYWAY, WHAT I MEAN IS... HOW'S LIFE BEEN TREATING YOU?
RED ROCKET 7
SNAP!

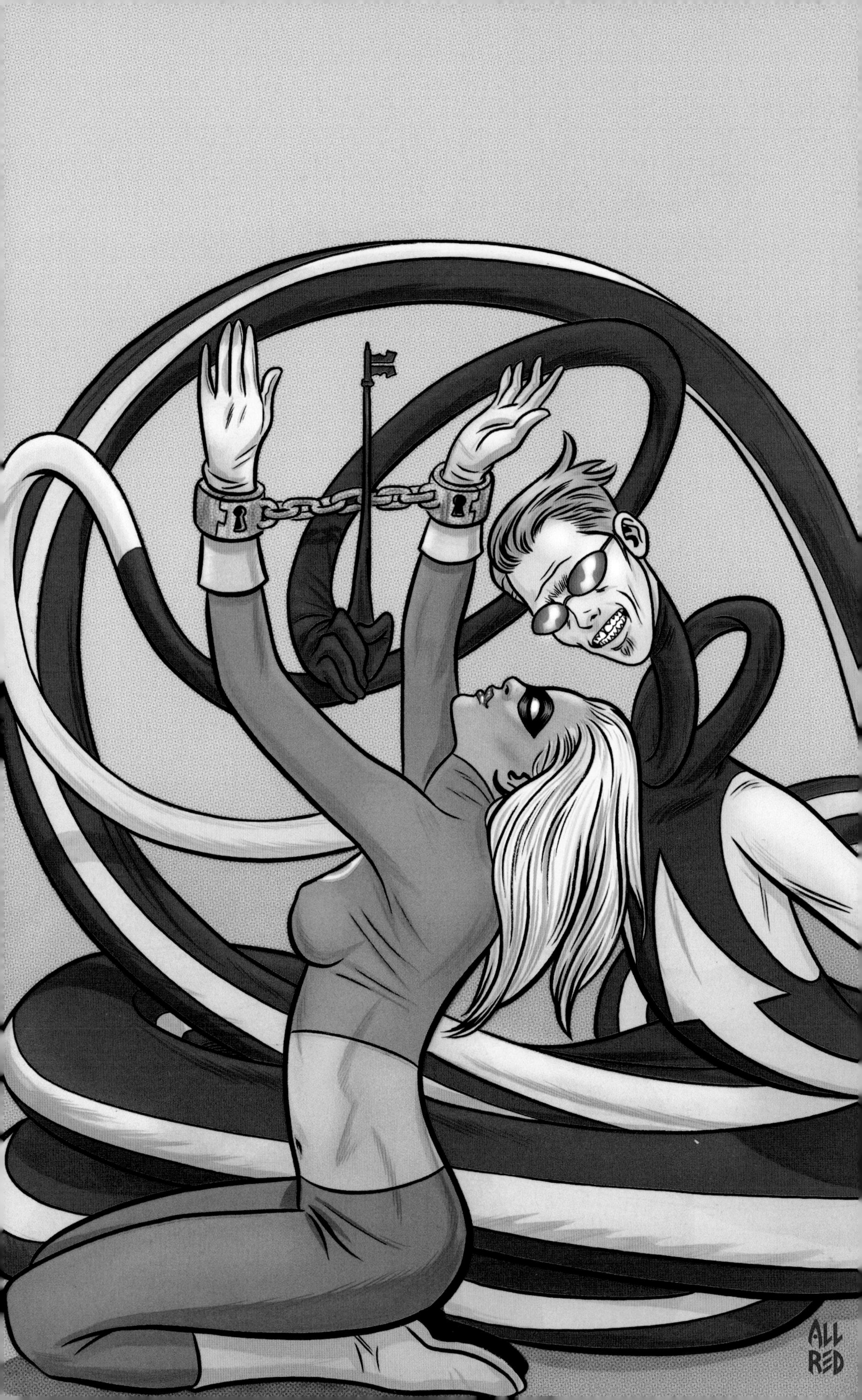
ALL
RED

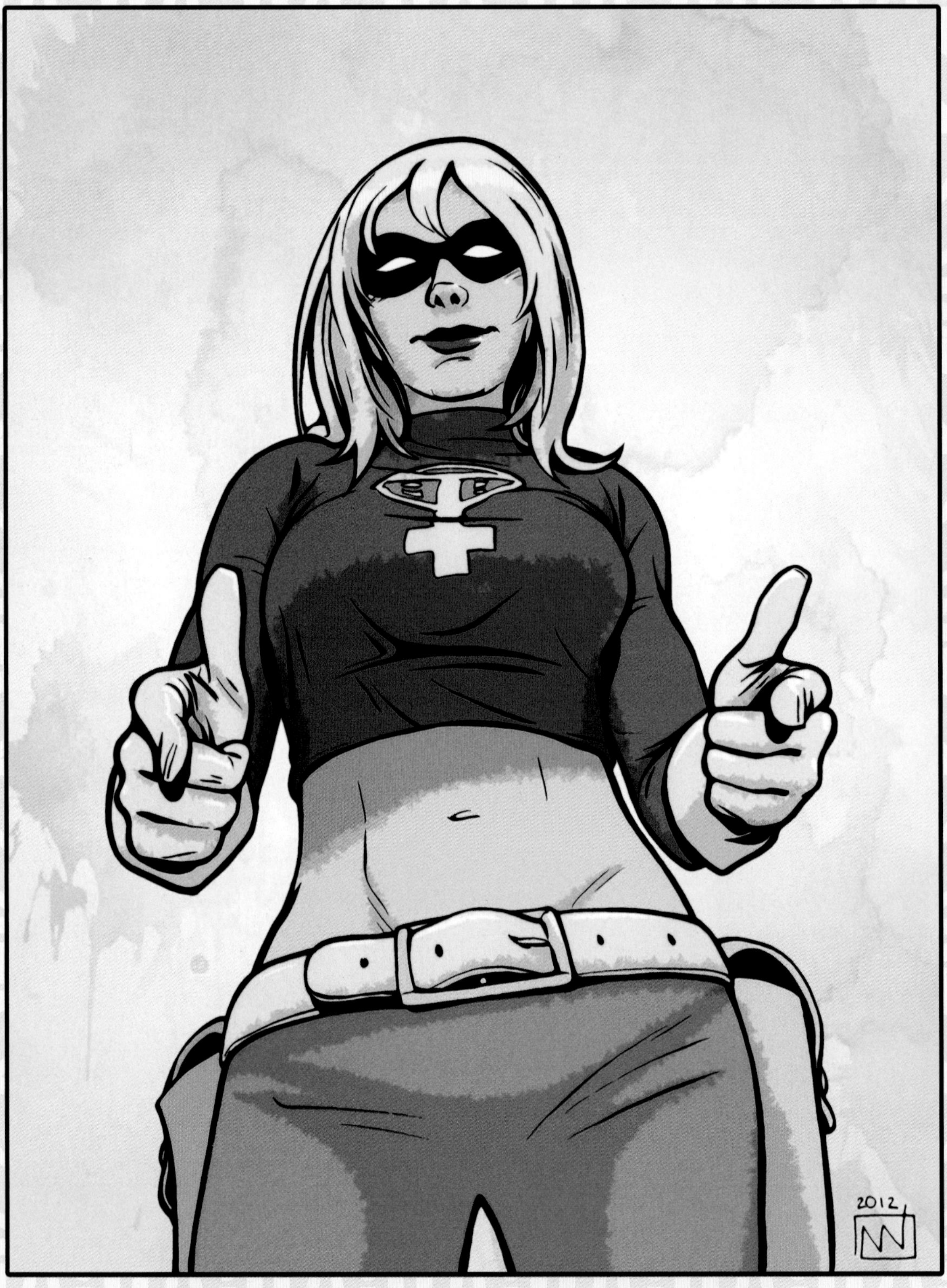
2012

Illustration by Natalie Nourigat natalienourigat.com

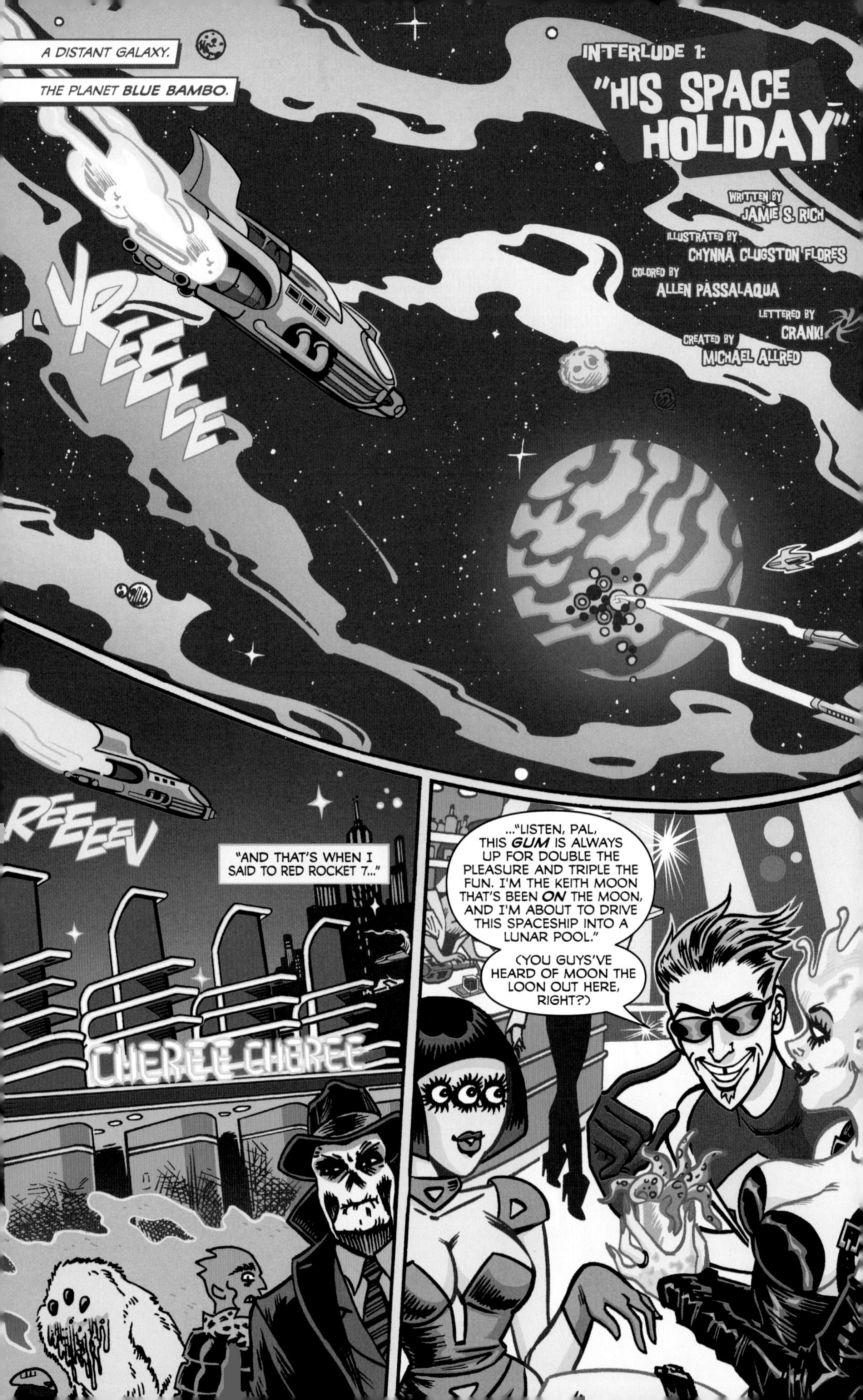
A DISTANT GALAXY.
THE PLANET BLUE BAMBO.
INTERLUDE 1:
"HIS SPACE HOLIDAY"
WRITTEN BY JAMIE S. RICH
ILLUSTRATED BY CHYNNA CLUGSTON FLORES
COLORED BY ALLEN PASSALAQUA
LETTERED BY CRANK!
CREATED BY MICHAEL ALLRED
VREEEEE
REEEEEN
CHEREE CHEREE
"AND THAT'S WHEN I SAID TO RED ROCKET 7..."
..."LISTEN, PAL, THIS GUM IS ALWAYS UP FOR DOUBLE THE PLEASURE AND TRIPLE THE FUN. I'M THE KEITH MOON THAT'S BEEN ON THE MOON, AND I'M ABOUT TO DRIVE THIS SPACESHIP INTO A LUNAR POOL."
(YOU GUYS'VE HEARD OF MOON THE LOON OUT HERE, RIGHT?)

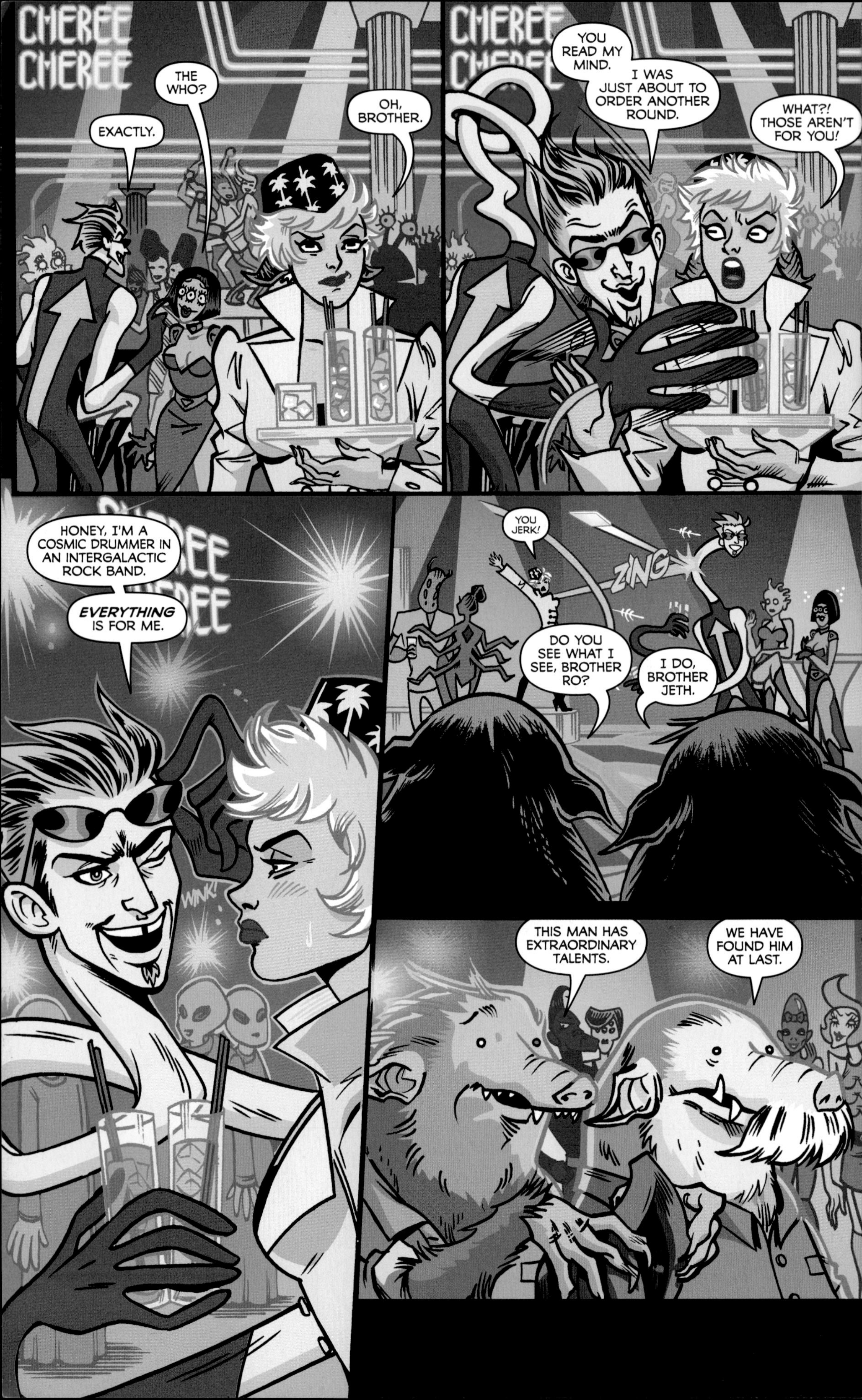
CHEREE CHEREE
THE WHO?
EXACTLY.
OH, BROTHER.
YOU READ MY MIND.
I WAS JUST ABOUT TO ORDER ANOTHER ROUND.
WHAT?! THOSE AREN'T FOR YOU!
HONEY, I'M A COSMIC DRUMMER IN AN INTERGALACTIC ROCK BAND.
EVERYTHING IS FOR ME.
WINK!
YOU JERK!
ZING
DO YOU SEE WHAT I SEE, BROTHER RO?
I DO, BROTHER JETH.
THIS MAN HAS EXTRAORDINARY TALENTS.
WE HAVE FOUND HIM AT LAST.

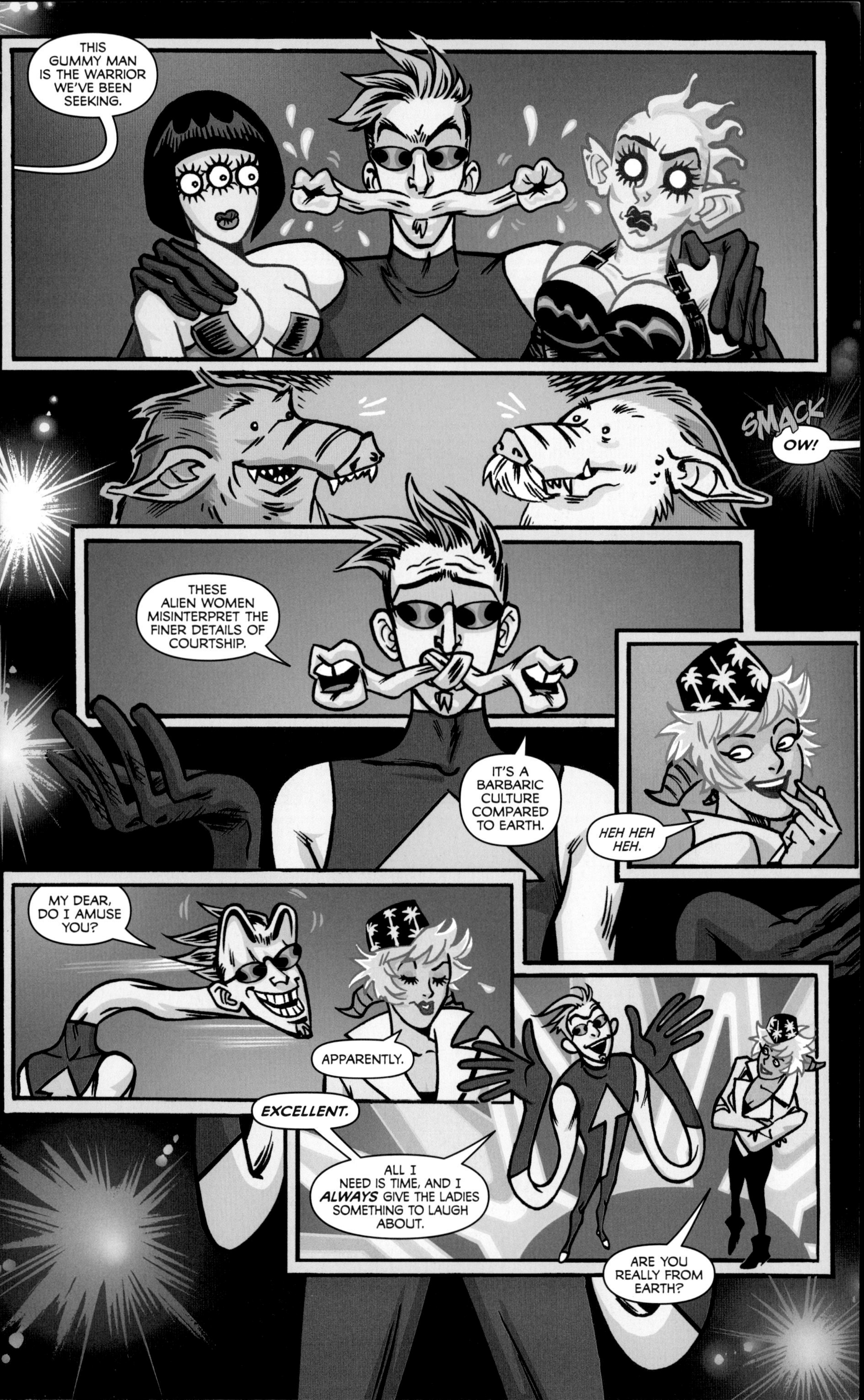
THIS GUMMY MAN IS THE WARRIOR WE'VE BEEN SEEKING.
SMACK
OW!
THESE ALIEN WOMEN MISINTERPRET THE FINER DETAILS OF COURTSHIP.
IT'S A BARBARIC CULTURE COMPARED TO EARTH.
HEH HEH HEH.
MY DEAR, DO I AMUSE YOU?
APPARENTLY.
EXCELLENT.
ALL I NEED IS TIME, AND I ALWAYS GIVE THE LADIES SOMETHING TO LAUGH ABOUT.
ARE YOU REALLY FROM EARTH?

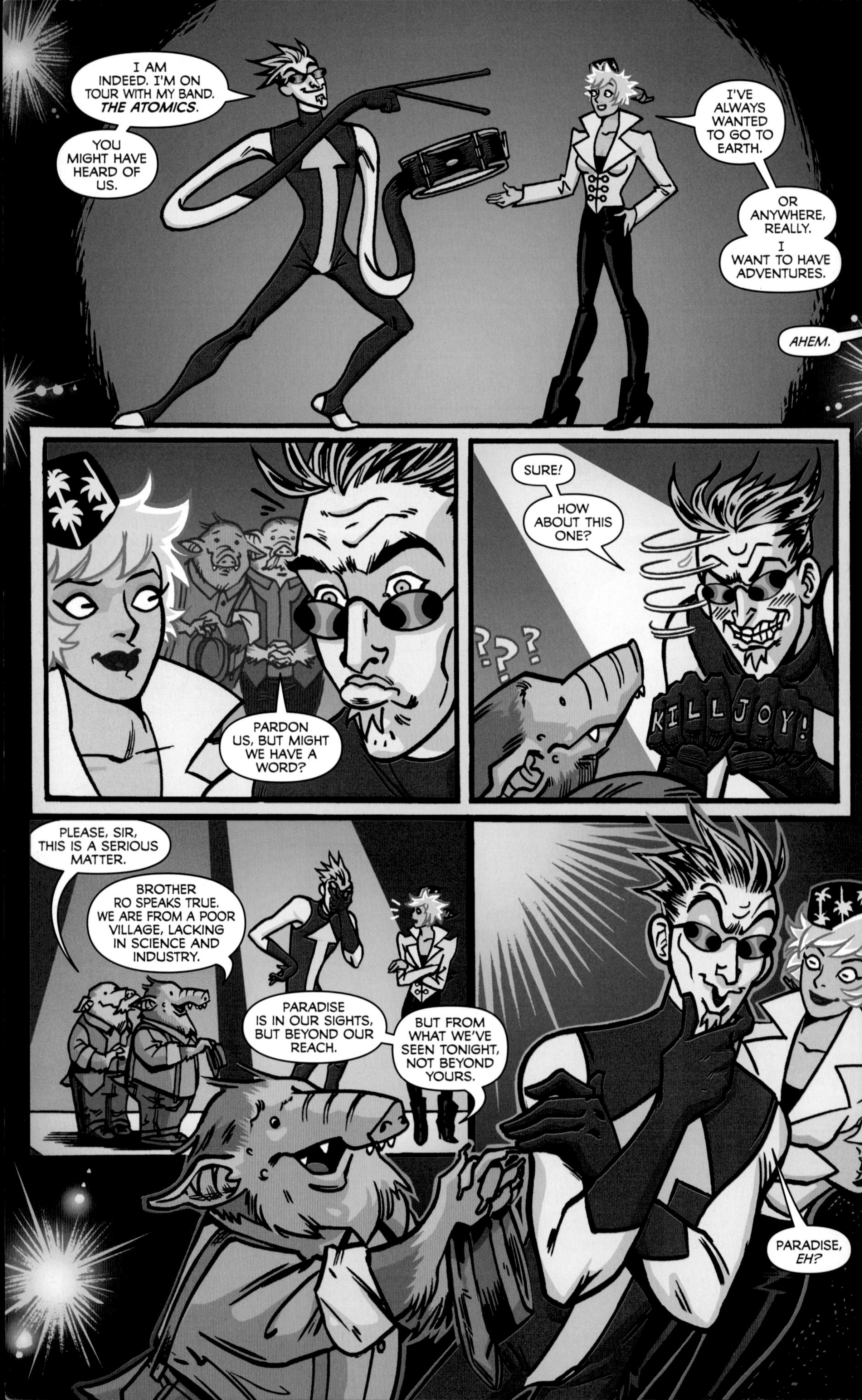

I AM INDEED. I'M ON TOUR WITH MY BAND. *THE ATOMICS*.
YOU MIGHT HAVE HEARD OF US.
I'VE ALWAYS WANTED TO GO TO EARTH.
OR ANYWHERE, REALLY.
I WANT TO HAVE ADVENTURES.
AHEM.
PARDON US, BUT MIGHT WE HAVE A WORD?
SURE!
HOW ABOUT THIS ONE?
KILLJOY!
PLEASE, SIR, THIS IS A SERIOUS MATTER.
BROTHER RO SPEAKS TRUE. WE ARE FROM A POOR VILLAGE, LACKING IN SCIENCE AND INDUSTRY.
PARADISE IS IN OUR SIGHTS, BUT BEYOND OUR REACH.
BUT FROM WHAT WE'VE SEEN TONIGHT, NOT BEYOND YOURS.
PARADISE, *EH?*

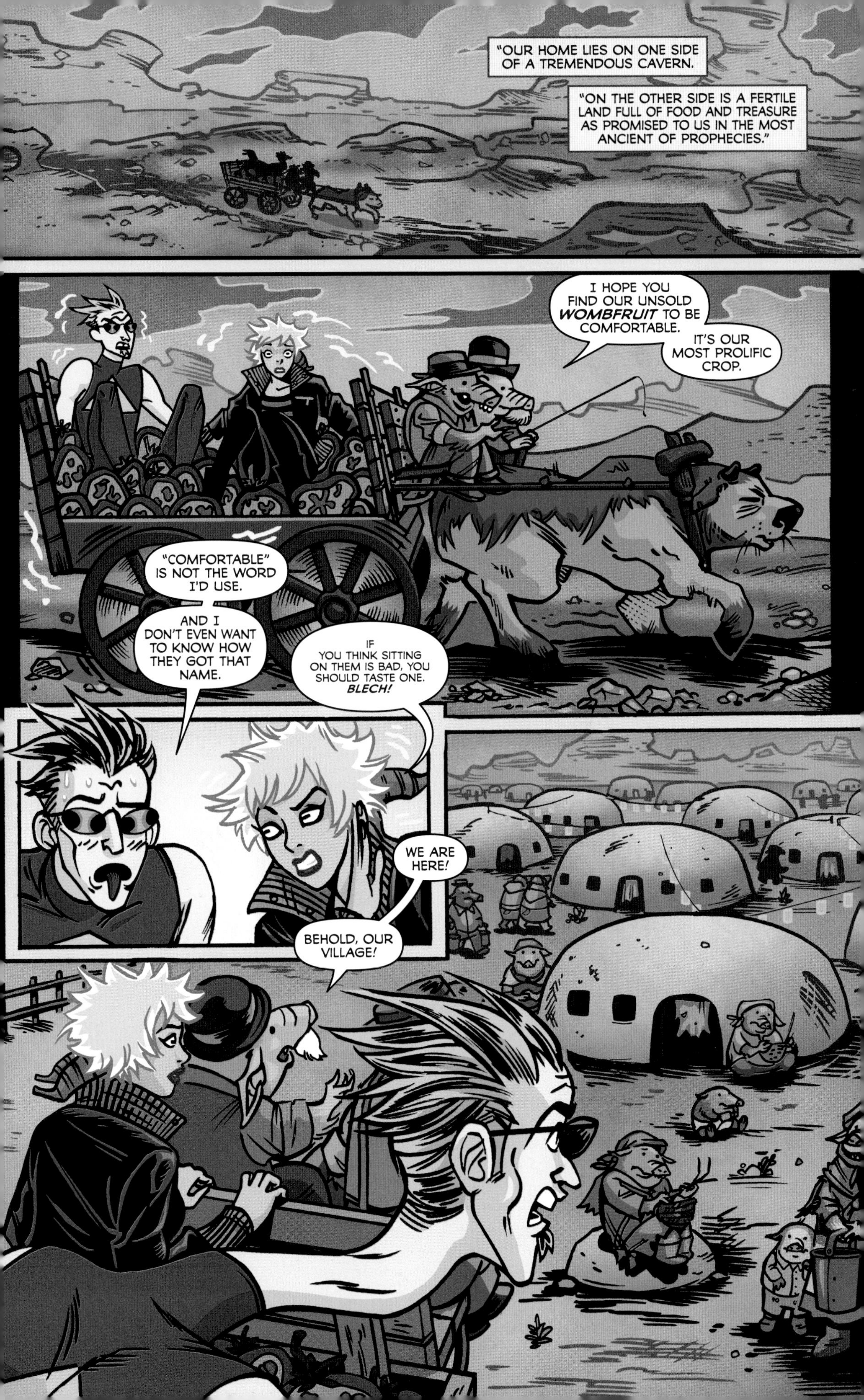
"OUR HOME LIES ON ONE SIDE OF A TREMENDOUS CAVERN.
"ON THE OTHER SIDE IS A FERTILE LAND FULL OF FOOD AND TREASURE AS PROMISED TO US IN THE MOST ANCIENT OF PROPHECIES."
I HOPE YOU FIND OUR UNSOLD WOMBFRUIT TO BE COMFORTABLE.
IT'S OUR MOST PROLIFIC CROP.
"COMFORTABLE" IS NOT THE WORD I'D USE.
AND I DON'T EVEN WANT TO KNOW HOW THEY GOT THAT NAME.
IF YOU THINK SITTING ON THEM IS BAD, YOU SHOULD TASTE ONE. BLECH!
WE ARE HERE!
BEHOLD, OUR VILLAGE!

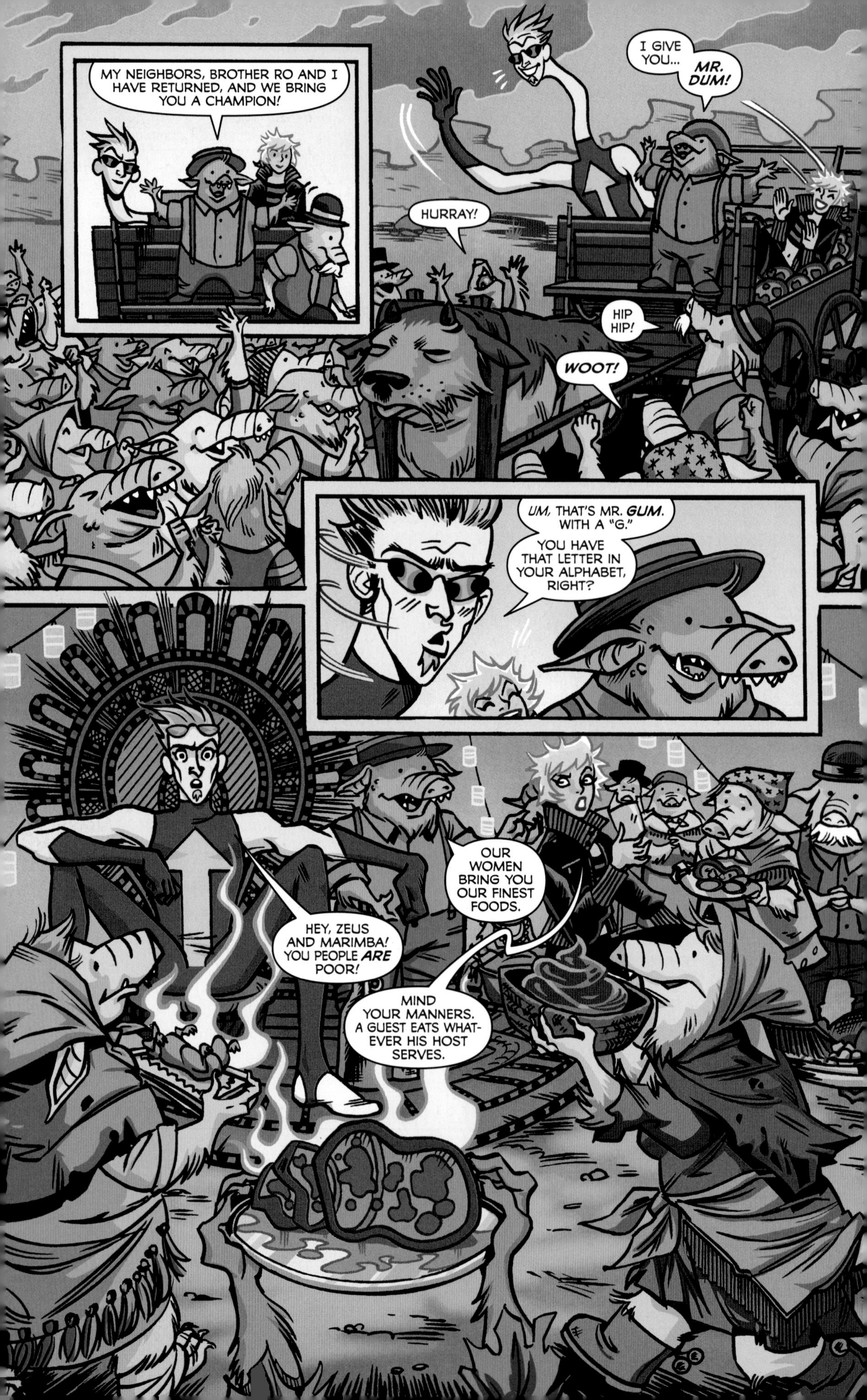
MY NEIGHBORS, BROTHER RO AND I HAVE RETURNED, AND WE BRING YOU A CHAMPION!
I GIVE YOU... MR. DUM!
HURRAY!
HIP HIP!
WOOT!
UM, THAT'S MR. GUM. WITH A "G."
YOU HAVE THAT LETTER IN YOUR ALPHABET, RIGHT?
HEY, ZEUS AND MARIMBA! YOU PEOPLE ARE POOR!
OUR WOMEN BRING YOU OUR FINEST FOODS.
MIND YOUR MANNERS. A GUEST EATS WHATEVER HIS HOST SERVES.

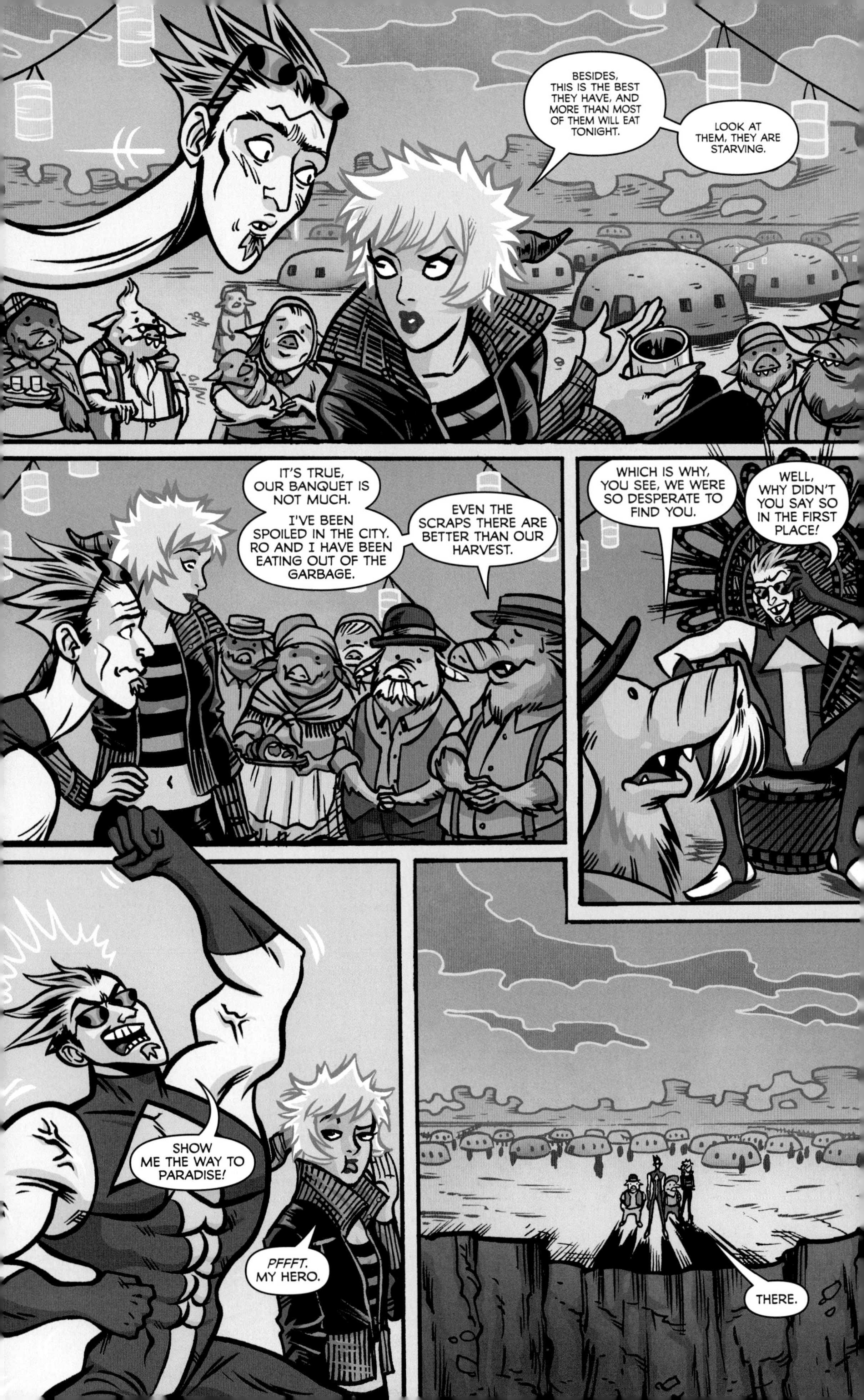
BESIDES, THIS IS THE BEST THEY HAVE, AND MORE THAN MOST OF THEM WILL EAT TONIGHT.
LOOK AT THEM, THEY ARE STARVING.
IT'S TRUE, OUR BANQUET IS NOT MUCH.
I'VE BEEN SPOILED IN THE CITY. RO AND I HAVE BEEN EATING OUT OF THE GARBAGE.
EVEN THE SCRAPS THERE ARE BETTER THAN OUR HARVEST.
WHICH IS WHY, YOU SEE, WE WERE SO DESPERATE TO FIND YOU.
WELL, WHY DIDN'T YOU SAY SO IN THE FIRST PLACE!
SHOW ME THE WAY TO PARADISE!
PFFFT. MY HERO.
THERE.

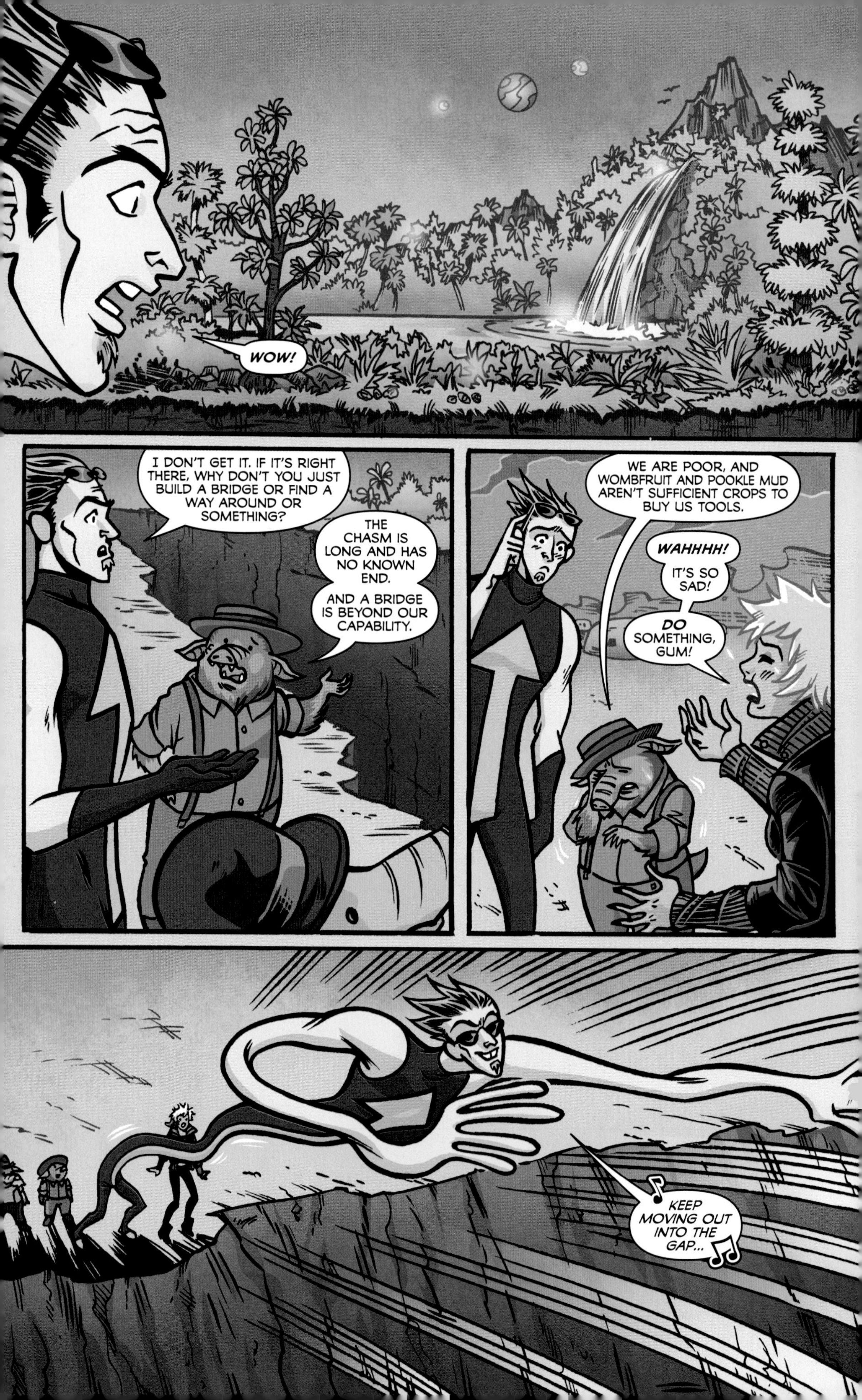
WOW!
I DON'T GET IT. IF IT'S RIGHT THERE, WHY DON'T YOU JUST BUILD A BRIDGE OR FIND A WAY AROUND OR SOMETHING?
THE CHASM IS LONG AND HAS NO KNOWN END.
AND A BRIDGE IS BEYOND OUR CAPABILITY.
WE ARE POOR, AND WOMBFRUIT AND POOKLE MUD AREN'T SUFFICIENT CROPS TO BUY US TOOLS.
WAHHHH!
IT'S SO SAD!
DO SOMETHING, GUM!
KEEP MOVING OUT INTO THE GAP...

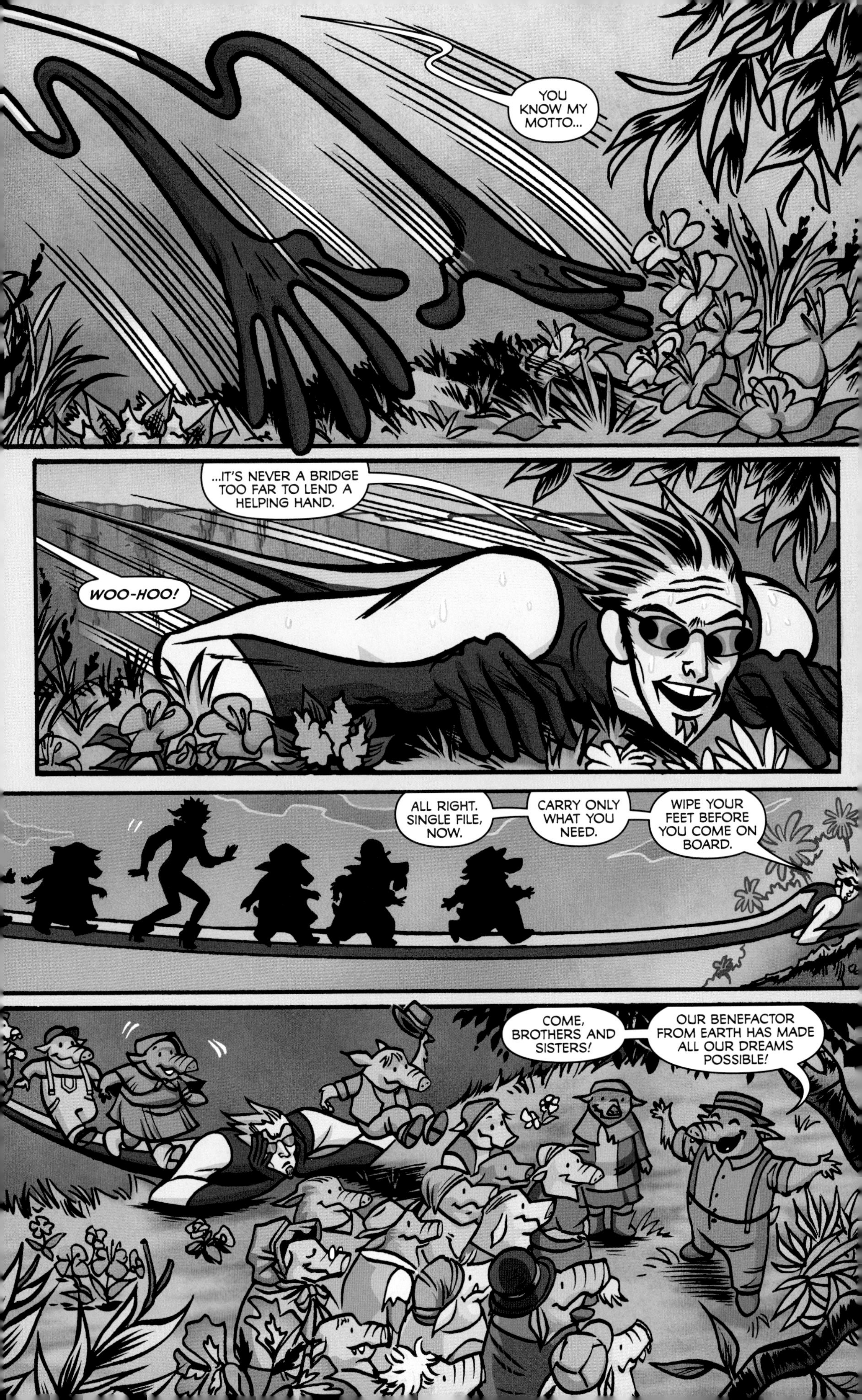
YOU KNOW MY MOTTO...
...IT'S NEVER A BRIDGE TOO FAR TO LEND A HELPING HAND.
WOO-HOO!
ALL RIGHT. SINGLE FILE, NOW.
CARRY ONLY WHAT YOU NEED.
WIPE YOUR FEET BEFORE YOU COME ON BOARD.
COME, BROTHERS AND SISTERS!
OUR BENEFACTOR FROM EARTH HAS MADE ALL OUR DREAMS POSSIBLE!

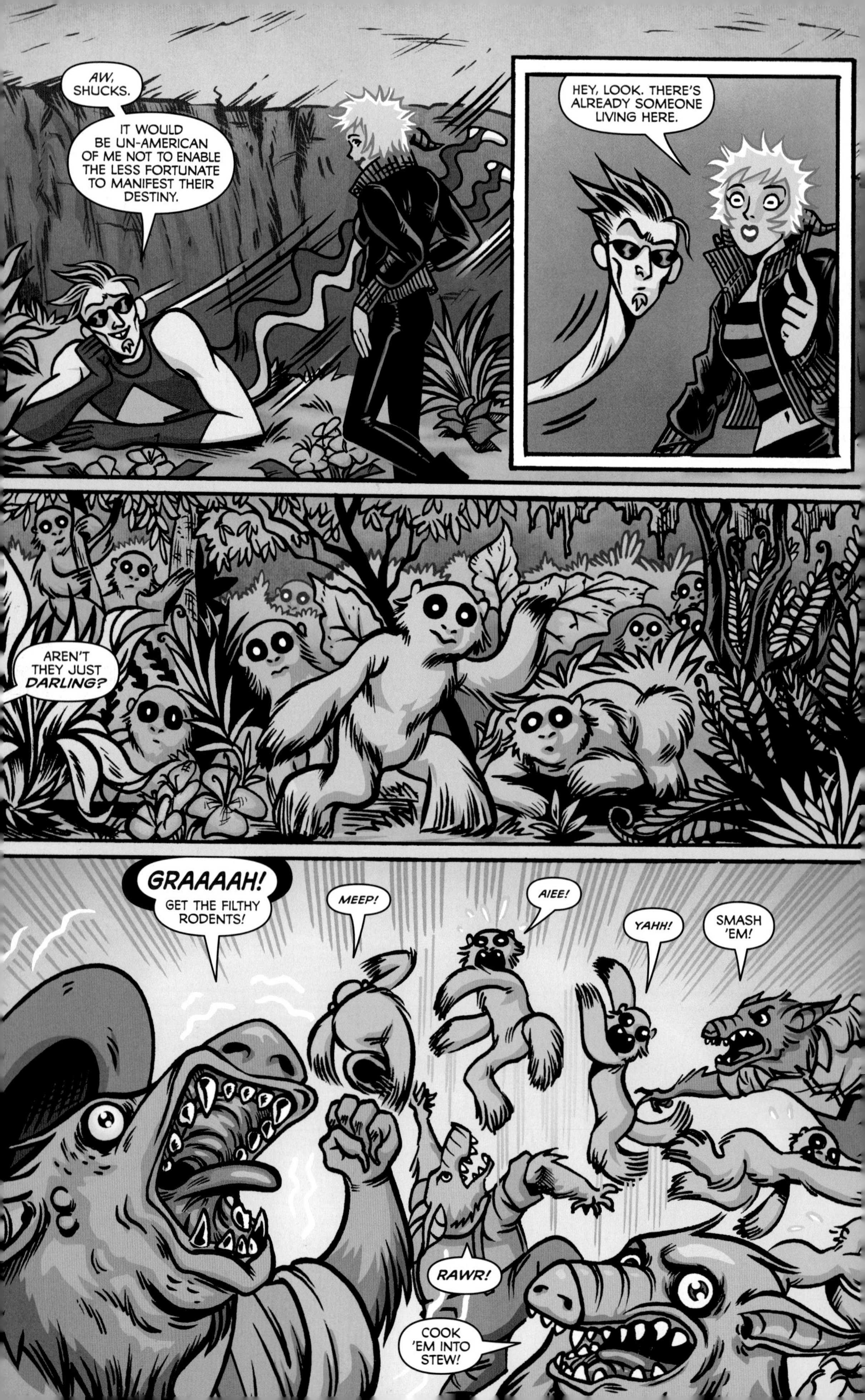
AW, SHUCKS.
IT WOULD BE UN-AMERICAN OF ME NOT TO ENABLE THE LESS FORTUNATE TO MANIFEST THEIR DESTINY.
HEY, LOOK. THERE'S ALREADY SOMEONE LIVING HERE.
AREN'T THEY JUST DARLING?
GRAAAAH! GET THE FILTHY RODENTS!
MEEP!
AIEE!
YAHH!
SMASH 'EM!
RAWR!
COOK 'EM INTO STEW!

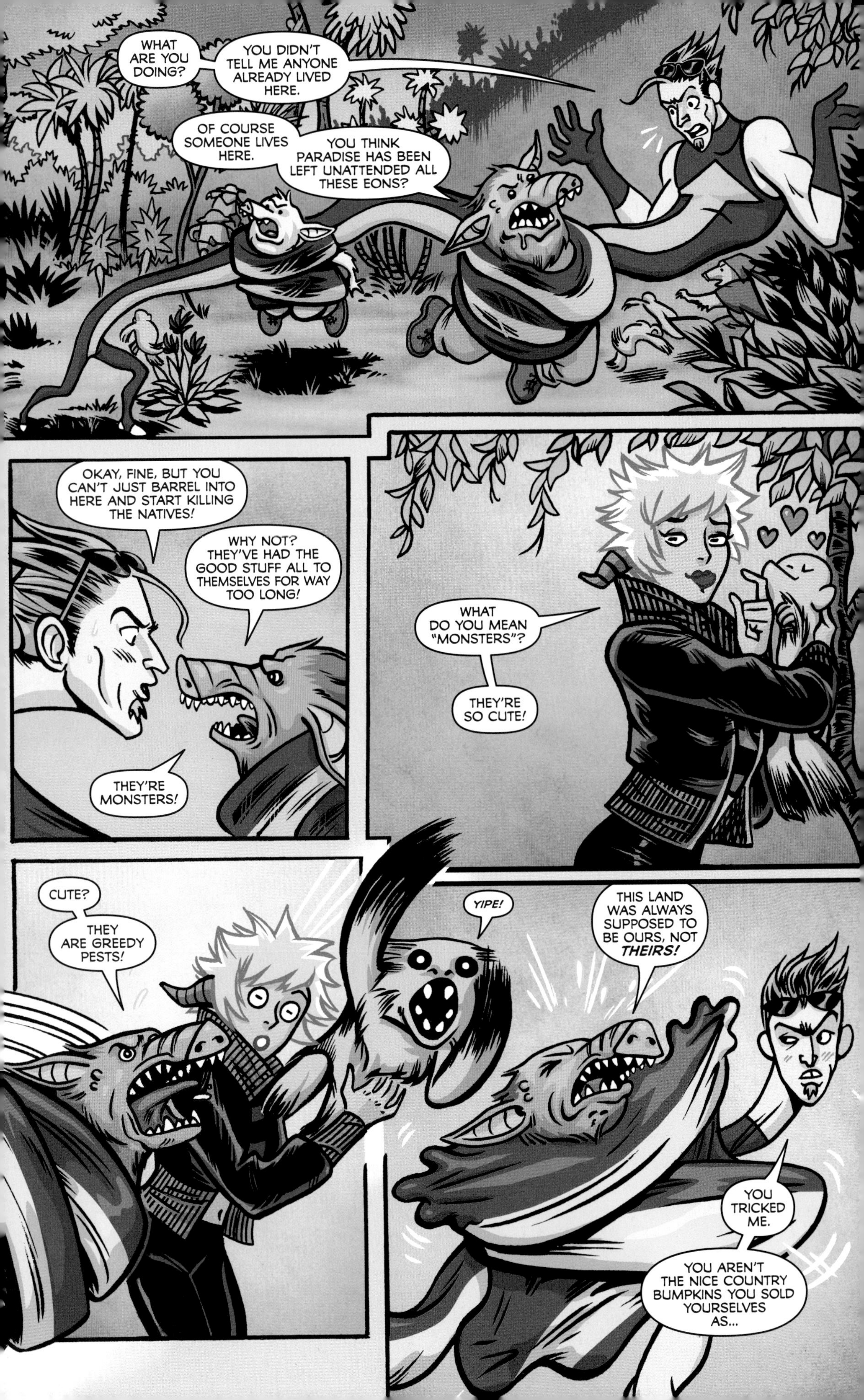
WHAT ARE YOU DOING?
YOU DIDN'T TELL ME ANYONE ALREADY LIVED HERE.
OF COURSE SOMEONE LIVES HERE.
YOU THINK PARADISE HAS BEEN LEFT UNATTENDED ALL THESE EONS?
OKAY, FINE, BUT YOU CAN'T JUST BARREL INTO HERE AND START KILLING THE NATIVES!
WHY NOT? THEY'VE HAD THE GOOD STUFF ALL TO THEMSELVES FOR WAY TOO LONG!
THEY'RE MONSTERS!
WHAT DO YOU MEAN "MONSTERS"?
THEY'RE SO CUTE!
CUTE?
THEY ARE GREEDY PESTS!
YIPE!
THIS LAND WAS ALWAYS SUPPOSED TO BE OURS, NOT ***THEIRS!***
YOU TRICKED ME.
YOU AREN'T THE NICE COUNTRY BUMPKINS YOU SOLD YOURSELVES AS...

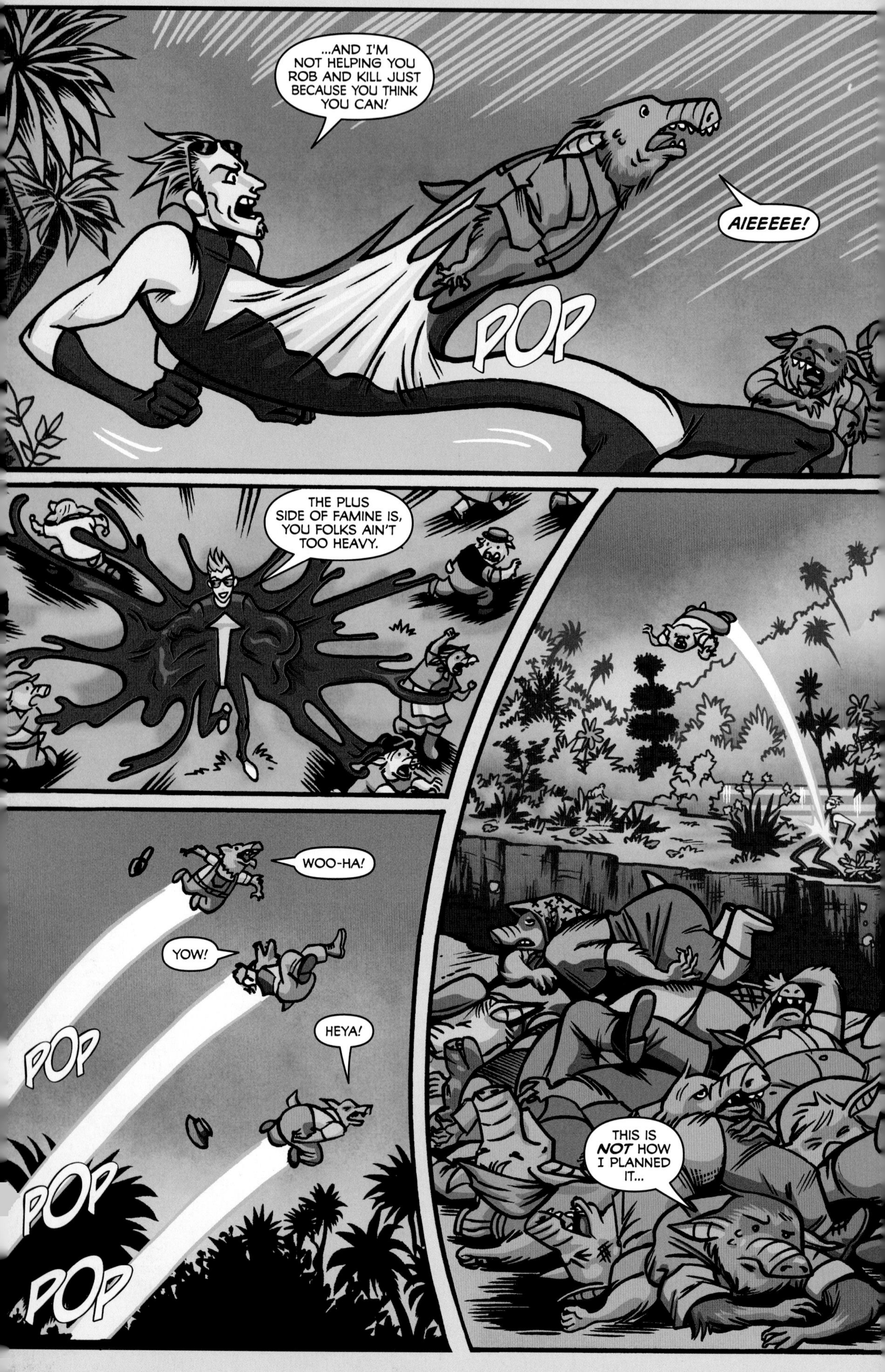
...AND I'M NOT HELPING YOU ROB AND KILL JUST BECAUSE YOU THINK YOU CAN!
AIEEEEE!
POP
THE PLUS SIDE OF FAMINE IS, YOU FOLKS AIN'T TOO HEAVY.
WOO-HA!
YOW!
HEYA!
POP
POP
POP
THIS IS *NOT* HOW I PLANNED IT...

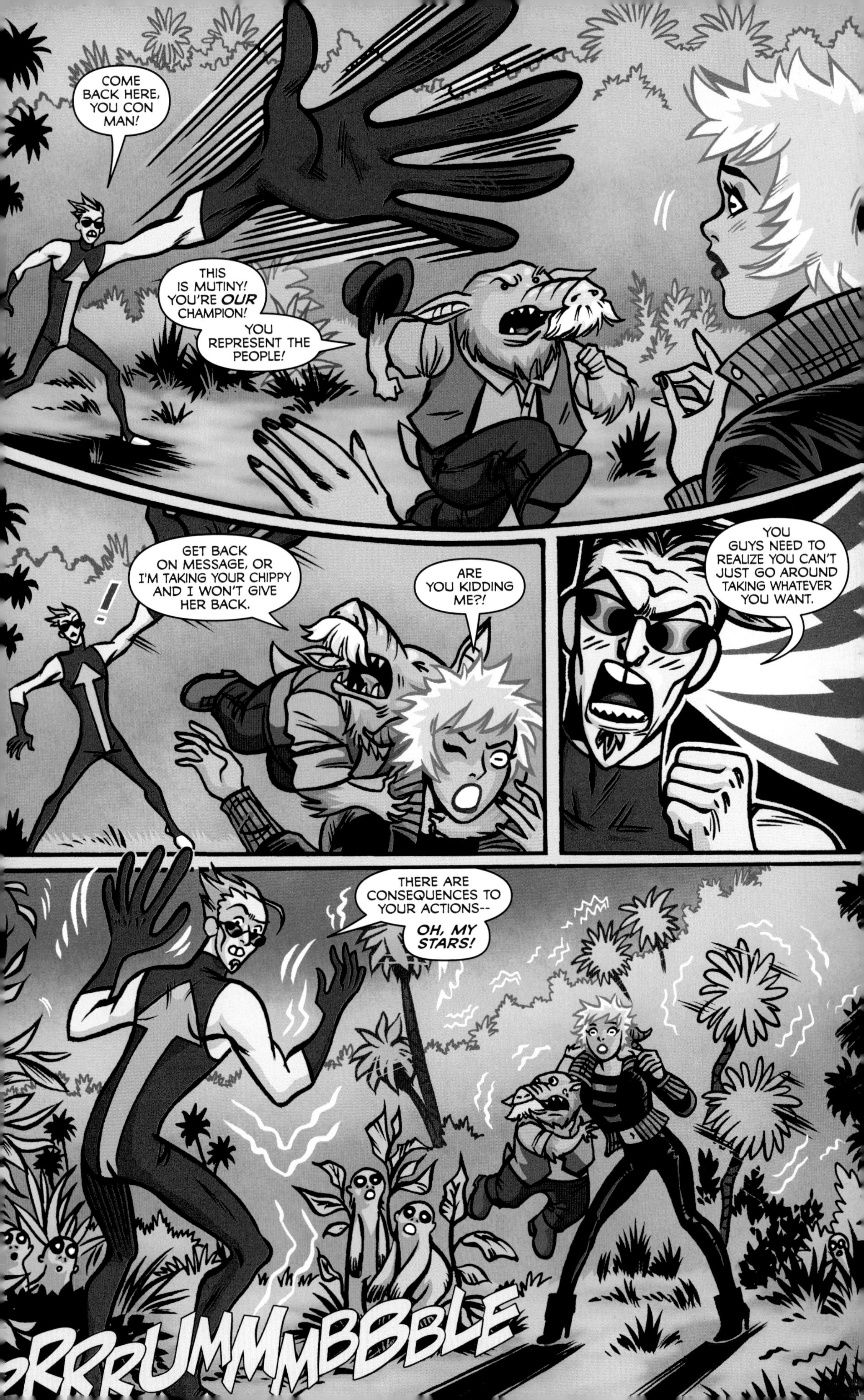
COME BACK HERE, YOU CON MAN!
THIS IS MUTINY! YOU'RE *OUR* CHAMPION!
YOU REPRESENT THE PEOPLE!
GET BACK ON MESSAGE, OR I'M TAKING YOUR CHIPPY AND I WON'T GIVE HER BACK.
!
ARE YOU KIDDING ME?!
YOU GUYS NEED TO REALIZE YOU CAN'T JUST GO AROUND TAKING WHATEVER YOU WANT.
THERE ARE CONSEQUENCES TO YOUR ACTIONS--
OH, MY STARS!
RRRUMMMMBBBBLE

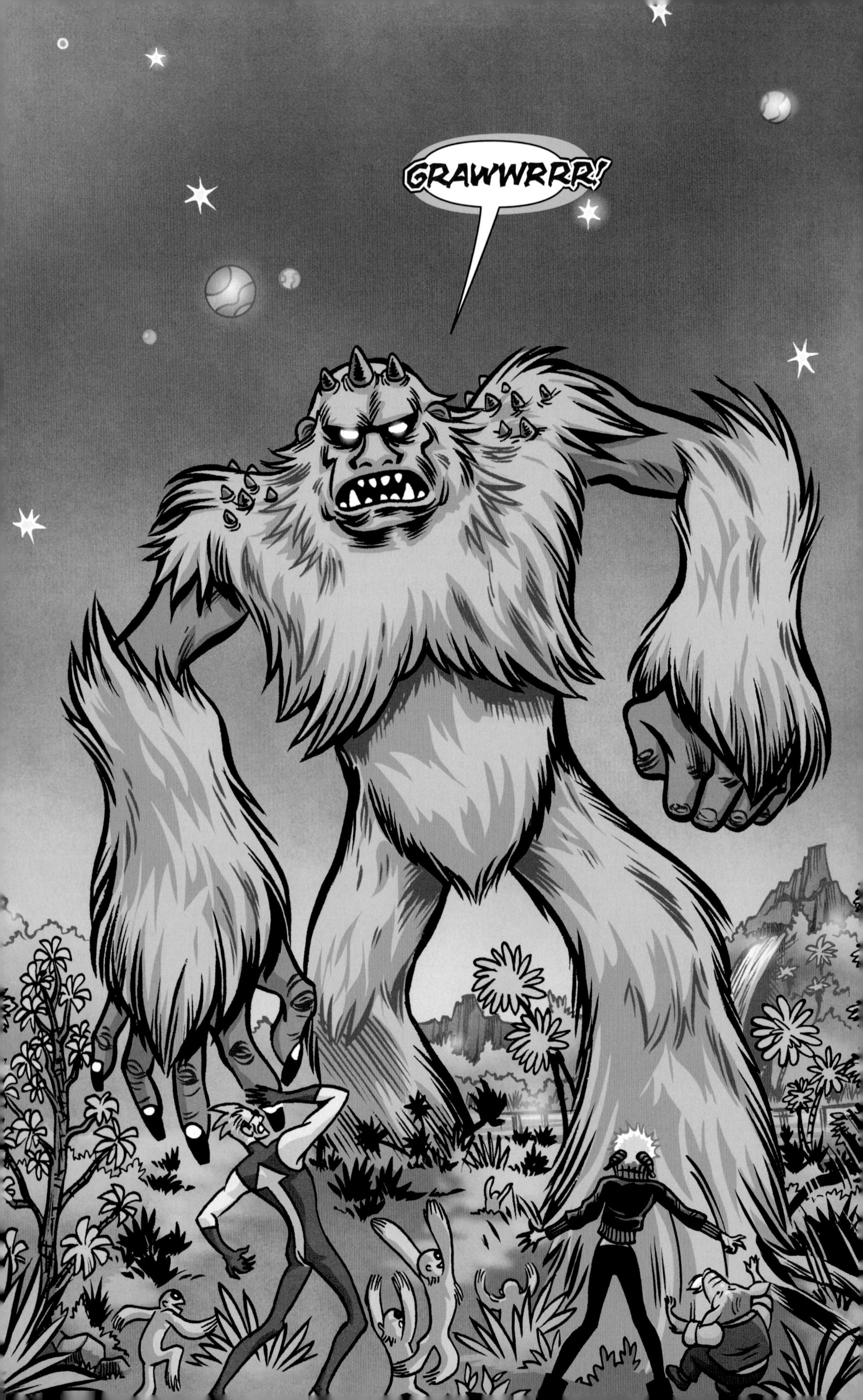
GRAWWRRR!

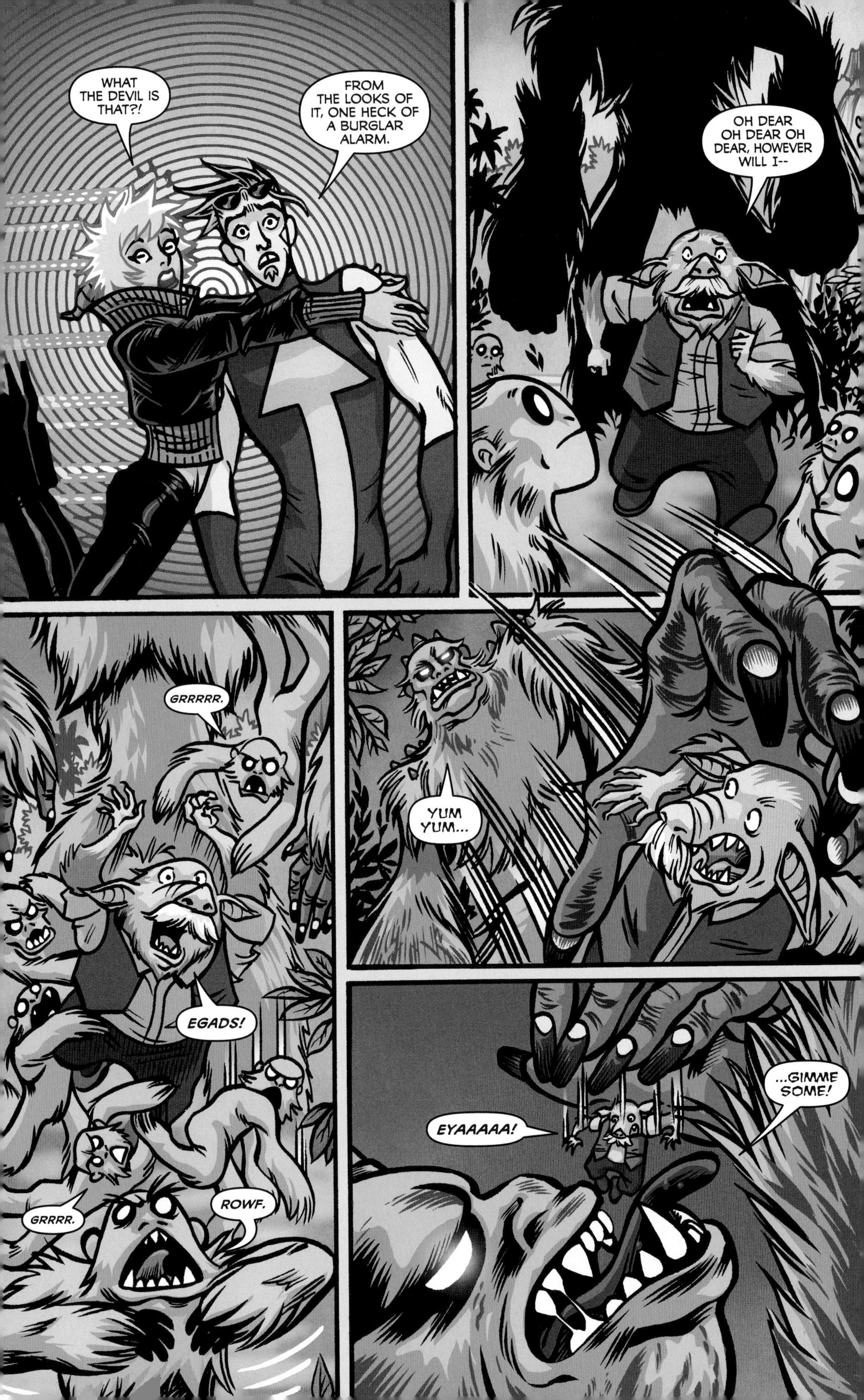
WHAT THE DEVIL IS THAT?!
FROM THE LOOKS OF IT, ONE HECK OF A BURGLAR ALARM.
OH DEAR OH DEAR OH DEAR, HOWEVER WILL I--
GRRRRR.
EGADS!
GRRRR.
ROWF.
YUM YUM...
EYAAAAA!
...GIMME SOME!

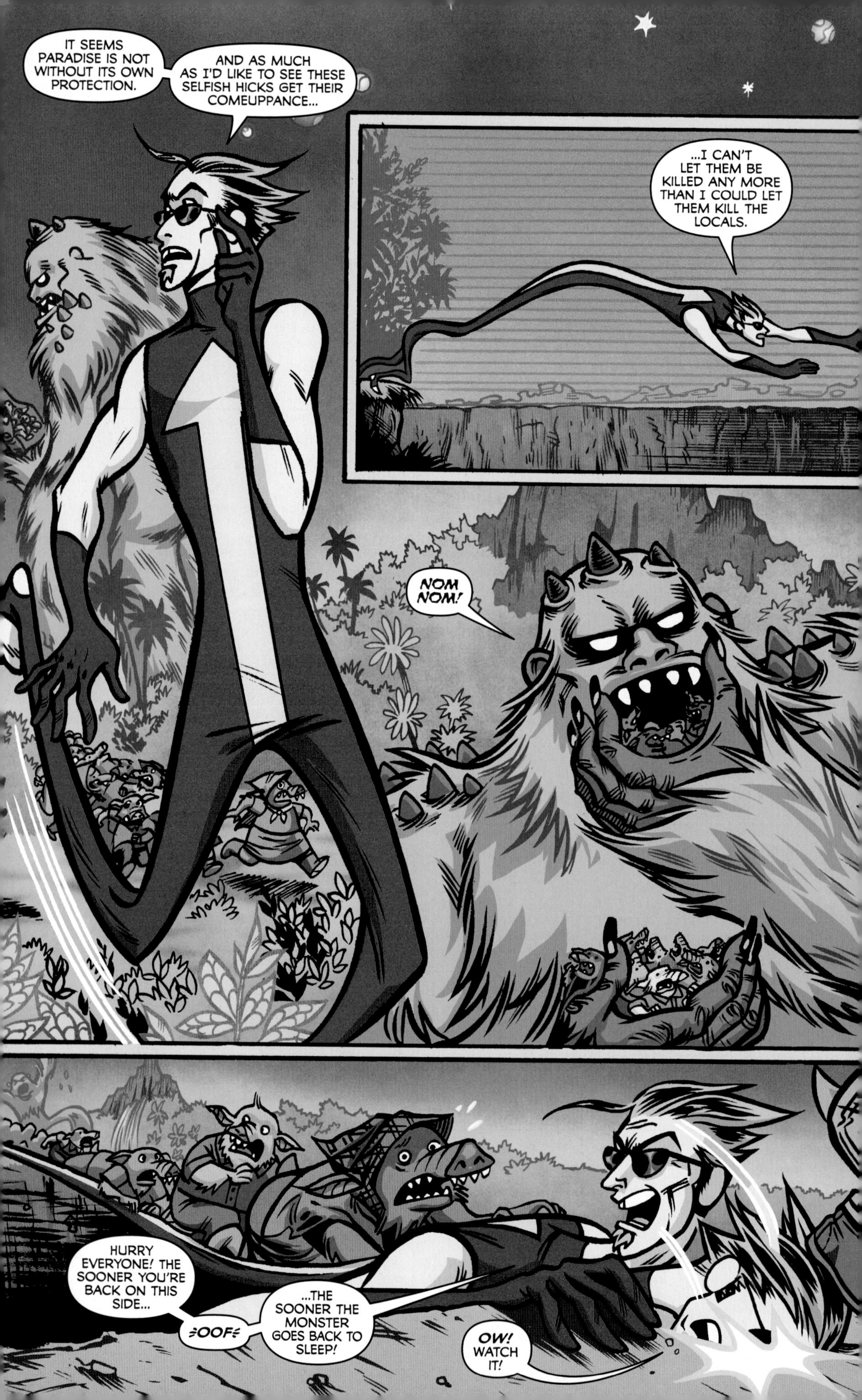
IT SEEMS PARADISE IS NOT WITHOUT ITS OWN PROTECTION.
AND AS MUCH AS I'D LIKE TO SEE THESE SELFISH HICKS GET THEIR COMEUPPANCE...
...I CAN'T LET THEM BE KILLED ANY MORE THAN I COULD LET THEM KILL THE LOCALS.
NOM NOM!
HURRY EVERYONE! THE SOONER YOU'RE BACK ON THIS SIDE...
OOF
...THE SOONER THE MONSTER GOES BACK TO SLEEP!
OW! WATCH IT!

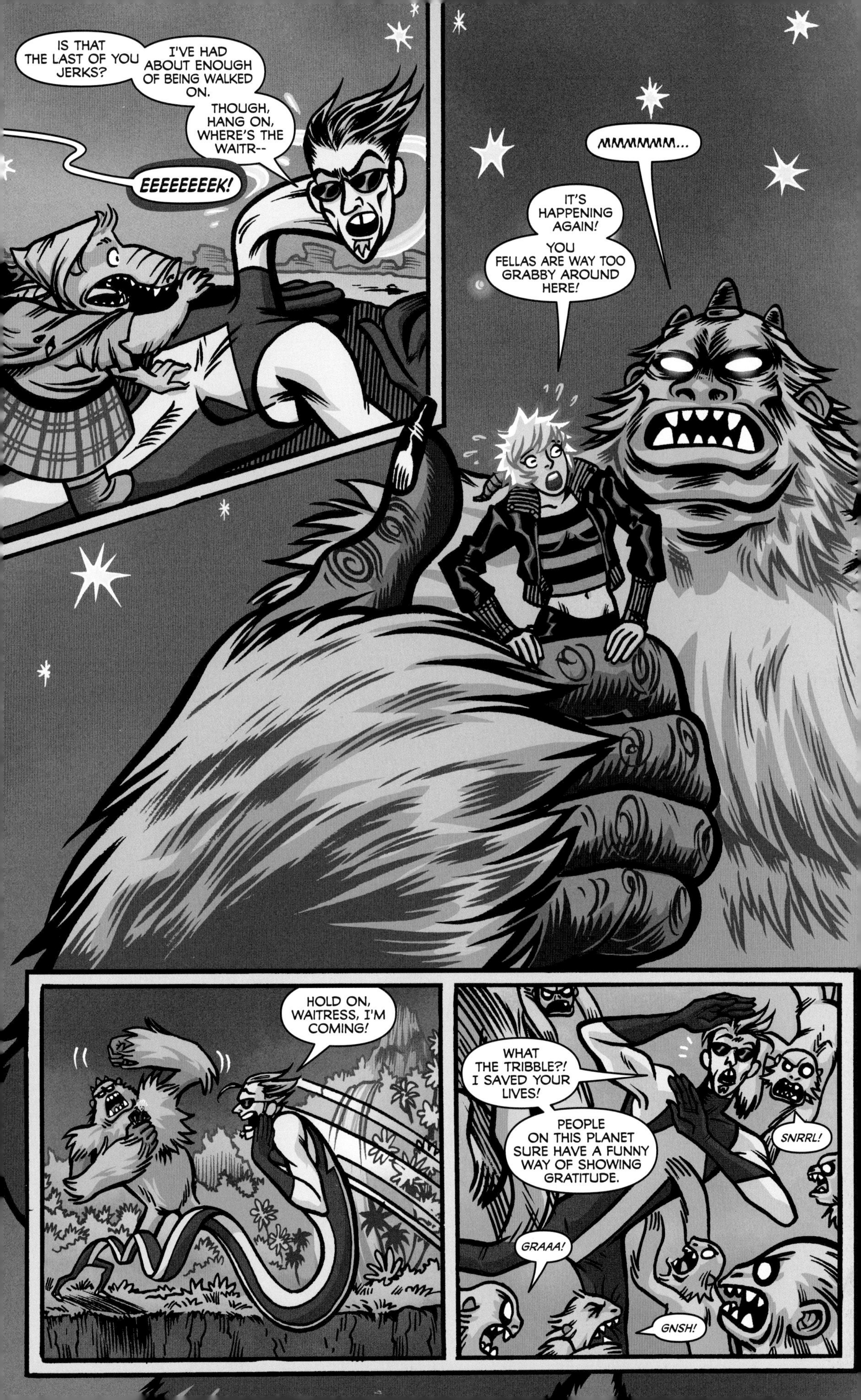
IS THAT THE LAST OF YOU JERKS?
I'VE HAD ABOUT ENOUGH OF BEING WALKED ON.
THOUGH, HANG ON, WHERE'S THE WAITR--
EEEEEEEEK!
MMMMMMM...
IT'S HAPPENING AGAIN!
YOU FELLAS ARE WAY TOO GRABBY AROUND HERE!
HOLD ON, WAITRESS, I'M COMING!
WHAT THE TRIBBLE?! I SAVED YOUR LIVES!
PEOPLE ON THIS PLANET SURE HAVE A FUNNY WAY OF SHOWING GRATITUDE.
SNRRL!
GRAAA!
GNSH!

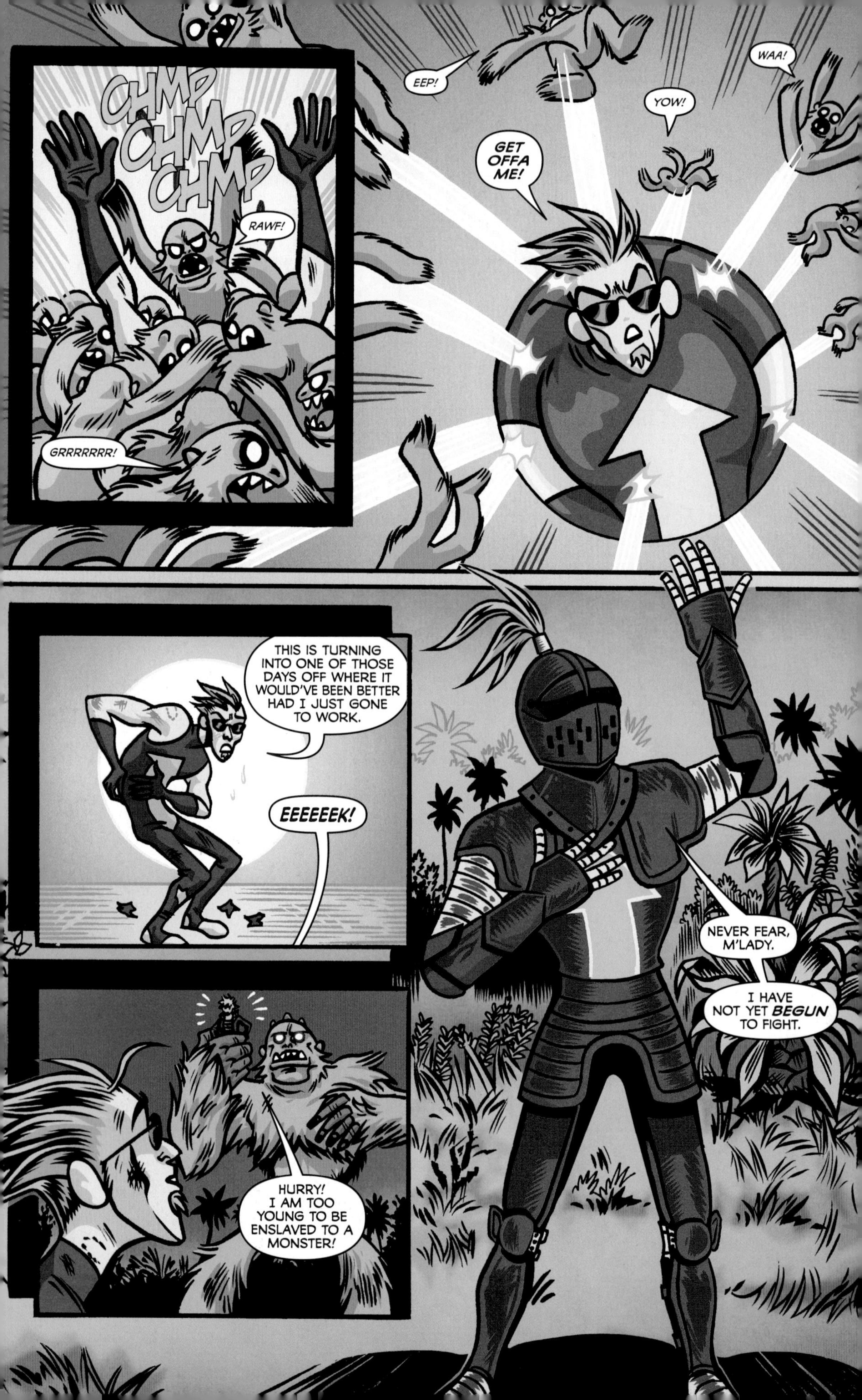
CHMP CHMP CHMP
RAWF!
GRRRRRRR!
EEP!
GET OFFA ME!
YOW!
WAA!
THIS IS TURNING INTO ONE OF THOSE DAYS OFF WHERE IT WOULD'VE BEEN BETTER HAD I JUST GONE TO WORK.
EEEEEEK!
HURRY! I AM TOO YOUNG TO BE ENSLAVED TO A MONSTER!
NEVER FEAR, M'LADY.
I HAVE NOT YET BEGUN TO FIGHT.

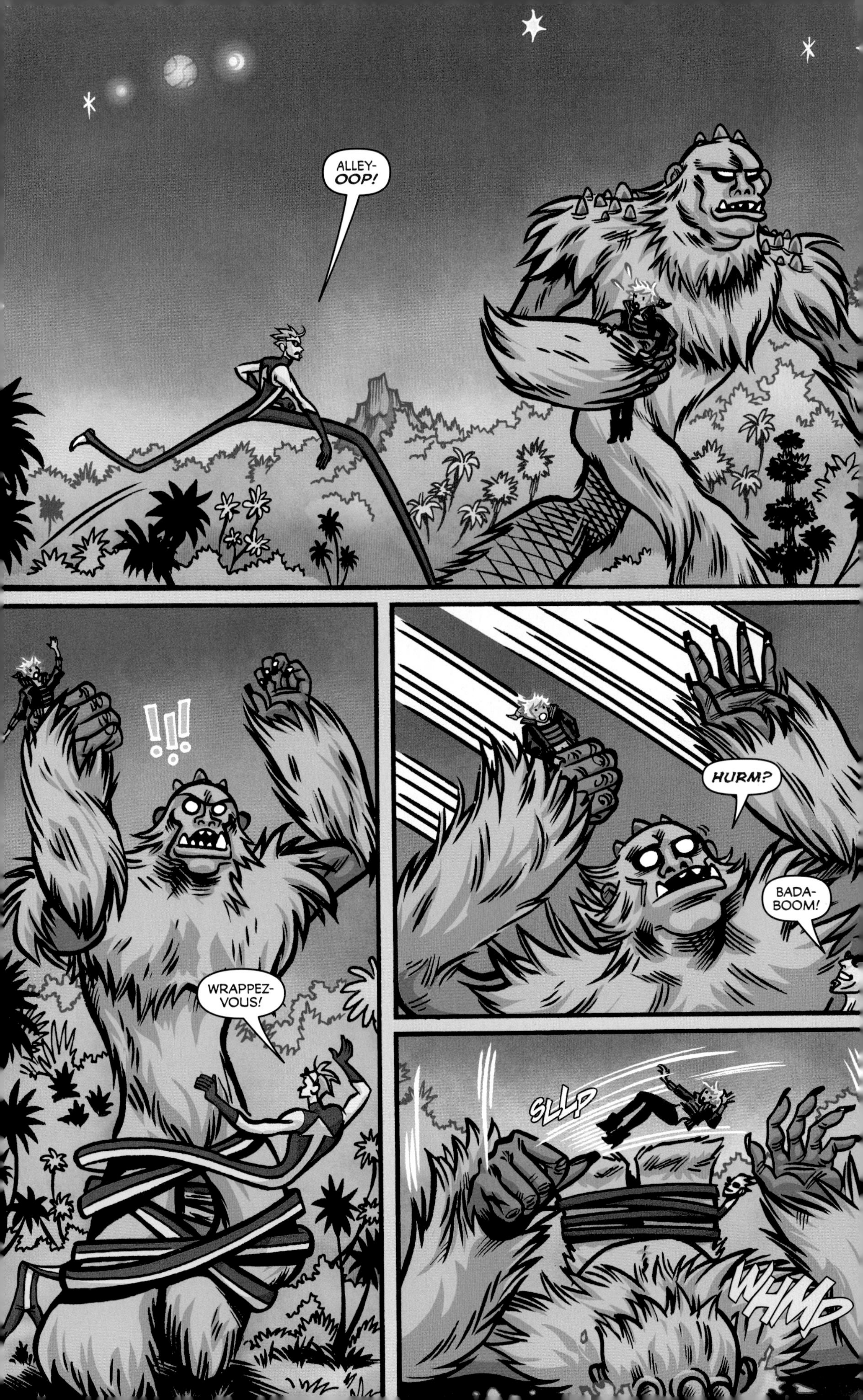
ALLEY-OOP!
!!!
WRAPPEZ-VOUS!
HURM?
BADA-BOOM!
SLLP
WHMP

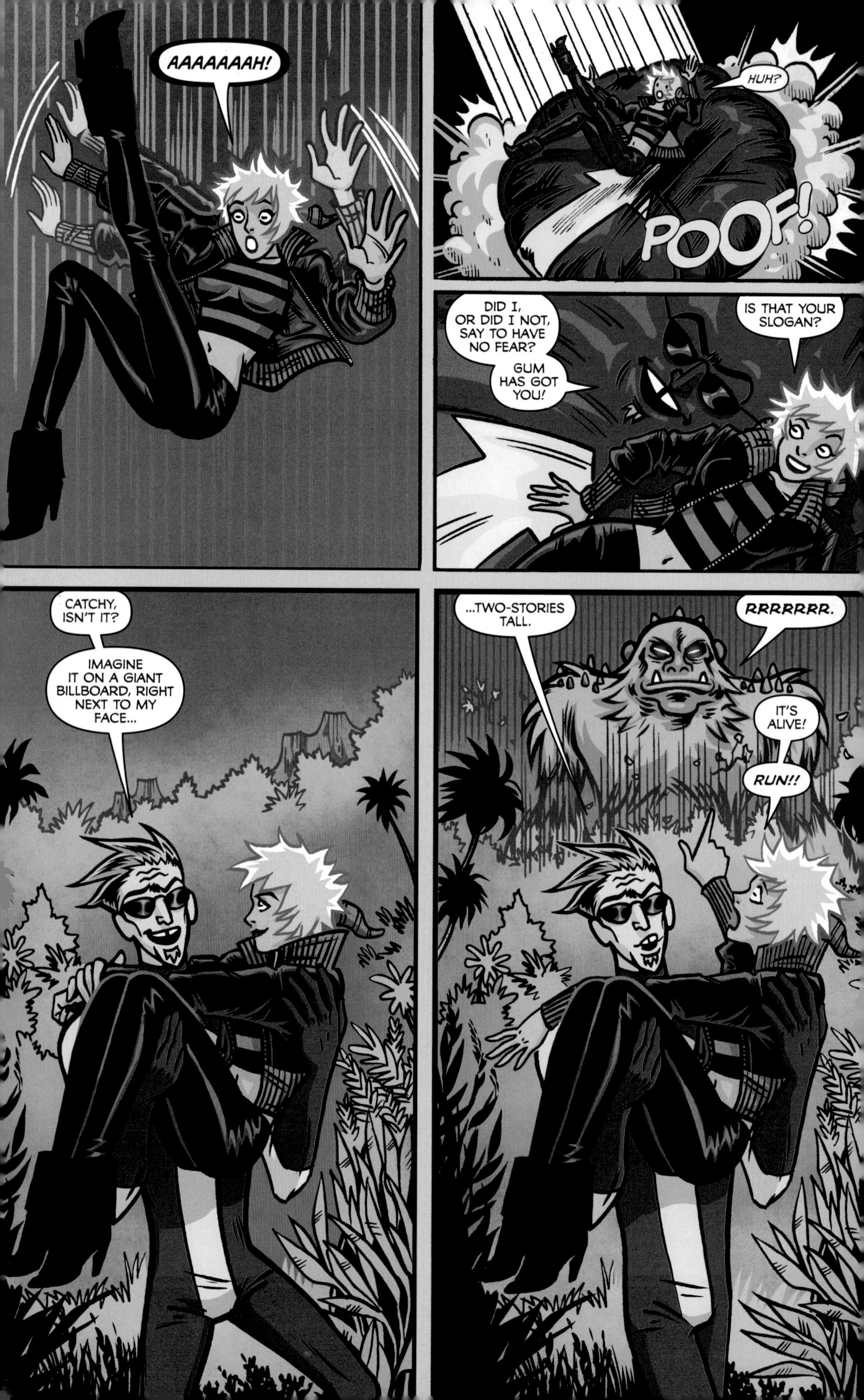
AAAAAAAH!
HUH?
POOF!
DID I, OR DID I NOT, SAY TO HAVE NO FEAR?
GUM HAS GOT YOU!
IS THAT YOUR SLOGAN?
CATCHY, ISN'T IT?
IMAGINE IT ON A GIANT BILLBOARD, RIGHT NEXT TO MY FACE...
...TWO-STORIES TALL.
RRRRRRR.
IT'S ALIVE!
RUN!!

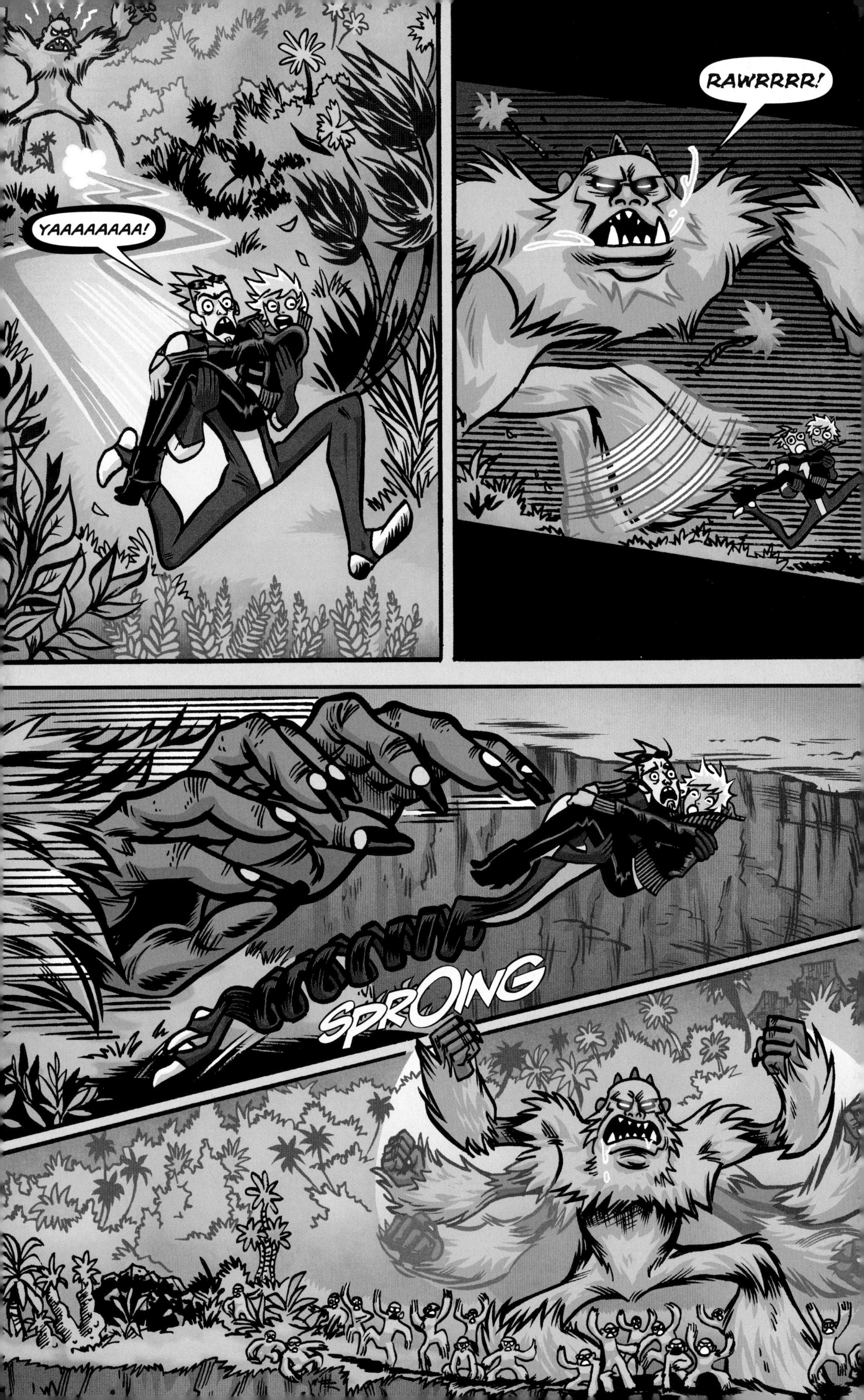
YAAAAAAAA!
RAWRRRR!
SPROING

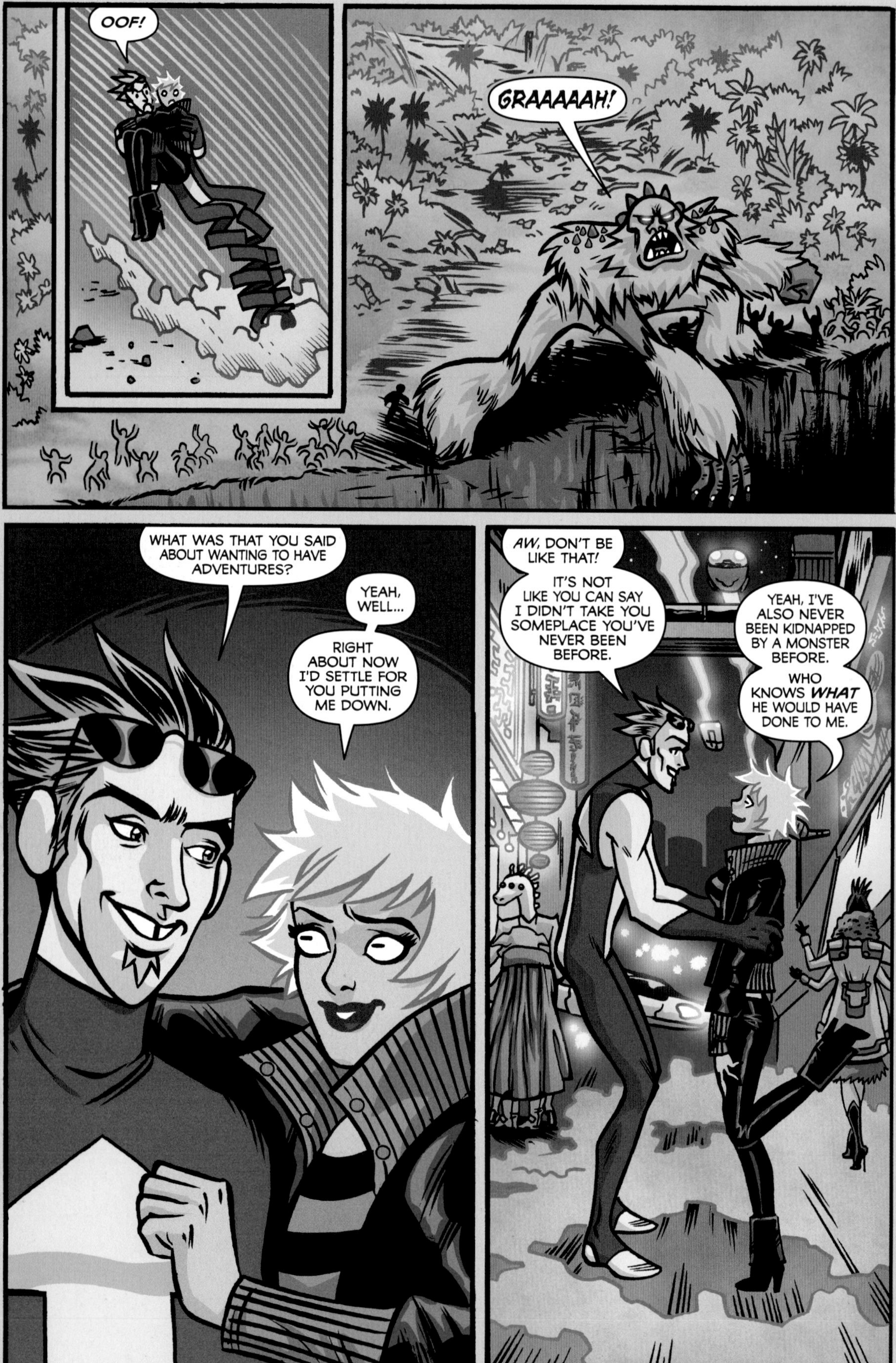
OOF!
GRAAAAAH!
WHAT WAS THAT YOU SAID ABOUT WANTING TO HAVE ADVENTURES?
YEAH, WELL...
RIGHT ABOUT NOW I'D SETTLE FOR YOU PUTTING ME DOWN.
AW, DON'T BE LIKE THAT!
IT'S NOT LIKE YOU CAN SAY I DIDN'T TAKE YOU SOMEPLACE YOU'VE NEVER BEEN BEFORE.
YEAH, I'VE ALSO NEVER BEEN KIDNAPPED BY A MONSTER BEFORE.
WHO KNOWS WHAT HE WOULD HAVE DONE TO ME.

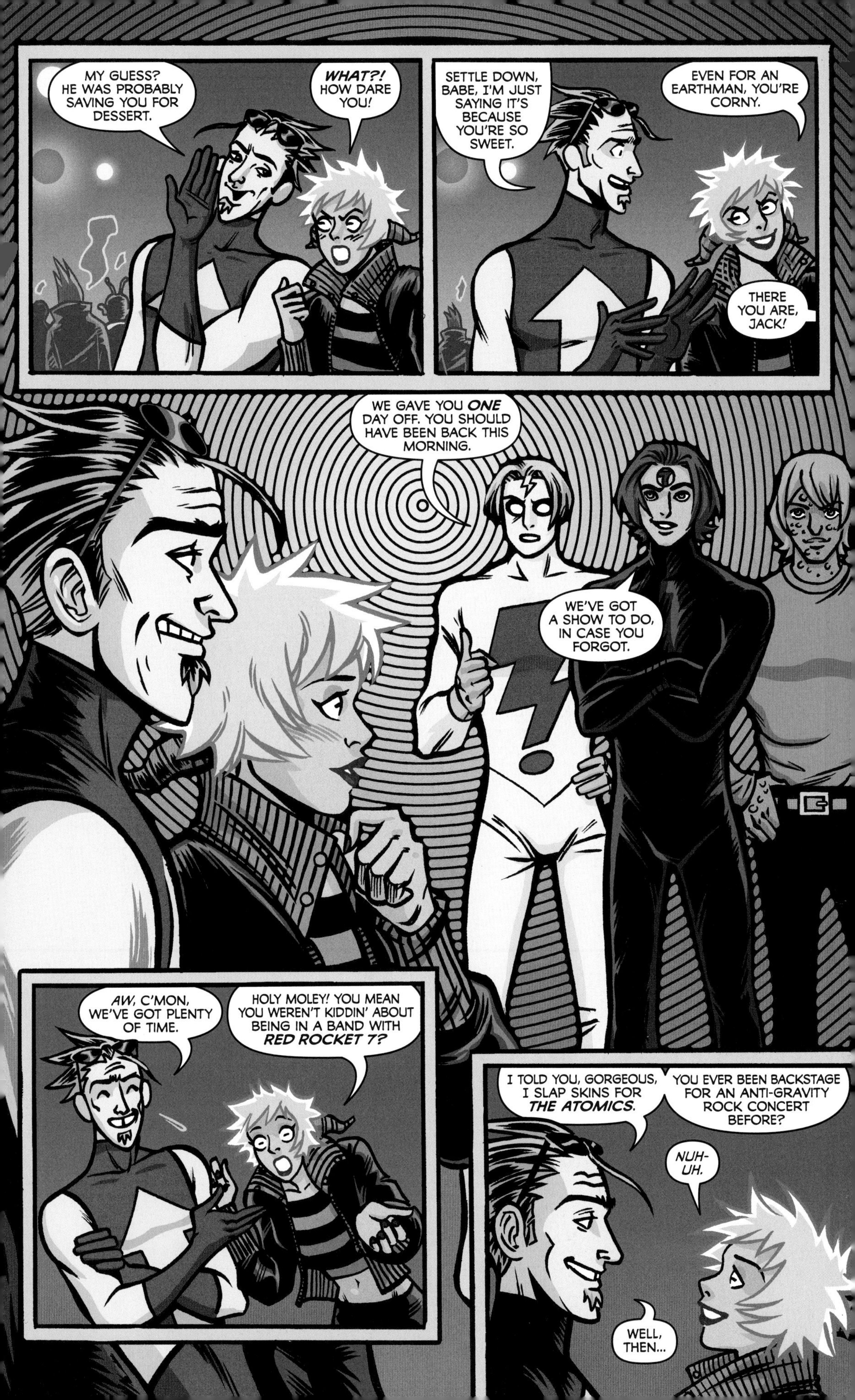
MY GUESS? HE WAS PROBABLY SAVING YOU FOR DESSERT.
WHAT?! HOW DARE YOU!
SETTLE DOWN, BABE, I'M JUST SAYING IT'S BECAUSE YOU'RE SO SWEET.
EVEN FOR AN EARTHMAN, YOU'RE CORNY.
THERE YOU ARE, JACK!
WE GAVE YOU ONE DAY OFF. YOU SHOULD HAVE BEEN BACK THIS MORNING.
WE'VE GOT A SHOW TO DO, IN CASE YOU FORGOT.
AW, C'MON, WE'VE GOT PLENTY OF TIME.
HOLY MOLEY! YOU MEAN YOU WEREN'T KIDDIN' ABOUT BEING IN A BAND WITH RED ROCKET 7?
I TOLD YOU, GORGEOUS, I SLAP SKINS FOR THE ATOMICS.
YOU EVER BEEN BACKSTAGE FOR AN ANTI-GRAVITY ROCK CONCERT BEFORE?
NUH-UH.
WELL, THEN...

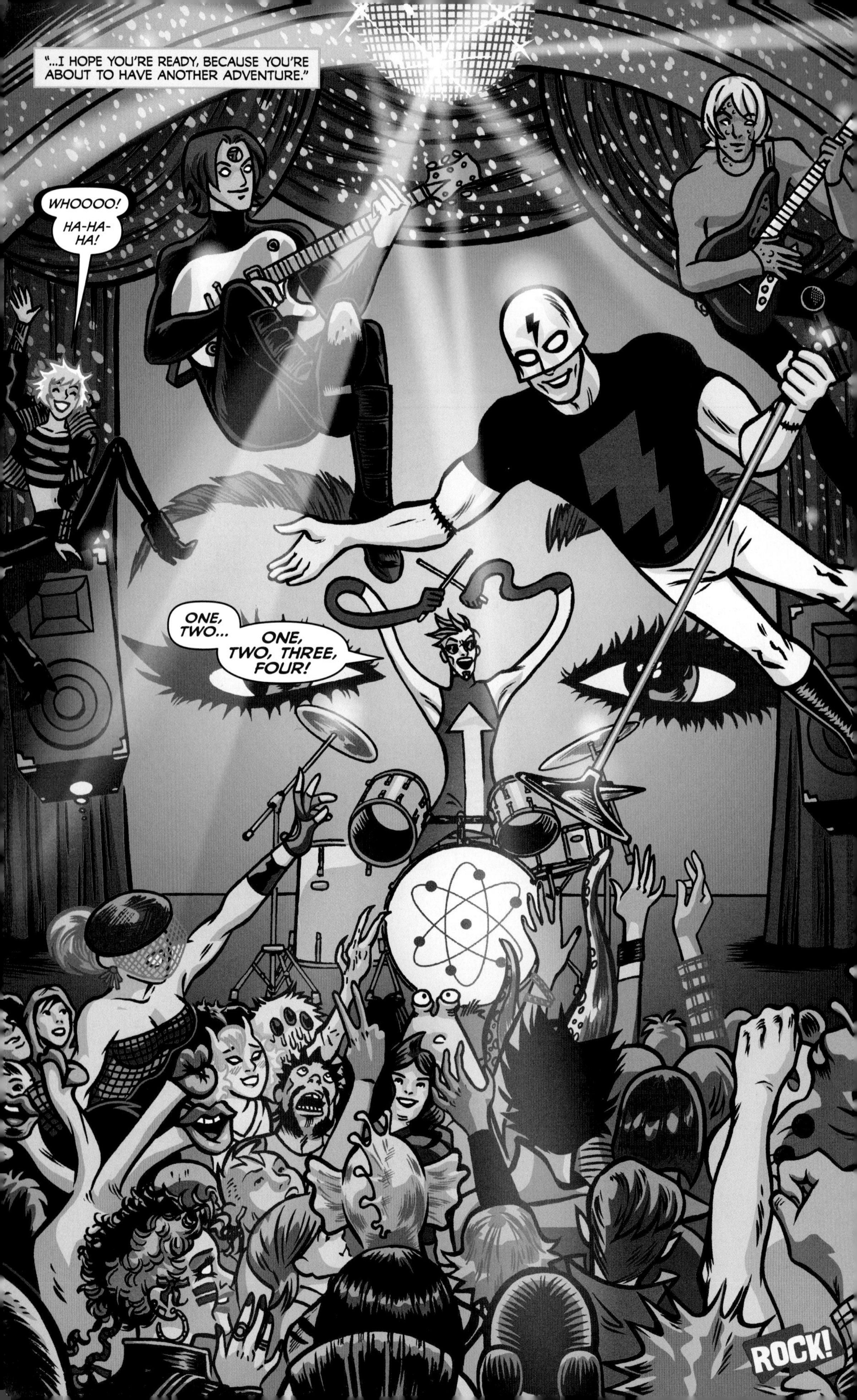
"...I HOPE YOU'RE READY, BECAUSE YOU'RE ABOUT TO HAVE ANOTHER ADVENTURE."
WHOOOO! HA-HA-HA!
ONE, TWO...
ONE, TWO, THREE, FOUR!
ROCK!

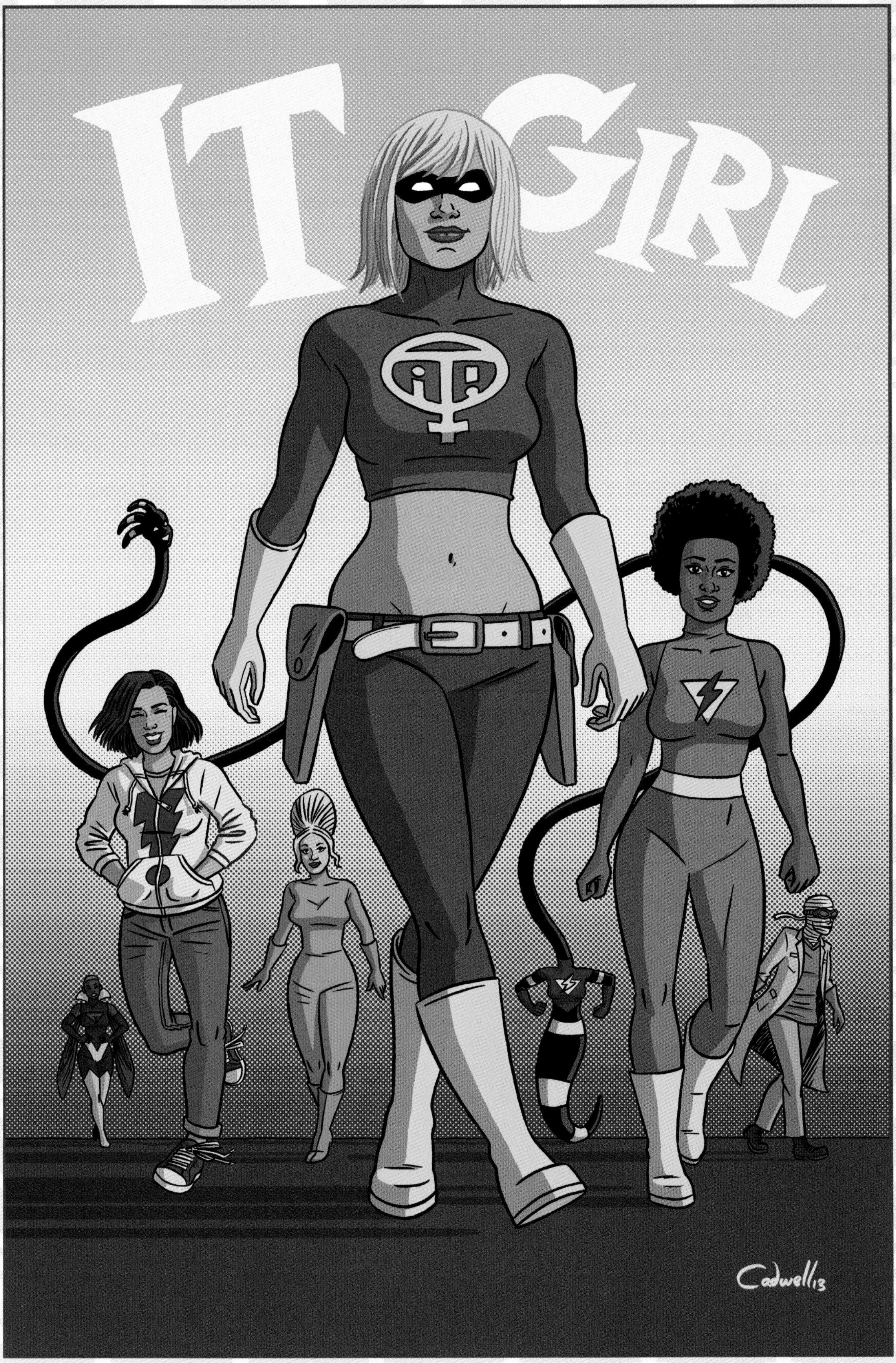
IT GIRL
Cadwell13

Illustration by Adam Cadwell

adamcadwell.com

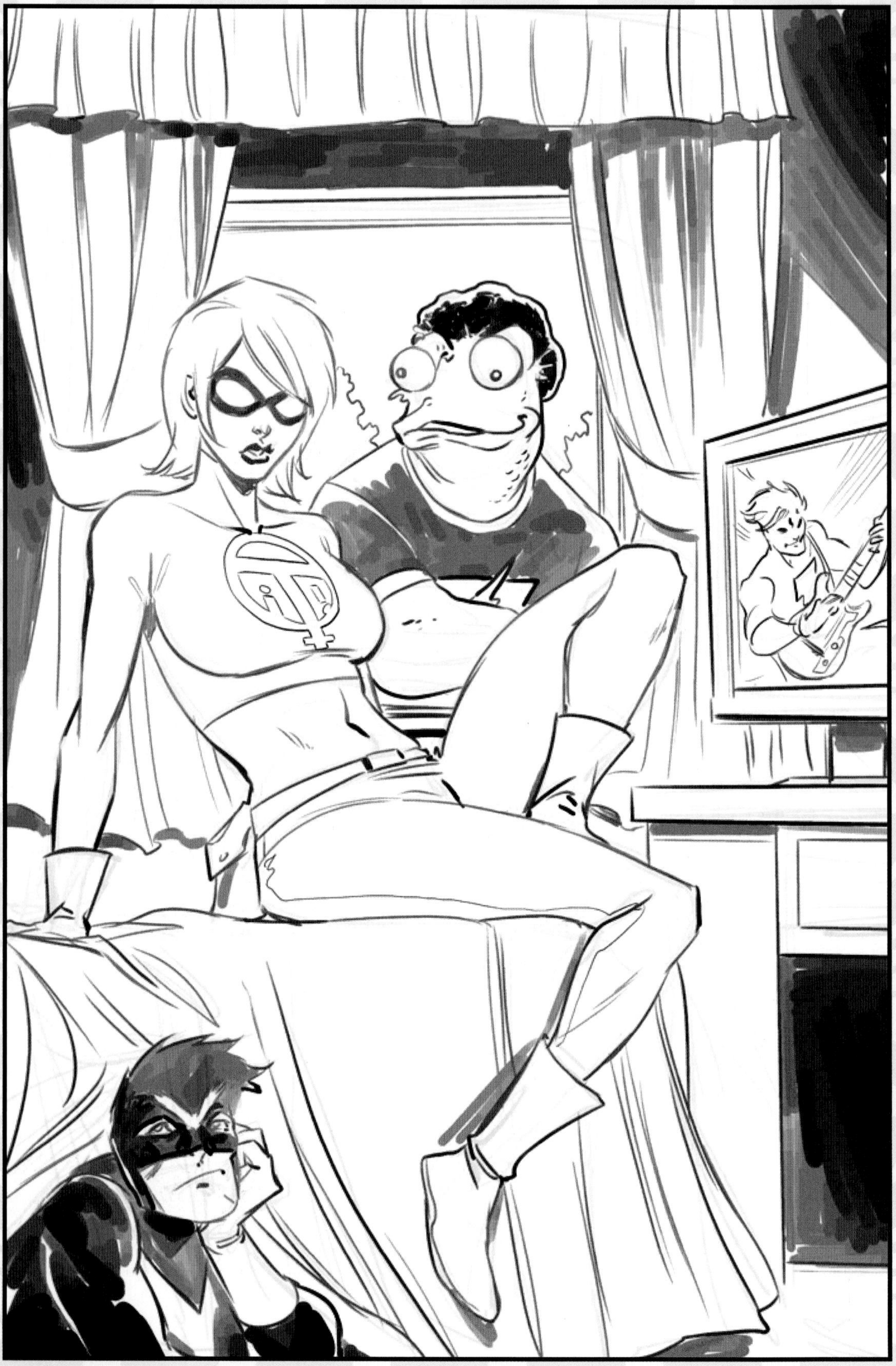

Mike Norton's first drawing of the characters.

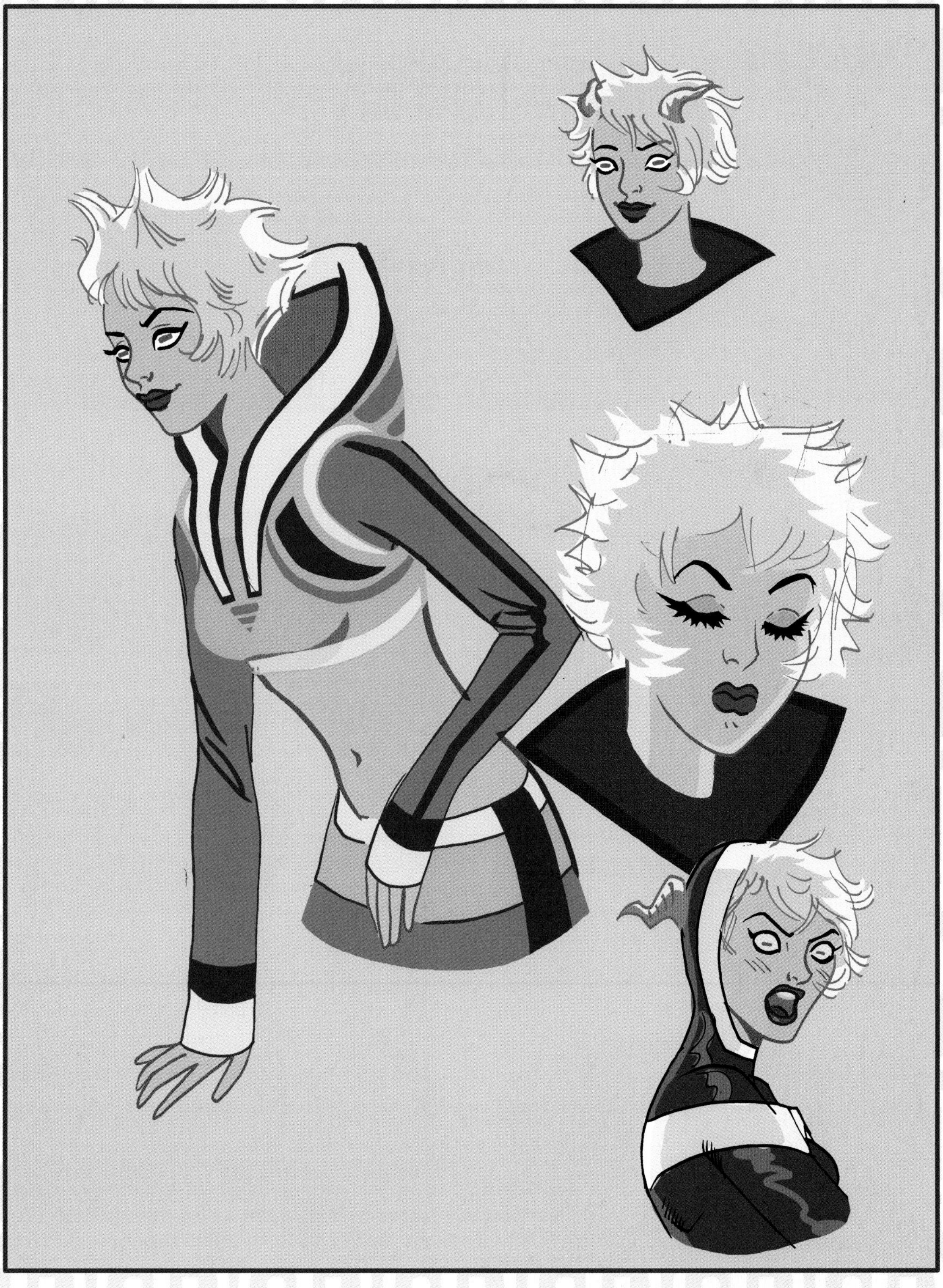

Chynna Clugston Flores' character sketches for the Waitress.

Michael and Laura Allred have been creating comics for more than two decades--he writes and draws, and she is an award-winning colorist. In 1992, they published the first ever issue of *Madman*, a genuine indie comics phenomenon and their most enduring creation. The series was originally published by Tundra before moving to Kitchen Sink, then Dark Horse, and finally, Image Comics. In 2000, they expanded the Madman universe by self-publishing *The Atomics*, an homage to silver-age superheroes, and the birthplace of It Girl. The husband and wife team have also paired up on *Red Rocket 7* (Dark Horse), *The X-Statix* (Marvel Comics), and *iZombie* (Vertigo), among others. They are currently collaborating with Matt Fraction on *FF*, a spin-off of the Fantastic Four. Mike is also a filmmaker and musician who records with his band The Gear. www.aaapop.com

Jamie S. Rich has edited *Madman* since 1997, and he is also an author, having written four prose novels and multiple comic book projects. He is best known for his work with Joëlle Jones on the books *12 Reasons Why I Love Her* and *You Have Killed Me*, both published by Oni Press. His current projects include the futuristic romance *A Boy and a Girl* with artist Natalie Nourigat, the rude-yet-magical comedy *Spell Checkers* with Nicolas Hitori de, and a new ongoing project with Joëlle, debuting in late 2013/early 2014. Rich regularly reviews movies for DVD Talk and the *Oregonian*. www.confessions123.com

Mike Norton has been working in comics for over 10 years now. He's made a name for himself working on books like *Queen and Country*, *Gravity*, *Runaways*, *All-New Atom*, *Green Arrow/Black Canary*, *Billy Batson & The Magic of Shazam*, and *Young Justice*. He is currently drawing two Image Comics series (*It Girl* and *Revival*), *The Answer* for Dark Horse Comics, and his weekly webcomic, *Battlepug*, which won the Eisner Award in 2012 for Best Digital Comic. He is also very, very tall. www.ihatemike.com

Allen Passalaqua is a professional comic color artist as well being involved in promoting culture, art and bringing together the creative community. Combining traditional and pop culture influences, Allen has been commissioned to create artwork for several National Parks, the San Diego Zoo, fine art design for The Grand Canyon, storyboarding Emmy-winning commercials, as well as various mass media outlet projects. Allen's comic book coloring work includes *Justice Society of America*, *Batman Confidential*, *JLA Classified*, *JSA Classified*, *Detective Comics*, and many others. He also is the ongoing color artist on the Eisner Award-winning *Battlepug*. www.angryf.com

Christopher Crank is a comics letterer currently based out of Cincinnati, OH. His recent work includes *It Girl and the Atomics*, *Revival*, *HACK/slash*, and the Eisner Award-winning webcomic *Battlepug!*
Outside of comics you can find him on Twitter (@ccrank), talking about junk at http://crankcast.net and playing music with the Vladimirs and Sono Morti (http://sonomorti.bandcamp.com/).

Chynna Clugston Flores is the creator of *Blue Monday* and has an unhealthy obsession with time travel, cheap lager, monster movies and nachos.
newavezombie.blogspot.com

MORE COMICS FROM WRITER
JAMIE S. RICH

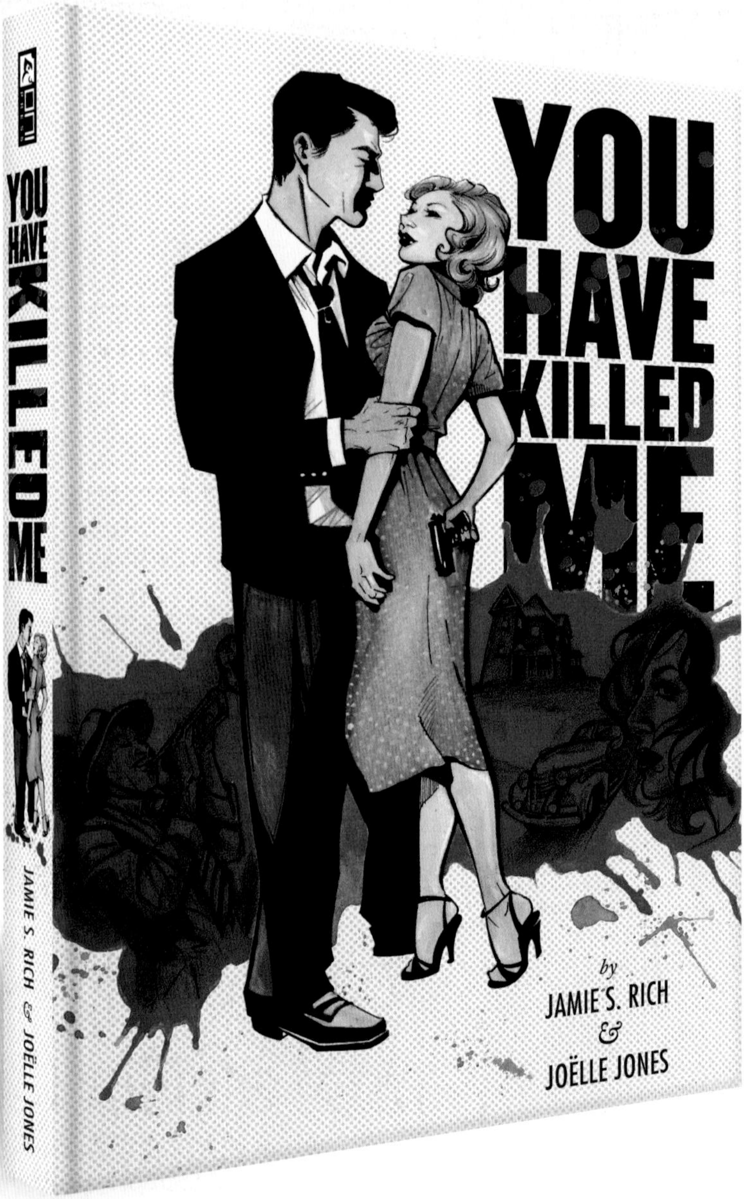
YOU HAVE KILLED ME
YOU HAVE KILLED ME
JAMIE S. RICH & JOËLLE JONES
by
JAMIE S. RICH
&
JOËLLE JONES

You Have Killed Me
by Jamie S. Rich & Joëlle Jones

ISBN: 978-1-932664-88-1

More info at www.onipress.com
Visit Jamie at www.confessions123.com

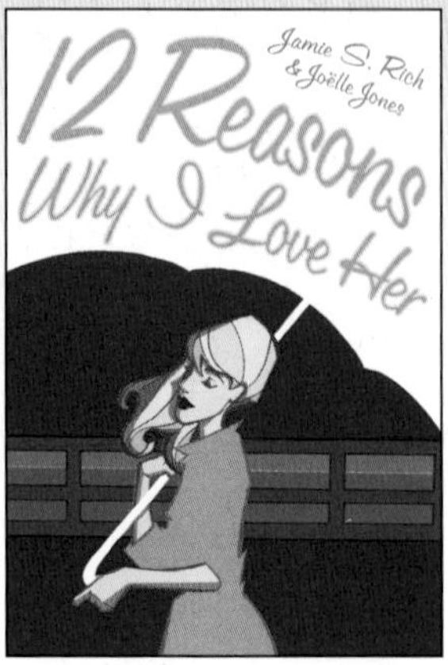
12 Reasons Why I Love Her
Jamie S. Rich
& Joëlle Jones

12 Reasons Why I Love Her
by Jamie S. Rich & Joëlle Jones
ISBN: 978-1-932664-51-5

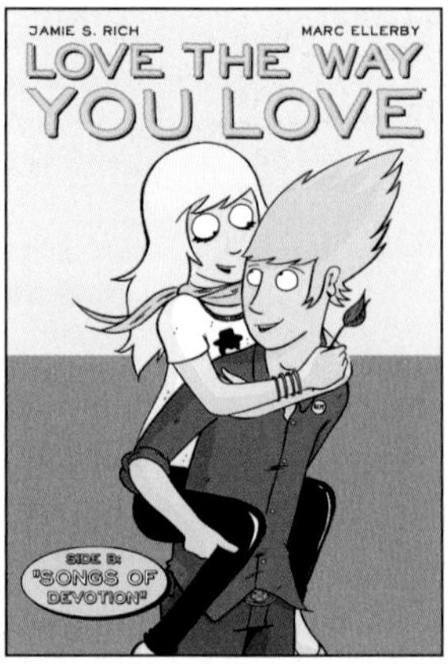
JAMIE S. RICH
MARC ELLERBY
LOVE THE WAY YOU LOVE
SIDE B: "SONGS OF DEVOTION"

Love the Way You Love
by Jamie S. Rich & Marc Ellerby
Side A - ISBN: 978-1-932664-66-9
Side B - ISBN: 978-1-932664-95-9

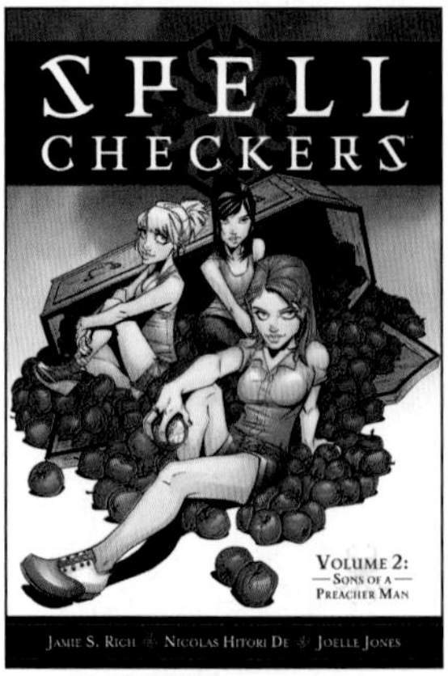
SPELL CHECKERS
VOLUME 2:
— SONS OF A —
PREACHER MAN
JAMIE S. RICH
NICOLAS HITORI DE
JOËLLE JONES

Spell Checkers
by Jamie S. Rich
Nicolas Hitori de & Joëlle Jones
Vol. 1 - ISBN: 978-1-934964-32-3
Vol. 2 - ISBN: 978-1-934964-72-9

ONI PRESS
REVOLUTIONIZE COMICS
www.onipress.com

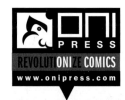

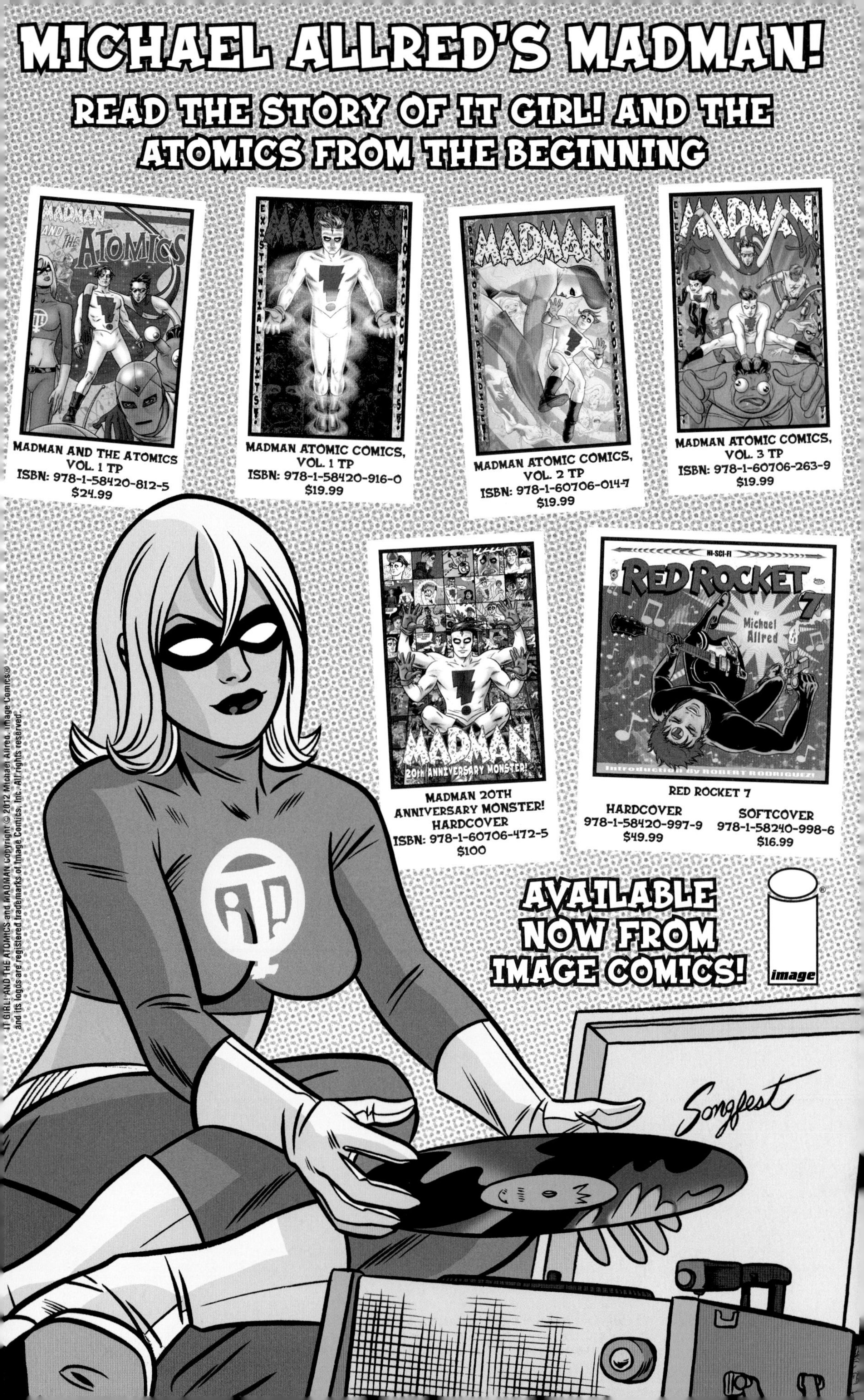
MICHAEL ALLRED'S MADMAN!
READ THE STORY OF IT GIRL! AND THE ATOMICS FROM THE BEGINNING
MADMAN AND THE ATOMICS VOL. 1 TP
ISBN: 978-1-58420-812-5
$24.99
MADMAN ATOMIC COMICS, VOL. 1 TP
ISBN: 978-1-58420-916-0
$19.99
MADMAN ATOMIC COMICS, VOL. 2 TP
ISBN: 978-1-60706-014-7
$19.99
MADMAN ATOMIC COMICS, VOL. 3 TP
ISBN: 978-1-60706-263-9
$19.99
MADMAN 20TH ANNIVERSARY MONSTER! HARDCOVER
ISBN: 978-1-60706-472-5
$100
RED ROCKET 7
HARDCOVER
978-1-58420-997-9
$49.99
SOFTCOVER
978-1-58240-998-6
$16.99
AVAILABLE NOW FROM IMAGE COMICS!
Songfest
IT GIRL! AND THE ATOMICS and MADMAN Copyright © 2012 Michael Allred. Image Comics® and its logos are registered trademarks of Image Comics, Inc. All rights reserved.